Digital Crime and Forensic Science in Cyberspace

Panagiotis Kanellis, Information Society S.A., Greece

Evangelos Kiountouzis, Athens University of Economics & Business, Greece

Nicholas Kolokotronis, University of Peloponnese, Greece

Drakoulis Martakos, National and Kapodistrian University of Athens, Greece

IDEA GROUP PUBLISHING

Hershey • London • Melbourne • Singapore

Acquisitions Editor:	Michelle Potter
Development Editor:	Kristin Roth
Senior Managing Editor:	Jennifer Neidig
Managing Editor:	Sara Reed
Copy Editor:	Nicole Dean
Typesetter:	Jessie Weik
Cover Design:	Lisa Tosheff
Printed at:	Integrated Book Technology

Published in the United States of America by
  Idea Group Publishing (an imprint of Idea Group Inc.)
  701 E. Chocolate Avenue
  Hershey PA 17033
  Tel: 717-533-8845
  Fax: 717-533-8661
  E-mail: cust@idea-group.com
  Web site: http://www.idea-group.com

and in the United Kingdom by
  Idea Group Publishing (an imprint of Idea Group Inc.)
  3 Henrietta Street
  Covent Garden
  London WC2E 8LU
  Tel: 44 20 7240 0856
  Fax: 44 20 7379 0609
  Web site: http://www.eurospanonline.com

Library of Congress Cataloging-in-Publication Data

Digital crime and forensic science in cyberspace / Panagiotis Kanellis
 ... [et al.], editor.
  p. cm.
 Summary: "Digital forensics is the science of collecting the evidence
that can be used in a court of law to prosecute the individuals who
engage in electronic crime"--Provided by publisher.
  ISBN 1-59140-872-5 (hardcover) -- ISBN 1-59140-873-3 (softcover)
-- ISBN 1-59140-874-1 (ebook)
 1. Computer crimes. 2. Forensic sciences. I. Kanellis, Panagiotis,
1967- .
 HV6773.D55 2006
 363.25'968--dc22
         2006009288

British Cataloguing in Publication Data
A Cataloguing in Publication record for this book is available from the British Library.

Digital Crime and Forensic Science in Cyberspace

Table of Contents

Section I: Cyberspace and Digital Forensics

> *Thomas M. Chen, Southern Methodist University, USA*
> *Chris Davis, Texas Instruments, USA*

> *Steven Furnell, University of Plymouth, UK*
> *Jeremy Ward, Symantec EMEA, UK*

Section II: Computer and Network Forensics

> *Sriranjani Sitaraman, University of Texas, USA*
> *Subbarayan Venkatesan, University of Texas, USA*

Section IV: Cyber Investigation and Training

Foreword

The digital crime phenomenon has achieved what I tend to call the "overwhelming" factor. A few years ago, incidents of this kind were few and almost entirely the works of computer and telecommunications aficionados that individually, or as members of groups, came to define what we now identify as the underground hacker (or cracker, depending on your point of view) culture. If such acts were carried out as is often claimed to prove and not to harm, today it is worrying to observe that increasingly the criminals of the digital age are driven by rather sinister motives and the numbers of incidents has increased with the publicity to match. Firstly, because even the "innocent" computer science student at a University lab starts to think differently if he knows that he can do what he pleases and go undetected especially if the rewards are high. Secondly, because digital crime acts are increasingly the collective and well-planned actions of organized crime syndicates and organizations.

Either as individuals or as organizations in the digital society we must understand what breaking the law electronically really means. Of course, what constitutes digital evidence in order to prosecute is controversial. The urgency of this is well-understood and it is becoming harder to simply ignore. Consider for example the findings of the *Digital Risk* survey which was carried out by the Economist Intelligence Unit (EIU) of 218 senior risk managers. Fifty five percent said that the biggest challenge their companies face in tackling IT risks is the growing sophistication of hackers and cyber criminals. Forty eight percent said IT and security problems pose a high risk to their business operations.

This book is important as it help us to understand the nature of cyber crime and as it familiarizes us with the various means by which crime can be detected and evidence collected. It provides a holistic coverage of the topic, i.e., offering technical as well as managerial perspectives and it goes a step further pinpointing issues pertinent to the education and skills that the cyber investigator must possess and of the various challenges that we face in training the professionals of the future. In essence it educates and informs the interested readers about what it really means to be ready to confront.

Solved digital crime cases will in the future read as good Sherlockian adventures. However, digital crime is not fiction, and this book is unique in exploring its multifaceted nature and defining the plateau where the battles between the good and bad guys are taking place. I hope you enjoy reading it as much as I did.

Kyriakos Tsiflakos
Partner, ERNST & YOUNG
Technology and Security Risk Services

Preface

*It is a capital mistake to theorize before one has data. Insensibly, one
begins to twist facts to suit theories, instead of theories to suit facts.*

Sherlock Holmes
Sir Arthur Conan Doyle's "A Scandal in Bohemia", 1891

Cain committed the first crime in the world and the history of crime is as old as the world
itself. Forensics—the process, means, and methods for collecting crime evidence—
can be said to date back to the 18th century stemming from forensic medicine and
studies of anatomy and fingerprints. Crime manifests itself in various ways and forms
and digital crime is the newest one. As the essence of the various forms of crime has
remained unaltered throughout the passage of time, it is safe to assume that digital
crime will exhibit this property too and it is this "permanence" factor that makes imperative for organizations and individuals to understand the issues and complexities that
arise.

In 2003, 82% of American companies surveyed by the Computer Security Institute,
faced security problems and dealt with damages that were estimated at $27.3 million.
And even though organizations already spend considerable amounts of money on
safeguarding their information assets, according to surveys published by monitoring
organizations such as the Computer Crime Research Centre in the U.S. (March 2004)
there will be an increase in the information security market because of cyber criminality
growth.

The *Organization for Economic Co-operation and Development* (OECD) defines "computer crime" as "any illegal, unethical, or unauthorized behavior relating to the automatic processing and the transmission of data". A common categorization of computer
crime is by dividing it to computer crimes and computer related crimes (Handbook of
Legislative Procedures of Computer and Network Misuse in EU Countries, 2002). Computer crimes encompass all offences against the confidentiality, integrity and availability of computer data and systems such as illegal access to computer systems or mali-

cious code writing. Computer-related crimes are "traditional crimes that can be, or have been, committed utilizing other means of perpetration which are now being, or are capable of being, executed via the Internet, computer-related venue (e-mail, newsgroups, internal networks) or other technological computing advancement. Examples are intellectual property rights infringement (e.g., software piracy) and payment system frauds (e.g., credit card fraud via the Internet).

The multiplicity of computer fraud incidents translates to the urgency for developing and maintaining a digital forensics capability as part of a holistic risk management framework. This urgency is projected through the directives and various announcements by a plethora of standards bodies and financial corporations. For example, the Basel Committee on Banking Supervision recommends in the 14th principle for risk management: "... banks should develop... a process for collecting and preserving forensic evidence to facilitate appropriate post-mortem reviews of any e-banking incidents as well as to assist in the prosecution of attackers... ."

At the *Digital Forensic Research Workshop* (DFRWS) in 2001, digital forensic science was defined as "...the use of scientifically derived and proven methods toward the preservation, collection, validation, identification, analysis, interpretation, documentation, and presentation of digital evidence derived from digital sources for the purpose of facilitating or furthering the reconstruction of events found to be criminal, or helping to anticipate unauthorized actions shown to be disruptive to planned operations." This volume is a collection of contributions that present the state of the art of many facets of digital forensics delving deep into the technical realm but also covering issues that reach beyond it as this process involves many stakeholders such as criminal prosecutors, law enforcement officials, IT managers, security administrators, internal and external auditors, government and private organizations, and others.

To this end, the book is subdivided into four sections (also depicted in Figure 1) covering to a large extent most aspects of digital forensics science.

Section I

In the first chapter of this section, Chen and Davis draw attention to a fundamental truth that underlines the phenomenon of digital crime; it is the ease of carrying out electronic attacks that adds to the temptation for attackers. Thus, an understanding of attackers and the methods they employ is a prerequisite to digital forensics. Although the authors acknowledge the fact that the range of possible attacks is almost unlimited, they provide an interesting taxonomy of attacks and proceed in providing an extensive overview of the major types encountered today and likely to continue into the foreseeable future. This chapter succeeds in providing the necessary background for a number of other chapters in this book that cover technical aspects of digital forensics in depth and in serving as a reminder that the increasing sophistication of attacks implies that digital forensics will have proportionately greater importance in investigating, diagnosing, and analyzing cyber crimes.

In turn, Furnell and Ward take the subject of electronic attacks a step further and focus on malware which, in the two decades since its first significant appearance, has become

Figure 1. Organization of the book

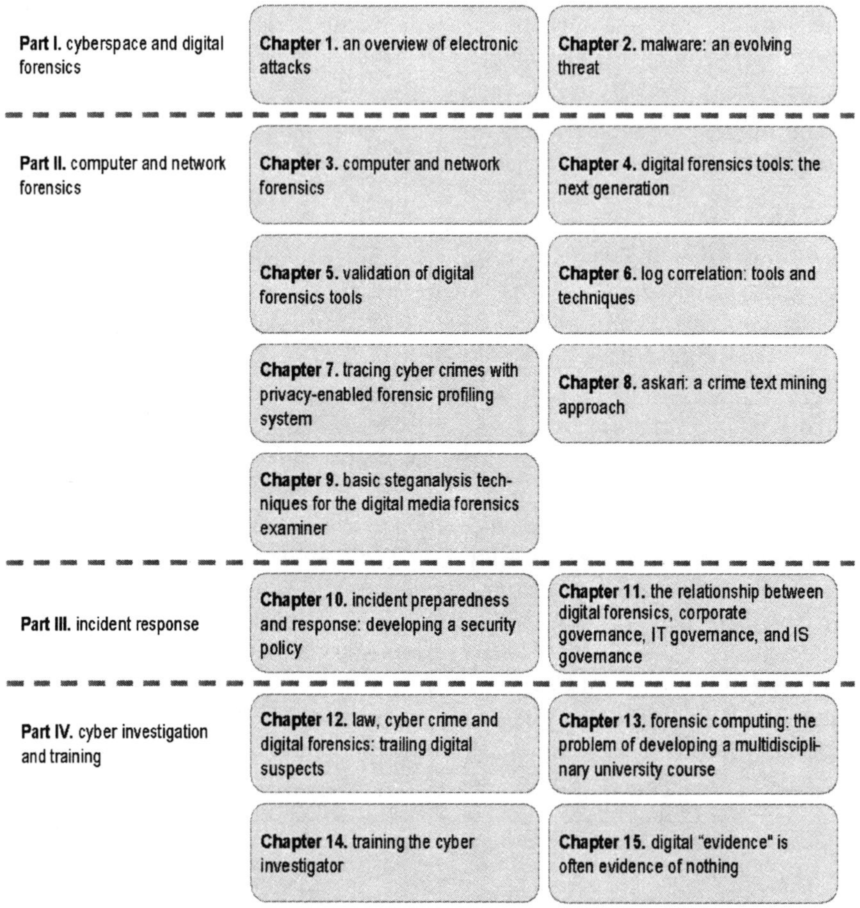

Part I. cyberspace and digital forensics	**Chapter 1.** an overview of electronic attacks	**Chapter 2.** malware: an evolving threat
Part II. computer and network forensics	**Chapter 3.** computer and network forensics	**Chapter 4.** digital forensics tools: the next generation
	Chapter 5. validation of digital forensics tools	**Chapter 6.** log correlation: tools and techniques
	Chapter 7. tracing cyber crimes with privacy-enabled forensic profiling system	**Chapter 8.** askari: a crime text mining approach
	Chapter 9. basic steganalysis techniques for the digital media forensics examiner	
Part III. incident response	**Chapter 10.** incident preparedness and response: developing a security policy	**Chapter 11.** the relationship between digital forensics, corporate governance, IT governance, and IS governance
Part IV. cyber investigation and training	**Chapter 12.** law, cyber crime and digital forensics: trailing digital suspects	**Chapter 13.** forensic computing: the problem of developing a multidiscipli-nary university course
	Chapter 14. training the cyber investigator	**Chapter 15.** digital "evidence" is often evidence of nothing

the most prominent and costly threat to modern IT systems. The essence of the chapter and consequently their contribution to this volume lies in the comprehensive coverage of the evolution of this particular type. The authors highlight that, as well as the more obvious development of propagation techniques; the nature of payload activities (and the related motivations of the malware creators) is also significantly changing, as is the ability of the malware to defeat defenses. This is certainly a moving target, but by tracing its history, a deeper understanding of its various manifestations can be gained and the inquisitive reader can draw similarities as well as differences with other types of electronic attacks. Engaged in this process, one has made the necessary first steps in order to untangle this complex ecosystem. On a hopeful note, and for malware in particular, the authors conclude that the risk and resultant impacts can be substantially mitigated by appropriate use of carefully planned and implemented safeguards.

Section II

As the phenomenon of crimes being committed using digital means is relatively new, and is expected to grow in the foreseeable future, Sitaraman and Venkatesan introduce aspects falling under the umbrella of computer and network forensics in the first chapter of this part. Roughly speaking, computer forensics deals with preserving and collecting digital evidence on a single machine whilst network forensics deals with such operations in a connected digital world. A number of sophisticated tools have been developed for forensic analysis of computers and networks and this chapter presents an overview of the most prominent ones. Following a critical analysis, it becomes apparent that most of the tools presented are suffering from limitations and only few have been validated for providing evidence that can be used in court.

As the technology pace is increasing sharply, current limitations of tools used by forensics investigators will eventually become obstacles in performing investigations in an efficient and reliable way. This has motivated Richard and Roussev to deal with the problem of identifying requirements that next generation of digital forensics tools should meet. The authors introduce the notions of *machine* and *human scalability* as two perspectives of the same problem, and present various approaches to address it. By taking into account the needs of digital forensics community, it is recommended the next generation of the digital forensics tools to employ high performance computing, more sophisticated evidence discovery and analysis techniques, as well as better collaborative functions.

The chapter written by Craiger, Swauger, Marberry, and Hendricks, takes the subject one step further, focusing on the validation of digital forensics tools. As noted by the authors, this should be an indispensable part of the software design and development process for tools being used in digital forensics; otherwise the results of cyber investigations cannot be introduced in courts. Contrary to typical software tool validation frameworks, special requirements are imposed if these are to be applied in the digital forensics context, most notably the lack of capability to conduct extensive validation due to time constraints. Important concepts and well-known methodologies currently used in forensic tool validation, along with the alternative *just-in-time tool validation* method, are described in detail.

In the sequel, the subject of this part is specialized by Forte in the study of tools and techniques widely used in log file correlation, presented from the perspective of digital forensics. The increasing number of information systems being connected over the network makes the difficulty of the cyber investigative process extremely high and necessitates the development of new more complex digital forensics investigative procedures. Log file correlation is comprised of two components, namely intrusion detection and network forensics. The author deals with the general requirements log files and associated tools should meet, and additional requirements imposed by the digital forensics community. Experimentations and results obtained from a research project are also presented leading to conclusions about the applicability of current practices in distributed architectures.

The chapter written by Kahai, Namuduri, and Pendse also treats the subject of network forensics focusing on intrusion detection and issues of tracing cyber crimes. Most organizations employ intrusion detection systems and other security measures to protect their network without enabling mechanisms in order to collect evidence and identify the attackers. This is attributed to the lack of tools and techniques for identification and IP trace back, as well as, to the inherent complexity of doing so in a universal cyber space. Motivated by this fact, the authors propose a forensic profiling system monitoring any anomalous activity in the network and accommodating real-time evidence collection. The proposed system is designed such that communication behavior of only suspicious sources is investigated, thus protecting the privacy of lawful users. It is argued that such a system may drastically reduce the time spent to filter system log files during forensic investigations.

The advancement of communication technologies has facilitated forms of organized crime, leading to a significant increase of concern about national security. Hence, the amounts of data that need to be analyzed by criminal investigators are in many cases prohibitively large. The identification of patterns revealing criminal behavior in large data sets is also considered by Chibelushi, Sharp, and Shah. Because such data sets contain large amount of information stored in textual and unstructured form, data mining, and in particular text mining, are two key technologies well suited to the discovery of underlying patterns. The authors review the use of these techniques in crime detection projects and describe in detail the text mining approach followed in ASKARI project. They propose an approach combining agent technology with text mining techniques to dynamically extract criminal activity patterns and discover associations between criminal activities across multiple sources. Limitations of proposed methodology are identified and directions for future research are also given.

The chapter by Agaian and Rodriguez focuses on the development of digital forensic steganalysis tools and methods by analyzing and evaluating the techniques most widely used. These techniques are mainly applied by digital forensics examiners to analyze, identify, and interpret concealed digital evidence (information appropriately embedded within multimedia objects with practically no visible effect). Many advanced open source steganography utilities are authored and distributed over the Internet and there are indications that cyber criminals may be using these freely available tools to hide communications in order to avoid drawing the attention of law enforcement agencies. As concluded in the DFRWS 2001, there are indications that cyber criminals may be using these freely available tools to hide communications in order to avoid drawing the attention of law enforcement agencies. To this end, it is of great importance to find means to effectively detect, estimate the length, extract, and trace the hidden information in all its forms; all such issues are presented by the authors in a simple and comprehensible manner. The results yielded have considerably improved currently achieved rates of detecting hidden information by existing algorithms, even in the presence of added noise, and this is validated by the extensive simulations performed.

Section III

No one can argue that the consequences following the aftermath of an attack that compromises the security of the information and telecommunications infrastructure are anything less than devastating. Of course impact and severity levels vary but the more organizations depend on information technologies even minor attacks will cause major disturbances. Some of the costs can be counted in dollars and severe financial loss emanating from loss of business. Others, such as poor public relations and lost customer confidence, cannot be directly measured but are of equal or greater importance. Incident preparedness and response that is part of a corporate security strategy is becoming increasingly important for organizations that must develop and demonstrate the required set of related competencies. Wylupski, Champion, and Grant examine the preparedness level and responses of three U.S. southwestern companies to their own specific threats to corporate cyber-security. They do so in sufficient detail and they paint a picture, which as reality itself, is a rather complex one. It becomes obvious by putting all the pieces together that effective intrusion preparedness and response relies on a combination of policies and processes, organizational commitment, and employee accountability. The authors place a heavy emphasis on the practical side of things by laying out the basic blocks one needs to define an effective security policy for corporate networks as well as provide a glimpse on emerging technologies that can be used as the means for implementing it. They do so without undermining and loosing sight of the role and importance of the human element that more often than not proves to be the weak link of even the most concrete security policies.

According to OECD, *"Corporate Governance"* is the framework by which business corporations are directed and controlled. Technology and systems are central to this framework pumping the information that without it no "directing" or "controlling" would be possible. In the 2½ years since the passage of the Sarbanes-Oxley Act in July 2003 both private and public organizations worldwide found themselves looking at the mirror with respect to the security and integrity of their information assets. So in the midst of it all there is also IT governance and information security governance. But where does Digital Forensics fit in the picture? von Solms and Louwrens argue that for any company that wants to create an effective Digital Forensics environment, it seems prudent to know precisely what the relationships between Digital Forensics, Information Security, IT Governance and Corporate Governance are. The reason being that if a Digital Forensics environment is created, and any of the relationships mentioned above are ignored, it may result in an environment that will not operate optimally. This has obvious implications for incident preparedness and response and how we are thinking and approaching it. The authors proceed in determining and defining these interrelationships. They investigate the overlaps and they provide detailed analyses of their content. Their conclusions help us to clarify the place and importance of digital forensics in relation to governance; a relation that organizations need to understand, nurture and manage.

Section IV

Many could argue that crime and punishment in the real world (as opposed to the digital and virtual one) is not that complicated an affair. At least if one makes the assumption that the mediators, in other words, the courts of justice abide by the rules as set in the books of law. Evidence is evidence and for each known crime there is the law that defines it as such. In the digital worlds we are not sure what constitutes evidence and each new day brings a new crime. To enhance the conditions under which cyber crime can be investigated, certain technical and organizational measures are necessary in an effort to detail further and support the legal framework. Mitrakas and Zaitch start their chapter with an overview of digital forensics from a criminology viewpoint prior to reviewing some pertinent legal aspects. Pursuant to the criminological typology of cyber crime, some definitions and specific features of cyber crime, this chapter reviews certain legal aspects of forensic investigation, the overall legal framework in the EU and US and additional self-regulatory measures that can be leveraged upon to investigate cyber crime in forensic investigations. The authors claim that while full-scale harmonization of forensic investigation processes across the EU and beyond is unlikely to happen in the foreseeable future, cross-border investigations can be greatly facilitated by initiatives aiming at mutual assistance arrangements based on a common understanding of threats and shared processes. They add that the involvement of users through self-regulation and accountability frameworks might also contribute to reducing risks in electronic communications that emanate from cyber criminal threats. In summary, the authors demonstrate how forensic readiness that complements the security set-up of an organization can improve security posture and provide coverage from cyber crime.

To be called a "science" or even a "discipline" one must have a distinct subject matter and some means of describing and classifying its subject matter. If we take practice aside for a moment, how well-defined as a field of study is digital Forensics? Is this a fully-fledged one or is it just emerging? These are interesting questions and one needs to dig deep into the nature and the core of the discipline, trace its roots, examine epistemological and ontological questions and perhaps draw parallels with other disciplines in order to reach a conclusion. Some answers to the above are given (directly or indirectly) from Stahl, Carroll-Mayer, and Norris by setting out to design a full undergraduate BS degree in forensic computing at a British University. Their experience is valuable as they bring out the issues and challenges for deciding what the knowledge base of a digital forensics professional should be. The authors emphasize the problem of interdisciplinary agreement on necessary content and the importance of the different aspects. Their contribution is important because its is bound to stir and simulate debate; something which as they point out will help us come to an agreement what the skills requirement for digital forensics professionals should be.

If the training issue was set in an academic context in the preceding chapter, Malinowski looks at it from a practitioner's perspective drawing on from his experience after being with the New York Police Department for over 20 years. Training possibilities for digital forensic investigators are presented, differentiating between civil service and industry needs for training, whereas any differences in considerations for providing such training are cited as well. While each organization has its own requirements, different paradigms and forums for training are offered. The chapter's added value is that it allows the reader to develop training plans that may be unique to his/her organization. This is achieved by providing solid foundations; those common subject matter areas that are felt critical to all organizations and needs, as well as, a "core" knowledge and skill base around that one needs in order to plan a training strategy.

The last chapter could have fitted well into any section of the book. Indeed, it could have been an integral part of this introduction. We decided to place it at the end of the volume, and in its own way this short chapter by Caloyannides provides a fitting epilogue. If we take for granted that it is impossible for more than one person to have the same fingerprints, then evidence is evidence. The author makes an argument that "Digital evidence is often evidence of nothing". The points that the author raises demand to be considered. In our opinion and regarding digital forensics in general, we would all be a little bit wiser after doing so.

Intended Audience

Generally, the book is intended for those who are interested in a critical overview of what forensic science is, care about privacy issues, and wish to know what constitutes evidence for computer crime. However, special attention has been given so that the book is would be of great value to the following target groups:

- *Academics* in the fields of computer science, software engineering, and information systems that need a source of reference covering the state of research in digital forensics.

The book has been designed so as to provide the basic reading material that could potentially serve as the backbone of an advanced course on cyber crime and digital forensics, covering current trends in cyber crime, tools used in computer and network forensics, technologies and interdisciplinary issues encountered, as well as, legal aspects of digital forensics. Hence, it is envisaged the book will be of assistance in identifying and further establishing research priorities in this area.

- *Security professionals*, as well as, internal and external auditors that must be aware of all aspects governing computer and network forensics.

Towards this direction, an overview of network attacks (including malware) launched to modern IT systems today is given, indicating most commonly used approaches followed by attackers. Further, the book also provides a detailed analysis of a wide variety of tools, both commercial and open source, commonly used to protect organizations from such attacks and also employed in all phases of digital forensics process.

Pros and cons of these tools are derived in a systematic manner and current trends are brought to the attention of the professional in order to assist him develop an effective security policy and informatively choose the proper action plan.

- *Information technology managers* that must have the necessary know-how in order to handle an investigation and deal with cyber-investigators.

All aspects (organizational, technical, legal) of the investigation and the evidence collection processes are carefully examined. The book reviews the current legal framework in the EU and U.S. that can be leveraged upon to investigate cyber crime in forensic investigations, and deals with the important issue of what constitutes digital evidence what does not. Furthermore, different paradigms for training cyber-investigators are considered and the core knowledge and skills that need to be developed are clearly identified.

Panagiotis Kanellis
Evangelos Kiountouzis
Nicholas Kolokotronis
Drakoulis Martakos

Acknowledgments

A book of this nature is indebted to a number of individuals and contributors. The editors would like to acknowledge the help of all involved in the collation and review process of the book, without whose support the project could not have been success-fully completed. Our sincerest thanks to Mrs. Aggeliki Kladi of Information Society S.A., who provided us with superb administrative support necessary to keep the project viable throughout its life.

Most of the chapter authors included in this book also served as referees for other chapter authors. We owe a tremendous amount of thanks to all those who provided constructive and comprehensive reviews. Special thanks also go to the publishing team at Idea Group Inc. whose contributions throughout the whole process from incep-tion of the initial idea to final publication have been invaluable and in particular to Ms. Kristin Roth, who kept the rhythm of the project by guiding us through its various stages and reminding us, always nicely, of the many deadlines we missed.

Finally, special thanks go to our colleagues at the National and Kapodistrian University of Athens and at the Athens University of Economics and Business for the time they invested in lengthy discussions resulting in much valuable input, ideas, and construc-tive criticism.

In closing, we wish to thank all of the authors for their insights and excellent contribu-tions to this book.

Panagiotis Kanellis
Evangelos Kiountouzis
Nicholas Kolokotronis
Drakoulis Martakos

Section I: Cyberspace and Digital Forensics

Chapter I

An Overview of Electronic Attacks

Thomas M. Chen, Southern Methodist University, USA

Chris Davis, Texas Instruments, USA

Abstract

This chapter gives an overview of the major types of electronic attacks encountered today and likely to continue into the foreseeable future. A comprehensive understanding of attackers, their motives, and their methods is a prerequisite for digital crime investigation. The range of possible cyber attacks is almost unlimited, but many attacks generally follow the basic steps of reconnaissance, gaining access, and cover-up. We highlight common methods and tools used by attackers in each step. In addition, attacks are not necessarily directed toward specific targets. Viruses, worms, and spam are examples of large-scale attacks directed at compromising as many systems as possible.

Introduction

Today computer systems are often invaluable for business and personal uses. Computer systems store valuable corporate and personal information while computer networks provide convenient data access and processing services. They are naturally very tempting targets, as shown by statistics that track the frequency and prevalence of cybercrimes. For example, an CSI/FBI survey found that 71% of organizations had experienced at least one attack in 2004, while the remaining organizations did not know the number of attacks (Gordon, 2005).

The ease of carrying out electronic attacks adds to the temptation for attackers. It is widely known that computer systems have numerous vulnerabilities, although not every attack exploits vulnerabilities (Hoglund & McGraw, 2004). In the second half of 2004, 54 new vulnerabilities per week were discovered on average, and 50% were serious enough to be rated as highly severe, meaning that exploitation of the vulnerability could lead to complete compromise of a system (Turner, 2005). Attackers are keenly aware of new vulnerabilities because it takes time for organizations to set up adequate protection. New vulnerabilities are announced along with a software patch, but organizations are sometimes slow to apply patches. In late 2004, exploit codes for new vulnerabilities appeared on average only 6.4 days after the announcement of the vulnerability; in early 2004, it was 5.8 days. Organizations that are slow to patch are often vulnerable to new exploits.

Attackers are also well aware that virtually all computers are interconnected by the Internet or private networks. Moreover, mobile and handheld devices with Internet connectivity have steadily grown in popularity. Networks make attacks easier to carry out remotely and more difficult to track to their sources.

This chapter gives an overview of electronic attacks, organized according to the basic steps of reconnaissance, gaining access, and cover-up. We focus here on network-enabled attacks, but this is not meant to imply that all electronic attacks are carried out remotely. Direct physical attacks on computers are also quite common but not covered here. This chapter also describes large-scale attacks such as viruses, worms, denial of service, and spam. An understanding of attackers and their attack methods is a prerequisite to digital forensics, which is concerned with the collection and analysis of evidence of electronic crimes. This chapter serves as necessary background for other chapters in this book that cover aspects of digital forensics in depth.

Types of Attackers and Motives

As one might expect, there are as many different types of attackers as there are different types of attacks. Attackers can be categorized in a number of different ways. For example, attackers may be either internal or external, depending on their relationship to the target. In the past five years, the fraction of attacks from inside have been roughly equal to the fraction from outside (Gordon, 2005). Insiders are worrisome because they have certain advantages such as trust and knowledge of the target organization that can increase the chances of a successful attack. Moreover, insiders do not have to overcome perimeter defenses designed for external attackers.

Attackers can also be viewed as amateurs or professionals. Many people probably visualize an attacker as the stereotypical male teenage "hacker" perpetuated by the mass media. While amateur hackers are undoubtedly responsible for a substantial fraction of viruses and worms and other vandalism, the involvement of professionals and perhaps organized crime is suggested by the sophistication of attacks and number of attacks apparently driven by profit motives (Swartz, 2004). Besides professional hackers, other professionals involved in electronic attacks include national governments, military agencies, and industrial spies.

The motivations for electronic attacks depend on the attacker. Because there are many different types of attackers, motivations can be almost anything ranging from fun and fame to extortion, profit, espionage, revenge, or a political agenda (Shinder & Tittel, 2002).

The stereotypical teenage hacker is believed to be usually interested in gaining fame or notoriety. On the other hand, organized crime and white collar attackers are more interested in profit. Attacks oriented towards invasion of privacy or theft of confidential data is a growing trend, as evidenced by an escalation in spyware and phishing attacks (described later in this chapter). Cyber attacks for political purposes have become a growing concern since international attention has turned to terrorism.

Types of Attacks

A taxonomy of attacks is offered in Figure 1. At the highest level, attacks can be targeted against specific hosts, the network infrastructure, or indiscriminately at as many hosts as possible. This chapter does not cover attacks against infrastructure; the interested reader is referred to the literature (Chakrabarti & Manimaran, 2002).

Attacks directed at specific hosts include sniffing, session hijacking, exploits of vulnerabilities, password attacks, denial of service, and social engineering. Social engineering can also be used in large-scale indiscriminate attacks. Other large-scale attacks include spam and malicious code (otherwise known as malware). Each of these attack methods are described later in this chapter.

Attack Phases

An attack to compromise a particular target is often carried out through a progression of steps, analogous to the steps of a physical attack (Chirillo, 2002; McClure, Scambray, & Kutz, 2001; Skoudis, 2002). As shown in Figure 2, the first step is reconnaissance to

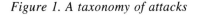

Figure 1. A taxonomy of attacks

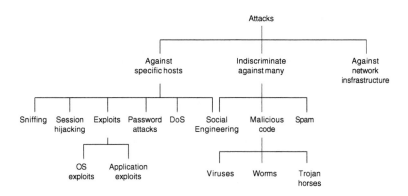

Figure 2. Basic steps in attacks against specific targets

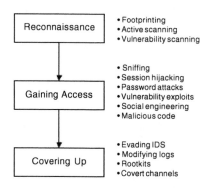

collect intelligence in preparation for attack. Knowledge of a target and its vulnerabilities can be critical to the success of an attack. The second step is gaining access, which could have many different goals such as control, theft, or destruction. During and after the attack, the attacker may take actions to try to avoid detection, such as changing system logs or installing a rootkit. We elaborate on each step in the remainder of this chapter.

Reconnaissance

In order to prepare for a successful attack, it would be common sense to first try to learn as much as possible about the target. The reconnaissance phase can reveal a surprising amount of information such as account names, addresses, operating systems, and perhaps even passwords. Moreover, most reconnaissance techniques are not viewed as malicious or illegal, and can be carried out relatively safely. Reconnaissance activities are so common that potential targets may not be alarmed.

Many different reconnaissance techniques are possible, and attackers do not follow a unique sequence of steps. We outline three general steps subsequently to progressively discover more information about a potential target. First, footprinting attempts to learn the location and nature of a potential target from public directories. Second, scanning provides more detailed information about a target by active probing.

Footprinting

The initial step in discovery is footprinting (also known as fingerprinting or enumeration) with the primary objective of locating and learning the nature of potential targets. For example, an attacker will want to know how many potential hosts are available and their IP addresses.

An abundant amount of information is readily available on the Web in large public databases. These databases can be interrogated by a number of utilities such as nslookup, whois, or dig (Kloth.net, 2005). Many of these databases have easy-to-use interfaces and do not require any advanced technical knowledge. In general, the information gained in footprinting is common, easily found, and presents a very low risk to corporate, government, and military entities.

The whois databases contain data about the assignment of Internet addresses, registration of domain names, and contact information. Domain names such as www.company.com are registered through the Internet Network Information Center (InterNIC), a consortium of several companies and the U.S. government (InterNIC, 2005). For a given domain name, the whois database can provide the registrant's name and address, domain servers, and contact information.

The American Registry for Internet Numbers (ARIN) database provides information about ownership of ranges of IP addresses (ARIN, 2005). It allows lookup of contact and registration information including IP addresses, autonomous system numbers, and registered organizations in the Americas. European IP address assignments can be discovered from Réseaux IP Euoropéens Network Coordination Centre (RIPE NCC). Likewise, Asian IP address assignments are maintained by the Asia Pacific Network Information Center (APNIC).

Another well-known and useful database is the Domain Name System (DNS). DNS is a hierarchy of servers used to associate domain names, IP addresses, and mail servers. For example, it resolves a domain name such as www.company.com to the IP address of the corresponding server. The hierarchy extends from the root DNS servers down to DNS servers for individual organizations and networks. These DNS servers contain information about other low-level DNS servers and IP addresses of individual hosts (DNSstuff, 2005).

From a digital forensic perspective, examination of an attacker's system should look for evidence of artifacts on the hard drive that show the Web sites and information gained during the footprinting process. This information is often found in the active cache or as remnants on the drive (Davis, Philipp, & Cowen, 2005).

Active Scanning

Footprinting may be viewed as similar to looking up names and numbers in a telephone book. To follow up, scanning is a more active step to learn about potential targets from their responses to various probes. There are many different ways to conduct scans, and most of them are automated for convenience and speed.

During a postmortem digital forensic examination of an attacker's host, it is important to look for tools similar to those described below. This will help an experienced examiner understand the probable skill level of the attacker. This step increases in importance when trying to understand the extent of a possible enterprise-wide compromise. Attackers generally like using the same tools over again, and in this early stage the attacker is likely to load some of these tools on other compromised hosts.

War Dialing

War dialing is an old and primitive method but still useful. Many organizations allow remote users to access an enterprise network through dial-up modems, but they can be misconfigured or overlooked by system administrators (Skoudis, 2002). War dialers are simply automated machines for dialing a set of phone lines to find accessible modems. A telephone number within an organization is usually easy to find through the Internet or telephone books, then an attacker could dial a surrounding range of numbers to discover phone lines with modems. Some war dialers include a nudging function that sends a predefined string of characters to a modem to see how it responds. The response may reveal the lack of a password, the type of platform, and perhaps a remote access program (such as the popular pcAnywhere). Many popular war dialers exist, including: *Toneloc*, *THC Scan*, *Phone Tag*, *Rasusers*, *Microsoft's Hyper-Terminal*, *PhoneSweep*, *Sandtrap*, and *Procomm Plus* (Packet Storm, 2005).

Although war dialers have been in use for decades, they can still be effective in attacks when a modem is not properly secured. Obviously, modems without password protection are completely vulnerable. Also, modems can be attacked by guessing the password. A successful attack through an unsecure modem can lead to compromise of an entire organization's network, effectively bypassing firewalls and other sophisticated defenses.

Ping Sweeps

The internet control message protocol (ICMP) is an essential part of the Internet protocol to enable notification of troubles and other control functions. ICMP includes a very useful utility called ping, typically used to verify that a specific host is operational (IETF RFC 1739, 1994). Ping messages consist of a pair of ICMP messages called Echo Request and Echo Reply. A host that receives an ICMP Echo Request message should reply with an ICMP Echo Reply.

Ping is frequently used by attackers to sweep or scan a block of IP addresses for active hosts. Many tools can easily perform a ping sweep. However, ping sweeps have two drawbacks for attackers. Ping sweeps can be noticed and alert potential targets of an imminent attack. Also, organizations will sometimes block ICMP messages as a matter of policy. To avoid this problem, TCP packets to well-known ports will also work. An initial TCP SYN packet (used to request a new TCP connection) to a target will prompt a TCP SYN-ACK reply.

Network Mapping

Ping sweeps will reveal the addresses of active hosts but no information about their networks. Traceroute is a widely used utility for mapping a network topology (Stevens, 1994). It takes advantage of the time-to-live (TTL) field in the IP packet header. When an IP packet is sent, its TTL field is set to the maximum time allowed for delivery; a limited lifetime prevents IP packets from looping endlessly in the network. Each router decrements the TTL field by the time spent by the packet in that router. Routers typically forward packets quickly and then must decrement the TTL value by the minimum unit of one. The TTL field essentially ends up serving as a hop count. If the TTL field reaches a value of zero, a router should discard the packet and send an ICMP Time Exceeded message back to the source IP address in the discarded packet.

The traceroute utility sends out a sequence of UDP packets, starting with a TTL field value of one and incrementing the value by one for each successive packet. When ICMP Time Exceeded messages are returned, they reveal the addresses of routers at incremental distances. Similarly, ICMP messages could be used instead of UDP packets.

Port Scanning

Applications using TCP and UDP are assigned port numbers conveyed in the TCP and UDP packet headers. The headers allow a range of 65,535 TCP and 65,535 UDP ports. Certain port numbers are "well known" and pre-assigned to common protocols, as listed in Table 1 (IETF RFC 1700, 1994). For example, Web servers listen for HTTP requests on TCP port 80. The other ports may be used dynamically as needed.

An attacker is almost always interested to discover which ports are open (or services are active) on a potential target. An open port means that the target will be receptive on that port. Also, exploits are often targeted to the vulnerabilities of a specific service. However, probing every possible port manually would be very tedious. A port scanner is an automated tool for sending probes to a set of specific ports in order to see which ports are open.

The most widely used tool for port scanning is probably the open-source Nmap. Nmap is perhaps the most capable port scanner, providing options for many different types of scans which vary in degree of stealthiness and ability to pass through firewalls. Other popular tools include Foundstone's superscan, hping, and nemesis (Insecure, 2005).

Table 1. Some well-known ports

Port	Description
TCP 20	FTP data
TCP 21	FTP control
TCP 23	Telnet
TCP 25	Simple Mail Transfer Protocol
TCP 53	Domain Name System
TCP 80	HTTP
UDP 161	Simple Network Management Protocol
TCP 179	Border Gateway Protocol

Operating System Detection

An attacker may attempt to discover a target computer's operating system because specific vulnerabilities are known for different operating systems (and their different versions). Eavesdropping on network traffic with a sniffer can find clues about a host's operating system (McClure, Scambray, & Kutz, 2001). Different operating systems exhibit specific behavior in setting TTL values in IP packet headers and TCP window sizes, for example. An active technique used by attackers is TCP stack fingerprinting which can be found in the popular Nmap tool. TCP stack fingerprinting takes advantage of the fact that while the TCP protocol is standardized in terms of its three-way connection establishment handshake, the standards do not cover responses to various illegal combinations of TCP flags. Operating systems can differ in their implementations of responses to illegal TCP packets. By probing for these differences with various illegal TCP packets, the operating system and even its particular version can be identified (Fyodor, 2005). Once an operating system is identified, an attacker could attempt exploits targeted to vulnerabilities known for that operating system.

Versatile Scanning Tools

A large number of free and commercial scanning tools are available. Many of these are used for legitimate purposes by system administrators as well to learn about or verify the configurations of hosts on their enterprise networks. We list here a number of tools that appeal to attackers because they conveniently combine several of the mapping and scanning functions mentioned earlier.

Sam Spade is a combination of useful reconnaissance tools with a Windows graphical user interface (Sam Spade, 2005). Its functions include ping, whois, IP block whois (ARIN database query), nslookup, traceroute, and a utility to verify e-mail addresses on a specific mail server. A version of Sam Spade is available as a Web-based tool, as shown in Figure 3.

Other examples of free scanning tools include CyberKit and Cheops (Cyberkit, 2005; Cheops, 2005). Cheops is a popular, easy-to-use utility for network mapping that can automatically draw out a network topology based on discovered hosts and distances. A screenshot of the Cheops interface is shown in Figure 4. It can also discover active services through port scanning and identifies operating systems by TCP stack finger-printing.

Northwest Performance Software's NetScanTools Pro is an example of a commercial tool. It includes ping, port scans, traceroute, netscanner (ping sweep), custom ICMP packet generation, whois, nslookup, IP packet capturing, e-mail address validation, and operating system identification. It uses an unusual method for operating system identification based on observing responses to four types of ICMP messages and variations of them. WildPackets' iNetTools is another commercial tool providing many of the functions as other scanners.

Figure 3. Screenshot of Sam Spade

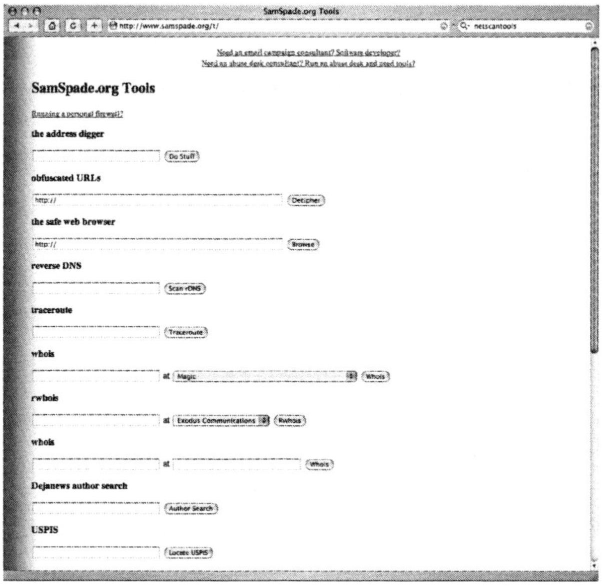

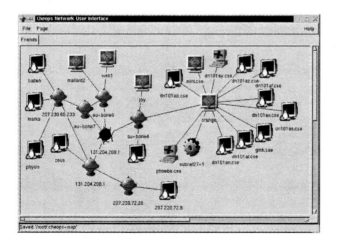

Figure 4. Screenshot of Cheops

Nmap was already mentioned earlier as a port scanner but it is more than a simple scanner. A screenshot of Nmap is shown in Figure 5. Other interesting options in Nmap include: scanning for RPC (remote procedure calls) services on a target machine; sending decoy scans with fake source addresses; sending scans with different timing options to avoid detection; and identifying a computer's operating system via TCP stack fingerprinting.

Figure 5. Screenshot of Nmap

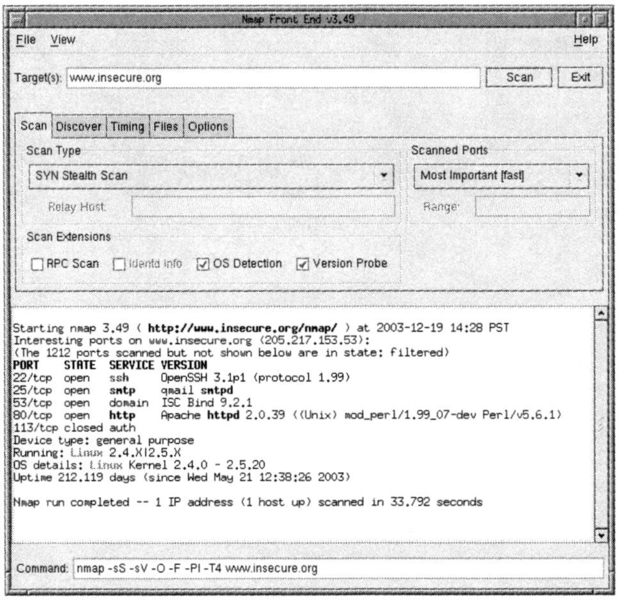

Vulnerability Scanning

Active scanning is invaluable to an attacker for learning a wide variety of information about a potential target, such as host addresses, network topology, open ports, and operating systems. The next basic step in reconnaissance is to scan for specific vulnerabilities that might be exploitable for an attack. Although one could manually scan each host for vulnerabilities, this method is not practical. Automated vulnerability scanners are readily available and often used by system administrators to evaluate the security of their internal network.

Attackers' toolkits have grown in sophistication over the years to the point that many functions are combined in the tools. For example, many tools perform active scanning and vulnerability scanning. Scanners evaluate several types of vulnerabilities, searching for one of three general system weaknesses that include faulty operating system code, faulty application code, or faulty configurations.

System Vulnerabilities

New vulnerabilities in operating systems are being discovered constantly (Koziol et al., 2004). The most critical vulnerabilities are often published by vendors along with a software patch. In practice, organizations find it hard to dedicate the time and effort needed to keep up regularly with security bulletins and patches. The time between the publication of a security vulnerability and the installation of patches leaves a window of opportunity for attackers to exploit that vulnerability. A Symantec report estimated that the average time between publication of a vulnerability and appearance of an exploit for that vulnerability is less than a week (Turner, 2005). Consequently, organizations should keep up with patching diligently.

Application Vulnerabilities

Vulnerabilities are found in applications as well as operating systems (Hoglund & McGraw, 2004). Applications introduce new risks to hardened operating systems by opening up new ports, installing new services, and otherwise spawning privileged processes that are sometimes faulty and susceptible to hijacking or buffer overflows. Commonly targeted applications include Web browsers and desktop applications such as Microsoft Word and Excel, which are capable of running downloaded code. A Web browser, for example, can be made to execute Javascript from an untrusted server that could make the client download and execute a malicious program.

Misconfiguration Errors

Network equipment requires significant technical expertise to configure properly. Incorrect configuration settings due to ignorance or accident can defeat any security offered by networking equipment. An example is a misconfigured firewall that could be too permissive in allowing incoming packets.

Additionally, many operating systems and service applications ship with default accounts and passwords (which are easy to find on the Web). These are intended to help ease the installation process, or simplify troubleshooting in case of lost passwords. Default passwords should be changed but can be overlooked or ignored. Attackers often look for the existence of default configurations because they offer an easy way to compromise a system.

Vulnerability Scanners

Most vulnerability scanners operate basically in a similar way (Skoudis, 2002). First, they try to search for active hosts within a given address range using ping or similar utility. Next, they run a basic set of scans to discover open ports and active services running on the hosts. Based on this information, they proceed to more customized probes to identify vulnerabilities. In the final step, they generate output in the form of a report. Some vulnerability scanners include a function for network mapping as well.

SATAN (Security Administrator's Tool for Analyzing Networks) was an early well-known vulnerability scanner developed in 1995. SATAN has two modern descendents, the open-source SARA (Security Auditor's Research Assistant) and the commercial SAINT (Security Administrator's Integrated Network Tool). SARA enhances SATAN's security engine and program architecture with an improved user interface and up-to-date vulnerability tests. SARA can discover information about hosts by examining various network services (ARC, 2005). It can also find potential security flaws, such as misconfigured network services, well-known system vulnerabilities, or poorly chosen policies. It can generate a report of these results or execute a rule-based program to investigate any potential security problems.

Nessus is a popular open-source vulnerability scanner (Nessus, 2005). It works in a client-server architecture, where the client and server may run on the same machine. The client consists of a tool for user configuration and a tool for recording and reporting results. The server consists of a vulnerability database, a knowledge base to keep track of the current scan, and a scanning engine. Nmap is included as the built-in port scanning tool. The vulnerability database is designed to be modular in the form of plug-ins. Each plug-in is designed to check for a specific vulnerability. Nessus contains over 500 plug-ins, and the user community continually contributes new ones. Vulnerabilities are rated and classified into categories such as finger abuses, Windows-related vulnerabilities, backdoors, CGI (common gateway interface) abuses, RPC vulnerabilities, firewall misconfigurations, remote root access, FTP, and SMTP (mail server vulnerabilities).

Commercial vulnerability scanners include TigerTools' TigerSuite Pro, McAfee's CyberCop ASaP, ISS's Internet Scanner, eEye Digital Security's Retina Network Security Scanner, and Cisco Systems' Secure Scanner.

Gaining Access

The attack phase to gain access to a target can take many different forms and serve different purposes, such as stealing confidential data, tampering with data, compromising the availability of a resource, or obtaining unauthorized access to a system. As shown previously in the taxonomy in Figure 1, attacks may be viewed in three broad categories: focused attacks directed at specific targets, large-scale attacks aimed indiscriminately at as many targets as possible, or attacks directed at the network infrastructure. The first two attack types are covered in this section. Quite often, large-scale indiscriminate attacks have the side effect of widespread disruption of networked systems, even if that is not the real intent.

The major types of attack covered here include sniffing, session hijacking, password attacks, exploits, social engineering attacks, Trojan horses, spyware and adware, viruses and worms, spam, and denial-of-service (DoS) attacks. This list is certainly not exhaustive, but intended to highlight the most common attack types seen today and most likely to be encountered in the near future. It should be noted that the taxonomy does not imply that methods are mutually exclusive; in fact, attack methods are often combined. For example, worms can simultaneously spread by social engineering and exploits, and carry out denial of service.

Sniffing

Sniffing is a passive attack that attempts to compromise the confidentiality of information. It might be considered part of reconnaissance (e.g., sniffing to learn passwords) prefacing an attack but can just as well be argued to be an attack to gain access to information. Sniffers traditionally used by network administrators for traffic monitoring and LAN troubleshooting have also been one of the most commonly used attack tools over the years. On a LAN, every host sees all of the traffic broadcast on the LAN medium, but normally ignore the packets that are addressed to other hosts. A sniffer program puts the network interface of a host into promiscuous mode to capture all packets seen on the LAN medium. Thus, the sniffer can eavesdrop on everything transmitted on the LAN including user names, passwords, DNS queries, e-mail messages, and all types of personal data.

Many free and commercial sniffers are available, including tcpdump, windump, Snort, Ethereal, Sniffit, and dsniff (Tcpdump, 2005; Snort, 2005; Ethereal, 2005; Dsniff, 2005).

Session Hijacking

Session hijacking gained national attention from Kevin Mitnick's alleged 1994 attack on Tsutomu Shimomura's computer (Shimomura & Markoff, 1996). Session hijacking is a combination of sniffing and address spoofing that enables the compromise of a user's remote login session, thus providing an attacker unauthorized access to a machine with the privileges of the legitimate user. Address spoofing is sending a packet with a fake source address. This is quite simple because the sender of an IP packet writes in the IP source address in the packet header. Address spoofing enables attackers to masquerade as another person.

If a user is currently engaged in an interactive login session (e.g., through telnet, rlogin, FTP), a session hijacking tool allows an attacker to steal the session. When most hijack victims see their login session disappear, they usually just assume that the cause is network trouble and try to login again, unaware of the hijacking attack.

Popular session hijacking tools include Juggernaut and Hunt (Hunt, 2005). The hijacking attack begins with the attacker sniffing packets of an interactive session between two hosts, carefully noting the TCP sequence numbers of all packets. To hijack the session, the attacker injects packets with a source address spoofing one of the hosts. The proper TCP sequence numbers must be used for the attack to work, because the receiving host must be convinced to accept the faked packets from the attacker.

Password Attacks

Password attacks attempt to gain access to a host or service with the privileges of a current user. Passwords continue to be very frequently used for access control despite their major weakness: if a password is guessed or stolen, an attacker could gain complete access. The most well-protected systems could be compromised by a single weak password. Understandably, many attacks are often directed at guessing or bypassing passwords.

Easy passwords to guess are the default passwords installed by many operating systems and service applications. For example, 3Com routers ship with Admin access with no password; Cisco CiscoWorks 2000 includes an admin account with password 'cisco' (Phenoelit, 2005). Extensive lists of default accounts and passwords are not hard to find by searching on the Web, and they are sometimes overlooked or ignored by system administrators.

The most powerful password attacks, called password cracking, can be performed if the attacker can obtain the password file (Shimonski, 2005). Computer systems store a list of user accounts and passwords in a password file, but the information is encrypted or hashed for protection against attackers. If an attacker can obtain the password file, the attacker has the advantage of time (translating into more CPU cycles) to crack the passwords by brute force (i.e., attempting all possible combinations of characters).

Brute-force password guessing can be very time consuming but is often not necessary. The natural human instinct is to choose passwords based on common words or names. A dictionary attack takes advantage of this tendency by guessing a set of common words and names. However, modern computer systems are usually programmed with policies to prevent users from choosing easily guessable passwords. Hence, the chance of guessing simple passwords is not as likely today as in the past.

More sophisticated hybrid password guessing tools combine dictionary attacks with limited brute-force attacks. They begin with guesses of common words but then methodically add characters to words to form new guesses. A few examples of password cracking tools include John the Ripper, Cain and Abel, Crack, Lincrack, L0phtcrack, Nutcracker, PalmCrack, and RainbowCrack (Password Crackers, 2005).

Exploits

As mentioned earlier, new vulnerabilities in operating systems and application software are being discovered constantly. A vulnerability is a description of a security hole which is not dangerous per se. However, given knowledge of a vulnerability and sufficient time, attackers will write an exploit to take advantage of that vulnerability (Hoglund & McGraw, 2004). The danger arises when the exploit appears and is shared among attackers. Vulnerabilities are associated with different levels of seriousness, where the most critical vulnerabilities can potentially lead to exploits that completely compromise a target host.

A vendor usually has knowledge of a vulnerability but withholds the information from the public at large until there is a fix for the problem. Then vulnerabilities are announced at the same time as a patch for fixing the vulnerability. Unfortunately, patches take time to download and apply, particularly for large organizations with many computers. For practical reasons, organizations and individuals can have a hard time keeping up to date with patches. If an organization is slow to patch however, it can be exposed to new exploits.

SANS maintains a "top 20" list of the most critical Internet security vulnerabilities (SANS, 2005). A buffer overflow vulnerability is one of the most commonly sought by attackers to exploit. Buffer overflow attacks are used particularly often by worms. This type of exploit is appealing to attackers because many applications and operating systems do not perform proper bounds checking and are thus vulnerable to a buffer overflow. Moreover, a successful buffer overflow attack could lead to complete control of a target host.

A well-known example is a stack-based buffer overflow attack, popularly known as "smashing the stack" (AlephOne, 1996). During a function call, various pieces of data are pushed onto the program stack: function-call arguments, return pointer, frame pointer, and local variables. This is illustrated in Figure 6(a). Normally, at the end of the function call, the pieces of data are popped off the stack, and the return pointer is used to resume execution of the main program. A stack-based buffer overflow depends on inputting more data than expected into the local variables. The excess data is written into the allocated buffer space and then overwritten onto the frame pointer and return pointer, as shown in Figure 6(b). If the excess data can be crafted carefully enough, the overwritten return pointer can be made to point back into the stack somewhere in the data

Figure 6. Buffer overflow attack

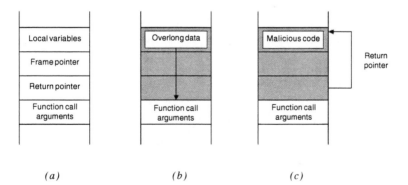

(a)   *(b)*   *(c)*

(a) Data pushed onto stack in normal function call. (b) Data overflows allocated space and overwrites return pointer in buffer overflow attack. (c) Return pointer now points back into stack, causing the malicious code to execute.

input by the attacker, as shown in Figure 6(c). Hence, when the main program resumes execution, the attacker's data (malicious code) will be run.

Obviously, a buffer overflow attack requires careful coding and significant technical knowledge about the target processor architecture. Hence, buffer overflow attacks are not easy to write from scratch. However, pre-written exploits are often shared among attackers and can be used without requiring a great deal of technical knowledge.

Social Engineering

Social engineering attacks take advantage of human interaction; social skills are used to trick the victim into a compromising action, such as revealing personal information or opening an infected e-mail message. Social engineering can be combined with many of the other attack methods to compromise security for just about any purpose. Although social engineering attacks are simple and low tech, they can be surprisingly effective if executed well.

In the past, the telephone was a favorite avenue for social engineering attacks. Today, many social engineering attacks are carried out through e-mail, due to the low risk and low cost of mass e-mailing. Also, e-mail works across different computing platforms and various types of devices. E-mail became the preferred medium after the success demonstrated by mass e-mailing viruses, such as the 2000 Love Letter and 2001 Anna Kournikova viruses. E-mail viruses typically offer a provocative reason to entice the recipient into opening an e-mail attachment, which results in a virus infection. More recently, e-mails might pretend to be security bulletins, bounced e-mail, notifications from an ISP or system administrator, or other official-looking messages.

Recently, a type of social engineering attack called phishing has escalated in frequency. Phishing attacks begin with e-mail seemingly from a reputable credit card company or financial institution that requests account information, often suggesting that there is a problem with an account or a transaction. These e-mails are carefully crafted to appear official and often include stolen corporate graphics. The e-mails typically include a link directing the victim to a Web site that appears to be genuine, but is actually fake. The purpose of the fake Web site is to capture any account or personal information submitted by the victim or download malicious code to the victim host. The Anti-Phishing Working Group counted 3,326 active phishing Web sites in May 2005, compared to 1,518 sites in November 2004 (Anti-Phishing Working Group, 2005).

Trojan Horses

Trojan horses are defined as malicious software that appear to be benign (analogous to the Greek wooden horse in the Trojan War) (Grimes, 2001). The purpose of the disguise is to entice a user into installing and executing the program. If executed, Trojan horses are capable of doing anything that other programs can do, running with the privileges of the associated user. Trojan horses can be combined with many of the other attack types (such as social engineering) to compromise security for just about any purpose.

In common usage, the term Trojan horses include some types of stealthy malicious code which attempt to hide their existence on a victim host. These Trojan horses are distributed by any number of stealthy ways including virus and worm payloads, peer-to-peer file sharing, and Web site downloads. Victims are often unaware of their installation.

The most worrisome Trojan horse may be backdoor programs, sometimes called remote access Trojans (RATs) because backdoors allow an attacker to remotely access a victim's machine (Grimes, 2002). Backdoors circumvent the usual access control security (e.g., login with password). Many backdoor Trojans are known and some are promoted for legitimate administrative uses, including Sub7, Back Orifice 2000, and VNC (Sub7, 2005; BO2K, 2005; RealVNC, 2005).

Adware and Spyware

Adware is software to monitor and profile a user's online behavior, typically for the purposes of targeted marketing. Adware is often installed at the same time as other software programs without the user's knowledge. Even when the user is alerted to the presence of the adware (often buried in the ignored licensing agreement), adware can be an attack on the privacy of the user when information about the user is communicated back to a marketing organization. Adware is primarily an annoyance, sometimes causing pop-up marketing windows during Web surfing.

A more serious and growing concern is another type of software that profiles and records a user's activities, called spyware. A Webroot report estimated that 88% of PCs were infected by spyware and 89,806 Web pages contained spyware for possible download during the first quarter of 2005 (Webroot, 2005). Similar to adware, spyware can sometimes be installed with a user's or system administrator's knowledge. For example, commercial versions of spyware are sold as means to monitor and regulate the online actions of children or an organization's employees. Often though, spyware can be installed stealthily on a machine as a Trojan horse or as part of a virus or worm infection. Spyware can record keystrokes (also known as keystroke loggers), Websites visited, passwords, screenshots, and virtually anything done on a computer. After capturing data, spyware can communicate the stolen data by various channels (e.g., e-mail, FTP, upload to the Web, or Internet Relay Chat) to an attacker. Spyware, like adware, is an attack on user privacy, but spyware is also more likely to compromise confidential data for identity theft.

Viruses and Worms

Viruses and worms are software designed for self-replication (Grimes, 2001; Harley, Slade, & Gattiker, 2001). While there is a certain disagreement among definitions, viruses are commonly considered to be snippets of program code that replicate by modifying (infecting) a normal program or file with a copy of itself. They are not complete (stand-alone) programs themselves but depend on execution of the infected program. When the host program or file is executed, the virus code is executed and takes over control to copy itself to other files. Usually human action is needed to execute the host program, so viruses are sometimes said to require human action to replicate (Webopedia, 2005).

In contrast, worms are stand-alone programs that replicate by spreading copies of themselves to other systems through a network. Worms have become more predominant than viruses in the past few years due to the growth of computer networks. Today, virtually all computers are connected to private networks or the Internet, which is an environment naturally friendly to worms. In particular, the widespread popularity of e-mail has made it easier for worms to spread across different computing platforms. E-mail continues to be the most popular vector for worm propagation.

Viruses have evolved in their complexity over the years, often in response to counter-measures put in place by anti-virus vendors. The first viruses often simply added their code to either the beginning or the end of the host file. In order to evade simple detection, viruses later began to intersperse their code throughout the host file. Another technique that viruses have adopted to evade detection is to encrypt their code within each host file instance, thus making it more difficult for a signature of the virus to be developed. When anti-virus programs began keying on the decryption algorithm as the signature, viruses became polymorphic, changing their decryption algorithm with each copy (Nachenberg, 1996). Taking it one step further, some viruses have become metamorphic, in other words, they change their logic (not just the decryption algorithm) with each infection instance (Szor, 2005).

Network-enabled worms have not had to evolve in the same way as file-infecting viruses. Functionally, a worm program must carry out a few specific steps to spread to another target after infection of a victim host.

First, an algorithm chooses candidates for the next targets. The simplest algorithm, which is used by quite a few worms, is to choose an IP address (32-bit number) at random. This is not efficient because the IP address space is not populated uniformly. More sophis-ticated target selection algorithms choose addresses within the same networks as the victim because local networks have shorter propagation delays to allow faster spreading. Other target selection algorithms may choose targets discovered from a victim's e-mail address book, mail server, DNS server, or countless other ways.

Second, some worms will perform scanning of selected targets. Scanning prompts responses from the potential targets that indicate whether the worm's programmed exploits can be successful. This process identifies suitable targets among the selected candidates.

The third step is the actual exploit or attack to compromise a suitable target. A common attack is to send e-mail to the target, usually carrying an infected attachment that has to be executed. More sophisticated e-mail worms are activated when their message is just previewed or read. Other worms might attack via file sharing, password guessing, or any number of exploits. It is also common for worms to combine multiple exploits to increase the likelihood of success and rate of spreading.

The fourth step after successfully gaining access is to transfer a copy of the worm to the target. Depending on the exploit, a copy of the worm might have been transferred during the exploit (e.g., by e-mail). However, some exploits only create a means of access, such as a backdoor or shell. The worm takes advantage of the access to transfer a copy of itself via any number of protocols including FTP, TFTP, or HTTP.

An optional last step is execution of the worm's payload, if there is one. The payload is the part of the worm's program that is directed at an infected victim and not related to its propagation. The payload could be virtually anything, and not necessarily destructive. In recent cases, payloads have included: opening backdoors and thus allowing remote access, installing spyware, downloading worm code updates from the Internet, or disabling anti-virus software.

Spam

Spam, the e-mail equivalent of unsolicited junk mail, has been a growing problem over the past few years. The volume of spam has been estimated as 60% of all e-mail traffic during the second half of 2004 (Turner, 2005). E-mail addresses are harvested from the Internet or generated randomly. They typically advertise a product, service, or investment scheme (which may well turn out to be fraudulent). E-mail is appealing because spammers can send enormous volumes of e-mail at much lower cost than postal mail. The necessary equipment is modest: a PC, software, and an Internet connection. Even if the response rate is very small, a sizable profit can be made easily.

At the very least, spam wastes network resources (bandwidth, memory, server processing) and necessitates spam filtering at ISPs and organizations. It also wastes the valuable time of users and system administrators. The seriousness of the problem has steadily grown as the volume of spam has escalated.

A growing concern with spam is evidence of collaboration between spammers, virus/worm writers, and organized crime. A substantial number of worms have been used as a delivery vehicle for Trojan horses that set up "bot networks." Bots are stealthy programs that listen for instructions from a remote attacker or allow backdoor access. A bot net is formed by a number of bots under coordinated control. Bot nets as large as 50,000 hosts have been observed (Honeynet Project, 2005). Bot nets are being used for distributed DoS attacks or spamming. Moreover, spam is increasingly being used for phishing (as described earlier). Phishing attacks attempting identity theft with increasing sophistication suggests the involvement of organized crime.

Denial of Service

Most people tend to think of denial of service (DoS) attacks as flooding, but at least four types of DoS attacks can be identified:

- starvation of resources (e.g., CPU cycles, memory) on a particular machine;
- causing failure of applications or operating systems to handle exceptional conditions, due to programming flaws;
- attacks on routing and DNS;
- blocking of network access by consuming bandwidth with flooding traffic.

There are numerous examples of DoS attacks. A "land attack" is an example of starvation. On vulnerable machines with Windows NT before service pack 4, the land attack would cause the machine to loop, endlessly consuming CPU cycles. The "ping of death" is an ICMP Echo Request message exceeding the maximum allowable length of 65,536 bytes. It caused earlier operating systems to crash or freeze (that programming flaw has been remedied in later operating systems).

The "Smurf" attack is an example of an indirect flooding attack, where the ICMP protocol is abused to cause many response packets to be sent to a victim machine in response to a broadcast packet. It is indirect because the real attacker's address is not seen in any packets. It is also interesting as an example of amplification: a single attacker's packet is multiplied into many packets by the recipients of the broadcast.

The most harmful flooding attacks take advantage of amplification through a distributed DoS network (Dittrich, 2005). A famous distributed DoS attack occurred in February 2000 taking down several Websites including Yahoo, eBay, e*Trade, and others for 1-3 hours (Harrison, 2000). Examples of automated distributed DoS tools include Trin00, TFN (tribe flood network), TFN2K, and Stacheldraht. In addition, viruses and worms have been known to infect victims with DoS agents.

Distributed DoS attacks generally proceed in two phases. The first phase is stealthy preparation of the DDoS network. The attacker attempts to compromise a large number of computers, often home PCs with a broadband connection, by installing a DoS agent (i.e., a Trojan horse). Distributed DoS tools such as Trin00 and TFN set up a two-level network. A small fraction of compromised machines are designated as "masters," waiting for commands from the attacker. The remainder of compromised machines are "daemons" waiting for commands from masters. The daemons carry out the actual flooding attack to a specified target.

Covering Up

Cover-up is the last basic step in an attack. During reconnaissance or an attack, an attacker would naturally prefer to avoid detection, which could trigger defensive actions. The problem is evasion of intrusion detection systems (IDSs) which are designed to catch attacks.

After a successful attack gaining access or control of a target, an attacker would like to hide evidence of the attack for the same reasons. Detection of a compromise would lead to defensive actions to defeat the attack, trace the attack back to the attacker, and increase defenses against future attacks.

Evading Intrusion Detection Systems

IDSs are designed to alert system administrators about any signs of suspicious activities. They are analogous in concept to burglar alarms, designed to react against intruders who are able to penetrate preventive defenses (e.g., firewalls). Network-based IDSs monitor the network traffic and might be implemented in a stand-alone device or integrated in firewalls or routers. Host-based IDSs are processes that run on hosts and monitor system activities. IDSs are now commonly used by organizations. Naturally, an intelligent attacker would want to avoid detection by IDSs.

Without special precautions, an attacker could be easily detected by an IDS during reconnaissance because scanning tools are noisy. A port scan might involve thousands of packets, while a vulnerability scan could involve hundreds of thousands of packets. These scans would have a noticeable impact on normal traffic patterns in a network. Moreover, these scans are exactly the signs that IDSs are designed to look for.

Most commercial IDSs attempt to match observed traffic against a database of attack signatures. This approach is called misuse or signature-based detection. Hence, an attacker could try to evade a signature match by changing the packets or traffic pattern of an attack. One approach to changing the appearance of an attack is to take advantage of IP fragmentation. An IDS must be able to reassemble fragments in order to detect an attack. An IDS without the capability for fragment reassembly could be evaded by simply fragmenting the attack packets. An IDS might also be overwhelmed by a flood of fragments or unusual fragmentation.

IDS evasion is also possible at the application layer. For example, an IDS may have a signature for attacks against known weak CGI scripts on a Web server. An attacker could try to evade this signature by sending an HTTP request for a CGI script, but the HTTP request is carefully modified to not match the signature but still run on the Web server.

Another strategy for evading detection by IDSs is to simply overload them with common, unimportant events to mask the actual attack. "Flying under the radar" of an IDS is somewhat easy to do when thousands of meaningless port scans and ping sweeps are filling the operators' consoles and logs, while a more sophisticated attack is executed.

Modifying Logs

Covering up evidence after an attack is particularly important if an attacker wants to maintain control of the victims. One of the obvious necessities is to change the system logs on the victim computers. Unix machines keep a running system log about all system activities, which can be viewed by system administrators to detect signs of intrusions. Likewise, Windows NT/2000/XP systems maintain event logs including logins, file changes, communications, and so on.

An attacker needs to gain sufficient access privileges, such as root or administrator, to change the log files. It is unwise for attackers to simply delete the logs because their absence would be noticed by system administrators searching for unusual signs. Instead, a sophisticated attacker will try to carefully edit system logs to selectively remove suspicious events, such as failed login attempts, error conditions, and file accesses.

Rootkits

Rootkits are known to be one of the most dangerous means for attackers to cover their tracks (Hoglund & Butler, 2005). Rootkits are obviously named for the root account which is the most prized target on Unix systems because the root user has complete system access. If an attacker has gained root access, it is possible to install a rootkit designed to hide signs of a compromise by selectively changing key system components. The rootkit cannot be detected as an additional application or process: it is a change to the operating system itself. For example, Unix systems include a program ifconfig that can show the status of network interfaces, including interfaces in promiscuous mode (or a sniffer). A rootkit could modify ifconfig to never reveal promiscuous interfaces, effectively hiding the presence of a sniffer. Another program find is normally useful to locate files and directories. A rootkit could modify find to hide an attacker's files.

Kernel-level rootkits have evolved from traditional rootkits (Wichmann, 2002). In most operating systems, the kernel is the fundamental core that controls processes, system memory, disk access, and other essential system operations. As the term implies, kernel-level rootkits involve modification of the kernel itself. The deception is embedded at the deepest level of the system, such that no programs or utilities can be trusted any more. Kernel-level rootkits might well be impossible to discover.

Covert Channels

Although logs and operating systems can be modified to escape detection, the presence of a system compromise might be given away by communications. For example, system administrators might recognize the packets from an attacker trying to access a backdoor through a particular port. Clearly, an attacker would prefer to hide his communications through covert channels.

Tunneling is a common method used to hide communications. Tunneling simply means one packet encapsulated in the payload of another packet. The outer packet is the vehicle for delivery through a network; the receiver has to simply extract the inner packet which is carried through the network unchanged. The outer packet is usually IP for routing through the Internet. Also, ICMP messages and HTTP messages have been used. Since the inner packet has no effect on network routing, any type of packet can be carried by tunneling.

Conclusions
and Future Trends

Computer systems are common targets for a wide range of electronic attacks. Instead of an exhaustive catalog, this chapter has attempted a quick tour of the most pressing types of attacks in preparation for later chapters with more details.

An understanding of attacks is a necessary prerequisite to designing proper digital forensic methods to collect and analyze evidence of attacks. Clearly, analysis of evidence to look for an attack can not be done properly without knowing the attack behavior. We have seen that attacks can be viewed as a sequence of phases proceeding from reconnaissance to access to coverup. Each step could leave digital evidence for crime investigators. Signs of reconnaissance could include existence of tools for scanning and network mapping. Attack tools such as session hijacking tools or sniffers would be obvious implications of crime. Evidence of coverup could include changed system logs or signs of a rootkit.

Predictions about the future of cyber attacks are difficult due to the unpredictability of cyber criminals. The perpetual struggle between cyber criminals and law enforcement means that both sides continually attempt to adapt. One side continually invents new types of attacks and attack tools, while the other side has historically followed. Extrapolating current trends, we might predict:

- attacks will increase in sophistication and coordination, out of necessity to evade more sophisticate law enforcement;
- attacks designed for profit and identity theft will increase;
- social engineering attacks will continue through e-mail, given its current success;
- spam volume will continue to increase, unless measures are taken to change the profitability for spammers;
- malicious code (viruses, worms, Trojan horses) has been the single most prevalent attack found in the CSI/FBI surveys over the last five years and will continue to be the most prevalent attack;
- malicious code will increase in new vectors such as instant messaging and mobile handheld devices (such as cell phones);
- attackers will seek to construct more and bigger bot nets.

Increasing sophistication of attacks implies that digital forensics will have proportionately greater importance in investigating, diagnosing, and analyzing cyber crimes. Digital forensic techniques will be challenged by attackers who will have access to more and better attack tools. These attackers will be capable of effective remote exploits and evasion of detection. Cyber crime investigators will need better knowledge of attacks and better forensic tools for collecting and analyzing electronic evidence.

References

Aleph One, Smashing the stack for fun and profit. Retrieved April 30, 2005, from http://www.insecure.org/stf/smashstack.txt

Anti-Phishing Working Group homepage. Retrieved July 30, 2005, from http://www.antiphishing.org

ARC, Security Auditor's Research Assistant. Retrieved July 30, 2005, from http://www-arc.com/sara/

ARIN, Whois database search. Retrieved July 30, 2005, from http://www.arin.net/whois/

BO2K homepage. Retrieved July 30, 2005, from http://www.bo2k.com

Chakrabarti, A., & Manimaran, G. (2002). Internet infrastructure security: a taxonomy. *IEEE Network, 16*, 13-21.

Cheops homepage. Retrieved July 30, 2005, from http://www.marko.net/cheops/

Chirillo, J. (2002). *Hack attacks revealed* (2nd ed.). Indianapolis, IA: Wiley Publishing.

Cyberkit homepage. Retrieved July 30, 2005, from http://www.gknw.com/mirror/cyberkit/

Davis, C., Philipp, A., & Cowen, D. (2005). *Hacking exposed: Computer forensics secrets and solutions.* New York: McGraw-Hill/Osborne.

Dittrich, D. (2005). *Distributed denial of service (DDoS) attacks/tools.* Retrieved April 30, 2005, from http://staff.washington.edu/dittrich/misc/ddos/

DNSstuff homepage. Retrieved July 30, 2005, from http://www.dnsstuff.com

Dsniff homepage. Retrieved July 30, 2005, from http://www.monkey.org/~dugsong/dsniff/

Ethereal homepage. Retrieved July 30, 2005, from http://www.ethereal.com

Fyodor, Remote OS detection via TCP/IP stack fingerprinting. Retrieved April 30, 2005, from http://www.insecure.org/nmap/nmap-fingerprinting-article.html

Gordon, L., Loeb, M., Lucyshyn, W., & Richardson, R. (2005). *2005 CSI/FBI computer crime and security survey.* Retrieved July 25, 2005, from http://www.gocsi.com

Grimes, R. (2001). *Malicious mobile code: Virus protection for Windows.* Sebastopol, CA: O'Reilly.

Grimes, R. (2002). *Danger: remote access trojans.* Retrieved July 30, 2005, from http://www.microsoft.com/technet/security/alerts/info/virusrat.mspx

Harley, D., Slade, D., & Gattiker, U. (2001). *Viruses revealed.* New York: McGraw-Hill.

Harrison, A. (2000). *Cyberassaults hit Buy.com, eBay, CNN and Amazon.* Retrieved on July 30, 2005, from http://www.computerworld.com/news/2000/story/0,11280,43010,00.html

Hoglund, G., & Butler, J. (2005). *Rootkits: Subverting the Windows kernel.* Reading, MA: Addison Wesley Professional.

Hoglund, G., & McGraw, G. (2004). *Exploiting software: How to break code.* Boston: Pearson Education.

Honeynet Project. (2005). *Know your enemy: Tracking botnets.* Retrieved July 30, 2005, from http://www.honeynet.org/papers/bots/

Hunt homepage. Retrieved July 30, 2005, from http://lin.fsid.cvut.cz/~kra/index.html

IETF RFC 1739. (1994). *A primer on Internet and TCP/IP tools.* Retrieved July 30, 2005, from http://www.ietf.org/rfc/rfc1739.txt

IETF RFC 1700. (1994). *Assigned numbers.* Retrieved July 30, 2005, from http://www.ietf.org/rfc/rfc1700.txt

Insecure, Nmap free security scanner, tools & hacking resources. Retrieved July 30, 2005, from http://www.insecure.org

InterNIC, The Internet's network information center. Retrieved July 30, 2005, from http://www.internic.net

Kloth.net, Online services. Retrieved July 30, 2005, from http://www.kloth.net/services/

Koziol, J., et al. (2004). *The shellcoder's handbook: Discovering and exploiting security holes*. Indianapolis, IA: Wiley Publishing.

Markoff, J., & Shimomura, T. (1996). *Takedown: The pursuit and capture of Kevin Mitnick, America's most wanted computer outlaw – By the man who did it*. New York: Hyperion Books.

McClure, S., Kutz, G., & Scambray, J. (2001). *Hacking exposed* (3rd ed.). New York: McGraw-Hill.

Nachenberg, C. (1996). *Understanding and managing polymorphic viruses*. Retrieved July 30, 2005, from http://www.symantec.com/avcenter/reference/striker.pdf

Nessus homepage. Retrieved July 30, 2005, from http://www.nessus.org

Packet Storm, Wardialers. Retrieved July 30, 2005, from http://packetstorm.linuxsecurity.com/wardialers/

Password Crackers, Russian password crackers. Retrieved July 30, 2005, from http://www.password-crackers.com/crack.html

Phenoelit, Default password list. Retrieved July 30, 2005, from http://www.phenoelit.de/dpl/dpl.html

RealVNC homepage. Retrieved July 30, 2005, from http://www.realvnc.com

Sam Spade homepage. Retrieved July 30, 2005, from http://www.samspade.org

SANS, The twenty most critical Internet security vulnerabilities (updated) – The experts consensus. Retrieved July 30, 2005, from http://www.sans.org/top20/

Shimonski, R. (2005). *Introduction to password cracking*. Retrieved April 30, 2005, from http://www-106.ibm.com/developerworks/library/s-crack/

Shinder, D., & Tittel, E. (2002). *Scene of the cybercrime: Computer forensics handbook*. Rockland, MA: Syngress Publishing.

Skoudis, E. (2002). *Counter hack: A step-by-step guide to computer attacks and effective defenses*. Upper Saddle River, NJ: Prentice Hall PTR.

Snort homepage. Retrieved July 30, 2005, from http://www.snort.org

Stevens, W. R. (1994). *TCP/IP illustrated, volume 1: The protocols*. Reading, MA: Addison-Wesley.

Sub7 homepage. Retrieved July 30, 2005, from http://sub7.net

Swartz, J. (2004). Crooks slither into Net's shady nooks and crannies, *USA Today*. Retrieved July 30, 2005, from http://www.usatoday.com/tech/news/2004-10-20-cyber-crime_x.htm

Szor, P. (2005). *The art of computer virus and defense*. Reading, MA: Addison Wesley Professional.

Tcpdump homepage. Retrieved July 30, 2005, from http://www.tcpdump.org

Turner, D., Entwisle, S., Friedrichs, O., Ahmad, D., Blackbird, J., Fossl, M., et al. (2005). *Symantec internet security threat report: Trends for July 2004 - December 2004.* Retrieved July 30, 2005, from http://www.symantec.com

Webopedia, The difference between a virus, worm and Trojan horse? Retrieved July 30, 2005, from http://www.webopedia.com/DidYouKnow/Internet/2004/virus.asp

Webroot. (2005). *State of sypware Q1 2005.* Retrieved July 30, 2005, from http://www.webroot.com

Wichmann, R. (2002). *Linux kernel rootkits.* Retrieved on July 30, 2005, from http://la-samhna.de/library/rootkits/

Appendix: Acronyms

APNIC	Asia Pacific Network Information Center
ARIN	American Registry for Internet Numbers
CGI	Common Gateway Interface
DNS	Domain Name System
DoS	Denial of Service
FTP	File Transfer Protocol
HTTP	Hypertext Transfer Protocol
ICMP	Internet Control Message Protocol
IDS	Intrusion Detection System
InterNIC	Internet Network Information Center
IP	Internet Protocol
ISP	Internet Service Provider
LAN	Local Area Network
RAT	Remote Access Trojan
RIPENCC	Réseaux IP Euoropéens Network Coordination Centre
SAINT	Security Administrator's Integrated Network Tool
SARA	Security Auditor's Research Assistant
SATAN	Security Administrator's Tool for Analyzing Networks
TCP	Transmission Control Protocol
TFN	Tribe Flood Network
TTL	Time to Live
UDP	User Datagram Protocol

Chapter II

Malware: An Evolving Threat

Steven Furnell, University of Plymouth, UK

Jeremy Ward, Symantec EMEA, UK

Abstract

In the two decades since its first significant appearance, malware has become the most prominent and costly threat to modern IT systems. This chapter examines the nature of malware evolution. It highlights that, as well as the more obvious development of propagation techniques, the nature of payload activities (and the related motivations of the malware creators) is also significantly changing, as is the ability of the malware to defeat defences. Having established the various facets of the threat, the discussion proceeds to consider appropriate strategies for malware detection and prevention, considering the role of modern antivirus software, and its use alongside other network security technologies to give more comprehensive protection. It is concluded that although malware is likely to remain a significant and ever-present threat, the risk and resultant impacts can be substantially mitigated by appropriate use of such safeguards.

Introduction

Malicious software (malware) such as worms, viruses, and Trojan horses are now amongst the most readily recognised threats to computing systems. Indeed, malware has been the principal computer security problem for the PC generation, and has certainly dominated the scene since mass adoption of the Internet began in the mid-1990s. However, the beginnings of the malware problem go back significantly beyond this. For example, while the precise origins of Trojan horse programs are unknown, the ultimate arrival of worms and viruses can be linked back to the earliest thinking about self-replicating systems, such as the proposal of "cellular automata" (von Neumann, 1948). Such "automata" introduce the concept that information can be encoded with simple rules in such a way that it is able to self-replicate and spread throughout a system. Effectively it is this concept that was used by Watson and Crick when, five years later, they published the structure of DNA— the molecule which encodes the information used to replicate organic life-forms. Some 30 years later, security researcher Frederick Cohen first used the term 'computer virus' to describe a self-replicating piece of code within an IT system (Cohen, 1994). In an interesting parallel development, Richard Dawkins' book *The Selfish Gene* (Dawkins, 1976), introduced the concept that all living organisms are the "puppets" of self-replicating pieces of code. These are the concepts that lie behind the examination of the evolution of the malware threat which is the subject of this chapter.

The discussion in this chapter aims to examine the evolution of the malware threat, and the consequent demands that it now raises in terms of protection. The next section presents some of the core terminology, and highlights the prevalence of the malware threat in relation to current systems. The third section considers the range of motivations that may lead to malware being written and released, which gives an insight into the reasons for the threat. The fourth section examines the ways in which malware has evolved, focusing upon the techniques that it may use to harm systems, as well as those that it uses to propagate and ensure its own survival. Having identified a clear threat, the next section identifies the various measures that should be considered in order to detect and prevent malware, including safeguards at both the system and network levels to provide a comprehensive overall strategy. The chapter concludes with an overall summary and thoughts on the future outlook. It should be noted that the discussion does not seek to address the software level implementation and functionality of the malware. However, readers interested in these aspects can find relevant information in a number of published sources (Skoudis & Zeltser, 2003; Harley, Slade, & Gattiker, 2001).

Background

At a general level, the term "malware" can denote any piece of computer code that has a malicious or unwanted effect on an IT system or network. While there are literally thousands of individual examples of malware, the key categories are typically considered to be the following:

- **Virus:** A replicating program that enters a system by infecting "carrier" materials such as disks, files, or documents. A virus may carry a payload, which will activate at some point after infection, causing unwanted and often damaging effects. It is worth noting that the term "virus" is often misused as a generic label for all forms of malicious software. This most often occurs in the context of media reports, and both reflects and explains the fact that many end-users perceive all forms of malware to be synonymous with the concept of a virus.

- **Worm:** Sharing a superficial similarity with the virus in terms of replicating between networked systems, worms differ in that they are able to spread autonomously, without the need to infect a carrier in the manner of a virus. Worms take advantage of the network connectivity between systems (Weaver, Paxson, Staniford, & Cunningham, 2003), and can spread as a result of fully automated activity (e.g. scanning random IP addresses and exploiting vulnerabilities to gain entry to remote systems) or user-initiated actions (e.g., opening bogus content from e-mail attachments or peer-to-peer file shares).

- **Trojan Horse:** Taking their name from the hollow wooden horse used by the Greeks to invade Troy, this category of malware refers to programs that fool users into executing them by pretending to perform a particular function, but ultimately prove to do something else (either instead of, or in addition to, the claimed function), resulting in unexpected and typically unwanted effects.

There are also various other terms that may be encountered in the discussion of dangerous or harmful code, including *backdoors* (routes opened up by attackers to allow unauthorized access into a system), *trapdoors* (entry points that are similarly unauthorized, but left behind by the original developers), *time bombs* (code set to trigger after a period of time has elapsed or when a specific date or time is reached), and *logic bombs* (triggered by a specific event, or event series, occurring within the system). However, for the purposes of this discussion, the descriptions above are considered to be appropriate as a top-level categorization.

Regardless of what we call it, malware is consistently one of the top-rated security issues, with many surveys effectively telling the same story. A selection of relevant results is presented in Table 1, almost all of which show viruses (and other malware) to be the most significant category of reported incident.

It is notable that even though malware was not the top-rated incident in the Ernst & Young survey (in the 2004 results that honour went to "Hardware failure", affecting 72% of respondents), it *was* still the top-rated concern when respondents were asked to indicate the security issue that they were most worried about in the year ahead, with 77% responding positively (as against 60% for employee misconduct involving information systems, and 56% for spam, in the second and third spots respectively).

It is perhaps unsurprising to discover that, in addition to being the most prevalent threat, malware is also the most costly. An indication of this comes from the CSI/FBI Computer Crime & Security Survey 2005, in which 639 respondents reported collective losses of over US$42.5 million to "virus" incidents. This was placed malware well ahead of any of the other twelve categories of breach that respondents were asked to comment upon (which included unauthorised access, theft of proprietary information, and denial of service), and accounted for a third of the reported losses in the survey overall.

Table 1. Survey findings showing the significant of malware incidents

Survey	Category	Associated statistic	Top-rated category
KPMG Global Information Security Survey 2002 (KPMG, 2002)	Virus incidents[a]	61% suffering breaches	✓
DTI Information Security Breaches Survey 2004 (DTI, 2004)	Virus infection and disruptive software	50% of respondents affected	✓
Ernst & Young Global Information Security Survey 2004 (Ernst & Young, 2004)	Major Virus, Trojan horse or Internet Worm	68% suffering incidents leading to loss of availability	✗
CSI/FBI Computer Crime & Security Survey 2005 (Gordon et al., 2005)	Virus[a]	~75% of respondents affected[b]	✓

[a] *The term "virus" was being used as a synonym for all malware in these surveys.*

[b] *The specific percentage was not stated in the published report, and so this value is inferred from an associated graph.*

Another notable point is that users now have significantly less chance of avoiding a malware encounter. The cause of this is largely attributable to increasingly inventive propagation mechanisms (discussed later in the chapter), and the leveraging of the Internet as a transport medium. As a result, malware distribution has become faster, more widespread, and experienced by far more people at firsthand. As an indication of this, we can consider the significant increase in malware-infected e-mail messages—one of the key infection vectors that the Internet has offered. Relevant figures here are reported by MessageLabs, which scans millions of e-mails per day as part of its managed e-mail security service. Back in 2000, these scans revealed that an average of one in every 790 e-mails contained a virus. However, as Figure 1 indicates, the situation changed considerably in subsequent years, and by 2004 one in every 16 messages was infected (MessageLabs, 2004). As such, the chances of avoiding infected messages have fallen considerably.

Given such a dramatic change, it is clear that those creating the malware are continually achieving a greater level of success, emphasising the importance of effective detection and prevention strategies. Prior to considering these, however, it is also worth examining why and how the perpetrators are pursuing their malicious objectives. This is the focus of the next two sections.

Figure 1. Chances of avoiding malware-infected email messages

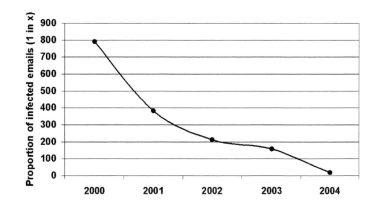

Motivations for Malice

Before looking at what the malware can do, it is relevant to consider the role of those who write and release the software. An appreciation of their evolving techniques and motives can contribute to understanding the threat that we face.

Typical motives can be classified according to one or more of the following reasons (Furnell, 2001):

- to see how far their creation can spread or how much attention it can attract (the former often influencing the latter),

- to cause damage or disruption (an aspect that could itself be motivated by factors such as revenge or ideology), which may take the form of a targeted attack against an individual, an organization, or a regime,

- to achieve a feeling of power or superiority over those who fall victim to the creation (the aliases of past virus writers, such as Dark Avenger and Black Baron, suggest some attempt to boost their own ego and sense of importance),

- to use the malware as a means of leveraging some form of personal gain,

- to give people a lesson in security, by providing a practical illustration of security weaknesses to users and vendors,

- to merely conduct an experiment and see what can be achieved with modern software, networking technology, etc.

Although interviews with malware writers are relatively rare, there are some reported comments that give an insight into the mindset. Perhaps following in the footsteps of the original research from Cohen, some latter day malware writers claim to be investigating the technical feasibility of new approaches, or to demonstrate a vulnerability of the platforms that they are targeting. For example, a published interview with former virus writer Marek "Benny" Strihavka, a former member of the 29A group, asked him about the purpose of the group and his own motives for writing viruses (Lemos, 2005):

The purpose of 29A has always been technical progress, invention and innovation of new and technically mature and interesting viruses . . . I always tried to come up with something new, never seen before. I coded viruses for platforms that were considered infect-resistant . . . This is not about any sort of "cyberterrorism."

A somewhat more direct justification comes from Onel de Guzman, a self-confessed malware writer and alleged to have created the infamous Loveletter worm. De Guzman's view was that Microsoft was ultimately to blame for the incident because the worm relied on the ability to exploit a weakness of the Outlook e-mail client (Landler, 2000):

For programmers like us, it is not wrong . . . I'm the user, I buy the product. If I use it in a wrong or improper way, why should I be blamed?

In addition to such reported quotes, it is also possible to get an indication of the author's claimed motives from messages that they often hide within their creations. Perhaps unsurprisingly, given the power and ego-oriented motives of many of their creators, one of the most common forms of message relates to boasting and bragging about their own skills. As an example, we can consider the following message, which is deposited in the System directory (in a file named "msg15.txt") following infection by a variant of the *Mydoom* worm (F-Secure, 2004):

Lucky's Av's ;P~. Sasser author gets IT security job and we will work with Mydoom , P2P worms and exploit codes .Also we will attack f-secure,symantec,trendmicro,mcafee, etc. The 11th of march is the skynet day lol . When the beagle and mydoom loose, we wanna stop our activity <== so Where is the Skynet now? lol.
This Will Drop W32.Scran P2P Worm

In this particular case, the text is ridiculing rival worm *NetSky* (the author of which referred to his creation as Skynet), and issuing an apparent threat to various antivirus companies.

It is also common for the authors to convey messages that attempt to justify or attribute blame for their actions. For example, the code from August 2003's *Blaster* worm contained the following message, which did not get displayed on-screen (Symantec, 2003b):

I just want to say LOVE YOU SAN!!

billy gates why do you make this possible ? Stop making money and fix your software!!

Meanwhile, the message embedded within the code of the *Klez* worm appeared to be an appeal for sympathy, with the original version, from October 2001, containing the following text (Symantec, 2001c):

I'm sorry to do so,but it's helpless to say sorry.

I want a good job,I must support my parents.

Now you have seen my technical capabilities.

How much my year-salary now? NO more than $5,500.

What do you think of this fact?

Don't call my names,I have no hostility.

Can you help me?

It is clear even from this brief set of examples that the (claimed) motivations may be quite varied. However, clues to the motives of the author can also be gleaned from what the malware attempts to do. For example, as later discussion shows, there has been an increase in the volume of malware that seeks to open a backdoor, which can then facilitate further criminal opportunities. Specifically, for each system compromised in this way, the attacker acquires an exploitable asset. As their number increases, these systems can represent a massive resource in terms of collective computing power and network bandwidth. With successfully replicating malware, thousands of PCs could be compromised, and then harnessed to operate as a robot network (botnet) under the attacker's control (as an example of the threat, the first six months of 2004 saw the number of botnets monitored by Symantec [2004b] rise from under 2,000 to more than 30,000). Having acquired such resources, the hackers can turn them to financial advantage in a number of ways. One established approach is to sell or rent the botnet to spammers as a means of sending junk mail and bypassing IP address blacklists, with reports suggesting that they can be rented for as little as $100 an hour (*Metro News*, 2004). Another proven option is extortion, based upon the threat of using the collective "fire power" of the compromised systems to launch a Distributed Denial of Service attack. Notable victims in this respect have included online gambling sites, which have reported being targets of demands from Russian organised crime syndicates (McCue, 2001).

Unfortunately, it is not only the motivations that may be varied. The creators of malware have also evolved myriad techniques to target and attack systems, and these are key to appreciating how the threat has evolved to its current prominence in spite of increased awareness amongst potential victims.

The Evolving Threat

Having established the existence of the malware problem, this section considers how the nature of the threat has evolved over time. Referring back to the malware categories defined earlier, it is worth noting that the discussion here is most specifically focused upon worms and viruses, as these are the forms of malware that have witnessed the most dramatic changes (Chen, 2003). Although Trojan horse programs still have a significant presence, the nature of their threat has not fundamentally evolved—they have always been able to do pretty much anything that can be achieved in software (albeit potentially constrained by the access privileges available to them). One of the most notable changes has been the route by which they might arrive in a system. Whereas the installation of a Trojan once relied upon manual action by an unsuspecting user, worms are now frequently used as a mechanism for dropping them into systems automatically. As such, the real change in this respect can equally be attributed to the evolution of worm techniques.

Tracing back the history of viruses and worms reveals a clear evolution in terms of the associated infection and propagation mechanisms, as well as the resulting actions on the target systems. Aside from an underlying fundamental change, which moved malware distribution away from reliance upon manual exchange of disks to leveraging of the Internet, the last fifteen years have witnessed some distinct phases:

- **Early 1990s:** Relied upon people to exchange disks between systems, to spread boot sector and file viruses,

- **Mid 1990s:** A move towards macro viruses, which enabled the malware to be embedded in files that users were more likely to exchange with each other,

- **Late 1990s:** The appearance of automated mass mailing functionality, removing the reliance upon users to manually send infected files,

- **Today:** Avoiding the need to dupe the user into opening an infected e-mail attachment, by exploiting vulnerabilities that enable infection without user intervention.

Figure 2. Message displayed by the Elk Cloner virus

```
      Elk Cloner:  The program with a personality

         It will get on all your disks
           It will infiltrate your chips
             Yes it's Cloner!

         It will stick to you like glue
           It will modify ram too
             Send in the Cloner!
```

However, the malware problem itself dates backs even further than this. For example, the first known virus incident can be traced to 1982, with the release of the "Elk Cloner" on Apple II systems. Written by 15-year-old Richard Skrenta, the program was like many viruses that would follow it: spreading between machines by infecting floppy disks, and loading into memory whenever a system was booted from an infected disk. After the 50th such boot, the virus would display the message shown in Figure 2 (Skrenta, 1982). Other than this nuisance aspect, however, Elk Cloner did nothing to intentionally disrupt the user or harm their system (although there was potential to destroy data if the program attempted to write itself to a disk that did not contain the operating system).

Although it is now referred to as a virus, this term had not been coined in the days of the Elk Cloner. It was not until two years later that this type of software behavior was given a name, in Fred Cohen's paper entitled "Computer Viruses—Theory and Experiments" (Cohen, 1984).

As some of the survey category headings from Table 1 have already illustrated, the term "virus" is now frequently used as a catch-all term to encompass all forms of malware and, together with hackers, the threat of the computer virus is the security issue that has most clearly permeated the public mind. Indeed, although other forms of malware such as worms and Trojan horses had emerged long before Cohen's paper, it was from his work that the biological analogy first arose, and this has been a lasting contribution to the way in which much of the subsequent literature has considered malware in general.

Figure 3 summarizes the timeline of some of the most significant developments to have occurred since the days of the Elk Cloner and Cohen's paper. It is notable that the last entry denotes the emergence of malware on a new platform, reflecting the increased capabilities of mobile phone devices and their desirability as a target for malware authors. At the time of writing, the malware problem has by no means become as established in this domain as it has within the PC context, but nonetheless equipping such mobile devices with antivirus protection has become an increasingly standard practice.

Figure 3. The evolution of viruses and worms

	1986	Boot sector viruses arrive (e.g. Brain)
	1987	File / Parasitic viruses appear (e.g. Jerusalem)
	1991	Polymorphic viruses (e.g. Tequila)
T I M E	**1996**	Word and Excel macro viruses (e.g. Concept, Laroux)
	1999	Self-distributing email malware (e.g. Melissa)
	2000	Metamorphic malware (e.g. Evol)
	2001	Widespread vulnerability exploitation and Blended threats (e.g. CodeRed, Nimda)
	2004	Smartphone viruses appear (e.g. Cabir)

In the two decades since Cohen's paper suggested the potential threat, the risk that he described was unquestionably borne out. Indeed, 2004 was significant for witnessing the arrival of the 100,000[th] malware threat (McAfee, 2004). However, while there are truly thousands of strains, it must be recognised that they do not all pose an equal threat. Indeed, in some cases, new malware will be identified and contained by antivirus laboratories before it has a chance to spread. Meanwhile, older strains will effectively die away as result of detection and eradication by antivirus software. So, of the thousands of strains that are known, only a fraction will represent an active threat at any time. Such malware is termed "in the wild", and the extent of the problem is gauged by The WildList Organization, which compiles a monthly list based upon reports received from trusted antivirus researchers and corporations world-wide. The classification is assigned to a virus if verified encounters are reported by two or more of the WildList correspondents within a given reporting period (WildList, 2005a). Unfortunately, although this brings the list down to hundreds rather than thousands of strains, it remains a considerable problem. For example, the chart in Figure 4 depicts the monthly WildList totals from the beginning of 2000 through to the end of 2004 (WildList, 2005b) (note: the gaps within each year are months for which there were no published figures). A clear upward trend is apparent, and it is notable that the figures became significantly higher towards the end of the period—which is again indicative of the increasing nature of the malware threat.

Another significant element of evolution, as already listed in Figure 3, has been the arrival of so-called blended threats, which combine the characteristics of malware with server and Internet vulnerabilities. According to the definition from Symantec, malware can be considered to qualify as a blended threat if it combines two or more of the following characteristics (Symantec, 2001a):

- Cause damage (e.g., launching a denial of service attack, dropping a Trojan Horse for later use),

- Spread via multiple methods (e.g., mass mailing, infecting visitors to compromised Web site),

Figure 4. WildList figures (2000-2004)

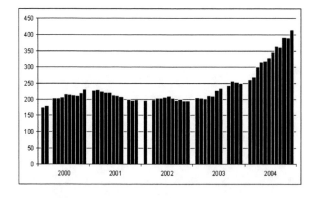

- Has multiple points of attack (e.g., adding script code to HTML files, infecting .exe files, making registry changes),

- Spreads automatically (e.g., scanning the Internet and other accessible networks for vulnerable systems),

- Exploits vulnerabilities (e.g., buffer overflows, default passwords, HTTP input validation vulnerabilities).

Much of the malware released since 2000 has been of the blended variety, and the effective combination of techniques has been responsible for the observed upsurge in the volume and cost of incidents.

Having established that the general nature of the threat has evolved, it is worth giving more specific consideration to the behaviour of the malware concerned. In this respect, key issues are:

- **Propagation:** How the malware spreads,

- **Payload:** What it does to an infected target,

- **Preservation:** How it ensures its own survival.

Although listed here as distinct issues, there is sometimes the possibility to perceive an overlap between these aspects (e.g., as a result of the propagation process itself causing disruptive effects, and being perceived as a payload). The various issues are now discussed in the subsections that follow.

Propagation Mechanisms

All malware requires a means to find its way onto victim systems. In the cases of worms and viruses, the ability to propagate is part of the inherent functionality, with replication within and between systems being the key to further infections. In general, a variety of techniques can be used and established methods have come to include:

- mass mailing (in some cases harvesting e-mail addresses from the victim system),

- vulnerability exploitation,

- traversing unprotected network shares,

- social engineering users into downloading and/or running the software on their system.

When considering possible infection vectors, it is important to recognize that malware writers are keen followers of fashion—at least in terms of watching the technologies that everyone else is using, and then hijacking the most popular ones as platforms for deploying new malware. Some notable examples of this include:

- **E-mail:** Since the late 90s, e-mail has proven itself to be an extremely powerful method of malware distribution. Although originally just another channel by which unsuspecting users might manually exchange macro-virus infected documents, the use of e-mail was quickly combined with automated features and scripting to enable mass-mailing to multiple recipients and effectively instantaneous global distribution. From the numerous examples that can be cited, landmark incidents that used this technique include *Melissa* (a Word 97 macro virus) in 1999 (Symantec, 1999a) and the *LoveLetter* (a worm based upon a malicious Visual Basic Script) the following year (Symantec, 2000a). A consequence of mass-mailing malware is the now standard advice to users to exercise caution and suspicion in dealing with e-mail attachments.

- **Peer-to-Peer (P2P) networks:** The early 2000s witnessed the widespread emergence and popularity of P2P networks, based upon software such as KaZaA and Morpheus, which became particularly notable as a source of illicit software, music and other pirated media files. With thousands of users drawn towards such networks, they became a natural target for malware, whose authors' realized that P2P could be used as a distribution channel by disguising the malware as other content, thus fooling users into downloading it in the belief that they are something else. Examples that have utilized P2P file sharing as their vector include the *Benjamin, Kwbot,* and *Mant* worms.

- **Instant Messaging (IM):** IM has become a popular end-user application in both domestic and workplace scenarios, enabling personal chatting as well as a convenient method of contact and information sharing within organizations. From the malware perspective, it has served to open another potential channel into the user systems and company networks. Examples of IM-based worms include *Choke* and *Kelvir*, both of which targeted Microsoft's MSN Messenger.

- **Blogs:** With the popularity of blogging, attackers have established bogus blog sites, from which visitors' systems can be compromised with malware (Websense, 2005). Users are tempted into visiting based upon the apparent topic of the blog, and once there render their systems vulnerable to the malware with which the site may have been baited.

All of these illustrate the opportunistic nature of the malware authors, and the fact that they are attuned to finding new ways to trick their victims. Indeed, in what could be viewed as both ingenuity and callousness, malware writers have also spotted the opportunity to use the notoriety of their creations as another means of enabling them to spread. Preying upon users' concern over the threat, malware often arrives masquerading as a security update, a virus warning, or claiming to be a "removal tool" for a strain that is receiving publicity at the time. Typical examples include the *Gibe* and *Qint* worms, both of which arrived in the guise of messages purporting to be from Microsoft, with bogus attachments that claimed to be security patches.

Table 2. Examples of malware payloads and their threats

Payload	Confidentiality	Integrity	Availability
Open backdoor	✓	✓	
Keystroke logging	✓		
Corrupt BIOS		✓	✓
Corrupt data / files		✓	✓
Launch Denial of Service			✓
Nuisance effects/messages		✓	✓
Rogue emails / Spamming		✓	
Disable antivirus software		✓	
Install Trojan horse		✓	

Payload Possibilities

The payload is the term used to refer to whatever the malware does when it is activated. In theory, this could effectively be anything that can be done under software control. In reality, however, malware payloads have tended to pursue a number of identifiable themes, with common top-level effects known to include deleting or modifying files, degrading the performance of the system, or causing it to become unstable, and compromising security by introducing backdoors or disclosing confidential information.

Of course, all malware will (to some extent) impact the integrity of the infected system—its mere presence having made a change to the legitimate state. Virus infections in particular will result in an unauthorized modification of their carrier (e.g., executable program, document, or disk boot sector). Beyond this, however, there could be further and more substantial integrity-related impacts, such as altering or corrupting data, or impairing the operation of the system itself. In addition, payload actions may potentially affect the other core security properties of confidentiality (i.e., by stealing or otherwise disclosing information) and availability (i.e., by impeding or preventing access to the system or its data for legitimate entities). Some examples of the range of potential payload activities are listed in Table 2, along with an indication of the security properties that such activities are most likely to compromise. The list is by no means exhaustive, but it represents a list of established activities, all of which have been observed in numerous malware cases over the years.

There are, of course, further impacts that may result as a consequence of the payload effects, such as disruption to activities, and financial costs associated with data loss and system recovery. In addition, impacts may not only affect the infected system. For example, as well as causing Denial of Service (DoS) for the local user, the payload may also cause the system to launch or participate in a DoS against a remote victim.

When analyzing malware, understanding the payload is a significant step towards understanding the threat. Having said this, a payload will not always be present—a situation that is often the case when it aims to provide proof-of-concept for a new propagation mechanism. Unfortunately, this also means that it can still pose a threat. A very good example can be provided here by the case of the *Slammer* worm, which was

Figure 5. The rising number of backdoor malware

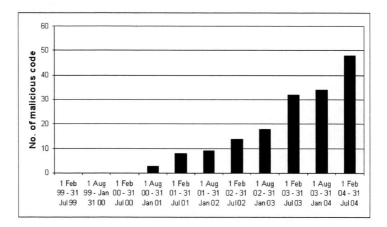

released in January 2003 and spread between systems by exploiting a known vulnerability in Microsoft's SQL Server 2000 and Microsoft SQL Server Desktop Engine (MSDE) 2000 software (Symantec, 2003a). Despite the lack of a payload, the worm was still able to cause a significant degree of disruption as a result of its speed of propagation and the consequent volume of traffic that it generated from compromised systems across the Internet. Resulting effects included the collapse of the South Korean telecommunications network, disruption to 13,000 Bank of America cash machines, and the failure of five of the Internet's 13 root name servers. Overall, the disruptive effects of the worm were estimated to have cost between $950m and $1.2bn in lost productivity (Lemos, 2003).

While early programs were very often destructive, a key difference in many of today's malware is that even when the payload is triggered, users remain oblivious. Indeed, while most end-user perceptions of malware still seem to be based upon the idea of something that infects the system, and then disrupts operations or destroys data in some way, it is important to recognize that the real threat is often to be found not in the initial infection, but in what this leaves behind. Rather than trashing the system, an increasingly frequent modus operandi is to open a "backdoor" that allows the system to be compromised in potentially more insidious ways. Indeed, this has become an ever more significant phenomenon over the past three years, as can be seen in Figure 5 (based upon numbers taken from Symantec DeepSight Alert, and identifying the number of unique instances of malicious code identified in each period) (Furnell & Ward, 2004).

In addition, the increasing tendency for malware to contain non-destructive payloads can be illustrated by plotting the relative numbers. This is illustrated in Figure 6, which shows the six-monthly totals for the number of new codes appearing without a destructive payload (i.e., those that *only* open a backdoor, or have no apparent payload functionality), as well as the percentages that these represented for the malware

Figure 6. The rise of non-destructive malware

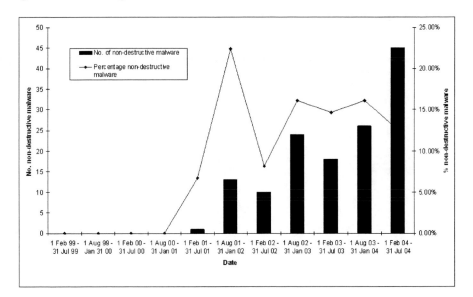

appearing in these periods overall. Although destructive variants are still dominant as a proportion of the total, the percentage of non-destructive malware is nonetheless significant, as is the overall rise in absolute numbers.

The nature of the payload action, and the point at which it should trigger, are important characteristics in determining the malware's potential lifespan within a system before discovery. If the payload is too extreme, then even a user without antivirus protection will be alerted to a problem, and if the resulting action is so destructive that it renders the system useless (e.g., corrupting the BIOS in the manner of the *CIH / Chernobyl* virus), then it removes the chance for further replication if the malware is a worm or virus. Similarly, if the payload triggers too soon after infection, then further opportunities to spread may be lost. Indeed, the ability to safeguard its own existence is another key element of most malware.

Self-Preservation Techniques

One of the desirable characteristics for effective malware is for it to be difficult to detect and destroy. In pursuit of this goal, malware writers have devised a number of techniques designed to conceal the existence of their creations within a system, and complicate the task for antivirus packages.

*   **Stealth techniques:** Malware can use stealth methods to hide evidence of its existence, and thereby increase the chances of avoiding detection. For example, if a virus has infected an executable program, the size of the affected file will almost

Figure 7. Examples of the registry keys removed by the Beagle.BN worm

```
HKEY_LOCAL_MACHINE\SOFTWARE\Microsoft\Windows\CurrentVer
sion\Run\"EasyAV"
HKEY_LOCAL_MACHINE\SOFTWARE\Microsoft\Windows\CurrentVer
sion\Run\"PandaAVEngine"
HKEY_LOCAL_MACHINE\SOFTWARE\Microsoft\Windows\CurrentVer
sion\Run\"Norton Antivirus AV"
HKEY_LOCAL_MACHINE\SOFTWARE\Microsoft\Windows\CurrentVer
sion\Run\"KasperskyAVEng"
```

inevitably have changed as a result. A stealth virus may attempt to conceal this by reporting the original, uninfected file length. This can be achieved by the virus intercepting disk-access requests.

- **Polymorphism:** Polymorphic malware is designed to complicate the task for antivirus software. Recognising that a principal method used by detection engines is signature matching, polymorphic malware encrypts itself differently for each infection, to avoid leaving a consistent detectable signature. A small portion of the code decrypts the rest when the malware is activated. The approach originated with the *Tequila* virus in 1991 (Symantec, 1991), and went on to become a common technique in subsequent malware.

- **Metamorphism:** Although polymorphic malware can adopt different disguises, the underlying code remains the same once decrypted. By contrast, metamorphic malware has the ability to *rewrite* itself, such that successive infections involve genuinely distinct code that still performs the same function. The metamorphic engine works by disassembling the code, permuting the instructions in some way (e.g. reordering or dividing the original instructions into separate blocks of code, linked by jumps), and then reassembling the result to yield the new instance of the malware. A well-known example is the *Evol* worm (Symantec, 2000b), which affects systems running a variety of Windows platforms.

- **Attacking security:** Recognizing that many systems are now equipped with antivirus and other forms of protection, it is now common for malware to attempt a pre-emptive strike against the programs that would otherwise seek to thwart it. Several techniques have been devised. For example, the *Gaobot* worm (Symantec, 2005a) attempts to block access to over 35 security-related Web sites (belonging to companies such as F-Secure, McAfee, Symantec, Sophos, and Trend Micro), in order to prevent the infected system from obtaining security updates that would enable detection or removal of the worm. It also maintains a list of over 420 processes (e.g., relating to antivirus and firewall software) that are then terminated if found running on the system. Meanwhile, one of the many variants of the *Beagle* worm (Symantec, 2005c) attempts to delete a variety of Windows registry entries (a subset of which are listed in Figure 7), in order to prevent the associated security software from running when the operating system starts up.

Example Incidents

Having identified various techniques, it is relevant to briefly highlight how they have been manifested in notable malware outbreaks. Some examples of related malware have, of course, been highlighted during the course of the preceding discussions. However, in order to give a view of how some of these techniques have appeared and evolved over time, Table 3 presents a series of some of the most significant malware strains from 1998 through to 2004. All of these targeted the Windows operating system, with the majority affecting all versions from Windows 95 onwards (the exception here is the *CIH* virus, which affected only Windows 95/98/ME and not the NT/2000/XP-based versions). Another common factor of all barring *CIH* was the ability to self-propagate between systems. However, looking at entries through the years, it is possible to observe some significant elements in the evolution of their techniques. For example, mass-mailers have evolved from using Outlook to having their own SMTP (Simple Mail Transfer Protocol) engines, and have become far more inventive in terms of how they apply the mass mailing technique. Rather than simply using addresses from the local address books, later worms incorporate techniques for harvesting addresses from an increasing range of other files, and use those found as both targets and spoofed origin addresses for subsequent mailings.

Having established that our systems have an increasingly significant range of threats to be concerned about, the discussion now proceeds to consider how we might take appropriate steps to protect them.

Detection and Prevention Strategies

The security industry has, of course, responded with a range of prevention, detection and inoculation technologies. Antivirus software is now one of the most widely used security countermeasures, with 96% of respondents to the aforementioned Computer Security Institute study claiming to use it (Gordon, Loeb, Lucyshyn, & Richardson, 2005), as well as all of those responding to the Ernst and Young (2004) survey. Developments in antivirus software have had to be rapid to match the pace of the evolving threat. Modern antivirus systems have to be highly complex, to deal with the complexity of the threat; this section will therefore seek only to summarize the main strategies used.For further information please refer to Szor's *The Art of Computer Virus Research and Defense* (Szor, 2005).

Table 3. Notable malware incidents over seven years

Year	Malware	Type	Infection and propagation techniques	Payload actions and impacts	Self preservation
1998	CIH (Symantec, 1998)	Virus	Becomes memory resident and infects 32-bit executable files on the host system when they are opened or copied. Manual actions (e.g. users sharing an infected file) enable propagation between systems.	Activates on 26th of the month (26th April only in the original versions). Overwrites the hard disk with random data and attempts to corrupt the Flash BIOS.	n/a
1999	Melissa, A (Symantec, 1999a)	MS-Word macro virus	Infects MS Word documents and templates. Performs one-off automated mailing using Microsoft Outlook, to the first 50 entries in the address book. All messages are disguised as "Important Message From USERNAME" (with USERNAME being taken from the MS Word setting on the infected system) and have the same message body: "Here is that document you asked for ... don't show anyone else ;-)"	Attaches the active document to the e-mail messages, potentially resulting in disclosure of confidential or sensitive information. Opening or closing an infected file at a number of minutes past the hour matching the current date (e.g., 10 minutes past on the 10th of the month) causes the following to be inserted into the document: "Twenty-two points, plus triple-word-score, plus fifty points for using all my letters. Game's over. I'm outta here."	Modifies security settings to disable macro warnings.
2000	KakWorm (Symantec, 1999b)	Worm	Spreads using unpatched versions of Microsoft Outlook Express, attaching itself to outgoing messages using the Signature feature.	Activates at 5 pm on the first day of the month, and shuts down the system.	n/a

Table 3. continued

2001	Nimda, A (Symantec, 2001b)	Virus Worm	Mass-mailing using own SMTP engine. Email addresses are harvested from .htm and .html files, as well as from messages held in email clients on the system. Can also spread via open network shares. Uses Unicode Web Traversal exploit to copy itself to vulnerable Microsoft IIS web servers	Opens the C drive as a network share, allowing access to the system. Also creates a guest account with administrator privilege. Infects executable files, and replaces a variety of other legitimate system files. May degrade performance and/or cause instability on the infected system.	n/a
2002	Klez-H (Symantec, 2002)	Worm	Mass-mailing via own SMTP engine. Attempts to harvest email addresses from over 20 types of file. Spoofs the sender address in mass-mailings. Randomly selects from 28 subject lines (seven of which also involve the random selection from 17 further random words for inclusion in the text).	Attaches a randomly selected file from the local system, which is sent as an attachment in mass-mailing, along with the worm. Infects executable files (hiding the originals and replacing them with copies of itself). Drops the Elkern virus into the program files directory and executes it.	Removes startup registry keys of AV products and deletes checksum database files

Malware Identification and Disinfection

Most antivirus systems are based around methodologies for identifying malware through "scanning" techniques and subsequently isolating them and then "disinfecting" the system. Scanners used by antivirus mechanisms can take one or all of the following forms:

- **Simple scanning:** This detects strings of bytes that are used by known malware.
- **Complex scanning:** This builds on simple scanning to refine the detection and identify exact matches—allowing the prevention of the variants that are such a feature of current malware.

Table 3. continued

2003	Sobig, F (Symantec, 2003c)	Worm	Mass-mailing via own SMTP engine. Harvests emails from .dbx, .eml, .hlp, .htm, .html, .mht, .wab and .txt files. Sends messages with one of nine possible subject lines, two possible message bodies and nine possible attachment names. Spoofs the sender details of its e-mails by using randomly selected email addresses from the local system as the 'From' address. Also attempted to propagate via network shares, but prevented by a bug in the code.	Capability to download and execute Trojan files on the local system. Subsequent potential to steal information from the local system.	n/a
2004	Netsky, P (Symantec, 2004a)	Worm	Mass-mailing via own SMTP engine. Harvests email addresses from files on local drives. Uses multiple e-mail subject, message and attachments. Copies itself to peer-to-peer file sharing directories, disguised using one of over 80 possible names.	n/a	n/a

- **Algorithmic scanning:** This generates an algorithm that can be used to match, and thus detect, a specific virus.

- **Code emulation:** This relies upon the use of a virtual machine to emulate the live environment. The virus executes in this virtual environment, where it can be understood, and thus detected and removed from the live system.

- **Heuristic analysis:** This looks for suspicious code combinations and is often used as a filter for algorithmic scanners.

- **Neural networks:** These can be used to reduce the number of false positives produced during the use of heuristic analysis. A neural network can be "trained" to detect only those code combinations that are truly malicious.

Once identified through the use of a combination of the scanning techniques mentioned above, malware must be isolated and, if necessary the infected system must be disinfected and repaired. At a general level, antivirus systems rely upon knowledge of the location and size of malicious code in order to enable the disinfection process to remove it from an infected host, program, or other medium. If the malware is polymorphic, it must first be decrypted, and most modern antivirus systems have a "generic decryptor" that relies upon the aforementioned code emulation technique to do this.

Despite the sophistication and complexity of their detection and disinfection techniques, antivirus systems are still largely limited to identifying only known threats. Hence, updating antivirus products regularly with new signatures is vitally important for the protection against malware to be viable. In addition, antivirus software relies upon end-users following best security practices and using it appropriately to scan unknown content entered at their systems. Improper use of antivirus software can significantly undermine its ability to offer protection against malware threats.

Malware Mitigation Techniques

Other mechanisms can be used to mitigate the malware threat. These include:

- Access control systems
- Integrity checking
- Behaviour blocking
- Sand-boxing
- User education

Access controls are built into operating systems to limit the rights of users and applications. Their purpose is to ensure the confidentiality of data on a system. However, by its nature malware represents a compromise of data integrity rather than confidentiality and thus is able to enter a system with all the rights that are appropriate to the user or application. Malware can therefore only be controlled by limiting the functionality of the system to basic applications that are not targets for infection, by isolating the system from contact with potential malware sources, or by limiting the data flow so as to break the chain of infectivity.

Unlike access controls, integrity checking relies on the fact that malware compromises the integrity of a program. Unfortunately, the ability of a system to check that all installed programs have not been changed has limited usefulness—given that applications frequently change, that it will not be possible to identify a program that is already infected, and that such a mechanism is very resource-intensive. However, integrity-checking can be run in combination with the scanning systems discussed, and could become of more use in future with developments in the PC architecture that will make applications inherently more secure.

Behavior blocking relies on the fact that malware often initiates actions of which the user is unaware, such as calling up an application or executable file. Behavior blockers will detect such actions and actively ask the user if this was intended. The problem with such a system is that most users will be unaware if the action is appropriate or not, and will find frequent messages irritating. Behavior blockers can be evaded by "slow infection" malware that only executes when a user unwittingly grants it permission to carry out an action and by malware whose code directly infects an action which a blocker has allowed to proceed.

However, behavior blocking can have a place, particularly when used in conjunction with heuristic analysis. In such cases the blocking action is transparent to the user. Indeed, the potential speed of infection by self-distributing e-mail malware (often referred to as "mass-mailers") has resulted in the development of specialized behavior-blocking and host-based defense tools of this kind. These are able effectively to act as host-based intrusion detection and prevention systems to identify the behaviour of many malware exploits such as *Slammer*, *Blaster*, *Mydoom*, *Netsky*, and *Sobig*. Put very simply, the technique blocks any attempt by the malware to execute a shell or command-prompt on a remote system.

Sand-boxing is a relatively recent concept that allows only trusted programs to run on the live system. All others run on isolated "virtual subsystems". Any infection will therefore not affect the live system, but can be detected and isolated in its subsystem. Sand-boxing has numerous potential draw-backs, including the difficulties of emulating all applications on virtual sub-systems, limitations imposed by networking, and the possibility that the 'trusted' system may become a point-of-failure. It is also possible that some malware may be able to exploit the live system and avoid the sand-box altogether. However, it is probable that sand-boxing may find an application in conjunction with other security solutions.

User education is a simple, but vital first line of defense in the mitigation of malware. It is important for all users of a system to realize that the actions they take can have a significant effect on the security of the system as a whole. They should be aware of the risks of opening or viewing e-mail attachments from an untrusted source and of the dangers of downloading untrusted software and of not keeping their antivirus system up-to-date. Administrators too should be aware of the risk of attaching any computer with out-of-date antivirus protection to a production system.

Network-Level Techniques

At the network level, malware defenses can include the use of router access control lists (ACLs), port-blocking on firewalls, deployment of network intrusion detection systems, and the use of honeypots and early-warning systems. Each of these is considered.

Network routers can be seen as the first line of defense against malware. They can be useful in preventing denial of service attacks and malware propagation attempts, by using ingress, egress filtering, and access control lists to deny traffic to/from specific subnets or ports. In fact, these features can resemble the functionality of firewalls, although not as sophisticated. Unlike a firewall, a router is not intended primarily to operate as a security device—its aim is to aid connectivity. It is also worth pointing out that routers themselves are subject to vulnerabilities and must be patched. In future it is possible that exploits will specifically target routers, with potentially devastating results.

Firewalls are a vital defense against malware. Through the use of appropriate firewall rules many malware exploits can be prevented. Specifically, blocking the ports to all unused services will prevent a significant amount of malware traffic, especially access to backdoors placed by malware. For example, blocking TCP port 3127 will prevent the *Mydoom* backdoor from operating, and blocking UDP port 1434 (associated with Microsoft SQL Server) will prevent *Slammer* from propagating. However, firewalls cannot easily block traffic to used services, such as TCP port 80, which is used by web servers. It is important to be aware that firewalls must be part of a "layered defense" system. For example, many organizations encourage home- and remote-workers to connect to networks using VPN (Virtual Private Network) tunnels. Such clients enter the network behind the perimeter-firewall, and unless they are provided with their own personal firewalls, the network is immediately vulnerable. It is also necessary to remember that firewalls have vulnerabilities, and are increasingly becoming targets for attackers. Firewall software must, therefore, be kept up-to-date as a matter of urgency.

Network intrusion detection and prevention systems can be used to produce alerts when the type of traffic generated by a malicious exploit is identified. In "logging mode" an alert is all that will be generated, allowing the system administrator to take appropriate action. In "blocking mode" the malicious traffic will be inspected and blocked before it reaches its intended target. Intrusion detection may use engines to identify anomalies in the flow of protocol traffic, as well as signature-based systems to identify specific attack types (Bace & Mell, 2001). The most effective systems combine both types.

Honeypot systems are designed to decoy attackers by providing a "virtual" system that appears to be vulnerable and can therefore easily be attacked (Spitzner, 2002). In a production environment, the general role of the system is to distract would-be intruders, capture details of an attack and direct it to a log-file. More advanced kinds of honeypot, collecting more extensive information, can be used in antivirus research to capture and analyze new types of viruses. Honeypots are thus a very useful addition to the malware defense armoury. As an aside, a similar but less sophisticated version of this concept is applied with spamtrap technologies, which can be used to attract and decoy spam messages using fake e-mail addresses.

Early warning systems are able to gather data from a number of different sensors. By correlating data-logs from firewalls, information from intrusion detection systems (both host and network) and honeypots they can provide the type of detailed analysis of malicious network traffic that will generate an alert to enable effective and timely action to be taken. Such systems are better if the information can be gathered from sensors placed in many locations across the Web; systems of this kind (such as Symantec's DeepSight system) are able to identify and track developing threats as they spread across the Web.

In summary, defense against malware must be layered and applied in depth. It must involve antivirus systems that are able to deploy the entire panoply of scanning and analysis techniques. These must be used at both the gateway and host and must be kept updated to ensure that they are able to deal with the constantly changing malware threat. The layered defense must also involve routers with well-configured access lists and firewalls on both network and hosts, with up-to-date policies. Network intrusion detection can play an important role, if it is appropriately deployed and monitored, as can honeypots and early warning systems. User security education must not be neglected, as secure user behavior forms an essential first line of defense.

Above all it is vital that critical vulnerabilities are identified and patched as soon as possible. Indeed, the timeframe between vulnerability disclosure and subsequent exploitation by malware has reduced dramatically. For example, back in 2001 it took some 330 days for a publicized vulnerability to be exploited by the *Nimda* worm, giving ample time for security-conscious administrators to patch their systems. By summer 2003 the pace of exploitation had increased significantly, with the *Blaster* worm appearing within 27 days of vulnerability disclosure. However, the challenge for system administrators has increased yet further, and during the last six months of 2004 there was an average of only 5.8 days between a vulnerability being published and a malware exploit for it being released (Symantec, 2005b). Additionally, much concern is being expressed about the potential for zero-day attacks, which involve the exploitation of a vulnerability that has not previously been publicly reported (Hilley, 2004). It is therefore more important than ever that close attention is paid to the issue of malware threat detection and prevention.

Conclusions

The discussion in this chapter has demonstrated that although malware has been widely recognized for over 20 years, it continues to be a significant and evolving threat. Security surveys from a variety of sources convey the worryingly consistent impression that malware is not only the most prominent threat, but that its prevalence and impacts is still increasing. As such, rather than diminishing, it is now considered to be a bigger problem than ever before.

The discussion has illustrated the increasing complexity of malware activity, in terms of propagation, payload, and preservation techniques. With a multitude of new infection vectors, plus a wider range of malicious actions that may be performed when infection occurs, the malware of today is in every way more problematic than earlier generations that preceded it. Much of this can be related to the additional opportunities that have arisen to leverage and exploit the underlying technology, particularly in relation to utilizing network connectivity. However, there is also a clear link to the individuals responsible for creating and releasing malicious code. The broad range of potential motivations means that there is certainly no single profile for a likely suspect, and the opportunities for financial gain are now likely to draw in many who would not previously have been interested.

Based upon what we have seen in the past, there is little doubt that malware will continue to develop. The threat that we face tomorrow has the potential to be significantly worse than that of today, with further infection vectors (such as mobile devices) having already begun to emerge. This situation has arisen despite apparent improvements in protective technologies. However, these technologies may continue to fail not because of inherent weaknesses but because of ineffective or inadequate deployment, or because so many vulnerabilities remain open, when they could be prevented by downloading software "patches". The evolving threat demands increased protection on many fronts, and can only be addressed by appropriate combinations of technology and awareness on the part of potential victims.

References

Bace, R., & Mell, P. (2001). *NIST special publication on intrusion detection systems.* National Institute of Standards and Technology (NIST). Retrieved March 15, 2006, from http://csrc.nist.gov/publications/nistpubs/800-31/sp800-31.pdf

Chen, T. (2003, September). Trends in viruses and worms. *Internet Protocol Journal, 6,* 23-33.

Cohen, F. (1984). Computer viruses: Theory and experiments. Originally appearing in *Proceedings of IFIP-SEC 84 an*d also appearing as invited paper in *Computers and Security, 6*(1), 22-35.

Cohen, F. (1994). *A short course on computer viruses* (2nd ed.). New York: Wiley Professional Computing.

Dawkins, R. (1976). *The selfish gene.* Oxford University Press.

DTI. (2004, April). Information security breaches survey 2004. *Department of Trade & Industry, URN 04/617.*

Ernst & Young. (2004). *Global information security survey 2004.* Assurance and Advisory Business Services. Ernst & Young. EYG No. FF0231.

F-Secure. (2004). MyDoom.AE. F-Secure Virus Descriptions, Retrieved October 16, 2004, from http://www.f-secure.com/v-descs/mydoom_ae.shtml

Furnell, S. (2001). *Cybercrime: Vandalizing the information society.* Addison Wesley.

Furnell, S., & Ward, J. (2004, October). Malware comes of age: The arrival of the true computer parasite. *Network Security*, 11-15.

Gordon, L., Loeb, M., Lucyshyn, W., & Richardson, R. (2005). *Tenth Annual CSI/FBI Computer Crime and Security Survey.* Computer Security Institute.

Harley, D., Slade, R., & Gattiker, U. (2001). *Viruses revealed.* Osborne/McGraw-Hill.

Hilley, S. (2004, March/April). The final countdown: 3,2,1 … Zero. *Infosecurity Today*, 58-59.

KPMG. (2002). *"Security Breaches", 2002 Information Security Survey.* KPMG Consulting, Inc. Retrieved March 16, 2006, from http://www.kpmg.com/microsite/informationsecurity/ iss_gloint_secbre.html

Landler, M. (2000). *'Love Bug' creator proclaims his fame.* Retrieved October 22, 2000, from SiliconValley.com

Lemos, R. (2003). *Counting the cost of Slammer*. Retrieved January 31, 2003, from CNET News.com

Lemos, R. (2005). *He's got the virus-writing bug*. Retrieved January 14, 2005, from CNET News.com

McAfee. (2004, September 20). *McAfee® AVERT Reports Detection of 100,000th Malicious Threat With Addition of Sdbot Variant to Its Database*. Press Release, McAfee, Inc.

McCue, A. (2001). *Russian mafia targets online businesses*. Retrieved November 21, 2004, from vnunet.com

MessageLabs. (2004). *MessageLabs Intelligence Annual Email Security Report 2004*. Retrieved March 16, 2006, from http://www.messagelabs.com/binaries/LAB480_endofyear_UK_v3.pdf

Metro News. (2004). *Fraudsters selling use of home PCs. Metro News*. Retrieved July 8, 2004, from http://www.metronews.ca/tech_news.asp?id=1862

Skoudis, E., & Zeltser, L. (2003). *Malware: Fighting malicious code*. Prentice Hall.

Skrenta, R. (1982). *Elk Cloner (circa 1982)*. Retrieved April 10, 2005, from http://www.skrenta.com/cloner/

Spitzner, L. (2002). *Honeypots: Tracking hackers*. Addison-Wesley Professional.

Symantec. (1991). *Tequila.A*. Symantec Security Response. Retrieved March 15, 2006, from http://securityresponse.symantec.com/avcenter/venc/data/tequila.a.html

Symantec. (1998, June). *W95.CIH. Symantec Security Response*. Retrieved from http://www.symantec.com/avcenter/venc/data/cih.html

Symantec. (1999a). *W97.Melissa.A. Symantec Security Response*. Retrieved March 29, 1999, from http://securityresponse.symantec.com/avcenter/venc/data/w97.melissa.a.html

Symantec. (1999b). *Wscript.KakWorm. Symantec Security Response*. Retrieved December 30, 1999, from http://securityresponse.symantec.com/avcenter/venc/data/wscript.kakworm.html

Symantec. (2000a). *VBS.LoveLetter and variants. Symantec Security Response*. Retrieved March 15, 2006, from http://securityresponse.symantec.com/avcenter/venc/data/vbs.loveletter.a.html

Symantec. (2000b). *W32.Evol. Symantec Security Response*. Retrieved March 15, 2006, from http://securityresponse.symantec.com/avcenter/venc/data/w32.evol.html

Symantec. (2001a). *Blended Threats: Case Study and Countermeasures*. White Paper. Symantec Enterprise Security. Retrieved March 15, 2006, from http://securityresponse.symantec.com/avcenter/venc/data/w32.evol.html

Symantec. (2001b). *W32.Nimda.A@mm. Symantec Security Response*. Retrieved September 18, 2001, from http://securityresponse.symantec.com/avcenter/venc/data/w32.nimda.a@mm.html

Symantec. (2001c). *W32.Klez.A@mm. Symantec Security Response*. Retrieved October 25, 2001, from http://securityresponse.symantec.com/avcenter/venc/data/w32.klez.a@mm.html

Symantec. (2002). *W32.Klez.H@mm. Symantec Security Response*. Retrieved April 17, 2002, from http://securityresponse.symantec.com/avcenter/venc/data/ w32.klez.h@mm.html

Symantec. (2003a). *W32.SQLExp.Worm. Symantec Security Response*. Retrieved January 24, 2003, from http://securityresponse.symantec.com/avcenter/venc/data/ w32.sqlexp.worm.html

Symantec. (2003b). *W32.Blaster.Worm. Symantec Security Response*. Retrieved August 11, 2003, from http://securityresponse.symantec.com/avcenter/venc/data/ w32.blaster.worm.html

Symantec. (2003c). *W32.Sobig.F@mm. Symantec Security Response*. Retrieved August 18, 2003, from http://securityresponse.symantec.com/avcenter/venc/data/ w32.sobig.f@mm.html

Symantec. (2004a). *W32.Netsky.P@mm. Symantec Security Response*. Retrieved March 21, 2004, from http://securityresponse.symantec.com/avcenter/venc/data/ w32.netsky.p@mm.html

Symantec. (2004b). *Symantec Internet Security Threat Report: Trends for January 1 - June 30 2004*. Vol. 5, September 2004.

Symantec. (2005a). *W32.Gaobot.CII. Symantec Security Response*. Retrieved February 5, 2005, from http://securityresponse.symantec.com/avcenter/venc/data/ w32.gaobot.cii.html

Symantec. (2005b). *Symantec Internet Security Threat Report: Trends for July 04– December 04*. Vol. 5, Retrieved March 2005, from http:// securityresponse.symantec.com/avcenter/venc/data/w32

Symantec. (2005c). *W32.Beagle.BN@mm. Symantec Security Response*, Retrieved April 15, 2005, http://securityresponse.symantec.com/avcenter/venc/data/ w32.beagle.bn@mm.html

Szor, P. (2005). *The art of computer virus research and defense*. Addison-Wesley.

von Neumann, J. (1948). *The general and logical theory of automata*. Hixon Symposium.

Weaver, N., Paxson, V., Staniford, S., & Cunningham, R. (2003, October 27). A taxonomy of computer worms. *In Proceedings of the 2003 ACM workshop on Rapid Malcode* (pp. 11-18). Washington DC.

Websense. (2005, April 12). *Toxic Blogs Distribute Malcode and Keyloggers*. Press Release, Websense, Inc.

WildList. (2005a). Frequently asked questions. *The WildList Organization International*. Retrieved March 15, 2006, from http://www.wildlist.org/faq.htm

WildList. (2005b). WildList Index. *The WildList Organization International*. Retrieved March 15, 2006, from http://www.wildlist.org/WildList/

Section II:
Computer and
Network Forensics

Chapter III

Computer and Network Forensics

Sriranjani Sitaraman, University of Texas, USA

Subbarayan Venkatesan, University of Texas, USA

Abstract

This chapter introduces computer and network forensics. The world of forensics is well understood in the non-digital world, whereas this is a nascent field in the digital cyberworld. Digital evidence is being increasingly used in the legal system such as e-mails, disk drives containing damaging evidence, and so on. Computer forensics deals with preserving and collecting digital evidence on a single machine while network forensics deals with the same operations in a connected digital world. Several related issues and available tools are discussed in this chapter.

Introduction

The widespread use of personal computers by domestic users and corporations in the past few years has resulted in an enormous amount of information being stored electronically. An increasing number of criminals use pagers, cellular phones, laptop computers and network servers in the course of committing their crimes (US DOJ, 2001). Computers are used in electronic crime in different ways. In some cases, computers provide the means of committing crime. For example, the Internet can be used to launch hacker attacks against a vulnerable computer network, or to transmit inappropriate images. In other cases, computers merely serve as convenient storage devices for evidence of crime. Such persistent electronic material may, in certain cases, constitute critical evidence of criminal activity.

Prosecutors and law enforcement agents need to know how to obtain electronic evidence stored in computers. Digital evidence may be found in magnetic storage media such as hard disks, floppy disks, flash drives, random access memory (RAM), and so forth. Electronic records such as computer network logs, e-mails, word processing files, and picture files increasingly provide the government with important (and sometimes essential) evidence in criminal cases. Even free space on the disk may contain important evidence. Manual review of such data is impossible. Proper collection and automated analysis procedures are essential to preserve computer data and present it as evidence in a court of law. *Computer forensics* deals with the "preservation, identification, extraction, documentation, and interpretation of computer media for evidentiary and/or root cause analysis" (Kruse, 2001).

The need for well-defined procedures for acquiring and analyzing evidence without damaging it and providing a chain-of-custody that will hold up in court was discussed in the First Digital Forensics Research Workshop (Palmer, 2001). A framework for digital forensic science was proposed. The framework outlined a linear process of investigation involving the following steps: identification, preservation, collection, examination, analysis, presentation, and decision. Based on this investigation framework, structured approaches such as End-to-End Digital Investigation (EEDI), and others, have been developed to facilitate complex investigations (Stevenson, 2003).

Network forensics involves determining how unauthorized access to a distant computer was achieved. Network forensics yields information about computer intrusions. Log files in the computer (the victim of the intrusion), routers, and internet service providers (ISPs) are used to track the offender.

A number of sophisticated tools have been developed for forensic analysis of computers and networks. Mohay, Anderson, Collie, McKemmish, et al. (2003) identify three main categories of forensic functionality: imaging, analysis, and visualization. Imaging is the first step where a copy of the evidence is made for subsequent analysis in order to prevent tampering of the original. Some tools widely used for imaging purposes are Norton Ghost, Safeback, Encase, Linux *dd*, and so on. A complete forensic analysis of the image is required to find information related to a specific case. Digital information is not always readily available. Some files may be deleted, corrupted, or otherwise hidden. Forensic analysis allows the recovery of deleted, hidden, password-protected, and encrypted files. Sleuthkit and WinInterrogate are some commonly used analysis tools. Visualization involves timelining of computer activity using information found in the various log files, and so forth.

Network forensics can be accomplished using tools such as Snort, TcpDump, and BlackIce. Intrusion detection systems use system logs and audit trails in the computer and/or information collected at routers/switches. A number of approaches have been proposed to detect intrusions and trace the origin (Sekar, Xie, Maltz, Reiter, & Zhang, 2004; Thurimella, Burt, Sitaraman, & Venkatesan, 2005).

Most computer forensics vendors offer a variety of tools and some of them offer complete suites. The Computer Forensic Investigative Toolkit (CFIT) developed by Defence

Science and Technology Organization (DSTO), Department of Defence, Australia (CFIT, 2001), for instance, provides tools for analyzing various kinds of data streams: from disk drives, network data, or telecommunications call records. Other widely used toolkits include The Coroner's Toolkit (TCT) (Farmer & Venema, 1999) and ForensiX (Goel, Shea, Ahuja, Feng, Feng, Maier, et al., 2003).

Software tools must meet Daubert Criteria: the tools must be tested for accuracy, reliability, and repeatability; peer-reviewed; and have a generally accepted methodology. The reliability of computer forensic tools is critical for the law enforcement community. Authorities such as National Institute of Standards and Technology (NIST) and National Institute of Justice (NIJ) have developed programs to test and validate forensic software.

This chapter provides an introduction to the various activities involved in a forensic investigation of digital crime and discusses some widely-used tools. With a brief overview of legal considerations while conducting forensic investigations, the chapter discusses some open problems and thoughts about future technologies.

Computer Forensics

A study by the University of California, Berkeley in 2001 indicates that 93% of new information created at that time was in the digital format. Computers are involved in today's crimes in multiple ways, as reported by the President's Working Group on Unlawful Conduct on the Internet (Unlawful Conduct, 2000). Computers can be *targets* of the crime where the damage is done to the integrity, confidentiality, and/or availability of the information stored in the computer. Unauthorized access is gained to a target system in order to acquire information stored in it or to disrupt its normal operations. In a second way, computers can be used as *data storage devices* to store stolen credit card numbers, social security numbers, medical records, proprietary information, and more. Computers can otherwise be used as *communication tools* where e-mails and chat sessions enable planning and coordinating many crimes. Sometimes computers can be used to communicate threats or extortion demands.

When a computer security incident or a computer crime is suspected, an investigator uses forensic tools to search through voluminous data for proof of guilt or innocence. Computer forensics is a methodology to acquire and analyze evidence in the digital format. Note that the nature of digital evidence is such that special procedures for obtaining and handling this evidence are required. Electronic evidence may be easily altered unless strict procedures are followed. For example, rebooting a system may cause the loss of any information in volatile memory and destroy valuable traces.

The passages to follow discuss the major steps involved in performing a computer forensic analysis and describe some tested and widely-used tools in investigations of computer crime.

Where is Computer Forensics Used?

Computer forensics techniques are essential to successfully prevent, detect, investigate, and prosecute electronic crime. Law enforcement is increasingly relying on computer forensics for prosecution as criminal use of computers becomes more widespread. Root-cause analysis is needed to prevent reoccurrence of a problem and forensics helps understand the full extent of the problem. Computer forensic tools constitute a necessary component to insure a successful arbitration (Arbitration, 2004).

Corporations are increasingly incorporating methods to save information to enable forensics. Because of the relative ease with which proprietary information can be stolen, protecting the companies' intellectual property, or "crown jewels" (Intellectual Property, 2004), is important. Loss of company trade secrets, confidential customer data, financial information, and other proprietary information is driving a multi-billion dollar crime wave. While companies focus on preventing outside hackers from stealing their informational crown jewels, its employees and former employees have the most unencumbered access to valuable protected data. Proper computer forensics procedures can help the companies in tracking cyber crimes.

Steps in Computer Forensics

There are many steps in a computer-related investigation for the retrieval and analysis of digital evidence. In general, three main steps, called the three A's, have been identified in the investigation process: Acquire, Authenticate, and Analyze. These three steps and the final step of Presentation are elaborated upon further in this section. Figure 1 shows a typical computer forensic investigation. When a suspect drive is obtained from a seized computer, a copy of the drive is made. The copy is then analyzed to identify valuable evidence such as log files, deleted files, and so forth. Analysis of identified evidence yields reconstructed files or other useful information.

Acquire the Evidence

The process of acquiring electronic evidence may vary from one case to another. A challenge in finding evidence is to know where to look for it. For example, some investigations may require examining the data stored in the hard disk while in certain cases of network intrusions, the evidence may exist only in the RAM. So, there is no single procedure for collecting evidence, and the use of a suitable methodology to secure digital evidence will depend on the type of evidence sought and the technology available at that time. The investigator should know which tool to use in order to make the evidence apparent. It is also important to identify and capture the evidence without losing its integrity and value so that it is admissible in court. There are several steps involved in acquiring the evidence as outlined in the following list:

Figure 1. A typical computer forensic investigation

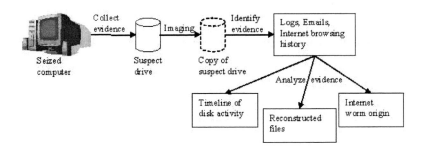

Chain of Custody: To protect the integrity of the evidence and argue that the evidence was not tampered while in custody, maintaining a chain of custody of the evidence collected is crucial. Chain of custody is a process used to maintain and document the chronological history of the investigation. The chain of custody tracking document for a piece of evidence records information such as who handled the evidence, what procedures were performed on the evidence, when the evidence was collected and analyzed, where the evidence was found and is stored, why this material was considered as evidence, and how the evidence collection and maintenance was done.

Identification: To identify potential evidence, the investigator needs extensive knowledge of computer hardware and software, including operating systems, file systems, and cryptographic algorithms. Evidence has to be identified among normal files, and may be found in slack space, unallocated space, registries, hidden files, encrypted files, password-protected files, system logs, etc. Evidence can be found on any number of media sources such as hard drive, floppy disk, CD-ROM, PDA, cell phones, flash drives, and more.

Collection/Preservation: The identified evidence has to be collected from available components. The evidence collection must not be delayed because valuable information may be lost due to prolonged computer use. In some cases, the evidence may have to be duplicated for analysis by making an exact bit-by-bit copy of the original using special "forensic" software and/or hardware. This process of making an identical copy of the original evidence is called imaging. The mutability of data creates a number of hurdles in the imaging process. Evidence could be altered easily while the copy is being made. The imaging utility must not introduce new data into the original evidence or the copy. The investigator must be able to prove in court that the copy is a valid one, and show that the imaging process is repeatable.

Transportation and Storage: All data recovered from the compromised system should be physically secured. Evidence such as hard disks can be damaged if not handled properly. Such magnetic media should be protected from mechanical or electromagnetic damage. The package has to be sealed to prove that it has not been tampered with during transportation. A chain of custody document must be associated with every piece of evidence.

A challenge in acquiring digital evidence lies in the fact that it is economically infeasible to seize all available resources for further investigation in today's digital age where information is mostly created, stored, and transmitted in an electronic form.

Authenticate the Evidence

It is essential that the evidence collected is an exact copy of the original at the time the crime was detected. The investigator must be able to persuasively show that the evidence originated from the computer under attack or the computer in the crime scene. Once the evidence is collected, it must be ensured that the evidence is not destroyed, altered, or tampered with.

Authentication of evidence using simple time-stamping techniques is an effective way to compare the duplicate with the original. A hash function H is a transformation that takes an input m and returns a fixed-size string, which is called the hash value h (that is, $h = H[m]$). One can think of the hash value as a "digital fingerprint". MD5 and SHA are two popular hash algorithms. When digital evidence is collected and duplicated, the hash values of the original and the copy are computed and recorded. They must be identical. More information about RSA's hash functions can be found in http://www.rsasecurity.com/rsalabs/node.asp?id=2176.

Analyze the Evidence

Multiple tools may need to be used to completely analyze the evidence seized. Tested and validated tools should be used, or if other tools are used, then the investigator must ensure that the evidence is not tainted. Some activities involved in the analysis include reading the partition table, searching existing files for relevant information such as keywords, system state changes, or text strings, retrieving information from deleted files, checking for data hidden in the boot record, unallocated space, slack space or bad blocks in the disk, cracking passwords, and so on. Performing analysis on a live system keeping in mind that the system utilities may have been modified by the intruder is a challenging task. In some cases, the complex computer and network activity makes the evidence dynamic and not conducive to reproduction.

Even deleted files can be retrieved from a disk by a trained forensic investigator; only completely overwriting a file will make it inaccessible by any standard means. In order to recover overwritten data, advanced techniques such as Scanning Tunneling Microscopy (STM) or Magnetic Force Microscopy (MFM) may be used (Gomez, Adly, Mayergoyz, & Burke,1992; Gutmann, 1996). These techniques exploit the fact that it is virtually impossible to write data to the same location every time because of physical limitations of the recording mechanisms. These devices incur huge costs in time and storage space and hence are not widely used. Other log-based techniques such as "Byteprints" have been proposed to recover previous consistent snapshots of files even if they have been overwritten (Sitaraman, Krishnamurthy, & Venkatesan, 2005). Such techniques do not need sophisticated and often expensive equipment.

The interpretation of the results of an analysis depends largely on the capability of the examiner. At this stage, the examiner can establish the meaning and relevance of the processed data and solve issues like the identity of the owner, purpose of the data, and so forth.

Report Generation

Presentation or generation of a report of the results of an analysis is a crucial step in an investigation. Every step in the forensic analysis has to be documented carefully. The examiner should be able to explain complex technological concepts in simple terms. The meaning and significance of the results obtained must be clearly conveyed.

Computer Forensic Tools

Forensic tools have been developed for the various steps of forensic analysis described previously. There is no single solution for all the diverse requirements of a computer forensic investigation. Forensic tools have been developed for different operating platforms. Some tools are open source tools while others are proprietary. Different tools

Table 1. Comparison of imaging tools

Imaging Tools	Platforms supported	Integrity checking	User Interface	Tested by CFTT	Source	Remote Backups
dd	Windows, Unix	MD5	Command line	Yes	Open source, free	Yes, with netcat utility
Encase	Windows, Linux, Solaris	MD5	Graphical	Yes	Proprietary	Yes
Safeback	Windows, Unix	SHA256	Graphical	Yes	Proprietary	Yes, via parallel port connection
Norton Ghost	Windows, Linux, DOS	Only by matching source and backup	Graphical	No	Proprietary	No

exist for performing evidence acquisition from live systems and analyzing the evidence. Some commonly used computer forensics tools based on the categories identified previously are listed below.

- **Imaging Tools:** dd, EnCase, Safeback, Norton Ghost, iLook, Mares, SMART, ByteBack, SnapBack, Drive Image, X-Ways Forensics
- **Analysis Tools:** Sleuthkit, WinInterrogate, ForensiX, SMART, DriveSpy, iLook, DiskSig Pro, Quick View, Thumbs Plus, CompuPic, Hex Editor, dtSearch, NTA Stealth, PDA Seizure
- **Forensic Toolkits:** The Coroner's Toolkit (TCT), Forensic Toolkit (FTK)

The available computer forensic tools may be evaluated against different criteria such as the completeness in functionality of the tool, the time taken by the tool to perform its function, the ease of use and user friendliness of the tool, cost of the tool, acceptability of the tool in court, and so on. Bearing these criteria in mind, Table 1 evaluates the imaging tools discussed in the following section in a comprehensive manner.

We next describe a few computer forensic tools that are commonly used by forensic investigators. These tools have been chosen for their popularity.

Imaging Tools

The process of imaging a hard drive involves making a bit-by-bit copy of the drive to a raw image file also called as the analysis drive. Imaging a suspect's hard drive is one of the most critical functions of the computer forensic process. It is extremely important that no data be written to the suspect's hard drive during this process. For this purpose, a software-based or hardware-based write-blocker technology is used. Write-blockers ensure that any write to the disk being imaged is blocked. It is also imperative that every bit copied to the analysis drive is exactly the same as that found in the suspect's drive. The integrity of the copy can be verified by generating fingerprints of the contents of the suspect's drive and the contents of the analysis drive using hash algorithms such as MD5 and comparing the fingerprints.

A number of imaging tools have been developed for use in a forensic examination. Four such tools have been described in more detail below. Investigators can use hardware devices also to make copies of system images.

dd

The *dd* utility is used to make a bit-wise copy of a file, a part of a file, physical memory, swap files, a logical drive, or an entire physical disk. It is free to use and download, and is available for Unix-based and Windows-based systems. It has an integrated checksum calculator using MD5, and an integrity checker which can compare the checksum of the data and the checksum of the image and indicate if they are different.

EnCase

Guidance Software's EnCase is available as an Enterprise Edition and a Forensic Edition. The EnCase Forensic Edition is a standard forensic tool used for full system analysis. EnCase Forensic can perform a sector-by-sector acquisition of a hard drive to collect and identify deleted files on the disk, including partially overwritten files, bad sectors, and slack space. EnCase automatically creates MD5 hash values to preserve the integrity of the evidence collected. The EnCase Enterprise Edition package has additional remote capabilities and network functionality. EnCase Enterprise has a polished interface, but it is expensive. Filters for viewing files are easily customizable. Encase Forensic's scripting interface lets investigators fine-tune evidence collection. Help documentation is complete and mature. More advanced features of these products can be found in www.encase.com.

SafeBack

SafeBack is an industry standard self-authenticating computer forensics tool commonly used by law enforcement agencies throughout the world. It is a DOS-based utility used to create evidence grade backups of hard drives on Intel-based computer systems. SafeBack copies all areas of the hard disk accurately. Remote operation via parallel port connection allows the hard disk on a remote PC to be read or written by the master system. In SafeBack 3.0, two separate mathematical hashing processes that use the SHA256 algorithm are used to maintain the integrity of Safeback files. A detailed audit trail of the backup process is provided for evidence documentation purposes. Other features of SafeBack can be found in http://www.forensics-intl.com/safeback.html.

Norton Ghost

Symantec's Norton Ghost 9.0 is a backup and restore utility that can work on Windows 9x, Me, NT; Linux®; and DOS systems. Its "hot imaging" feature allows the creation of backup images without restarting Windows®. Time and space is saved by making incremental backups. Automatic backups can be scheduled for updated images. An interested reader can find more about Norton Ghost 9.0 at http://www.symantec.com/sabu/ghost/ghost_personal/.

Analysis Tools

Forensic analysis activities differ based on the type of media being analyzed, the file system used, and so on. Some activities involved in forensic analysis were discussed in prior passages. Some of the widely-used analysis tools are further described.

DriveSpy

DriveSpy is a forensic DOS shell. It is designed to emulate and extend the capabilities of DOS to meet forensic needs. It can examine DOS and non-DOS partitions using a built-in sector (and cluster) hex viewer. Configurable documentation capabilities are included in DriveSpy to record all the activities of an investigation. DriveSpy can save and restore compressed forensic images of a hard drive. MD5 hash of an entire drive, a partition or selected files can also be obtained. Using DriveSpy, extensive architectural information for entire hard drives and individual partitions can be obtained. A complete list of features of DriveSpy can be found in http://www.digitalintelligence.com/software/disoftware/drivespy/.

dtSearch

dtSearch is a fast and precise text-retrieval tool that is very useful in a computer forensic investigation. It can instantly search gigabytes of text across a desktop, network, and Internet or Intranet site. dtSearch allows indexed, unindexed, fielded, and full-text searching, and is used by forensic investigators in e-mail filtering and analyzing acquired forensic evidence. dtSearch products work under Win & .NET platforms; a Linux version of the dtSearch Engine for programmers is also available at www.dtsearch.com.

ILook Investigator©

ILook Investigator toolsets are computer forensic tools used to acquire an image from seized computers, and analyze the images obtained. ILook is offered only to law enforcement agencies. ILook Version 8 is a multi-threaded, Unicode compliant, fast forensic analysis tool that runs on Windows 2000 and Windows XP platforms. ILook Version 8 consists of two components. The IXimager component is an imaging tool designed to follow forensic best practices. It supports the use of SCSI, SATA, Firewire, and USB devices. The ILookv8 Investigator component contains the analysis tools which allow the investigator to examine data captured by the IXimager. More details can be found in http://www.ilook-forensics.org/.

The Sleuth Kit (TSK)

The Sleuth Kit is a collection of Unix-based command-line forensic analysis tools based on the design and code of The Coroner's Toolkit (TCT). It consists of file system tools and media management tools. The file system tools such as fsstat, fls, ffind, icat, dcat, and more are used to analyze the file systems in a hard drive in a non-intrusive manner. All file system tools support NTFS, FAT, Ext2/3, and UFS1/2 file systems. The media management tools are used to examine the layout of disks and other media. Some examples of media management tools include mmls and img_stat. The Sleuth Kit supports DOS partitions, BSD partitions (disk labels), Mac partitions and Sun slices (Volume Table of Contents). With these tools, locations of partitions can be identified and data extracted from them can be analyzed with file system analysis tools. The Autopsy Forensic Browser is a graphical interface to the tools in The Sleuth Kit. The interface is not as well-developed as that of Encase or ProDiscover. The Sleuth Kit can be used to create timelines of file activity which is very useful in a forensic investigation. www.sleuthkit.org provides more information about its various tools.

Forensic Toolkits

Forensic toolkits usually provide tools for performing many activities of a computer forensic investigation. Note that no single toolkit has been developed that encompasses all the forensic activities that an investigation might require. Following are two toolkits that can be used to perform a variety of forensic activities.

The Coroner's Toolkit (TCT)

The Coroner's Toolkit (TCT) is a collection of tools by Dan Farmer and Wietse Venema. These tools are used to perform a post-mortem forensic analysis of a UNIX system. Grave-robber, ils, mactime, unrm, lazarus, findkey, and so forth are some components of TCT. The grave-robber tool captures information based on the order of volatility of the evidence. Grave-robber collects details about memory and active processes before the memory gets overwritten and the process dies. Ils and mactime tools display access patterns of files dead or alive, and are used for timestamped evidence gathering. The unrm and lazarus tools recover deleted files from unused portions of the disk drive. Findkey recovers cryptographic keys from a running process or from files. The tools can be downloaded from www.fish.com/tct.

Forensic Toolkit (FTK)

AccessData's Forensic Toolkit (FTK™) has an interface that is easy to understand and use. It automatically retrieves and sorts deleted and partially overwritten files. FTK also integrates dtSearch, a text retrieval engine, which provides powerful and extensive text search functionality. FTK's customizable filters allow sorting through thousands of files to quickly find the required evidence. FTK can also be used to perform e-mail analysis. FTK's interface is more straightforward and easier to understand than that of EnCase. More details about FTK are available in www.accessdata.com.

Network Forensics

With the growth of the Internet, cyber attacks and security breaches have increased. Existing methods such as examining log files from servers, firewall records, intrusion-detection events, host-based forensic disk-imaging and searching software, packet dumps, and so on, are not sufficient in functionality to identify the sophisticated attacker using tools such as cryptography, among others. Network forensic tools use specialized analysis engines capable of capturing and correlating data from multiple network entities. In the following sections, some network forensic activities and existing tools are discussed.

Common Network Forensic Activities

When a network intrusion is detected, the first step to be taken is the identification and collection of volatile data. Subsequently, the perusal of the various logs using special forensic tools may yield information about the intrusion such as the entry point, the vulnerability being exploited, and more. Special attention should be given to system clock offsets, especially in the case where time synchronization protocols such as NTP or external timing sources had not been used. The following are some relevant network forensic activities.

Network Monitoring and Logging

Proactive logging provides valuable information. Monitoring the network for suspicious connections or new processes real-time is an effective way to detect and stop intrusions. Intrusion alerts of intrusion detection systems (IDSs) trigger the forensic analysis but do not provide any information about what happened after the attack. Monitoring chat rooms and other modes of communication may be helpful. The increasing number of computers on networks and the size of the Internet makes monitoring network traffic very challenging. The time duration for which logs should be maintained at the various points in the network is not clearly defined. This is directly influenced by the amount of storage available. Obtaining network logs from different jurisdictions is difficult due to lack of cooperation.

E-Mail Tracing

E-mails are used in committing crimes. If an e-mail is related to a crime, it should be recorded as evidence and the e-mail header may be useful to trace the suspect. The e-mail tracing process requires the investigator to know how "e-mail" works. Some parts of the e-mail header cannot be spoofed so easily such as the last server that the e-mail passed through. The router and firewall logs may help verify the path taken by the e-mail message. E-mail servers usually maintain a log of all the e-mail messages that have been processed, and hence, even if the user deletes an e-mail, it may be recovered from the e-mail servers. Legal and jurisdictional matters create tough challenges to trace e-mails successfully. Log data may not be properly maintained by Internet Service Providers (ISPs). Encrypted e-mails, e-mails with stripped headers, and so forth, make the e-mail tracing process more difficult.

IP Traceback

Most denial-of-service attacks involve a number of packets sent to the victim system. All relevant packets have apparently valid source IP addresses. The packets have no information that could be used to determine their originating host. IP Traceback involves identifying the source of such attack packets. Some IP traceback techniques include actively querying routers about traffic they forward, creating a virtually overlay network using logging mechanisms for selective monitoring of packet flows, and identifying the attack path by reconstruction, using a collection of packets, marked or especially generated by routers along the attack path. There is no solution that successfully identifies the source in all attacks.

Attack Traceback and Reconstruction

Internet attacks such as worms and viruses are becoming more sophisticated and spread very quickly in an automatic fashion. The worms do not need any human interaction to propagate, they are self-contained, self-propagating pieces of code. Tracing the true source of such malicious flows is gaining importance as a network forensic activity (Sekar, Xie, Maltz, Reiter, & Zhang, 2004). Figure 2 shows a typical data communication path between two nodes in a network. The flow details are maintained by both the source node, A, and the destination node, E, of the flow. If a malicious bitstream is detected at node E, node E looks up its table of incoming flows to determine the source of this malicious flow. Node E can then use a query-response protocol to determine the origin of the bitstream (Thurimella, Burt, Sitaraman, & Venkatesan, 2005). The flow details can alternatively be stored in edge routers instead of end hosts in order to avoid modifications to all the end hosts.

Figure 2. Tracing an Internet worm's origin

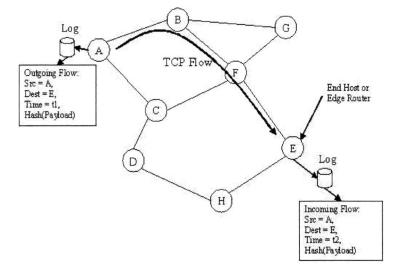

The reconstruction of the attack will allow system administrators to understand the mechanics of the spread, and thus enable patching vulnerable systems and preventing future attacks. The tracing of the origin of an Internet attack is useful for prosecution or damage mitigation purposes.

Network Forensics Tools

Several tools such as Snort, BlackIce, TcpDump, Paraben's Network E-mail Examiner, NetAnalysis, and others have been developed to perform network forensic activities. Network forensic tools may be classified into host-based tools and network-wide tools. Host-based tools examine packets that arrive at a particular host and present statistical data about the traffic at the host to the investigator. Network-wide tools, on the other hand, have multiple components that reside in different parts of the network and communicate with each other in order to present network-wide information. In the following passage, we discuss commonly available network forensic tools based on these categories.

Host-Based Forensic Tools

Host-based network forensic tools reside on a single host in the network and help understand network activity by capturing and analyzing packets that arrive at that host. These tools usually provide a lot of information in the form of logs for the user to analyze. Some popular host-based tools have been discussed further.

Sandstorm's NetIntercept 3.0

NetIntercept helps understand network activity and identify perpetrators of cyber crime. It can reassemble packets into streams, and can perform full inspection and analysis of contents of e-mails, Web pages, and files. NetIntercept offers secure remote administration, and decrypts SSH2 from modified servers. Users can drill down through connections, and catch header or port spoofing. Clear text passwords and contents of unencrypted remote login sessions can be displayed. It is very useful in studying external break-in attempts, and to analyze hundreds of thousands of network connections from archives. See http://www.phonesweep.com/products/netintercept/ describes all the features of NetIntercept 3.0.

TcpDump

TcpDump is a command line tool used for network monitoring, protocol debugging, and data acquisition. Tcpdump prints out the headers of packets on a network interface that match a given boolean expression. TcpDump is available for use in multiple operating platforms such as Linux, BSD, HP-UX, SunOS, Solaris, and a version of TcpDump called WinDump is available for Windows 95, 98, ME, NT, 2000, XP, 2003, and Vista. WinDump is free and is released under a BSD-style license. WinDump puts the network interface in promiscuous mode; in other words, it will grab all the packets it sees, not just the ones destined for it. In order to see traffic to and from other hosts, the tool needs to be run on a shared-access network such as a non-switched Ethernet.

Pcap

The Packet Capture library provides a high-level interface to access packets and send packets on the network. The Pcap library is the basis for many Unix network monitoring tools. The Pcap library in turn uses a set of Unix kernel functions known as Berkeley Packet Filter (BPF). WinPcap is a Win32 port of libpcap consisting of two main components, namely, a kernel-level packet-filter driver based on the BPF functionality, and a high-level programming library, libpcap, for Windows. The packet-capture driver is a device driver that adds the ability to capture and send raw network packets to Windows 9x, Windows NT, and Windows 2000 in a way similar to the BPF of Unix kernels.

Snort

Snort is an open-source network security tool that was initially developed for the Unix platform in 1998 and has now been ported to the Win32 platform. Snort is a simple, command line tool used to watch network traffic, look for rule-based intrusion signatures, alert and log when a match is made, perform protocol analysis, troubleshoot the network, and control unauthorized applications. The tool has a small memory footprint and requires very little processing power. Snort can listen to all traffic to one computer or it can put the network adaptor in promiscuous mode and listen to all traffic on the wire.

Network-Wide Forensic Tools

Network-wide forensic tools consist of multiple monitors that can be installed at different points in the network and used for distributed network surveillance. Information required to perform certain network forensic activities such as IP traceback, attack reconstruction or e-mail tracing has to be collected from hosts in the same domain as the victim host, or from cooperating or hostile parts outside the victim's domain. Such network monitoring tools integrate data from the different monitors and provide a complete and comprehensive view of the network activity. A popular network forensic tool with network-wide deployment capability is described next.

Niksun NetDetector 2005

NIKSUN's NetDetector 2005 is a full-featured appliance for network security surveillance, detection, analytics, and forensics. It performs signature and statistical anomaly detection and continuously captures and stores network events. With a powerful GUI, it is capable of advanced reconstruction of Web, e-mail, IM, FTP, Telnet, VoIP applications, and superior forensic analysis at the packet level. It can be integrated with Cisco IDS, Micromuse NetCool, and IBM/Tivoli Risk Manager. Appliances may be distributed throughout the enterprise and then centrally managed along with aggregated reporting and analysis. More details about NetDetector are in http://www.niksun.com/ Products_NetDetector.htm.

Testing and Reliability of Forensic Tools

There is a critical need in the law enforcement community to ensure the reliability of computer forensic tools. NIST and NIJ have developed standards to test the reliability of forensic tools.

Computer Forensic Tool Testing (CFTT)

The goal of the Computer Forensic Tool Testing (CFTT) project at NIST is to establish a methodology for testing computer forensic tools by development of general tool specifications, test procedures, test criteria, test sets, and test hardware. The activities of forensic investigations are initially separated into discrete functions or categories, such as hard disk write protection, disk imaging, string searching, and so forth. A test methodology is then developed for each category. Each assertion, derived from testable requirements, is then tested within the overall testing framework to produce results that are repeatable and objectively measurable. Test results are then reported to manufacturers and law enforcement organizations.

As an example, disk imaging tools are tested for the following capabilities namely, the accuracy of copy by comparing disks, an unchanged source disk, an uncorrupted image file, and reliable error handling of faulty disks. Rigorous tests force the vendors to improve their tools and make them acceptable in court. The results of the tests can be used by law enforcement agencies and other investigators to choose the right tools for the investigation, and to decide when and how to use them.

The forensic tools that have been currently validated by CFTT include hard drive imaging tools namely Safeback, EnCase, Ilook, and Mares, write block software tools namely RCMP HDL, Pdblock, and ACES, and write block hardware devices namely A-Card, FastBlock, and NoWrite.

The lack of standards or specifications of tools and multiple versions of tools make it difficult to test forensic tools. Reliably faulty hardware and obscure knowledge domain (Windows drivers) make the testing task more challenging. More details about CFTT can be found in http://www.cftt.nist.gov/.

National Software Reference Library (NSRL)

NIST's National Software Reference Library (NSRL) is designed to provide international standard court-admissible reference data that tool makers and investigators can use in investigations. This project is supported by the U.S. Department of Justice's National

Institute of Justice (NIJ), federal, state, and local law enforcement. NSRL is designed to collect software from various sources and incorporate file profiles computed from this software into a Reference Data Set (RDS) of information. The RDS contains digital signatures of known, traceable malicious software applications like hacking scripts and steganography tools. Cryptographic functions such as MD5 and SHA1 are used to generate the digital fingerprint (or hash). Repeatability and traceability are important goals of the NSRL project.

The RDS can be used to review files on a computer by matching file profiles in the RDS, and determining which files are important as evidence. With the signatures, law enforcement investigators can ignore these benign files on seized computers, system administrators can identify critical system files that have been perturbed, digital archivists can identify applications versus user-created data, or exact duplicate files. The NSRL can be used to prosecute intellectual property crimes. A law enforcement agent can have easy and definitive access to prove that a given piece of software is or is not a copy of specific software. The review of files is only as good as the hashed collection, hence software vendors must help in creating an extensive RDS by donating a copy of their software to the NSRL. More information about NSRL can be found in http://www.nsrl.nist.gov.

E-Crime

Electronic Crime Program (E-Crime), which consists of methods and training programs for forensic analysis, has been developed by NIJ in collaboration with NIST. Electronic Crime Program is designed to address any type of crime involving digital technology, including cyber crime and cyber terrorism. The goal is to enable the criminal justice community to better address electronic crime by building capacity for and conduits among Federal, State, and local agencies; industry; and academia. The E-Crime program and its current activities can be found in http://www.nlectc.org/training/cxtech2004/2004CXTech_NIJ_E-Crimes.pdf.

Legal Considerations

While investigating computer crimes, one has to know the laws that cover such crimes. Authorizations are needed to access targets for evidence. In order to preserve the admissibility of evidence, proper handling of evidence by a computer forensics expert is required (Nelson, Phillips, Enfinger, & Steuart, 2004). Manuals such as that of the U.S. Department of Justice explain the laws related to search and seizure of computers for digital evidence gathering (US DOJ, 2002). The International Organization on Computer Evidence (IOCE) has working groups in Canada, Europe, the United Kingdom, and the United States to formulate international standards for recovery of computer-based evidence. Different warrant requirements and other legal constraints apply to different categories of data such as recent, older, interceptable, not interceptable, etc. Investigators should always consult the legal department of their corporation to understand the limits of their investigation. Privacy rights of suspects should not be ignored. Legal issues associated with cyber crimes are still being developed by legislators and may change in future.

Future Trends

The field of computer forensics is still nascent. Tools are continually being developed to handle electronic content and the diverse operating environments. The US Department of Justice in a recent report (US DOJ, 2002) identified finding information in the "information ocean", anonymity, traceability, and encryption as the four major challenges in relation to forensic evidence collection and analysis. Finding valuable evidence from the massive amount of information is nearly impossible. Digital evidence may be found in monolithic computers, or in a distributed form in multiple computers. Computer networks allow people to have a false identity thereby maintaining anonymity. This anonymity is misused by some sophisticated users who commit unlawful acts. With the computers connected to the Internet, evidence may be spread across several jurisdictions and vast geographical distances. Law enforcement agencies in different jurisdictions will have to cooperate and coordinate in the evidence collection process.

Computers are increasingly embedded in larger systems with more sophisticated methods of storing and processing data. Evidence collection from such systems is complicated and presentation of the collected evidence in court is a daunting task. Traceability, which deals with establishing the source and destination of computer-based communications, is very difficult to achieve because of the diversity of the Internet. Cryptography presents an additional threat to forensic analysis. Robust encryption tools can be installed easily and allow the criminals to communicate and store information in a form that is not easily accessible to law enforcement.

For subsequent forensic analysis, the detection of steganography software on a suspect computer is important. Many steganography detection programs work best when there are clues as to the type of steganography that was employed in the first place (Kessler, 2004). Finding steganography software on a computer would give rise to the suspicion that there are actually steganography files with hidden messages on the suspect computer and maybe provide some clues about the types of such files. The tools that are employed to detect steganography software are often inadequate. The detection of steganography software continues to become harder due to the small size of the software coupled with the increasing storage capacity of removable media.

Integrated evidence gathering and analysis tools are being developed. Note that there is no complete solution for all forensic needs. Very few tools are validated and approved for use in legal proceedings. Currently there are no standardized procedures for conducting computing investigations. Also, there is a shortage of skilled forensic examiners and a lack of standard certification processes. An effective forensic investigator must be familiar with systems administration practices and have a fundamental understanding of computers, operating systems, databases, and computer networks. An increased awareness of the legal issues involved in a computer forensic investigation is also essential.

A variety of portable devices such as cell phones, PDAs, and more, are used today for data communications, and can have valuable digital evidence. Development of new forensic tools for analyzing the storage media of such portable devices is gaining impetus. Computer forensic techniques and tools should adapt well to new technology products and innovations. Automated techniques for detection and prevention of malware such as viruses and worms are being developed.

Conclusions

The need for security measures to guard against Internet attacks and cyber crime is well recognized. Digital forensics is the solution to find the perpetrator of a computer-related crime after the incident, and to gather intelligence to prevent such attacks in the future. This chapter provided an introduction to the two main components of digital forensic analysis of computer crimes namely, computer forensics and network forensics. The various steps involved in a forensic investigation have been outlined. Some popular computer forensic tools and network forensic tools have been described in detail. Although a number of tools are available today, few tools have been validated for providing evidence that can be used in court. In addition to developing more sophisticated forensic analysis tools, the focus of future research will be the integration of digital forensic techniques with mainstream computer and network security techniques.

References

Arbitration. (2004). *The use of computer forensics in arbitration*. Online Security.

CFIT. (2001). *Operational Information Security*. Information Networks Division. Defense Science and Technology Division. CFIT User Manual.

Farmer, D., & Venema, W. (1999) *The coroner's toolkit (TCT)*. Retrieved April 2005, from http://www.porcupine.org/forensics/tct.html

Goel, A., et al. (2003). Forensix: A robust, high-performance reconstruction system. *The 19th ACM Symposium on Operating Systems Principles* (SOSP). New York: ACM Press.

Gomez, R., Adly, A., Mayergoyz, I., & Burke E. (1992) Magnetic force scanning tunneling microscope imaging of overwritten data. *Magnetics, IEEE Transactions on, 28*(5), 3141-3143.

Gutmann, P. (1996) Secure deletion of data from magnetic and solid-state memory. In *Proceedings of Sixth USENIX Security Symposium.*

Intellectual Property. (2004, Winter). How intellectual property gets stolen: Can you count the ways?. *The Norcross Group Newsletter: The (Forensic) Fish Wrap, 1*(1), 5. Retrieved April 2005, from http://norcrossgroup.com/TNG%20Newsletter.pdf

Kessler, G. (2004). An overview of steganography for the computer forensics examiner. *Forensic Science Communications, 6*(3).

Kruse, W., & Heiser, J. (2001). *Computer forensics: Incident response essentials.* Addison Wesley.

Mohay, G., et al. (2003). *Computer and intrusion forensics.* Norwood, MA: Artec House.

Nelson, B., et al. (2004). *Guide to computer forensics and investigations.* Boston: Thomson Course Technology.

Palmer, G. (2001). *A roadmap for dgital forensics research.* Technical Report. First Digital Forensic Research Workshop (DFRWS). Retrieved March 2006, from http://www.dfrws.org/dfrws-rm-final.pdf

Sekar, V., Xie, Y., Maltz, D., Reiter, M., & Zhang, H. (2004). Toward a framework for internet forensic analysis. In *Proceedings of the Third Workshop on Hot Topics in Networks* (HotNets-III). ACM SIGCOMM. San Diego, CA, USA.

Sitaraman, S., Krishnamurthy, S., & Venkatesan, S. (2005). Byteprints: A tool to gather digital evidence. In *Proceedings of the International Conference on Information Technology (ITCC 2005).* Las Vegas, Nevada, USA.

Stevenson, P. (2003). *A comprehensive approach to digital incident investigation.* Elseiver Information Security Technical Report. Retrieved April 2005, from http://people.emich.edu/pstephen/my_papers/Comprehensive-Approach-to-Digital-Investigation.pdf

Thurimella, R., Burt, A., Sitaraman, S., & Venkatesan, S. (2005). Origins: An approach to trace fast spreading worms to their roots. In *Proceedings of the South Central Information Security Symposium (SCISS 2005).* Austin, Texas, USA.

Unlawful Conduct. (2000). *The electronic frontier: The challenge of unlawful conduct involving the use of the internet.* President's Working Group Report. Retrieved April 2005, from http://www.usdoj.gov/criminal/cybercrime/unlawful.htm

US DOJ. (2001). *Electronic crime needs assessment for state and local enforcement.* National Institute of Justice. Research Report, NCJ 186276. Washington DC.

US DOJ. (2002). *Searching and seizing computers and obtaining electronic evidence in criminal investigations.* United States Department of Justice. Retrieved from http://www.usdoj.gov/criminal/cybercrime/s&smanual2002.htm#introduction

Chapter IV

Digital Forensics Tools: The Next Generation

Golden G. Richard III, University of New Orleans, USA

Vassil Roussev, University of New Orleans, USA

Abstract

Digital forensics investigators have access to a wide variety of tools, both commercial and open source, which assist in the preservation and analysis of digital evidence. Unfortunately, most current digital forensics tools fall short in several ways. First, they are unable to cope with the ever-increasing storage capacity of target devices. As capacities grow into hundreds of gigabytes or terabytes, the traditional approach of utilizing a single workstation to perform a digital forensics investigation against a single evidence source, such as a hard drive, will become completely intractable. Further, huge targets will require more sophisticated analysis techniques, such as automated categorization of images. We believe that the next generation of digital forensics tools will employ high-performance computing, more sophisticated evidence discovery and analysis techniques, and better collaborative functions to allow digital forensics investigators to perform investigations much more efficiently than they do today. This chapter examines the next generation of digital forensics tools.

Introduction

A wide variety of digital forensics tools, both commercial and open source, are currently available to digital forensics investigators. These tools, to varying degrees, provide levels of abstraction that allow investigators to safely make copies of digital evidence and perform routine investigations, without becoming overwhelmed by low-level details, such as physical disk organization or the specific structure of complicated file types, like the Windows registry. Many existing tools provide an intuitive user interface that turns an investigation into something resembling a structured process, rather than an arcane craft.

Unfortunately, the current generation of digital forensics tools falls short in several ways. First, massive increases in storage capacity for target devices are on the horizon. The traditional approach of utilizing a single workstation to perform a digital forensics investigation against a single evidence source (e.g., a hard drive) will become completely inadequate as storage capacities of hundreds of gigabytes or terabytes are seen more often in the lab. Furthermore, even if traditional investigative steps such as keyword searches or image thumbnail generation can be sped up to meet the challenge of huge data sets, much more sophisticated investigative techniques will still be needed. For example, while manually poring over a set of thousands (or even tens of thousands) of thumbnails to discover target images may be possible, what will an investigator do when faced with hundreds of thousands of images? Or millions?

The next generation of digital forensics tools will employ high performance computing, more sophisticated data analysis techniques, and better collaborative functions to allow digital forensics investigators to perform examinations much more efficiently and to meet the challenges of massive data sets. In this chapter, we examine some of the technical issues in next-generation tools and discuss ongoing research that seeks to address them.

Challenges

To see the challenges faced by the next generation of digital forensics tools, we examine the looming problems of scale that will soon overwhelm current-generation tools. The primary challenges are fueled by fundamental trends in computing and communication technologies that will persist for the foreseeable future. Storage capacity and bandwidth available to consumers are growing extremely rapidly, while unit prices are dropping dramatically. Along with the consumer's desire to have everything online, where music collections, movies, and photographs will increasingly be stored solely in digital form, these trends mean that even consumer-grade computers will have huge amounts of storage. From a forensics perspective, this translates into rapid growth in the number and size of potential investigative targets. To be ready, forensic professionals need to scale up both their machine and human resources accordingly.

Currently, most digital forensic applications are developed for a high-end, single or dual-CPU workstation that performs queries against a set of target media. In many cases, this approach already requires too much time, even for targets of modest size. More importantly, fundamental trends in hardware dictate that this single workstation approach will hit an insurmountable performance wall very soon. Patterson (2004) performed a quantitative survey of long-term trends in hardware with respect to capacity, bandwidth, and latency. From a forensics perspective, the most consequential result is the observed divergence between capacity growth and improvements in latency. Specifically, over the last 10 years, for representative "high performance" hard disk drives, the capacity has grown 17 times (from 4.3 to 73.4 GB), while average latency (disk seek time) has improved only 2.2 times (from 12.7 to 5.7 ms). Similarly, the gap between capacity and transfer rate has also grown as transfer rate (throughput) has improved only 9.6 times (from 9 to 86 MB/s). In practical terms, the gap is even bigger among high-capacity (250GB+) drives targeted at the mass retail market. These are typically EIDE/ATA drives that are optimized for capacity and cost, with throughput and latency being somewhat less important.

Since most current digital forensics operations, such as computing cryptographic hashes, thumbnail generation, file carving, and string searches, are I/O-bound, the performance of existing investigative tools will become completely unacceptable as the size of the problem (determined by capacity) grows significantly faster than the ability to process it (determined by drive latency and transfer rate limitations). We refer to the ability to scale up machine resources to match the growth of the forensic targets as *machine scalability*.

A generally overlooked side of the scalability problem, which we refer to as *human scalability*, is the ability to make efficient use of human resources in a digital forensics investigation. This includes the presence of more advanced processing capabilities to relieve experts from routine work (e.g., searching for contraband images) as well as support for collaboration, which allows multiple experts to efficiently work together on a case.

An alternative view of scalability is to consider turnaround time of time-sensitive digital forensic investigations. For example, consider a situation where law enforcement officers have seized a computer belonging to a suspected kidnapper. In this situation, it is *critical* that investigators be able to concentrate all available machine/human resources (perhaps in an ad-hoc manner) and thoroughly examine the available information for clues as rapidly as possible. Turnaround of minutes or hours is needed, rather than days or weeks.

For all practical purposes, current tools do not deal with scalability issues of the kind described above. In the following sections, we discuss in more detail both the machine and human aspects of the scalability problem and present some approaches to address them.

Machine Scalability

At a high level, the technical aspects of the digital forensic process can be described as follows: for each file in a given file system, a number of type-specific operations— indexing, keyword searches, thumbnail generation, and others—are performed. Digital evidence such as deleted files, file slack, directory structures, registries, and other operating system structures can be represented as special file types, so the model applies to these types of evidence as well. To be credible, an investigator must thoroughly examine the content of the entire forensic target. Even in cases where a partial examination is acceptable, a substantial amount of data must be processed. Thus, the turnaround time of a forensic inquiry is inherently limited by disk transfer rate and seek time.

Current tools, such as the Forensics Toolkit (FTK) from AccessData Corp., attempt to reduce the need to read an entire forensics image repeatedly (e.g., for each search operation) by performing an initial preprocessing step that builds index structures to speed up keyword searches, disk carving, and to provide file categorization. While this technique is effective in many scenarios, it is limited by the computational resources available on a single workstation. First, it may take several days just to perform the preprocessing step. Second, the system indexes only strings that it judges to be of use in the investigation: for example, character sequences that appear to be similar to English words and those that are useful for file carving. Regular expression searches, as well as simple searches for character sequences that are not in the index, such as words in foreign languages with different encoding, still require an exhaustive examination of the entire target image. On targets of hundreds of gigabytes or terabytes, investigators may (necessarily) be disinclined to perform searches that may take days of execution time, particularly as caseloads grow. Finally, the index structure of a large target will also become large, which will prevent it from being kept in main memory.

Generally, there are two possible approaches to improve machine scalability—improve the efficiency of the algorithms and their implementations to get more from the current hardware platforms or enable the use of more machine resources in a distributed fashion. These two approaches are to a great extent complementary; however, the former is likely to yield only incremental improvements in performance, whereas the latter has the potential to bridge the hardware performance gaps discussed earlier.

As already discussed, any kind of digital forensics analysis is inherently I/O-constrained because of the need to process vast amounts of data; however, it can also become CPU-constrained if more sophisticated analytical techniques, such as automatic image classification, are used. A distributed solution can address both the I/O and the CPU constraints. For example, a 64-node Beowulf cluster with 2GB of RAM per node can comfortably cache over 100GB of data in main memory. Using such a system, the cost of the I/O transfer of a large forensic image can be paid once and any subsequent I/O can be performed at a fraction of the cost. Taking the idea a step further, the data cached by each node can be made persistent so that if the system needs to shutdown and restart, each node need only autonomously read in its part of the data from a local disk. At the same time, having multiple CPUs performing the CPU-intensive operations obviously has the potential to dramatically improve execution time. Therefore, in the following section, the focus of the discussion is on the application of distributed computing techniques in a digital forensics environment.

Distributed Computing and Digital Forensics

Most digital forensics operations are naturally file-centric with very few (if any) dependencies among the processing of different files. Thus, choosing an individual file as the primary distribution unit minimizes synchronization and communication among the nodes of the cluster. Consequently, the first essential step in employing distributed computing is to distribute the files comprising the digital evidence over a compute cluster.

From a caching perspective, maximizing speedup is relatively straightforward—files should be spread such that as many of them as possible are kept in RAM during processing. Large files that are much bigger than the available physical memory on any given machine may have to be split into pieces and/or processed separately. It is desirable, but not crucial, that there be enough physical memory to cache all useful files during processing. Any cache requests exceeding the available RAM resources will automatically be handled by the host virtual memory system. Although no experimental results have been published, common experience from general operating system usage suggests that, depending on access patterns, overloading by as much as 50% can have only modest impact on performance, and as much as 100% may be tolerable.

Maximizing CPU utilization is a bit more complicated. One approach is to scatter the files of a particular type evenly across the processing nodes. The rationale is that, whenever an operation is issued—for example, a regular expression search—all nodes will have a similar amount of work to complete and, therefore, CPU utilization will be maximized. However, more sophisticated processing that attempts to correlate different objects (such as the image classification technique discussed later) may be hampered by this file distribution pattern, increasing the need for network communication. In such cases, concentrating the files in fewer nodes and crafting a suitable communication pattern may yield better results.

Another twist is the recent trend toward routine use of symmetric multi-processor (SMP) and multi-core systems, especially in high performance compute clusters. In an SMP, all CPUs have uniform access to a shared memory pool and often have dedicated high-speed communication among the processors. Clearly, to optimize performance, such architectural features must be taken into consideration during the distribution and processing phases.

Distributed digital forensics tools are still in their infancy but even preliminary results from research prototypes clearly demonstrate the benefits of the approach. *DELV* (Distributed Environment for Large-scale inVestigations) provides a look at how distributed systems can be applied to digital forensics (Roussev & Richard, 2004). An investigator controls the investigation on a single workstation through a GUI similar to those provided by other forensic tools in common use. Behind the scenes, however, digital forensics operations are farmed out to nodes in a commodity *Beowulf* cluster and the returned results are aggregated and dynamically presented to the user as soon as they become available. Thus, to perform a complicated regular expression search against a large target, for example, the investigator enters a single expression and the search is performed in parallel across all (or some subset of) the cached evidence. As hits accumulate, they are displayed for the user.

There are three notable differences in the user experience between *DELV* and most traditional single-machine digital forensics tools. First, the system does not perform any preprocessing—it simply loads the forensic image and is ready to perform queries. The system supports two different modes to load target images. The first is "cache" mode, in which a central coordinator node reads the entire image and distributes data over the network to compute slaves. In the other "load" mode, the coordinator instructs the slaves to individually load certain data from the target image, which is on a shared fileserver. Preliminary experiments have shown that the concurrent loading provided by "load" mode was much better able to utilize the read throughput of a high performance RAID storage, with measured speed-up of up to 30%. Nodes can use their local disk to cache their part of the evidence so subsequent loads of the image take only a fraction of the original time.

Another difference is that, since all work is performed remotely, the investigator's machine remains responsive and available to do follow-up work on partial results (e.g., opening a matching file) as soon as they become available. It is also possible to start new queries, such as text searches, while previous ones are still running, with little noticeable change in the overall performance. This is due to the fact that many operations are I/O-bound and once the I/O bottleneck is overcome through caching, the CPUs can easily handle simultaneous queries. More generally, it is reasonable to expect the execution time of overlapping I/O-bound operations to be very close to that of a single query.

The final difference is that investigative operations execute in a fraction of the time required on a single workstation. Specifically, the 8-node experiments in Roussev and Richard (2004) point to a super-linear speedup for I/O-bound forensics operations. The speedup in this case is likely to be a constant factor unrelated to the concurrency factor (number of nodes) but reflects the time savings from not accessing the disk. Nonetheless, the gap between cluster and single workstation performance grows as a function of the target size. This occurs because the growing mismatch between available workstation resources and actual processing needs leads to other adverse side effects such as virtual memory system thrashing and competition for RAM resources between index structures and evidence. For CPU-bound operations, such as detection of steganography, the observed *DELV* speedup is approximately equal to the concurrency factor.

Although this area of research is still in its early stages, these results provide food for thought in terms of improving the processing model of digital forensics tools. One important issue is to improve investigation turnaround time. For example, if the complete target can be kept cached in RAM, costly preprocessing (such as string indexing), designed to speedup I/O-bound operations such as string searches, can be completely eliminated in favor of an on-demand distributed execution of the operation. Another attractive possibility is to perform the preprocessing step in parallel on the cluster and then use the results on local workstations. This may not be possible if the specific processing needed is only available from a proprietary software package, such as *FTK*. However, it might still be possible to pool the RAM resources of the cluster and create a distributed RAM drive. Assuming a fast enough network (e.g., gigabit or better), such a network "drive" should outperform a local hard disk when a significant fraction of the disk operations are non-sequential.

Looking forward, distributed computing also allows the sophistication of investigative operations to be improved substantially. For example, automated reassembly of image fragments (Shanmugasundaram, 2003) and analysis of digital images to determine if they have been tampered with or were computer-generated (Farid & Lyu, 2003), watermark detection (Chandramouli & Memon, 2003), automatic detection of steganography (Chadramouli, Kharrazzi, & Memon, 2004), and correlation and attribution (de Vel, Anderson, Corney, & Mohay, 2001; Novak, Raghavan, & Tomkins, 2004) of documents all have significant computational requirements and will be made practical by the application of high-performance computing.

Some digital forensics operations straddle the machine vs. human scalability line. Sophisticated image analysis is one example, in which deeper analysis of images can save a significant amount of human effort, but the analysis may only be feasible if sufficient computational resources can be applied. Content-based image analysis, which also fits into this category, will be discussed in a subsequent section.

On-the-Spot and "Live" Digital Forensics

Another approach to improving machine scalability is to improve preliminary identification of evidence. Currently, the best practical solution in large-scale investigations is to either seize all sources of evidence or use a portable high performance storage system to obtain a copy of any potential evidence. There are several reasons that make this approach problematic. The first has already been discussed—as forensics targets grow in size—insurmountable logistical problems will arise in the collection, preservation, and analysis steps of an investigation. In some cases, a forensic target may be a currently unidentified machine (or machines) in a large network, such as a computer lab at a library. In other cases, the forensic target might be a huge fileserver, whose operation is critical for the well-being of a company. Performing an imaging operation on every machine in a large laboratory setting will be a very daunting task, as will be imaging a multi-terabyte fileserver. Even if logistical problems with the imaging process are overcome, a huge interruption of service is necessary during a traditional imaging operation, during which normal operation of the computer systems is impossible. Finally, analyzing the drives of a large group of machines (or of a terabyte fileserver) will consume considerable resources.

A more efficient solution is to perform a safe screening of the target systems and take only the relevant data and systems to the lab. Such screening can be performed using the local computational and communication resources of the targets. A straightforward solution that overcomes some (but not all) of the logistical problems described above is creation of better imaging tools, where files that are not interesting (e.g., operating systems files or file types irrelevant to an investigation) are not included in the captured image. In many cases, however, the number of files that might be excluded may be rather small, in comparison to the size of the entire target. Thus, other approaches should be explored, in addition to creating better drive imaging tools.

The Bluepipe architecture (Gao, Richard, & Roussev, 2004) permits an on-the-spot investigator to perform simple queries and to capture and preserve digital evidence, using only a small amount of hardware (e.g., a PDA or laptop). Bluepipe uses a client/ server architecture, with a server running on the target machine and one or more Bluepipe clients controlling the investigation. Client and server communicated via a SOAP-based protocol. Bluepipe clients may also serve as proxies, which allows remote investigators to gain remote access to the target over a trusted connection, as well as collaborate with investigators on the spot.

To begin an inquiry, an investigator performs several steps: she plugs in USB dongles to enable wireless communication with the target computers, boots the target computers using Bluepipe boot CDs, and launches the Bluepipe client application on her PDA or laptop. The Bluepipe boot CD invokes the server-side Bluepipe application, initializes the connection between client and server, and exposes the secondary storage devices of the target to the Bluepipe server application. The investigator then uses the client GUI on the PDA (or laptop) to issue queries and receive results. All processing on the target side consists of collections of read-only operations—called Bluepipe patterns—against the secondary storage on the target machine. An audit log tracks all operations performed on the target; this log is transmitted to the client at the end of the inquiry. Because some investigatory operations are expected to complete quickly and some require substantial processing time, Bluepipe supports both synchronous and asynchronous communication.

A Bluepipe pattern is an XML document describing a set of related operations to be executed on the target machine, combined with some additional parameters that govern priority and frequency of progress updates. The goal of a pattern might be to determine whether a particular application is installed on the target, to extract a system timeline, or to perform case-specific keyword searches. All Bluepipe patterns preserve the state of secondary storage on the target machine. Supported pattern operations include checking for existence of files with specific names or hash values, searching files for keywords, retrieving files, and generating directory and partition table listings. Bluepipe patterns are stored on the client and transmitted to the Bluepipe server for execution as they are selected by the investigator. Results of the pattern execution are then transmitted back to the client.

A few simple examples illustrate the use of Bluepipe patterns to perform preliminary analysis of a target machine. The following pattern was used to obtain a partition table listing of a target with a single IDE hard drive:

```
<BLUEPIPE NAME="partitions">
<!— get a lot of drive/partition info—>
<LISTPARTITIONS LOCAL="drives.txt"
GENHASHES=TRUE/>
</BLUEPIPE>
```

The result of executing this pattern, a text file named "drives.txt", illustrates that the target machine's single hard drive contains five partitions with at least two operating systems installed:

hda

Model Number: IC25T060ATCS05-0.

Serial Number: CSL800D8G3GNSA

device size with M = 1024*1024: 57231 Mbytes

Partition table:

Disk /dev/hda: 240 heads, 63 sectors, 7752 cylinders

Units = cylinders of 15120 * 512 bytes

Device Boot	Start	End	Blocks	Id	System
/dev/hda1	1	6173	46667848+	7	HPFS/NTFS
/dev/hda2	7573	7752	1360800	1c	Hidden Win95 FAT32 (LBA)
/dev/hda3 *	6174	7364	9003960	83	Linux
/dev/hda4	7365	7572	1572480	f	Win95 Ext'd (LBA)
/dev/hda5	7365	7572	1572448+	82	Linux swap

MD5 hash for drive: 463e65ec8d9f51bdd17c0347243f467b

The next pattern, named "findcacti", searches for pictures of cacti using a hash dictionary. A single target directory is specified, "/pics", which is searched recursively. Files that match are retrieved and stored on the client in a directory named "cactus". No file size restrictions are imposed. The %s and %h placeholders in the message will be replaced by the filename and hash value of each matching file.

```
<BLUEPIPE NAME="findcacti">
<!— find illegal cacti pics using MD5 hash dictionary —>
<DIR TARGET="/pics/" />
<FINDFILE
 USEHASHES=TRUE
 LOCALDIR="cactus"
 RECURSIVE=TRUE
 RETRIEVE=TRUE
 MSG="Found cactus %s with hash %h ">
<FILE ID=3d1e79d11443498df78a1981652be454/>
<FILE ID=6f5cd6182125fc4b9445aad18f412128/>
```

```
<FILE ID=7de79a1ed753ac2980ee2f8e7afa5005/>
<FILE ID=ab348734f7347a8a054aa2c774f7aae6/>
<FILE ID=b57af575deef030baa709f5bf32ac1ed/>
<FILE ID=7074c76fada0b4b419287ee28d705787/>
<FILE ID=9de757840cc33d807307e1278f901d3a/>
<FILE ID=b12fcf4144dc88cdb2927e91617842b0/>
<FILE ID=e7183e5eec7d186f7b5d0ce38e7eaaad/>
<FILE ID=808bac4a404911bf2facaa911651e051/>
<FILE ID=fffbf594bbae2b3dd6af84e1af4be79c/>
<FILE ID=b9776d04e384a10aef6d1c8258fdf054/>
</FINDFILE>
</BLUEPIPE>
```

The result of executing this pattern on a target appears below. Notice that the DSC00051 and bcactus5 image files have identical content:

Beginning execution for pattern "findcacti".

DIR cmd, added "/pics".

FINDFILE cmd.

Found cactus /pics/BBQ-5-27-2001/DSC00008A.JPG with hash
6f5cd6182125fc4b9445aad18f412128

Found cactus /pics/BBQ-5-27-2001/DSC00009A.JPG with hash
    7de79a1ed753ac2980ee2f8e7afa5005.

Found cactus /pics/CACTUS_ANNA/DSC00051.JPG with hash
3d1e79d11443498df78a1981652be454.

Found cactus /pics/GARDEN2002/bcactus5.JPG with hash
3d1e79d11443498df78a1981652be454.

Pattern processing completed.

Sending pattern log. Remote filename is "findcacti.LOG".

Ultimately, tools like Bluepipe do not attempt to replace traditional methods in digital forensics—instead, they improve the triage process and also improve the efficiency of digital forensics investigators. Another type of tool, which also improves triage but operates on live machines, is described below.

An interesting trend in next-generation digital forensics is "live" forensics investigation—analysis of machines that are allowed to remain in operation as they are examined. The idea is appealing, particularly for investigation of mission-critical machines, which would suffer substantial downtime during a typical "dead" analysis. The mobile forensic platform (Adelstein, 2003), now called the OnLine Digital Forensic Suite in its commercial incarnation, allows live investigation of computer systems, permitting an investigator to obtain evidence and perform a thorough examination remotely. The researchers observe, quite correctly, that in large computer networks, unauthorized activity can have devastating consequences and must be dealt with very quickly. Unfortunately, most organizations simply do not have the staff to examine each local network potentially involved in an attack. In addition, in any geographically dispersed organization, the less time the investigators spend traveling, the more time they have to investigate the incident. The MFP is a network appliance, deployed on an organization's local network, which exposes a secure, Web-based investigative interface to an organization's computers. The machines may be investigated while they perform their usual functions, without raising the suspicion that they are under investigation.

A live investigation using the MFP will involve collecting evidence from one or more targets. The MFP organizes an investigative effort into inquiries, each of which represents an investigator's effort to collect data from a target. During a particular inquiry an investigator may collect a machine's state, including running processes, a list of who is currently logged in, and networking information such as currently executing servers and which ports they are listening on. During the inquiry, the investigator may also capture memory dumps of physical memory and running processes, examine the registry (for Windows) and copy files from the target to the MFP network appliance. Any analysis is then performed on data acquired during a particular inquiry—should the investigator wish to snapshot the machine's state again, an additional inquiry is created. Time-consuming operations, such as capturing the physical memory of the target or imaging the entire disk, run as background threads in the MFP and do not block the user interface.

One important difference between a traditional "dead" digital forensics investigation—where a machine is seized, its drives imaged, and analysis performed on these copies—and a "live" investigation, using the MFP, is that the investigator is not an outsider. The MFP requires administrative privileges on the machine under investigation and uses the operating system and hardware resources of the target. As such, it may not be possible to investigate machines whose operating systems have been completely compromised, through the installation of kernel-level rootkits, or machines whose administrator account passwords have been (maliciously) changed. For these kinds of situations, a traditional "dead" analysis is likely required, though all contextual evidence, such as running processes, active connections, and in-memory structures will be lost when the machine is taken down.

Human Scalability

Improving human scalability means making better use of an investigator's time, automating tasks that are routine or tedious, and saving brainpower for tasks that require human intelligence. One benefit of applying high-performance computing to digital forensics investigations is that the abundance of computational resources allows the creation of tools that are much more responsive to an investigator. That is, investigators might continue to work on other aspects of a case while searches and other processing occurs in the background. Highly responsive, multithreaded GUIs are a requirement for next-generation digital forensics tools.

Another benefit is that high-performance computing allows substantially more sophisticated investigative techniques to be supported. For example, the average computer user will likely have a substantial collection of multimedia objects, such as images, audio, and video files. Existing tools provide almost no automation for investigation of multimedia—essentially, an investigator must examine each file in turn. There are a number of digital signal processing techniques that can be employed to speed up the analysis of multimedia. However, such approaches require substantially more computational resources than a single- or dual-CPU system can offer, so high performance computing is a de facto prerequisite for the practical use of such techniques. The next section discusses early research efforts aimed at automating the processing of multimedia evidence as well as some ideas on the kind of support that can be expected in the coming years.

Automated Image Analysis

Digital forensic investigators are often presented with the task of manually examining a large number of digital pictures in order to identify potential evidence. This can be especially daunting and time-consuming if the target of the investigation is very broad, such as a Web hosting service. Current forensic tools are woefully inadequate in facilitating this process and their support is largely confined to generating pages of thumbnail images and identifying known files through cryptographic hashes. Several more sophisticated techniques for processing images are discussed below.

Content-based image retrieval (CBIR) techniques (Chen, Roussev, Richard, & Gao, 2005) have the potential to dramatically improve the performance of image-based searches in at least two common scenarios—queries for contraband images and queries for images related to some known images (e.g., a picture of a particular person). A CBIR system works by extracting and storing a set of image features—essentially, mathematical properties of an image—for each target image. One mathematical approach to extract these features is described in Chen et al. (2005); the interested reader is referred there for the details. Intuitively, the feature set can be thought of as a form of "fingerprint" of the image and can be used later to automatically identify the original image and some versions of it. Based on the feature information of a target set of images, the system builds a database that can later be queried by submitting images or feature sets. The query result is a ranking of the images in the database, such that the one with the highest degree of similarity is at the top.

To use CBIR for contraband discovery, the feature set database is updated by various law enforcement agencies with the feature sets of discovered contraband images. Thus, all images on an investigative target can be automatically compared to the ones in the features database. To use CBIR for image queries, the system first builds a database from all the images on the target and then allows the investigator to submit image queries that rank target images by similarity.

The CBIR approach has several properties that make it particularly suitable for digital forensics purposes:

- **Source independence:** The original images are *not* stored and it is *not* possible to recover them in any form from the stored feature data. This is particularly important in storing information about contraband images, since direct storage of the images themselves is often illegal. Even if legality is not an issue, the use of features instead of originals essentially eliminates the security and public relations risks associated with maintaining the database.

- **Scalability:** The storage requirements for the image feature sets are a small fraction of those of the original image. For high resolution images, less than 1% is typical. This allows the resulting system to scale much better than one based on direct image-to-image comparison and will certainly offer better response time for database queries.

- **Stability:** In addition to discovering exact copies of query images, a CBIR repository system has the added advantage that it can readily identify common image variations. In Chen et al. (2005), the ability of a CBIR system to match a transformed image to its original was evaluated. The system was over 99% accurate in identifying a target image, even after substantial reductions in size or quality. 90-degree rotations and mirroring transformations had a similar effect on the system's effectiveness. In contrast, most existing image query techniques are based solely on cryptographic hashes. This type of matching is very fragile, because only identical files can be discovered. Finally, the stability of CBIR methods further improves the scalability of the system as only a single feature set needs to be stored for a group of derived images.

Image clustering can be built on top of the CBIR approach and seeks to help an investigator by automatically separating target images into clusters of similar images. The idea is to enable the investigator to quickly get an idea of the image content of a large target by looking at a few representative images from each cluster. The flip side of this kind of analysis is to find "anomalies" in the image distribution. For example, it may of interest to flag images that are stored in the same directory, but which have very different content. Obviously, image clustering will not replace human judgment in the forensic process, but it has the potential to drastically reduce the time required to find evidence of interest.

Streaming Media Analysis

Looking forward, ordinary users will increasingly have large libraries of streaming multimedia content. Today, there are practically no tools for automating the examination of such evidence, beyond extraction and searching of any embedded textual information. Part of the problem is that the single-CPU machine is already pushed to the limit and therefore automated (CPU-hungry) analysis is simply not practical. However, a distributed platform offers enough power to tackle the problem. Some ideas for research in this area include:

- **Automated video summarization:** The forensic system can be tasked to extract a series of "important" images that characterize the video stream to be shown to the investigator. Image processing techniques, such as image clustering or feature identification, can then be applied to the individual images.

- **Voice identification/characterization:** Voice analysis tools have been used for a while but are generally not available for routine inquiries. Potential applications include finding occurrences of a specific person's voice in an audio file or identification of the voices of children. The idea is to automate these processes and enable their use on large-scale targets.

- **Searchable multimedia:** The basic idea is to combine automated video summarization with speech-to-text conversion in order to produce an HTML-like summary that can be browsed and searched with conventional tools.

Multi-User Tools

Another aspect of the improvement in human scalability is the efficient pooling the knowledge and expertise of a team of investigators. There are at least two kinds of support that teams need—real-time and long-term. Real-time support is needed to allow teamwork on the same case, so that investigators can see each other's actions and results, and can coordinate on different aspects of a case. The same technology can also be used for training purposes, allowing an inexperienced investigator to observe the approaches taken by more experienced investigators.

Real-time collaboration support becomes particularly relevant if the team has access to a high performance compute cluster. On one hand, the distribution of data and computation *enables* the parallel execution of multiple operations (perhaps submitted by different team members). At the same time, the cluster becomes a valuable resource that virtually *requires* the ability to dynamically share it across teams/cases for proper utilization.

Providing real-time collaboration support will require more sophisticated user interfaces, to control the collaboration, additional security mechanisms beyond those provided in typical single-user tools, and more sophisticated concurrency control, to protect the integrity of a digital forensics investigation. Real-time collaboration support is currently being implemented as part of the work described in Roussev and Richard (2004) and Gao et al. (2004).

Long-term collaboration support refers to the ability of the digital forensics infrastructure to efficiently store and present technical knowledge accumulated through the processing of different cases. Digital forensics knowledge bases are an obvious choice for supporting the exchange of forensic expertise within the lab and across the digital forensics community. In general, even though a knowledge base may present a unified interface to access the "lessons learned", care must be taken because internal and external sources may have different sharing restrictions, trustworthiness, and structure. Internal sources are, presumably, based on existing cases and an appropriate level of confidentiality must be maintained. Alternatively, lessons could be anonymized.

The work described in Mandachela (2005), called a digital forensics repository (DFR), is an early attempt to address the needs of long-term collaboration through a specialized knowledge base. The central idea, borrowed from Harrison (2002), is to build a repository of lessons. A lesson is any technical article that describes a procedure/method for solving a particular forensic problem, such as imaging a specific type of device. Lessons may be created from reports generated by popular digital forensics suites, imported from the Web, or created manually. The system also supports RSS feeds to distribute new lessons and features such as a "lesson of the day".

Conclusion

The technical challenges facing next-generation digital forensics tools are dominated by issues of scale. Current single-CPU systems are quickly approaching a point where their poor performance will make them unusable, due to a fundamental imbalance between the resources needed to process a target and resources available on a single forensics workstation. The only way to address this imbalance is to base the next generation of digital forensics tools on a high performance computing platform, while simultaneously trying to improve the user experience of investigators using the tools and improving the evidence acquisition process. While some problems with current tools—such as lack of multithreading, which often results in unresponsive user interfaces during intensive tasks—are easily corrected with incremental improvements to the applications, new approaches are required to deal with these issues of scale. In addition to sophisticated evidence caching schemes and the use of more CPUs, better collaborative capabilities are also needed, to allow investigators to work together on difficult cases.

Early experimental results in distributed digital forensics confirm that this approach is indeed a practical one, in many cases yielding speedups that well exceed the concurrency factor. A distributed computing approach also allows interactivity to be improved and will enable deployment of sophisticated methods for multimedia processing into next-generation tools. For example, next generation tools should offer investigators far more powerful facilities for images and video than simple thumbnailing, including automatic categorization of images, image searches that are immune to typical image transformations, and summarization and searching for video files. Distributed computing will make implementation of these facilities possible—a resource-starved, single CPU workstation simply isn't up to the task.

Some new tools are also becoming available to provide better evidence evaluation and collection. These fall roughly into two categories—tools that may be used to evaluate "dead" targets on the spot, even by relatively inexperienced investigators, and tools which permit "live" investigation, while a mission-critical machine continues to function. There are some qualms in the digital forensics community about how live forensics fits into the traditional investigative model, where exact copies of evidence (typically, hard drives) are captured and then investigated. Live machines are a moving target and there is no single "image" that defines that state of the machine. This will require some adjustments to the investigative model, as will many of the advances on the horizon for digital forensics.

References

Adelstein, F. (2003). MFP: The mobile forensic platform. *International Journal of Digital Evidence, 2*(1).

Chandramouli, R., Kharrazzi, M., & Memon, N. (2004). *Image steganography and steganalysis: Concepts and practice.* Lecture notes in computer science. Springer-Verlag, Vol. 2939.

Chandramouli, R. & Memon, N. (2003). On sequential watermark detection. *IEEE Transactions on Signal Processing, Special Issue on Signal Processing for Data Hiding in Digital Media and Secure Content Delivery, 51*(4).

Chen, Y., Roussev, V., Richard, G. III, & Gao, Y. (2005). Content-based image retrieval for digital forensics. In *Proceedings of the First International Conference on Digital Forensics (IFIP 2005).*

de Vel, O., Anderson, A., Corney, M., & Mohay, G. (2001). Mining email content for author identification forensics. *SIGMOD Record, 30*(4).

Farid, H. & Lyu, S. (2003). Higher-order wavelet statistics and their application to digital forensics. *IEEE Workshop on Statistical Analysis in Computer Vision.*

Gao, Y., Richard, G. III, & Roussev, V. (2004). Bluepipe: An architecture for on-the-spot digital forensics. *International Journal of Digital Evidence (IJDE), 3*(1).

Harrison, W. (2002). A lessons learned repository for computer forensics. *International Journal of Digital Evidence (IJDE), 1*(3).

Mandelecha, S. (2005). *A prototype digital forensics repository.* M.S. thesis, Department of Computer Science, University of New Orleans.

Novak, J., Raghavan P., & Tomkins, A. (2004). Anti-aliasing on the Web. In Proceedings of *the 13ᵗʰ International Conference on the World Wide Web.*

Patterson, D. (2004). Latency lags bandwidth. *Communications of the ACM, 47*(10).

Roussev, V., & Richard, G. G. III. (2004). Breaking the performance wall: The case for distributed digital forensics. In *Proceedings of the 2004 Digital Forensics Research Workshop (DFRWS 2004).*

Shanmugasundaram, K. (2003). Automated reassembly of fragmented images. In *Proceedings of the IEEE International Conference on Acoustics, Speech, and Signal Processing.*

Chapter V

Validation of Digital Forensics Tools

Philip Craiger, University of Central Florida, USA

Jeff Swauger, University of Central Florida, USA

Chris Marberry, University of Central Florida, USA

Connie Hendricks, University of Central Florida, USA

Abstract

An important result of the U.S. Supreme Courts Daubert decision is that the digital forensic tools must be validated if the results of examinations using those tools are to be introduced in court. With this audience in mind, our chapter describes important concepts in forensic tool validation along with alternative just-in-time tool validation method that may prove useful for those who do not have the capability of conducting extensive, in-depth forensic tool validation efforts. The audience for this chapter is the law enforcement agent and industry practitioner who does not have a solid theoretical background—from training or experience—in software validation, and who is typically time-constrained in the scope of their validation efforts.

Introduction

As with all other forensic disciplines, digital forensic techniques and tools must meet basic evidentiary and scientific standards to be allowed as evidence in legal proceedings. In the United States, the requirements for the admissibility of scientific evidence and expert opinion were outlined in the precedent setting U.S. Supreme Court decision Daubert vs. Merrell Dow Pharmaceuticals, Inc., 509 U.S. 579 (1993). The U.S. Supreme Court found that evidence or opinion derived from scientific or technical activities must come from methods that are proven to be "scientifically valid" to be admissible in a court of law. The term "scientifically valid" suggests that the tools and techniques are capable of being proven correct through empirical testing. In the context of digital forensics, this means that the tools and techniques used in the collection and analysis of digital evidence must be validated and proven to meet scientific standards.

Traditional software validation testing is performed as a routine part of any software development effort. Software validation has been well studied, and the basic tenets of a successful validation approach have been codified in numerous standards accepted by such international bodies as the IEEE. There are significant references and standards covering the role of validation testing during software development, as illustrated in the references to this chapter.

There is often some confusion between the terms validation and verification as applied to software testing. The definitions provided in "General Principles of Software Validation; Final Guidance for Industry and FDA Staff" (http://www.fda.gov/cdrh/comp/guidance/938.html):

- **Software verification** provides objective evidence that the design outputs of a particular phase of the software development life cycle meet all of the specified requirements for that phase. Software verification looks for consistency, completeness, and correctness of the software and its supporting documentation, as it is being developed, and provides support for a subsequent conclusion that software is validated. Software testing is one of many verification activities intended to confirm that software development output meets its input requirements. Other verification activities include various static and dynamic analyses, code and document inspections, walkthroughs, and other techniques.

- **Software validation** is a part of the design validation for a finished device…considers software validation to be 'confirmation by examination and provision of objective evidence that software specifications conform to user needs and intended uses, and that the particular requirements implemented through software can be consistently fulfilled.' In practice, software validation activities may occur both during, as well as at the end of the software development life cycle to ensure that all requirements have been fulfilled. …the validation of software typically includes evidence that all software requirements have been implemented correctly and completely and are traceable to system requirements. A conclusion that software is validated is highly dependent upon comprehensive software testing, inspections, analyses, and other verification tasks performed at each stage of the software development life cycle.

Validation of Digital Forensic Tools

If the developer or manufacturer validates software, one would presume that it should address requirements as specified in Daubert. The problem is that end users of the software rarely receive information as to the methods or results of the validation testing performed on the software. Consequently, end users are not capable of offering evidence or testimony in court to support the assumption that the software used in an investigation worked as intended. Some companies will provide representatives to give expert testimony about the validity of their software if required during a court case, but that is not something the average examiner—local or state law enforcement agent or industry practitioner—can rely upon or expect.

A good deal of forensic software is developed on an ad hoc basis, often by small labs or individuals who recognize a need and provide a product to address it. Because of its ad hoc nature the software tools often do not undergo extensive development testing or planning. This software is sometimes shared among practitioners, or provided to the public as open source software. Practitioners who will use this software in examinations will be required to perform their own validation testing in order to assure both themselves and the courts of the suitability of their tools and results.

Our experience suggests that most practitioners have little or no training or experience in software validation. Consequently, there are several practical matters that limit the law enforcement agents or industry practitioner's ability to perform validation at the same level rigor as the professional software engineer or developer. Foremost is that law enforcement agents and industry practitioners would need documentation tailored to their level of expertise in the field of digital forensics. Second is that in practice there are typically time constraints that limit the scope of the practitioners validation efforts to only a subset of the functions of the tool that will be used in the current examination.

In practice, there are few opportunities for digital forensic practitioners to conduct thorough validation tests. One reason is time: several law enforcement agencies, including, local, state, and federal agencies, have informed us of several months to years of backlogged cases involving digital forensic examinations, some as long as two years. Clearly need is outstripping production. Any process that will reduce the amount of time spent examining a system, while maintaining a high level of quality control, is advantageous to the forensic practitioner as well as to the judicial system. Below we describe a more efficient method of test validation that meets the pressing needs of forensic practitioners.

Limitations in Organized Digital Forensics Validation Efforts

The National Institute for Standards and Technology's (NIST) Computer Forensics Tool Testing (CFTT: www.cftt.nist.gov) division is one government entity that formally tests computer forensics software. CFTT performs extremely rigorous scientific tests to validate software tools used in digital forensic examinations. CFTT has and continues to perform testing on numerous computer forensic software applications, and has identified various problems that have been addressed by the software vendors. Unfortunately, the ability of one organization to examine all forensic software products and their variations is limited due to the sheer magnitude of the task (Craiger, Pollitt, & Swauger, in press).

The digital forensics community cannot rely on a single certifying body to test and evaluate all forensic software, as the sheer pace of change and number of software products is overwhelming (Craiger et al., in press). In addition, software tools written by forensic examiners—that are not commercial products—often provide additional functionality examiners find useful (such as EnCase scripts). Such software, unless it is widely distributed and used, will not rise to the attention of major validation organizations.

Validation Testing Methods

In the following sections, we describe two software validation methods that are appropriate for our practitioner audience: white- and black-box testing. These methods meet the needs of practitioners because: (a) they are simple yet effective methods that require little in-depth knowledge of software validation testing and (b) they are efficient in that they allow the examiner to quickly test only those functions that will be used in the current case.

White-Box Testing

White-box testing (WBT) involves examination of the source code on which the application is built as well as tests comparing the performance of the software against requirements. A requirement is a specification of something that the software must do. Requirements are developed during the software design requirements phase, one of the first phases in the software engineering process.

A formal examination of the source code is called a code walkthrough and has two major requirements. First, the source code on which the application is built must be available for review. Most commercial vendors are reluctant to make source code available to external reviewers due to intellectual property concerns. Thus, code walkthroughs conducted by parties external to a vendor are not common.

The second requirement is that team members conducting the walkthrough ideally consist of individuals with solid technical skills and expertise in two areas. Some members, such as programmers and software engineers, will have expertise in programming and software engineering. In addition, a code walkthrough requires participation by parties with domain knowledge of the tasks to be performed with the software. In the context of digital forensics this will include forensic experts with knowledge about media composition, file systems, forensic tasks, and so forth.

Code walkthroughs are sufficiently labor intensive—moderate size applications may contain hundreds of thousands or even millions of lines of code—which they may take months or even years to complete. Code walkthroughs, while thorough, are of limited use to members of the computer forensic community dealing with the rapidly changing software environment associated with digital evidence recovery tools.

Black-Box Testing

Black-box testing (BBT) evaluates software by comparing its actual behavior against expected behavior. Unlike WBT, BBT assumes nothing about the internal structure of the application (i.e., the source code). In BBT the software serves essentially as a "black box" and the performance of the application is evaluated against functional requirements.

In a digital forensics context, BBT is performed using a tool to perform forensics tasks under various conditions, such as; different file systems, various digital artifacts, different hardware, and various software parameters (switches and settings, etc.). The results of these tests across different conditions are compared against the software design requirements. If the tool performs as specified in the requirements then we have a level of confidence that the tool will work as expected under similar conditions. A positive outcome indicates we have validated the tool for the current task and conditions only; however, this confidence in the tool does not extend to conditions not covered in the test validation. For instance, a validation study may demonstrate that a tool passes a test for searching for non-fragmented ASCII encoded keywords. This result does not generalize to other text encodings, such as UNICODE, UTF-8 or even to ASCII text fragmented across non-contiguous clusters. Representations about a tool's capability only extend as far as the conditions covered during tool testing.

BBT can be performed more quickly than WBT because it does not include a code walkthrough; however, it can still be a time consuming process as a thorough validation test may include several dozens to hundreds of test scenarios, each of which includes different combinations of hardware, test media, and software parameters. In a typical thorough validation it is crucial to exercise a tool over its full range of user selectable parameters and against a number of different data sets or test samples. Although one or two tests may produce positive results, there can always be situations where the tool will fail, situations that are unusual enough to have not been tested or addressed by the designers. Some peculiar combination of set-up parameters, operating criteria, and so on, may reveal a hidden error (i.e., software bug) that, while rarely occurring, may invalidate a tool's functionality for a particular set combination or variables.

Just-in-Time Validation

Just-in-time validation is a testing methodology that involves testing software tools using only those parameters (file systems, file types, software switches, hardware, etc.) that will be used in the actual collection and/or analysis of the evidence. For instance, if a forensic examiners task is to use tool X to identify graphical images on an NTFS formatted volume, then the tool validation test should use only those parameters (file system=NTFS, file types=graphics, etc.) that duplicates the actual task. The set of parameters used in the test will be a subset of the total set of parameters available to be tested. However, only testing those conditions that are required at the time can save effort that would otherwise go into testing test scenarios that are irrelevant for the current case.

Just-in-time validation may be conducted using either a validated reference data source or using a comparative analysis, each of which we describe below. First we describe tool validation procedures as promoted by the Scientific Working Group on Digital Evidence that will serve as the basis for our tool tests.

SWGDE Guidelines for Validation Testing

The best source for guidance for digital forensic tool validation is from the Scientific Working Group for Digital Evidence (SWGDE) Recommended Guidelines for Validation (Scientific Working Group for Digital Evidence, 2004). SWGDE is composed of members from law enforcement (local, state, federal), industry, and academia whose goal is to create standards for digital evidence (www.swgde.org).

SWGDE's guidelines for validation testing describe the procedures one should follow in validating digital forensics software. The guidelines specify that tool validation includes creating a test plan, performing the tests specified in the test plan, and documenting the results. Below we will use SWGDEs guidelines to demonstrate just-in-time validation of a tool's capability for identifying and recovering deleted files on a floppy disk.

Using the SWGDE guidelines our first step is to develop our test plan. A test plan specifies the tool and its functionality to be tested, as well as how the tool will be tested. The test plan includes a description of the purpose and scope of the test, the requirements (tool functionality to be tested), a description of the testing methodology, the expected results, a description of the test scenarios, and a description of the test data.

In our example we will test tool X's capability to identify and recover deleted files, a very common forensic task. Our purpose and scope might be written as: "To validate tool X's capability to identify and recover deleted files on a FAT12 formatted floppy disk." Next we specify three requirements that the tool must exhibit:

1.   The tool must be able to identify deleted files and mark them in an unambiguous fashion so that the examiner may differentiate deleted from non-deleted files.

2.   The tool should be able to identify and display metadata for deleted files, to include the files size, modified, access, and created times.

3.   The tool must be able to recover, and export, the logical contents of the deleted file to the host file system.

Based on the requirements we can then specify the expected results for the test:

1.   The tool shall mark each deleted file to differentiate deleted from non-deleted files.

2.   The tool shall display and unambiguously label the deleted files metadata.

3.   The tool shall write the contents of the deleted file to the host file system using a unique name for each file recovered.

Table 1. Example test plan

Test #	Environment	Actions	Requirement	Expected Result
001	1. 1.4MB Floppy 2. FAT12 3. File A in directory A	Recover and Export Deleted File (logical file only)	Recover and Export Deleted File (logical)	1. Tool shall recover and export each file to the host file system. 2. Hash of the recovered file shall match the hash of the original file.

4. The hash of the recovered file shall match that of an original copy of the file. (This ensures that the file recovered is exactly the same as the original.)

Next we specify the test scenarios. A test scenario specifies the conditions under which the tool will be tested, as well as the pass/fail criteria for each test scenario. For instance, a test scenario for recovering deleted files might look something like Table 1.

Finally, we describe our test data. In this case our test media is a 1.4MB floppy disk, formatted with the FAT12 file system. Our digital artifacts (files) to be recovered include two sets of files: a non-deleted and a deleted version of File A (a small file < 1K), and a non-deleted and a deleted version of File B (a moderately sized file of ~ 60K). Our next step is to prepare the test media that will be used in our testing.

To ensure a scientifically rigorous test we must first sterilize our media to ensure no file remnants remain on the test media, which could bias our results. The test media preparation methodology occurs as follows:

1. "Sterilize" the media by writing a series of characters over the entire writeable area of the media, from the first to the last sector. Typically, 0s (zeros) are written to the entire disk. (In our experience, using 0s make its easier to determine whether a complete sterilization of the media was accomplished). Sterilization is accomplished easily using Linux command line utilities (see Craiger, 2005). Most commercial tools provide this capability.

2. Format the floppy disk to create a file system. The choice is important as we wish to extrapolate from our test to the real-world media we will use. In this case, it is a FAT12 formatted floppy.

3. Copy our test files to the media.

4. Delete some of the files.

5. Write block the floppy to prevent from changing the contents inadvertently.

6. Create a *forensic duplicate* (exact copy) of the image. Again, Linux command line utilities may be used (Craiger, 2005), or any commercial tool that provides that capability.

7.   Calculate a hash (e.g., MD5 or SHA-1) for both duplicate and original. These hash values should match.

Running the Test Scenarios

The forensic duplicate now constitutes our validated reference data source. We are now prepared to run the test according to our test plan. Figures 1 through 3 demonstrate a test scenario using X-Ways Forensics (www.x-ways.net or www.winhex.com) capability of identifying and recovering deleted files on a FAT12 floppy.

Figure 1. Unique marking of deleted files

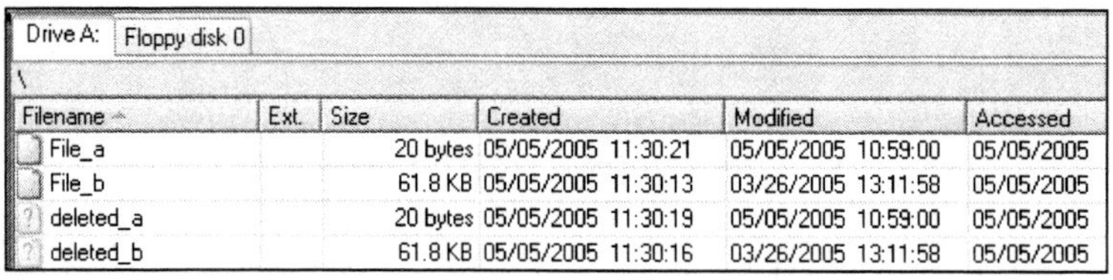

Figure 2. File recovery menu item

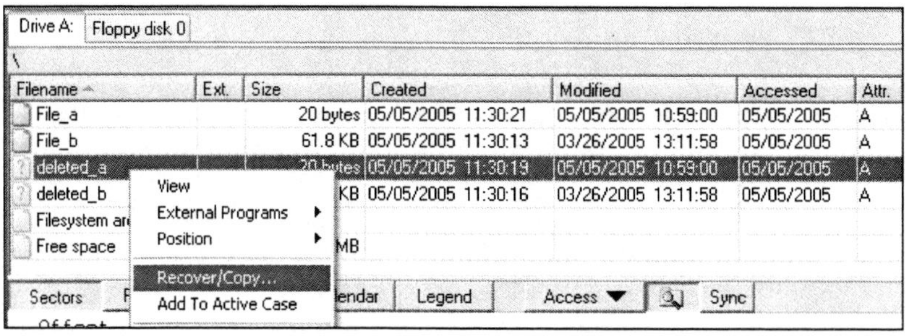

Figure 3. Hashing of original and recovered files

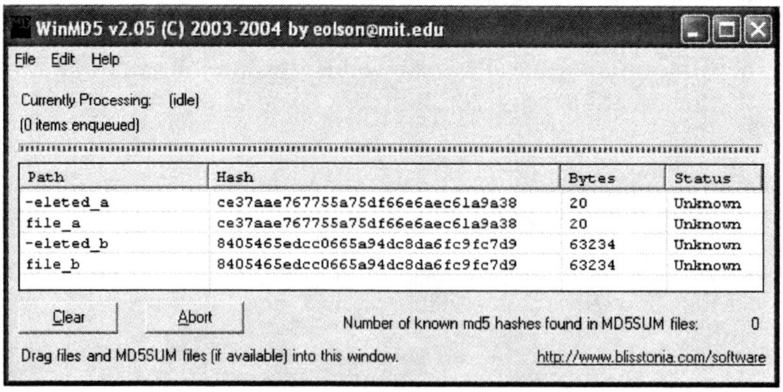

Figure 1 shows that we open our forensic duplicate in the tool and note that it displays our four known files on our validated reference data source. Figure 1 indicates that the tool unambiguously identifies deleted files using a "?". The tool thus passes our first requirement.

The next requirement specifies that the tool allow for the recovery of deleted files. Figure 2 demonstrates that the tool provides a menu selection to recover deleted files. We select the menu item, specify the location of the file, and the tool writes the recovered file to the host file system. Our tool thus passes the second requirement.

Requirement three is important as it determines whether the logical portion of the file was successfully recovered. To be forensically sound, the hash of the recovered files *must* match the hash of the original files. Figure 3 demonstrates that the original and deleted files are hashed using the MD5 cryptographic hash, a 128-bit hashing algorithm. Note that the deleted and original files hashes match, indicating that the tool successfully recovered the file, and thus, it passes the final requirement.

The results of our tests were consistent with the expected results, indicating a positive outcome of the tool validation test.

This example was a simple test of a tool's requirement for identifying and recovering deleted files using the SWGDE guidelines for tool testing using BBT. Next we discuss a second method of testing that can be performed without a validated reference data source.

Comparative Analysis

The example above illustrates the use of a validated reference data source (i.e., test media with known contents) to validate the functionality of a software tool using BBT. A second method, what we call a comparative analysis, is useful when a validated reference data source is either unavailable, or the creation of which would require a significant investment of time and resources that would imprudently delay the actual examination of the evidence. Note that comparative analysis also uses BBT as the test design method.

The key to a comparative analysis is to compare the results across multiple independent tools. Tools are independent in the sense that they are written by independent teams of programmers, and are usually from different commercial vendors or are open source alternatives. Versions 1.0 and 1.1 of the same tool would not constitute independent tools. If all three tools return the same result, then we have supporting evidence that the software functions as intended. We have a stronger claim for validation when one or more of the tools have been validated using a reference data set. For instance, if tools Y and Z were previously validated using a reference data set, then we have stronger evidence of validation when tool X produces the same results as tools Y and Z. The claim is weaker if only one of the other tools has been validated. If none of the other tools have been validated, the confidence is the weakest, although the fact those three tools created by three separate programming teams returned the same result can be interpreted as triangulating on those results.

Table 2. Comparing results of tools

	Find Keyword		
	UNICODE	**ASCII**	**UTF-8**
Tool X	Y	Y	Y
Tool Y	Y	Y	Y
Tool Z	Y	Y	Y

The actual testing procedure is the same as that described previously in the BBT section. A test plan is created, and then each of the tools is tested, following the test plan, and using the test media. After the tools have been tested, we compare the results for each tool as demonstrated in Table 2.

Table 2 illustrates the simple case where three tools are used to recover three files differing in the type of encoding (A = UNICODE, B = ASCII, C = UTF-8). Each of the tools successfully identified the keyword in the different encodings. The results suggest that we can have a measure of confidence in the three tools given that they triangulated on the same result. We have more confidence in our results if one of the tools had been validated previously using a validated reference data source.

What if the tools do not produce the same results? Reality may not be so clear-cut for the simple reason that even the best designed software will contain bugs (as demonstrated by the prevalence of service packs and interim patch releases one sees on a weekly basis). Below we discuss software errors and how to calculate error rates.

Metrics and Errors

There are several validation metrics against which software may be tested, two of the most common of which are performance (speed) and errors. Typically speed will not be of utmost importance to the forensic practitioner. For the digital forensics practitioner the most significant metric will be whether the software performed as expected, as measured by the error rate of the tool.

In the Daubert decision, known or potential rates of error, and error type should be considered when evaluating a scientific technique. Two statistical error types of interest are false positive (Type I) and false negative (Type II) errors. False positive errors occur when a tool falsely identifies a positive result when none is present. For instance, using a validated reference data source, Tool X identifies a file as deleted when in actuality it is not. False negative errors occur when a tool fails to identify results that are actually there. For instance, Tool X fails to identify a file as deleted when in actuality it is.

As an example, consider a forensic tool whose purpose is to scan digital media to detect .jpg graphic image files. The primary design requirement of the software, from a forensic point-of-view is to detect obfuscated jpg image files, for example, when a user changes a jpg extension as a means of hiding the files true type. The tool works by scanning file headers and footers (i.e., the first and last few bytes of a file that determine the files real type) and comparing the files true type with its extension. Normally, the file header/footer and extension will match. However, a simple way of hiding a file is by changing its extension.

For test media we use a hard drive with 50 files, five of which are jpg files. Of these five jpg files, two have an extension other than a normal jpg file (.jpg or .jpeg). The hard drive constitutes our reference data set.

The tool's performance is evaluated by comparing the tool's results with the expected results: which is the tool's ability to detect extensions that do not match the files signature. One expected result is that the tool should identify all instances of .jpg image files, regardless of the extension, using header information. A second expected result is that the tool should not misidentify any non-jpg files as .jpg image files.

Table 3 shows the result of a test where the tool found all instances of jpg files on the hard disk.

In this example, the tool successfully passed the test by (a) detecting all instances of the jpg images, both with and without the correct extensions, and (b) not identifying non-jpg files as jpg files. Out of the 50 files on the test hard drive, all 50 were correctly identified by type. In this case, the tool has proven 100% accurate (correctly identified divided by the total number) with an error rate of 0%.

Now let us consider the case where the tool missed several jpg files as illustrated in Table 4. In this example, the tool failed to detect some jpg files on the test hard drive. Of the 50 files, only 48 were correctly identified. In this case, the tool has displayed an accuracy of 96 percent and displayed two false-negative, or Type II, errors.

Table 3. Search results for JPG detection tool

Known JPG Files	Tool X Discovered JPG Files
Test1.jpg	Test1.jpg
Booty.jpg	Booty.jpg
Hidden.txt*	Hidden.txt
Byebye.zip*	Byebye.zip
Test2.jpg	Test2.jpg

Table 4. Search results for JPG detection tool

JPG File	List of Discovered JPG Files
Test1.jpg	Test1.jpg
Booty.jpg	Booty.jpg
Hidden.txt*	(FAIL)
Byebye.zip*	(FAIL)
Test2.jpg	Test2.jpg

Table 5. Search results for JPG detection tool

JPG Files	List of Discovered JPG Files
Test1.jpg	Test1.jpg
Booty.jpg	Booty.jpg
Hidden.txt*	Hidden.txt
Byebye.zip*	Byebye.zip
Test2.jpg	Test2.jpg
	Document.doc (FAIL)

Now, let us consider the results as seen in Table 5. In this example, the tool successfully identified all jpg format files on the test hard drive, however it misidentified a Microsoft Word file (with the .doc extension) as a jpg image. In this case, the tool correctly identified 49 of the 50 files, resulting in a correct score of 98%, or a 2% error rate, and returned a false-positive, or Type I, error.

(Although not relevant for just-in-time validation, full-blown validation tests would include the above test run using other test media in order to generate more reliable statistics. For example, if the tool was run three times with the results as indicated above, the average accuracy would be (100 + 96 + 98)/3, or 98%, with a standard deviation of 2 (2%) and displayed both Type I and Type II errors. The larger the number of test samples, or the larger the number of relevant data in the test sample, and the more times the tool is tested against different test media, the higher the confidence in the results of the test.)

Identifying Error Causes for Validation Testing

When a test of a software application results in test failures the most important task is to attempt to determine the cause of the test failure. In the examples above, the bit patterns of the files that were not correctly identified should be examined, and their location relative to disk sector or cluster boundaries should be reviewed. It could be that the tool is coded in such a way that it is not looking at the entire header or footer field, or has a coding error that allows it to misread the header, footer, or extension information. In addition, it may be possible that the tool has a problem accurately identifying these fields if they lay across cluster/sector boundaries, or if they lie in non-contiguous clusters. In the example used in this chapter above, further testing and analysis of the test hard disk should be performed to determine if any identifiable cause for the failures could be found. Further testing based on this and other scenarios should be performed to gather further data.

It should be noted that a limited number of failures does not necessarily completely discredit the use of the test tool software. The failure needs to be interpreted with respect to both the entirety of the test results and the nature of the failures. Depending on the manner in which the tool is to be used, a certain error rate may be acceptable if that error rate and the error types are known and taken into account in the analysis of the data recovered.

Test Scenarios

Note that just-in-time validation is efficient because of the judicious selection of test scenarios. Just-in-time validation only includes test scenarios that are immediately relevant to the current task. Contrast this with full-blown validation testing, the purpose of which is to draw inferences about an entire population of tasks, some of which include highly improbable boundary conditions.

Selecting or creating test scenarios for full-blown validation testing is one of the most challenging aspects of validation testing. The set of test scenarios should consist of a number of heterogeneous examples that duplicate conditions that will be found in real world forensic tasks. In addition to common types of data, the test scenarios must include boundary cases. Boundary cases are conditions or examples of things the tool must be capable of detecting even if they are rarely found in most situations. Recovering a 100GB file is an example of a boundary condition for the task of recovering a deleted file. If the tool correctly reports the results from real-world examples as well as boundary cases, then we can say with some authority that the software functions as expected.

A test scenario would ideally include test media containing a complete set of variables and data to thoroughly exercise the application. The advantage of running the tool against a known standard is that the results are known a priori given that the examiner knows what exists on the test media. The disadvantage is the time and effort to create the test media1, which can be extensive, and the potential lack of knowledge about the range of variables that can exist. For example, consider the case of a test of a simple keyword extraction software package, which searches a hard disk for the presence of a keyword or keywords. To perform even a moderately extensive test of this application, the following conditions must be tested, with corresponding test cases produced: (1) five different HD sizes must be used that fall within the traditional hard disk size boundaries; (2) each drive must be presented with both the default and non-default cluster/sector size; (3) the disks must be partitioned in a variety of common formats (FAT 32, FAT 16, NTFS, and EXT3); (4) the keyword(s) that are to be searched for should be present in various formats, including at a minimum: Unicode, ASCII, UTF-7, UTF-8, and RTL; (5) the keyword(s) to be searched for should be placed on the disk in such a way that various locations relative to the physical clusters are presented for test, in other words, lying entirely within one cluster, and crossing cluster boundaries for both the contiguous and non-contiguous cluster cases; (6) and the keyword(s) that are to be searched for should be placed on the hard disk embedded in other characters with no leading or trailing spaces, embedded in other characters but with one leading and trailing space (e.g., null character), and alone with no leading or trailing characters.

This is only a partial, although fairly comprehensive, approach to performing a validation test of a keyword search and extraction algorithm/software package. Certainly additional encodings and other disk partitioning and cluster sizes could be tested. In addition, to more fully test the software, a wide variety of different keywords could be tested, as the algorithm may always find a specific combination of characters that it might not detect (though one can carry this to extremes if one is pedantic enough). As it is, even testing for only one keyword using the above approach, 1800 different individual test cases must be prepared, and if only one partition type is used on each hard disk, 20 hard drives must be prepared for testing. This represents a significant amount of time and effort for both test preparation as well as test performance, with test preparation taking significantly more time than it takes to perform the test.

In the creation of test scenarios for computer forensic applications, this requires that an expert with extensive knowledge of both computer hardware and operating system standards is involved with the test scenario and test media creation. This expertise is required to ensure that the test scenario and media does not overlook important conditions or data that would diminish the validation tests thoroughness.

Conclusions

The Daubert decision will continue to have a major impact on the practice of computer forensics practice as courts and litigants become more technically savvy. The case will also serve to modify expectations of scientific testing of computer forensics tools used to create evidence in these court cases. The thrust of this chapter was to provide an overview of tool validation for digital forensics examiners with limited training and experience in tool testing. Unfortunately, there is very little literature that directly and specifically addresses digital forensic tool validation. The best sources are the SWGDE Guidelines (2004) and documents at National Institutes for Standards and Testing Computer Forensic Tool Testing site (www.cftt.nist.gov).

As the number of forensic software applications continues to increase, and the environment that the tools must operate in continually evolves with the development of new operating systems and computer applications, traditional, intensive software validation will continue to be unable to keep pace with the requirements of the forensic community for validated software. Individual forensic practioners, as well as major labs and accrediting bodies, must be capable of performing validation of tools to some degree of rigor if the results of such tools are to continue to be accepted as evidence in legal proceedings. The approaches presented in this chapter, when applied with due diligence and documentation, will be called upon more and more to provide the required validation and assurance that forensic software applications perform as required.

References

Center for Biologics Evaluation and Research, U.S. Food and Drug Administration. U.S. (2002). *General principles of software validation; Final guidance for industry and FDA staff*. Retrieved from http://www.fda.gov/cdrh/comp/guidance/938.html

Craiger, J. (in press). Computer forensics procedures and methods. To appear in H. Bidgoli (Ed.), *Handbook of Information Security, Volume III*. New York: John Wiley & Sons.

Craiger, J., Pollitt, M., & Swauger, J. (in press). Digital evidence and law enforcement. To appear in H. Bidgoli (Ed.), *Handbook of Information Security, Volume III*. New York: John Wiley & Sons.

IEEE Computer Society. (2004). IEEE 1012 Software Verification and Validation Plans. Retrieved from http://standards.ieee.org/reading/ieee/std/se/1012-2004.pdf

IEEE Standards Association. (1993). IEEE 1059 Guide for Software Verification and Validation Plans. Retrieved from http://standards.ieee.org/reading/ieee/std_public/description/se/1059-1993_desc.html

IEEE Standards Assocation. (1997). IEEE 1074 Standard for Developing Software Life Cycle Processes. Retrieved from http://standards.ieee.org/reading/ieee/std_public/description/se/1074-1997_desc.html

Scientific Working Group for Digital Evidence. (2004). Recommended Guidelines for Validation Testing. Retrieved from www.swgde.org

Chapter VI

Log Correlation:
Tools and Techniques

Dario Valentino Forte, CFE, CISM, Italy

Abstract

Log file correlation comprises two components: Intrusion Detection and Network Forensics. The skillful and mutualistic combination of these distinct disciplines is one of the best guarantees against Points of Failure. This chapter is organized as a tutorial for practitioners, providing an overview of log analysis and correlation, with special emphasis on the tools and techniques for handling them in a forensically compliant manner.

Digital Forensics: Background

The increasingly widespread use of distributed systems requires the development of more complex and varied digital forensic investigative procedures of both the target (the attacked machine) and the analysis platform (forensic workstation). Our discussion here of log analysis and related issues will focus on UNIX-based platforms and the various UNIX "dialects" such as Solaris, AIX, xBSD and, of course, LINUX.

Figure 1. The investigative process

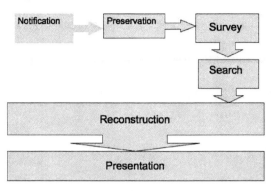

A Digital Forensics Primer

Forensic operations are essentially platform independent, although the same cannot be said for all file systems and log files. In order to adhere to the rules of due diligence contained in the IACIS (International Association of Computer Investigative Specialists, www.cops.org) code of ethics, we must have a clear idea of the general characteristics of file systems and their corresponding log files.

First, let us understand what is meant by "investigative process" in a digital forensics context. This process comprises a sequence of activities that the forensic examiner should carry out to ensure compliance with juridical requirements now common to all countries.

The investigative process may be broken down into six steps (Spafford & Carrier, 2003) as illustrated in Figure 1.

- **Notification:** When an attack is detected by an automatic device, internal personnel, or via external input (for example by a system administrator in another company, or by another business unit in the same company) a first report is generated. The next action usually entails setting up and deploying a response team, whose first task is to confirm that an attack has indeed occurred.

- **Preservation:** This critical incident response step represents the first digital forensic action. The main objective here is to ensure that no alterations are made to the scene of the crime so as not to preclude any future investigative or analytical measures. The "digital crime scene" is usually duplicated via the creation of an image disk so that detailed analyses may subsequently be performed in a properly equipped laboratory.

- **Survey:** This is the first evidence collection step. The scene of the crime is examined for any obvious digital evidence and hypotheses are developed to orient further investigation.

- **Search:** The hypotheses developed in the Survey stage are tested with the help of analysis tools. More detailed evidence is collected in this step, allowing investigators to abandon the "cold" trails and concentrate on the "hot" ones.

- **Reconstruction:** Detailed testing is performed here to link up the pieces of evidence and reconstruct the event. New evidence, or a need thereof, is often discovered here.

- **Presentation:** Here the findings are assembled into a coherent whole and presented to those who ordered the investigation.

There are two basic cases requiring forensic analysis:

1. Reconstruction of an attack (Post Mortem Analysis);
2. Examination of a computer that may have been used to carry out some sort of criminal violation.

In the first case, the computer examined is the target of an attack, in the second it is a *tool* used to perpetrate one.

Log files are subject to the same rules applied in file system analysis. Below we discuss a number of major issues in this regard.

Characteristics and Requisites of Log Files

Log files have certain fundamental requisites for network forensics purposes. They are:

- **Integrity:** The log must be unaltered and totally free of any tampering or modification by unauthorized operators.

- **Time Stamping:** The log must ensure a reasonable certainty as to exactly when a certain event was registered. This is absolutely essential for making post-incident correlations.

- **Normalization** and **Data reduction:** Normalization refers to the extraction of a datum from the original format of the log file without altering its integrity. This datum can then be correlated with others of a different type. Data reduction (a.k.a. filtering) is a procedure for identifying pertinent events and correlating them according to selective criteria.

Figure 2. Log flow

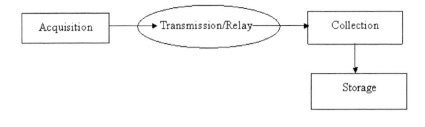

Log Integrity

The integrity of log files must be guaranteed from the moment they are generated. Regardless of how it is acquired (Sniffer, Agent, Daemon, etc.) a log usually flows as portrayed in Figure 2.

When a network sniffer, a system agent, or a daemon acquires an event log it transmits it to a machine that is usually different from the one where the event occurred. Once the log has reached the destination machine (called the log machine) it may be temporarily memorized in a preassigned slot or input to a database for later consultation. The log machine disk capacity is determined by policy and once it has been reached, the original logs are stored elsewhere and then deleted to make room for new files from the source object. This method is known as log rotation.

Log file integrity can be violated in several ways. An attacker might exploit a non-encrypted transmission channel to intercept and modify the transiting log. He might also spoof the IP (Internet Protocol) sending the logs to make the log machine think it is receiving log entries and files that actually come from a different source.

Log File Integrity and Syslog

Despite its popularity and widespread use, the Syslog logging protocol is intrinsically insecure. The *RFC 3164* states that Syslog transmissions are based on UDP (User Datagram Protocol), which is a connectionless protocol and thus unreliable for network forensic purposes unless separate LANs (Local Area Networks) are used for the transmission and collection of log files. Although, even here, some cases may be difficult to interpret. The protocol specifications themselves cite gaps in the definition of the standard. Although some of these shortcomings are remedied in *RFC 3195*, the standard is far from being widely implemented and most logging systems do not conform to its recommendations.

The main problems in using this protocol to gather data for forensic purposes or routine log reviews fall into three categories:

- Transmission-related

- Message integrity

- Message authenticity

We will look at examples of attacks for each of these categories to highlight the drawbacks of using this logging protocol.

Syslog: Transmission Issues

As pointed out, *Syslog* relies on UDP to transmit messages. This makes communication between the two parties unreliable by definition. On top of this, messages generated during network transmission between the source and the destination may be lost entirely. This can only be resolved by using a reliable protocol like TCP (Transmission Control Protocol) as a transport substrate. This protocol uses transmission notification, following an initial handshake phase.

Some implementations of the *Syslog* daemon (e.g., *syslog-ng*) allow you to choose the communication channel. Another solution is to use a point-point connection (e.g., serial line) or a dedicated subnet to collect system logs. However, a hacker with access to the communication network between source and destination could listen in on the communication channel and delete any messages he detects. This misdeed cannot be detected because there is no message notification or sequential numbering.

Syslog: Message Integrity Issues

A second intrinsic problem with the protocol is that it has no mechanism, except at the IP packet level, to safeguard message integrity. This means an attacker can capture a transiting message, alter it, and reintroduce it into the network without leaving any trace. And the problem will not be solved merely by adding a checksum field or a hash to the message. All our hacker needs to do is recalculate the error control code or the message hash and overwrite the existing one to avoid suspicion by the destination host.

Syslog: Message Authenticity Issues

Finally, there is no message source verification mechanism. In effect the remote log collector does nothing more than listen to the specific port and write the messages it receives to disk. This admits a host of problems related to exploiting the collector's "trust" in the source. For example, once the hacker has gained access to the system, he might generate false alerts and transmit them to the remote host until its disk space is full. He could then manipulate the system secure in the knowledge that his activities, although monitored, cannot be registered on the remote host. This type of intrusion does not

Figure 3. Pseudo-code of simple program causing disruption of service on a remote host

```
while (true){
        ip.addr = ip.log_host;


        udp.dport = 514;


        udp.data = random_string();

}
```

require any special expertise. A possible program designed to create a disservice of this type on a remote host log with a few lines of pseudo-code might run like Figure 3.

The packet does not even need to contain all its previous fields, making it even easier to produce harmful messages.

Another way of taking advantage of the lack of message authenticity control might be to forge ad hoc messages to distract the attention of the system administrator from real threats taking place.

Once collected, *Syslog* data must be stored safely to be used as proof in any investigation of a system violation. However forensic analysis requires that the proof, in other words the logs, satisfy the following criteria:

- **Admissibility:** They must be admissible as evidence according to the rules of the courtroom.

- **Authenticity:** It must be proven that the logs contain evidence of the incident in question.

- **Completeness:** The logs must represent the entire history of the incident, not just a part.

- **Trustworthiness:** There can be no doubt as to how the data were collected, their authenticity and exactly how they have been handled and transmitted.

- **Credibility:** They must be easily understood and believable in the courtroom.

Various new versions of *Syslog* have been developed to bring it more closely into line with the above requirements. Currently numerous such implementations exist, including: modular *syslog*, *SDSC Syslog*, *Syslog Ng*, and *Kiwi*. Each of these has its own strengths and weaknesses (especially when implemented in a distributed environment). Nevertheless they are all vulnerable to attack once the attacker identifies the type of traffic involved. We will discuss these problems futher.

More Integrity Problems: When the Logs Arrive on the Log Machine

Another integrity problem regards how files are handled after they have been received by the log machine. If the log machine is subject to attack, then the log integrity is at risk. Individual files may have their content modified or even wiped. The integrity issue also regards how the issue of the *paternity* of log files is handled; in many courtrooms, you have to be certain which machine generated the log files and who did the investigation.

There are several methods for resolving the problem. The first is specified in RFC 3195, which identifies a possible method for reliable transmission of *Syslog* messages. It is especially useful if there are many intermediate relays (transmission nodes between the source and the log machine). The main problem here is that RFC 3195 is not yet an established protocol because it has not been incorporated into enough systems.

Hence, practically speaking, most system administrators and security analysts view SCP (Secure Copy) as a good workaround. The most evident contraindication is its unsuitability for intrusion detection purposes, since the time of the intrusion cannot be determined from the log file. And the problem of transmission security between the acquisition and the collection points still remains. In response to the problem, at least in UNIX-based architectures, the practice of using *cryptcat* to establish a relatively robust tunnel between the various machines is gaining wider acceptance.

The procedure is as follows:

On log-generating host:

    1. you must edit /etc/syslog.conf in this mode:

    .   @localhost

    2. then run command:

    # nc -l -u -p 514 | cryptcat 10.2.1.1 9999

On log-collecting host:

    1. run syslog with remote reception (-r) flag (for Linux)

    2. run command:

    # cryptcat -l -p 9999 | nc -u localhost 514

The above configuration will establish an encrypted connection among the various transmission nodes. An alternative would be to use a *Syslog* variant such as *Syslog-ng*, which performs relay operations automatically and with greater security.

The methods described above offer a good practical compromise between real-world needs and the theory that a hash must be generated for every log entry (which is impossible in a distributed environment). Transaction atomicity (transactions are done or undone completely) and log file reliability must still be achieved. We must be sure that log files are not altered once they have been closed, for example by being intercepted during the log rotation phase. The most important aspect of this phase is the final-record message, indicating the last record written in the log, which is then closed and hashed. This sequence of operations may turn out to be critical after correlation when a whole, trusted log has to be provided to judicial authorities.

Log Time Stamping Management

Log file time stamping is another important issue. Each report has to be 100% reliable, not only in terms of its integrity in the strict sense (IP, ports, payloads, etc.), but also in terms of the date and time of the event reported. Time stamping is essential for two reasons: atomicity of the report, and correlation. The most common problems here are the lack of synchronization and the lack of time zone uniformity.

The lack of synchronization occurs when the acquisition points (network sensors and *Syslog* devices) are not synchronized with a universal standard (an atomic clock) but only among themselves. If this is the case, reliance is usually placed on the NTP (Network Time Protocol), but this has a number of vulnerabilities, especially in distributed architectures connected to the public network. Furthermore, NTP does not guarantee uniformity unless a series of measures recommended by certain RFCs is adopted for certain types of logs as we will describe below. Some technology manufacturers have come out with appliances equipped with highly reliable processors that time stamp every entry, synchronizing everything with atomic clocks distributed around the world. This sort of solution, albeit offering a certain degree of reliability, increases design costs and obviously makes management more complex. In a distributed architecture, it takes the

Figure 4. Log architecture with time stamping machine

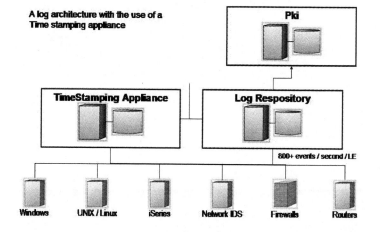

form of an appliance interacting with a PKI that authenticates the transaction nodes to prevent report repudiation set up as seen in Figure 4.

This type of architecture requires a hefty budget, but there are less extensive architectural options that adhere to basic best practices.

Given that one of the most commonly used log formats is *Libpcap* (used by TcpDump, Ethereal) over TCP connections (hence three-way), it is possible to attribute a further level of timestamping, as per *RFCs 1072* and *2018*, by enabling the Sack OK option (Selective Acknowledgement OK). This option can return even a 32 bit time stamp value in the first four bytes of each packet, so that reports among transaction nodes with the Sack OK option enabled are synchronized and can be correlated. This approach may be effective provided that the entire system and network are set up for it.

Regarding time zones, in internationally distributed architectures, some information security managers believe it is wise to maintain the local time zone of the system or network object. The disadvantage here is that it complicates log correlation. Currently, more and more time zones are simply being based on GMT. This simplifies management, but the choice has to be incorporated into a policy.

Normalization and Data Reduction

If all reports had a single format there would be no need for normalization. In heterogeneous architectures this is obviously not the case. Normalization is also known as *event unification*, and there is a physiological need for it in distributed architectures. Let us imagine, for example, an architecture in which we have to correlate events recorded by a Web site, by a network sniffer, and by a proprietary application. The Web site will record

Figure 5. Normalization

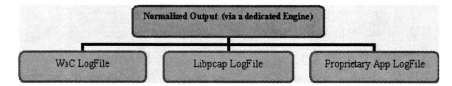

Figure 6. Multi-layered log architecture

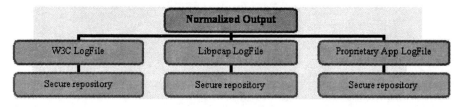

the events in w3c format, the network sniffer in LibPcap format, and the proprietary application in some other format. Somehow these reports have to be unified. The solution consists of finding points in common among the various formats and creating a level of abstraction as illustrated in Figure 5.

An attacker may once again seek to violate log integrity by homing in on the links between the various acquisition points and the point of normalization. We will discuss this next.

The point of normalization (normally an engine) and the point of correlation may be the same machine. This is clearly a potential point of failure from the standpoint of network forensics and thus must be handled in such a way as to guarantee integrity and limit possible losses of data during the normalization process. The current state-of-the-art entails using MD5 and SHA-1 to ensure integrity, while dealing with the data loss issue by carrying out an in-depth test of the event unification engine, keeping the "source" logs in the normalized format. In Figure 6, each source log is memorized on ad hoc supports, adding another layer to Figure 5.

In order to manage the secure repository section and still use a series of reliable "source log files", the machines in the second line of Figure 6 have to be *trusted*, in other words, hardened, and have cryptosystems that can handle authentication, hashing and reliable transmission as briefly discussed previously.

Correlation and Filtering

In performing log correlation and filtering, the security architect and the manager have to deal with the problems described above from the architectural point of view.

Correlation Defined

Correlation: A causal, complementary, parallel, or reciprocal relationship, especially a structural, functional, or qualitative correspondence between two comparable entities. (dictionary.com)

In this chapter we use *correlation* to mean the activity carried out by one or more *engines* to reconstruct an event that may relate to some violation.

Filtering is the extraction and arrangement (by protocol type, time, IP, MAC Address, etc.) of data. It may be performed by the same engines doing correlation.

A fairly complex architecture may be set up like Figure 7.

If SCP or some similar method is used to collect data from the individual acquisition points (before the logs get to the normalization engines), this might slow down the subsequent steps, which are more complex than the "simple" acquisition and generation of logs. Hence a Tunneling and Authentication (Tp) system is required that is based on a secure communication protocol such as a level 3 ISO/OSI.

Log File Interpretation

Usually, when a security administrator reads the result of a correlation performed by a certain tool, he is only seeing the tip of the iceberg. There is a very complex set of processes upstream of the GUI display. There are two basic approaches to log analysis contained in the literature, as discussed in the next section.

Top-Down Approach

A forensic examiner working with an automated log and event correlation tool generally uses this approach. While in intrusion detection a top-down approach means starting from an attack and backtracing to its point of origin, in network forensics it means starting from a GUI display of the event to get back to the source log, with the dual purpose of:

1.   Validating the correlation process used by the automatic log and event correlation tool

Figure 7. Correlating normalized events

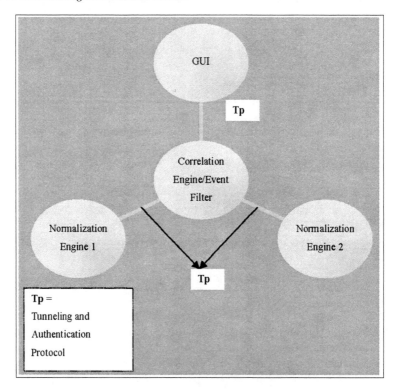

2.   Seeking out the source logs that will then be used as evidence in court or for subsequent analysis

Figure 7 represents a top-down approach to get back to the source logs represented in the previous figures. Once retraced, the acquired logs are recorded onto a CD-ROM or DVD, and the operator will append a digital signature.

Bottom-Up Approach

This approach is applied by the tool starting from the source log to arrive at the "presentation" level of the investigative process. An IDS (intrusion detection system) follows this approach in identifying an ongoing attack through a real time analysis of events. In a distributed security environment the IDS engine may reside (as hypothesized in Section 4.1) on the same machine hosting the normalization engine. In this case the IDS engine will then use the network forensic tool to display the problem on the GUI.

This is also the approach used when log analysis and correlation is done without the aid of automated tools. In this case *log parsers* are used to analyze source logs for a bottom-up correlation. A parser is usually written in a language such as Perl or Python, although there are also some written in Java to allow a cross-platform approach. .

Requisites of Log File Acquisition Tools

In order to ensure forensically compliant correlations, logging infrastructure must meet a number of requisites specified in the literature:

- TCPdump support, both in import and in export;

- State-of-the-art hashing algorithms;

- Data reduction capabilities as described in previous sections;

- Data Recovery: extraction of connections and payload from intercepted traffic for interpretation of the file formats involved in the transaction;

- Covert channel recognition capability (not absolutely essential but highly recommended);

- Read Only During Collection and Examination. This is an indispensable feature for this type of tool;

- Complete Collection. This is one of the most important requisites. All packets should be captured, or at least all losses must be minimized and documented;

- Intrinsic Security, especially for connections between points of acquisition, collection repositories, administrative users, etc.

Experimentation: Using GPL Tools for Investigation and Correlation

There are a number of GPL (General Public License) tools providing the essentials for a bottom-up technique. This approach is simpler and less costly than its top-down counterpart based on automated correlation and GUI display techniques. Next, we will discuss a number of these tools and the related projects.

The IRItaly Project

IRItaly (Incident Response Italy) is a project that was developed at the Crema Teaching and Research Center of the Information Technology Department of the Università Statale di Milano. The project addresses information attacks, defensive systems, computer and network forensics, and data recovery methods. Its main aim is to inform and sensitize the Italian scientific and business communities, and private and public organizations about incident response issues.

It is organized into two sections, one providing detailed and exhaustive guidance and instructions, and the other comprising a bootable CD-ROM. Best practices for incident response are presented for analyzing the victim machines and reconstructing how the attack was waged. The final goal, of course, is to provide methods for hardening the system and preventing future attacks.

All operations are conceived and designed with special attention to log identification and storage methods to ensure their validity as evidence in a disciplinary hearing or courtroom. The CD-ROM provides a set of actions to undertake in response to an intrusion along with a detailed analysis of each:

- Intrusion response preparation;
- Analysis of available information regarding the intrusion;
- Collection and storage of information (evidence);
- Elimination of implanted tools (rootkits) used to gain and maintain illicit access to the machine;
- Restoration of the systems to normal operating conditions.

Additionally, detailed information is provided as to:

- Management of different file systems;
- Data backup procedures;
- Disk imaging;
- Secure electronic communication;
- Cryptographic algorithms;
- Log file acquisition, analysis, and safeguarding tools.

The CD also provides model incident report and the all important chain of custody forms to improve organization and facilitate interactions among the organizations involved in analyzing the incident.

The IRItaly bootable CD-ROM may be used to carry out an initial examination of the victim computer. Tools are included to analyze disks (TASK/autopsy), create disk images, and examine logs. After booting, a terminal interface is launched that the examiner can use to start certain applications such as TCPDump, Ethereal, Snort, Swatch and so on.

The correlation process involves the comparison of logs present on the victim machine with those on other machines. In this case, the IRItaly CD essentially works in very small environments or even in one-to-one contexts, as illustrated in Figure 8.

Figure 8. IRItaly CD-ROM normal use

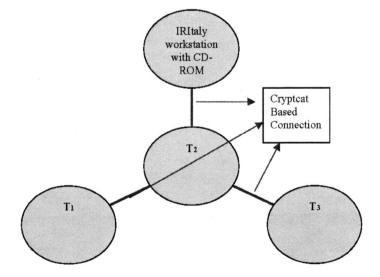

Here, T1, T2 and T3 are various targets that may be booted with the IRItaly CD and connected to the main forensic workstation via Netcat or Cryptcat. The main limitation of the CD is that it cannot be used in a distributed architecture. However, as discussed in the following section, work is underway to develop a new version of the CD with additional tools that should overcome a number of the initial limitations.

Further Developments: IRItaly Version 2

The IRItaly Project has already begun work to resolve the limitations of its first CD. The work will entail the release of a new version of the CD-ROM, which will contain a full implementation of the new Python FLAG.

The original FLAG was designed to simplify the process of log file analysis and forensic investigations. Big cases often mean lots and lots of data that needs to be analyzed and correlated. FLAG uses a database as a backend to assist in managing these large volumes, allowing it to remain responsive and expedite data manipulation operations.

Since FLAG is web based, it can be deployed on a central server and shared by a number of users. Data is organized by case to keep things orderly. Bookmarks are also used extensively to organize and report findings.

FLAG started off as a project in the Australian Department of Defence. PyFlag is the Python implementation of FLAG—a complete rewrite of FLAG in the much more robust Python programming language. Many additional improvements have been made. Some of its most important features are:

Disk Forensics:

- Supports NTFS, Ext2, FFS and FAT;
- Supports many different image file formats, including sgzip (compressed image format), Encase's Expert Witness format, as well as the traditional dd files;
- Advanced timelining for complex searching;
- NSRL hash support for quick file identification;
- Windows Registry support, includes both win98 variant as well as the Window NT variant;
- Unstructured Forensics capability allows recovery of files from corrupted or otherwise unmountable images by using file magic.

Network Forensics:

- Stores tcpdump traffic within an SQL database;
- Performs complete TCP stream reconstruction;

- Has a "knowledge base" making deductions about network communications;
- Can construct an automatic network diagram based on TCPDump, or real time.

Log Analysis:

- Allows arbitrary log file formats to be easily uploaded to database;
- GUI driven complex database searches using an advanced table GUI element.

The new IRItaly CD-ROM will also contain new log analysis capabilities in the form of SecSyslog. As we saw above, Syslog has problems of integrity, one of the components of the all important CIA paradigm (Confidentiality, Integrity, Availability). Integrity could be violated by compromising authentication between machines, spoofing addresses, or intercepting traffic. SecSyslog seeks a solution to this problem through the use of covert channels, working along these lines:

1. It uses TCP in addition to the "simple" and inadequate UDP to establish connection between the machines;

2. The "Syslog" packets are crypto-encapsulated in the UDP packets. Thus, someone intercepting the transmission would not understand what kind of traffic is passing the line;

3. Once at destination, the Syslog packets are "deciphered" by the SecSyslog deamon and the messages can be analyzed.

SecSyslog is an example of a "good dual use" of hacker techniques. It may solve a number of integrity and confidentiality problems related to the lack of security and forensic compliance of many logging architectures.

SecSyslog and Covert Channels in Detail

The commonly accepted definition states that a covert channel is "any communications channel which can be used to transmit information using methods that violate existing security policies[i]" (U.S. Department of Defense, 1985).

A second definition similarly describes a covert channel as "any method that allows the transmission of information via one or more global system variables not officially designed for that purpose[ii]" (Shieh, 1999)

Categories

Covert channels can be divided into two main categories: *storage channels* and *timing channels*. Their purpose is basically the same; they differ only in how the information is made available. The former use a shared *global variable* (an area of memory for IT specialists, for example, or a letter for a prisoner) which acts as a transmission channel in which one of the two communicating parties can make changes to be read directly or indirectly by the other. The latter allow us to transmit information by modulating the use of particular system resources (CPU time, receipt of a packet and the response, etc.), so as to exploit the differences from normal operation as a means for codifying the information transmitted. Hybrid covert channels combining the two methods described above are also possible to make the hidden channel even more difficult to detect.

While earlier covert channel research focused on information flows between different processes in the same system, interest has lately shifted to information sent from one host to another exploiting the network protocols of today's Internet.

Network Covert Channels: Current Use

TCP/IP protocols offer many ways to establish covert channels and transmit data between hosts in order to:

- bypass perimeter security devices;

- evade network sniffers and NIDS;

- encapsulate information, encrypted or otherwise, in ordinary packets for secret transmission in networks that prohibit such behavior (this is known as *TCP/IP Steganography*).

Here we will not only discuss techniques for manipulating TCP/IP headers, but also those used for ICMP (Internet Control Message Protocol) and higher levels such as HTTP (HyperText Transfer Protocol) and DNS (Domain Name Service).

Let us now look at some of the common techniques used to create covert channels and the tools used to implement them.

Information Coding in IP Headers

TCP and IP headers provide numerous fields in which information can be sent secretly. Figure 9 shows the header format for the IP protocol.

In this case the only field that can be used to set up a covert channel that is not easy to detect is the *Identification* field. We will take a closer look at this next.

The header of the TCP protocol provides several possibilities, but again the covert channel will only be covert if it is difficult to detect, and so the best field to use here is *SN (Sequence Number)*. The TCP header looks like Figure 10.

The Sequence Number field can be exploited either by using the Initial Sequence Number or by using the Acknowledge Sequence Number.

Figure 9. IP protocol header format

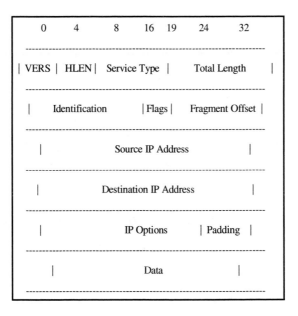

Figure 10. TCP protocol header format

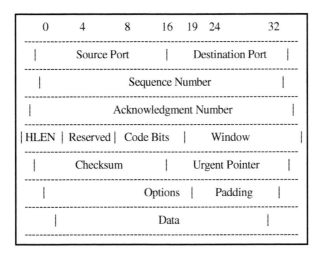

Manipulating the IP ID Field

The ID field of the IP protocol contains a unique value so routers and hosts can correctly reassemble the fragmented packets they receive. This field can be manipulated by substituting a value (an ASCII value for example) into the ID field that contains coded information. The transmission mechanism is not altered in any way, and the recipient only has to read the ID field and use a decoding algorithm to translate it back into the ASCII value that the source wanted to send.

Here is a brief example of traffic received by *TCPdump* showing how the text string "MICKEY" can be transmitted to a Web server. The decoding algorithm subtracts one from the ID field and then performs Mod 256 to obtain the original ASCII value.

Ascii('M') = 77   Ascii('I') = 73   Ascii('C') = 67
Ascii('K') = 75   Ascii('E') = 69   Ascii('Y') = 89

10:38:59.797237 IP (ttl 47, id 26702) foo.bar.com.57459 > test.bar.com.www: ...
Decoding: ... (26702 − 1) mod 256 = 77 = 'M'

10:39:00.797237 IP (ttl 47, id 34378) foo.bar.com.48376 > test.bar.com.www: ...
Decoding: ... (34378 − 1) mod 256 = 73 = 'I'

10:39:01.797237 IP (ttl 47, id 36164) foo.bar.com.17583 > test.bar.com.www: ...
Decoding: ... (36164 − 1) mod 256 = 67 = 'C'

10:39:02.797237 IP (ttl 47, id 23884) foo.bar.com.26587 > test.bar.com.www: ...
Decoding: ... (23884 − 1) mod 256 = 75 = 'K'

10:39:03.797237 IP (ttl 47, id 27206) foo.bar.com.18957 > test.bar.com.www: ...
Decoding: ... (27206 − 1) mod 256 = 69 = 'E'

10:39:04.797237 IP (ttl 47, id 20048) foo.bar.com.31769 > test.bar.com.www: ...
Decoding: ... (20048 − 1) mod 256 = 79 = 'Y'

This method uses a forged ad hoc packet with correct destination and source fields and the coded information contained in the ID field. The remote host receives the data by listening to port 80 with a daemon that can distinguish the covert channel packets from regular HTTP requests, decode the former and send the latter to the Web server.

The method is fairly robust and easy to implement, although it is vulnerable to failure if there is a firewall or a NAT (Network Address Translation) machine in place between the two hosts.

Initial Sequence Number Method

In the TCP protocol the ISN value guarantees flow reliability and control. Every byte transmitted by the TCP stream has an assigned sequence number. Each connection (each connected pair of sockets) can be used for several flows and the stronger the ISN calculation algorithm the more streams are available. When the connection is established, the client host must determine the ISN value and launch the so-called "three-way handshake".

Because of its size (32 bit), the ISN field is ideal for transmitting clandestine information. The field can be exploited in an analogous manner to our example above. An ISN value is generated from the ASCII character that we wish to code and transmit. The packet with just the SYN flag active is the one that contains the coded data. The recipient only has to read the ISN value and, in the following example, divide this by 65536*256 = 16777216. Below is an example showing transmission of the string "MICKEY".

Ascii('M') = 77   Ascii('I') = 73   Ascii('C') = 67

Ascii('K') = 75   Ascii('E') = 69   Ascii('Y') = 89

12:11:56.043339 foo.bar.com.57645 > test.bar.com.ssh: S 1300938487:1300938487(0)

Decoding: ... 1300938487 / 16777216 = 77 = 'M'

12:11:57.043339 foo.bar.com.46235 > test.bar.com.ssh: S 1235037038:1235037038(0)

Decoding: ... 1235037038 / 16777216 = 73 = 'I'

12:11:58.043339 foo.bar.com.46235 > test.bar.com.ssh: S 1140809246:1140809246(0)

Decoding: ... 1140809246 / 16777216 = 73 = 'C'

and so on.

If someone is paying very close attention, they might notice that the calculated ISNs are very close to each other and get suspicious. However, with 32 bits available, ISN calculation algorithms could be used that produce much more scattered results, making the covert channel all that much less prone to detection.

Acknowledge Sequence Number Method

This method depends on IP spoofing to allow the sender to 'bounce' the packet off a remote server and on to the proper destination. The technique fools the recipient into thinking that the server off which the packet was bounced is actually the source host. Thus the real source remains anonymous. This type of covert channel is very difficult to detect, especially if the bounce-server is heavily loaded.

This technique exploits a feature of TCP/IP protocols whereby the destination server responds to the connection request by sending a packet with an ISN increased by one. The sender needs to forge an ad hoc packet where the following fields are changed:

- Source IP;
- Source port;
- Destination IP;
- Destination port;
- TCP Initial Sequence Number containing the coded data.

The choice of the destination and source ports is entirely arbitrary. The destination IP must be that of the bounce-server, and the source IP that of the destination host. The packet is thus sent by the client to the bounce-server, which proceeds to forward it to the destination machine (with the ISN increased by one) for decoding.

A correctly configured router/firewall should not allow a packet with an active ACK flag to pass unless it recognizes that the destination host is responsible for opening the connection. Widespread use of stateful racket filters makes this method increasingly ineffective, but it may still work if the configuration can be altered. The use of well known bounce-servers (.mil or .gov websites, for instance) may also block other types of filters on the destination host network.

Covert Channels Using ICMP Tunnels

Although the technique was developed way back in 1996, many systems are still vulnerable to a covert channel using an ICMP tunnel. The only requirement is that the system permits ICMP_ECHO traffic.

Many consider ICMP traffic to be benign, and it is in its objectives since what it does is to report delivery problems. ICMP packets are encapsulated in IP datagrams. The first 32 bits of the ICMP header are always the same and the rest of the header may contain any of fifteen different types of message allowed by the protocol.

The ICMP messages that are vulnerable to being used as covert channels are ICMP_ECHO (query) and ICMP_ECHOREPLY (reply). Since we can send queries and get responses, the protocol is a potential vehicle for hidden data-streams. The utility *Ping*, for example, sends and receives just such messages. So how do we send and receive data using an ICMP tunnel?

ICMP_ECHO messages allow you to enter information in the Data field, which is normally used to hold information on delay times and so on. However, the Data field is not subject to control by any particular device and can therefore be used to send arbitrary data, thus creating a covert channel.

HTTP/S Tunnel

There are a number of ways to design a covert channel based on HTTP. One could look at what type of server is to be implemented (http daemon, proxy or CGI), how traffic could be manipulated to help mask the channel (proxy chains, generation of noise, etc.), or what type of functions are required. Having examined these aspects, we can chose which http methods to use (GET, CONNECT, POST...) and figure out how to apply the model in practice.

As with any covert channels, steganographic or cryptographic techniques may also be useful to further confuse anyone observing the traffic and enhance the disguise.

These tunnels generally require two synchronized units: one inside the target network and the other on the outside. The external server should be accessible from the inside but must not raise the suspicions of any controlling mechanism, automatic or otherwise, when contacted. The server must act as if it is capable of processing HTTP requests, and the client should send suitably coded information in the guise of normal HTTP requests.

HTTP-based covert channels can thus take a great variety of forms, making them an attractive vehicle for those wishing to hide illicit traffic.

Many open-source and closed-source tools use HTTP tunnels for a wide variety of purposes. For example, tools designed to trace a stolen computer as soon as it connects to the network may send the location information invisibly via e-mail using an HTTP tunnel. The SOAP protocol (originally: Simple Object Access Protocol, but the acronym has been dropped from more recent versions), a Remote Procedure Call (RPC) over HTTP, is based on the use of HTTP tunnels.

As we see, covert channels are not used exclusively for illicit purposes. Studying the loopholes in network protocols can lead to useful projects.

Two tools we might mention, if only for academic purposes, are hcovert and GNU http-tunnel, whose code is freely available over the Internet. To find out more about HTTP tunneling, see "Exploitation of data streams authorized by a network access control system for arbitrary data transfers: tunneling and covert channels over the HTTP protocol," at www.gray-world.net.

DNS

The possibility of using ordinary DNS requests/responses to send data has aroused great interest recently. Dan Kaminsky (*"Black Ops of DNS"*, 2004) demonstrated tools that allowed him to achieve SSH (Secure Shell) sessions and to transmit and receive audio traffic via normal DNS servers. However, others before him had already exploited the weaknesses of the DNS protocol.

DNS uses a hierarchical naming system (.com; .bar.com; .foo.bar.com) and this leads to a number of interesting outcomes. If we can control a DNS server via the authority of a certain domain name, we can change the tables which provide the information needed to satisfy the client requests. We can then create a covert channel using certain records from the DNS table. And we get a bonus of a lot of 'bandwidth'. Using the CNAME record to code transmitted information we can send and receive up to 110 bytes per packet, while the TXT record gives us a whopping 220 bytes per packet. This is an enormous amount of data compared to what we can do with TCP and IP headers.

Many tools use this technique. We should mention NSTX and the many rumors circulating to the effect that botnets and other malignant code may be able to exploit DNS servers for illicit data exchange. It will come as no great surprise if the next generation of viruses and worms use this method to get synchronized and launch another DDoS (Distributed Denial of Service) attack like others we have seen in recent years.

The DNS protocol is similar in several ways to the HTTP protocol:

- It works on blocks of data;
- It does nothing until the client submits a specific request;
- It works on character sets (Base32 / Base64).

As we have seen above, many tools have been developed to exploit HTTP tunnels. Given the similarities between DNS and HTTP, there must be numerous ways of using DNS for our purposes and numerous tools similar to the ones existing for HTTP. Dan Kaminsky has shown us how these techniques can be effectively implemented with his OzyManDNS, a proof-of-concept downloadable off the Internet.

We should mention in closing that while the first request filtering products are becoming available for HTTP and numerous other protocols, the same is not true for DNS, and there are various reasons why it is not likely to happen near term. Meanwhile, intense DNS traffic could easily raise suspicion. This is only partly counterbalanced by the high bandwidth (max 220 bytes per packet) the method offers. It is still far more effective to use a HTTP tunnel when a sizable transmission bandwidth is required.

SecSyslog: A Syslog Daemon Using Covert Channels

There are a number of open- and closed-source implementations of the *Syslog* protocol. Each of these adds functionality to the protocol's original features and remedies specific weaknesses. Given the importance of logs both for troubleshooting and for legal proceedings, there is a strong consensus that it is essential to guarantee that messages reach their destination, unaltered, secure, and secret. Each version has its advantages and disadvantages with regard to the others. The choice is purely a matter of personal preference, based—to be sure—on a detailed understanding of the specific version and its additional features, weighed against the added complexity of configuration.

We will describe herein a possible implementation of a new system logging solution using covert channels and list its advantages and disadvantages with respect to other software.

Why Use DNS Covert Channels?

Why might it be useful to use a covert channel? Let us imagine the case of a company that has many branch offices and needs to centralize its logs. How can it send these without keeping the *Syslog* service publicly open?

Some *Syslog* daemons allow you to authenticate clients. Although this is easy to configure, the *Syslog* messages are still transmitted unencrypted and require the log service to be public on the net. It might be a good idea to tunnel the messages in SSH encrypted sessions, but this simply shifts the problem onto another service that you may want to close with a firewall. Another solution might be a VPN (Virtual Private Network), but configuration and maintenance can be expensive.

None of the above ideas is inherently wrong. Any decision has to take into account a variety of factors: simplicity, cost, availability, and so on. What advantages does a covert channel offer in this case, especially considering the peculiarities of the DNS service?

If we want to implement a project using covert channels we have to consider what tasks need to be performed. When we understand the requisites we can decide which techniques are best suited to providing the desired solution. We could start by examining the data transmission bandwidth required.

What kind of data does a *Syslog* client transmit to the server? How frequently are log messages sent to the server? As we mentioned earlier, if we need to contact the server frequently it might be a good idea to hide the covert channel in a very common type of traffic, like HTTP GET or DNS queries to avoid raising suspicions.

Syslog is simply a system for exchanging text strings. This does not exclude *a priori* the use of HTTP tunneling, but this offers much more bandwidth than is really necessary. The *Syslog* daemon only needs to send strings of a few characters at a time. Conversely, techniques using TCP and IP headers provide limited bandwidth so that a single message might generate an enormous volume of traffic which would quickly attract attention.

DNS tunneling techniques are interesting and as yet little used. The fact that there are still no application filtering techniques, unlike those for HTTP, represents a big advantage for this method.

One other advantage is the very widespread availability of DNS servers. Every medium or large company has one or more internal DNS servers, some of which are also accessible to various clients in the subsidiaries. The service is often not even filtered.

In practical terms, a DNS covert channel can be used to send logs invisibly from branch systems to a centralized SecSyslog server at another site, miles away, by simply bouncing the data off the DNS server at the second branch. What better solution for sending *Syslog* messages between geographically distant locations transparently yet almost invisibly? What better way to hide a data flow than passing it directly under the nose of someone wishing to intercept the messages?

Figure 11. Architectural overview of the SecSyslog project

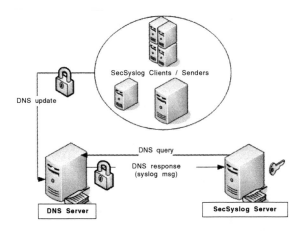

Such observations explain why sending logs with SecSyslog via a covert channel is so powerful, and why DNS tunneling provides an excellent solution to the problem.

Suggested Implementation

Figure 11 gives a rough illustration of how the SecSyslog project might work. We then go on to describe the problems faced and possible solutions we are currently evaluating. As the project is still only in the design stage, these might not be the best or most workable solutions, but it nevertheless illustrates a possible application of DNS to establish a covert channel.

Basically the idea is to transmit information by bouncing it off a DNS server on which certain hosts (SecSyslog clients, the sources of information) may write data to send, making opportune modifications to the tables in a particular area managed by the server. Meanwhile, the real destination—the SecSyslog server—makes a number of queries to obtain records from the DNS server, which answers these by forwarding the data originally transmitted by the client.

The first problem is to ensure that the requests sent to the DNS server reach their destination, i.e., to guarantee the integrity of the transmission. DNS is based on UDP but it can also answer TCP requests. In the DNS communication mechanism the client tracks all UDP requests and waits for the answer 'task executed'. If no answer is forthcoming within a given timeframe the client sends a second identical request through a TCP session.

At any rate, if the dimension of the packet containing the request is higher than 512 octets, it is immediately sent via TCP. This way the problem is resolved by the DNS service protocol itself.

Authentication of Clients

Interaction with the DNS server involves modifying its tables, but we cannot allow the DNS server to be open to editing by just anyone. Basic principles of security require that we look at a way to authenticate the subjects who are authorized to make the necessary changes.

The implementation of the Dynamic Update mechanism on the DNS servers can be of use to us in solving this problem. By configuring the system accordingly (using allow-update{} inside the zone definition) we can ensure that only update requests with specific signatures will be executed. In effect, the DNS server defines, for each zone managed, who can alter the tables and who cannot.

We can also use the allow-query{} construct to define which hosts may ask to read records for a specific zone and get their queries answered. Such mechanisms (or DNS server equivalents other than BIND, which we use) allow us to control who can send and who can receive SecSyslog messages.

Message Authenticity and Integrity

The transmitted logs will only be legally valid if we are able to guarantee the authenticity and integrity of the *Syslog* messages received through the covert channel. SecSyslog provides these guarantees via DNS Security Extensions, using asymmetric key cryptography and various hashing algorithms. Encryption also provides a further level of secrecy to the message and prevents unauthorized publication of the logs.

The DNS server publishes the public key for write access via specific records (KEY and SIG), thus allowing the clients to download it and verify its authenticity by checking the signature. The DNS server may periodically adopt a new key, so it is helpful to implement a mechanism to synchronize the key update with the client downloads.

Once the *Syslog* message is encrypted, the results of the three most widely used hashing algorithms—MD5, SHA1, and RIPE-160—are added, in specific order, below the message. The encrypted message and the three hash values thus constitute the effective payload which is sent to the DNS.

How Communication Works

The communication algorithm for publication of the *Syslog* message and downloading by the server is illustrated in Figure 12. The SecSyslog client takes the following steps to publish the messages:

1. The client encrypts the outgoing message and calculates the three hashes, adding them at the bottom to complete the payload.
2. The client updates the message header by inserting the timestamp of the previous packet, the length of the encrypted message, the number of parts contained within it, the current part number, and the message ID.

Figure 12. Communication steps between SecSyslog clients and servers

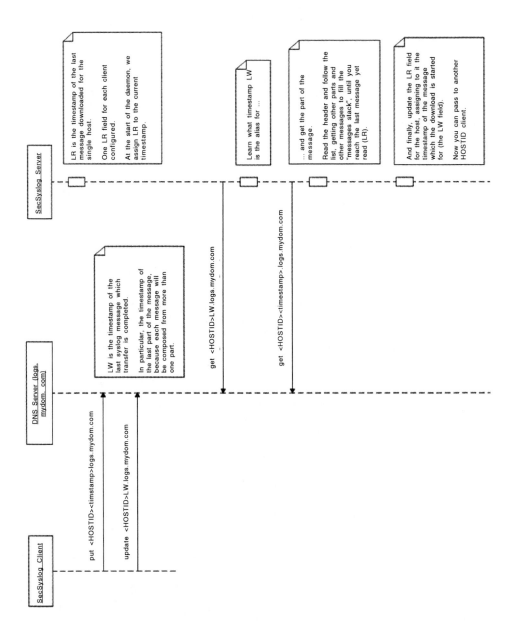

Figure 13. Format of packets sent by clients to DNS servers

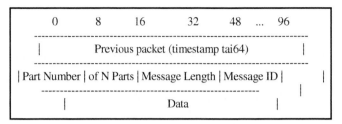

3.   The client updates the DNS zone by publishing the header and payload in a TXT field for the host by the name of <HOSTID><timestamp>, where the timestamp is the current time (calculated at the moment the packet is composed) in tai64 format. This value must be stored for inclusion in the header of the packet to be sent later, so as to recreate the full list of packets transmitted.

4.   When the last packet containing the last part of the *Syslog* message has been published to the DNS, the client must update its own CNAME field, the <HOSTID>LW. This record is used as a list 'index', i.e., a starting point for reading the messages to be downloaded by the server. In other words the timestamp of the header represents the 'marker' for the previous item.

The tasks performed by the SecSyslog server to download the messages are as follows:

1.   For the controller host, the server asks the DNS for the alias corresponding to the last published message, sending a query to <HOSTID>LW;

2.   The server now knows the last message published by that client and can thus query the TXT record to download the last packet sent, requesting the <HOSTID><timestamp> corresponding to the alias;

3.   The server reads the packet header, finds the timestamp of the previous packet and continues to download packets corresponding to that timestamp, in effect repeating step 2, until it reaches the timestamp of a message that has already been downloaded;

4.   Having filled the message stack, the server can now process the data received to write the messages into log files for the configured host;

5.   After a brief wait, the server can check another of the configured hosts and download new *Syslog* messages. The waiting time must be brief enough to enable it to check all the hosts before the DNS cache expires (TTL).

Note that with a little tuning of the TTL, the DNS server cache will not be unnecessarily overpopulated since the old *Syslog* messages sent to the client are automatically deleted from the DNS daemon when the cache expires.

In Figure 13, we see the format of the packet sent by the client and published to the DNS server. This example uses the TXT record which allows it to publish 220 bytes, 18 of which for the header.

Further Steps and Conclusions

The internal tool validation process remains one of the most pressing problems in digital forensics, and this also regards the tools we have discussed here. The IRItaly Project is developing a checklist of state-of-the-art tools that should be in every forensic investigator's toolbox. The priority is to guarantee a minimum of compliance with best practices and a solution to the integrity and security problems discussed above.

IRItaly has completed the daemon architecture and is writing the code to be submitted for thorough testing. Implementation studies will largely be geared to verifying in practice what we have described above, with particular reference to the forensic compliance of the implemented daemon. We believe this project may represent a valid alternative to the advanced Syslog systems cited above. We also believe that SecSyslog can satisfy digital forensic needs when circumstances require it. In most criminal trials where we have been called as expert witness, the defense attorney has questioned the integrity of the *Syslog* materials produced as evidence, citing *Syslog's* vulnerability to interception and attack by hackers. We believe that the SecSyslog daemon will soon be ready for peer review (we are aiming to publish our results on sourceforge by the end of 2005) and stable implementation in architecture requiring secure and forensically compliant stealth-based syslogging.

This chapter is intended as a tutorial for log and event correlation. To ensure compliance with the general principles of digital forensics, the tools used have to meet a series of requisites. The IRItaly Project is currently working towards this objective. At the moment, the most important problem to resolve regards how to deal with distributed architectures, particularly with regard to top-down and bottom-up (real-time) approaches. There is currently a gap between the two approaches. They are pursued, respectively, by ISVs and in the GPL realm. The latter has a lot less money to throw around and thus cannot use the same methodology. The hope here is to guarantee a minimum of autonomy to those operators who are not able to invest large sums in complex distributed systems.

References

Kaminsky Dan (2004). *Black Ops of DNS*. Retrieved from http://www.doxpara.com/dns_bh

RFC 3164: The BSD syslog Protocol, IETF. Retrieved from http://www.ietf.org/rfc/rfc0793.txt

RFC 3195: Reliable Delivery for syslog, IETF. Retrieved from http://www.ietf.org/rfc/rfc3195.txt

Shieh, S. (1999). *Estimating and measuring covert channel bandwidth in multilevel secure operating systems.*

U.S. Department Of Defense. (1985). *Trusted computer system evaluation criteria.*

Additional Reading

Albitz, P., & Liu, C. (2001). *DNS and BIND* (4th ed.). O'Reilly.

Alhambra and daemon9 (1996). Project Loki: ICMP tunneling. *Phrack Magazine,6*(49). http://www.phrack.org/phrack/49/P49-06

Bejtlich, R. (2005), *The TAO of network security monitoring* (pp. 505-517). Addison Wesley.

Carrillo, J., Ospina, C., Rangel, M., Rojas, J., & Vergara, C. (2004). *Covert channels sobre HTTP.* Retrieve from http://www.criptored.upm.es/guiateoria/gt_m142m.htm

Chuvakin, A. (n.d.). *Advanced log processing.* Retrieve from www.securityfocus.com

Comer, D. (1995). *Internetworking with TCP/IP, vol. 1.* Prentice Hall.

Dyatlov, A., & Castro, S. (2003). *Exploitation of data streams authorized by a network access control system for arbitrary data transfers: Tunneling and covert channels over the HTTP protocol.* Retrieved from http://www.gray-world.net/projects/papers/html/covert_paper.html

Forte, D. (n.d.). Analyzing the difficulties in backtracing onion router traffic. *The International Journal of Digital Evidence*, Utica College. http://www.ijde.org/archives/02_fall_art3.html.

Forte, D. (n.d.). The art of log correlation, tool and techniques for log analysis. *In Proceedings of The ISSA Conference 2004.* Johannesburg, South Africa

Forte, D., & Al. (2005, November). Forensic computer crime investigation. In T. Johnson & T. Johnson (Eds.), *Forensic Sciences.* CRC Press.

Forte, D., & Al. (2005, November). Forensic analysis of UNIX systems. In H. Bidgoli (Ed.), *HandBook of information security.* Wiley.

Forte, D., Zambelli, M., Vetturi, M., & Maruti, C. (n.d.). SecSyslog: An alternative approach based on covert channels. In *Proceedings of the First International Workshop on Systematic Approaches to Digital Forensic Engineering (SADFE 2005).*

Owens, M. (2002). *A discussion of covert channels and steganography.* Retrieved from http://www.sans.org/rr/whitepapers/covert/678.php

RFC 0791: Internet Protocol, IETF, http://www.ietf.org/rfc/rfc0791.txt

RFC 0793: Transmission Control Protocol, IETF, http://www.ietf.org/rfc/rfc0793.txt

RFC 1072: TCP Extensions for Long-Delay Paths, IETF, http://www.ietf.org/rfc/rfc1072.txt

RFC 2018: TCP Selective Acknowledgment Options, IETF, http://www.ietf.org/rfc/rfc2018.txt

RFC 2136: Dynamic Updates in the Domain Name System, IETF, http://www.ietf.org/rfc/rfc2136.txt

RFC 2535: Domain Name System Security Extensions, IETF, http://www.ietf.org/rfc/rfc2535.txt

Rowland, C. (1997). *Covert channels in the TCP/IP protocol suite*. First Monday. Retrieve from http://www.firstmonday.org/issues/issue2_5/rowland/

Simple Nomad (2003). README for the ncovert2 tool. Retrieve from http://ncovert.sourceforge.net/

Steven, M., & Stephen, L. (2005). *Embedding covert channels into TCP/IP*. Retrieve from http://www.cl.cam.ac.uk/users/sjm217/papers/ih05coverttcp.pdf

Szor, P. (2005). *The art of computer virus research and defense*. Addison Wesley.

Wang, W. & Daniels, T. (2005). Network forensics analysis with evidence graphs. In *Proceedings, (Demo Proposal) Department of Electrical and Computer Engineering*. Iowa State University. DFRWS, New Orleans.

Endnotes

[1]   *Trusted Computer System Evaluation Criteria*. The translation is ours.

[2]   The translation is ours.

Chapter VII

Tracing Cyber Crimes with a Privacy-Enabled Forensic Profiling System

Pallavi Kahai, Cisco Systems, USA

Kamesh Namuduri, Wichita State University, USA

Ravi Pendse, Wichita State University, USA

Abstract

Security incidents that threaten the normal functioning of the organization are on the rise. In order to resist network attacks most organizations employ security measures. However, there are two sides of the problem at hand. First, it is important to secure the networks against new vulnerabilities. Second, collection of evidence without intruding on the privacy, in the event of an attack, is also necessary. The lack of robust attribution mechanism precludes the apprehension of cyber criminals. The implementation of security features and forensic analysis should be such that the privacy is preserved. We propose a forensic profiling system which accommodates real-time evidence collection as a network feature and uses a mechanism to keep the privacy intact.

Motivation

The Computer Crime and Security Survey 2003 conducted by Computer Security Institute (CSI) in association with the San Francisco Federal Bureau of Investigation's (FBI) Computer Intrusion Squad concluded that the theft of proprietary information was responsible for most of the financial losses, with the average reported loss of about $2.7 million per incident. Denial of service attacks alone were responsible for more than $65 million in total losses among the organizations that participated in the survey. The survey indicated that the threat to large corporations and government agencies originates from both inside and outside their electronic boundaries: 78% of the respondents quoted the internet as the source of attack and 36% attributed the attacks to internal systems. Viruses and worms can penetrate through thousands of computers through duplication and acquire information such as a company's e-mail directory or an individual's banking information. Among the organizations surveyed, 251 were able to quantify the losses as over $200 million. There has been an upward trend in the number of cyber crimes and also in their nature in 2004. In Massachusetts, organized crime groups hacked into the State Registry of Motor Vehicles databases paving the way for identity theft. A new trend noticeable in 2004 was "phishing", the use of spam impersonating a bank wherein an individual can be conned to provide confidential information.

Clearly, cyber crimes and other information security breaches are rampant and diverse. Most organizations employ methods such as encryption technologies, network monitoring tools, firewalls and intrusion detection, and response mechanisms to secure their networks. Configuring security features does not guarantee that the information system is absolutely foolproof. Evidence collection, "trace and trap" mechanism, and identification of the attacker are as important as intrusion detection. While there are several intrusion detection mechanisms available today, present technology lacks the tools and techniques for identification and IP traceback. Apprehending and prosecuting cyber criminals is complicated because of the intercontinental nature of the cyber space. Negotiations across jurisdictional boundaries, both corporate and national, are questionable because of the considerable variance between the regulations and policies of different government and corporations. This is generally because of the non-uniform legislative measures concerning privacy in different countries. Millions of computer systems around the world were affected by the May 2000 Love Bug virus initiated by a resident of the Philippines, which crippled email systems from the British Parliament to the Pentagon to networks in Asia. The virus caused billions of dollars of damage, mostly due to lost work time. Investigation was hampered by the lack of a Philippines law that specifically addresses computer crimes. The warrant was finally sought under the Access Devices Regulation Act of 1998. The law was written chiefly to target credit card fraud but also covered the use of any unauthorized access device in order to obtain goods or services. Moreover, countless instances of illegal access and damage around the world remain unreported, as victims fear the exposure of vulnerabilities and the potential for copycat crimes. Mechanisms of cooperation across national borders to solve and prosecute crimes are complex and slow. Cyber criminals can therefore, defy the conventional jurisdictional domains.

Privacy vs. Security

Privacy is the state of being free from unsanctioned intrusion. With the growth of the internet and the dependence of the corporate world on electronic and digital media, privacy is threatened. The Electronic Privacy Information Center (EPIC), a public interest research center established to focus public attention on emerging civil liberties issues and to protect privacy has laid out some directives for internet and digital privacy. These include privacy principles for email, digital rights management, and European Union data protection directive. Most of the networks belonging to different organizations employ policies that safeguard the privacy of the employees. The privacy policies and practices adopted by a company require support by technologies that implement these policies. In order to back the claims laid out by the companies, Privacy-enhancement Technologies (PeTs) are used. PeTs include data encryption, anonymous remailer services, or anonymous Web browsing (Olivier, 2004).

The internet security glossary [RFC 2828] defines security incident as "a security-relevant system event in which the system's security policy is disobeyed or otherwise breached". The mechanism of handling a security incident is called incident response. The policies that govern the collection and archiving of data responsible for the security incident are handled by forensic investigation. Forensic investigation may violate the privacy policies, but as long as only the data considered as suspicious and relevant to the case is investigated, the privacy may remain intact. Besides, the suspected perpetrator loses the right to privacy. Privacy considerations are outlined in the Guidelines for Evidence Collection and Archiving [RFC 3227].

We propose a forensic profiling system that tracks the security incidents in the network which can eventually be used for forensic investigation. Since the mechanism involves tracking of suspicious activities only this helps the investigation process become less time-consuming and the organization can resume normal functioning quickly. The suspicious activities that are logged on to a dedicated server are used for investigation after the compromise has occurred. The process does not involve interception of data in transit as is the case with network sniffers or other data interception tools. Electronic Communication Privacy Act of 1986 (ECPA) restricts the ability of businesses to intercept e-mails and other forms of electronic communications, while generally permitting the recovery of stored data on company networks. The mechanism adopted is thus compliant with the privacy act.

Related Work

Early intrusion detection systems were modeled to detect anomalous activities on a single host. The well-known host-based Intrusion Detection Systems (IDS) are TRIPWIRE that acts as a system integrity verifier and SWATCH which is a log file monitor. In order to monitor the activities of the entire network, network-based IDS came into existence. The network based IDS such as Snort, e-Trust, NetSTAT and Event Monitoring Enabling

Responses to Anomalous Live Disturbances (EMERALD) proposed by Porrras and Neumann (1997) are involved in intrusion detection related to large-scale distributed networks. Ning, Wang, and Jajodia (2001) describe a hierarchical model to support attack specification and event abstraction in distributed intrusion detection. For detection of coordinated attacks over large scale networks Yang, Ning, and Wang (2000) suggest an architecture, CARDS (Coordinated Attack and Response Detection System). The backbone of CARDS consists of independent but cooperative components. Deviation from normal behavior does not necessarily indicate the occurrence of an attack. Collaboration between the different intrusion detection and response systems has been the focus of recent research. The MIRADOR project funded by the French Defense Agency includes an intrusion alert correlation module, Corrélation et Réaction aux Intentions Malveillantes (CRIM) as described by Cuppens (2001) and Cuppens and Mi'ege (2002). CRIM provides the interface for alert clustering, alert merging, and alert correlation. A distributed intrusion detection architecture proposed by Huang, Jasper, and Wicks (1999) is based on attack strategy. A similar approach proposed by Barrus and Rowe (1998) suggest a cooperative behavior not only between different network-intrusion detection systems but also among hosts in the network. The Common Intrusion Specification Language (CISL) proposed by Kahn, Bolinger, and Schnackenberg (1998) presents a language for communication between the different intrusion detection systems in a network. Common Intrusion Detection Framework (CIDF) only provides a means for communication between the different components of the network but does not facilitate on-demand information gathering. Ning, Wang, and Jajodia (2000) provide an extension to CIDF (Kahn et al., 1998) and discuss the modeling of requests between the different components in a network. A description language that supports communication between different intrusion detection systems is described by Michel and M'e (2001).

Alert aggregation and alert correlation mechanisms are being widely investigated. Debar and Wespi (2001) developed aggregation and correlation algorithm for intrusion detection alerts whereas Valdes and Skinner (2001) provide a mathematical framework for multi-sensor data fusion. Most of the alert correlation methods are restricted to known attack scenarios. A formal framework for alert correlation and detection of multi-stage attacks has been developed by Ning, Cui, and Reeves (2002). Alert correlation is performed if the consequence of a previous alert serves as prerequisite for the current alert. But the alerts generated by the IDS do not confirm the possible consequence. For instance, if a buffer overflow attack is detected by the IDS it does not imply that the possible consequence was true, that is, the attacker was successful in acquiring the root privileges. In order to determine if the attack was indeed successful, participation from other network components is important. A distributed model that extends to forensics is ForNet, suggested by Shanmugasundaram, Memon, Savant, and Bronnimann (2003), that provides network logging mechanism to aid digital forensics over wide area networks. Our work proposes a privacy-enabled real-time forensic evidence collection mechanism where each node in the network is capable of detecting security incident. The evidence in the form of log entries indicative of the malicious activity does not violate the privacy of the individuals that have access to that particular system.

Most of the work done regarding privacy deals with the policies and procedures that ensure privacy of data that could be violated during a forensic investigation. Since popular forensic tools such as Encase have the capability of retrieving sensitive information, Korba (2002) suggested proper authentication mechanisms for access to these security products during forensic investigations. Researchers have proposed to issue role-based permissions to each network device, which will control access to viewing data and search results for an investigator. A secure servlet installed in each network device can be used to log, monitor and control the session of an investigator as proposed by Patzakis (2003). Since most of the evidence files collected during investigation could violate the privacy of an individual, suggestions have been made to encrypt the evidence files using strong public key encryption techniques such as the AES, so that a third party is unable to access those evidence files. Apart from privacy concerns during a forensic investigation, enterprise privacy has also been dealt with. Since enterprises collect a large amount of personal data from their customers, they should follow the standards of enterprise privacy to secure the personal data of their customers. In order to keep the promises of privacy to customers, a platform for enterprise privacy practices (E-P3P) has been suggested by Ashley, Hada, Karjoth, and Schunter (2002) that defines a privacy policy model. An internal privacy officer using the E-P3P would formalize the desired internal handling of collected data inside the enterprise. A distributed privacy system has also been suggested in which the information gatherer and information provider are required to setup privacy preferences, where the information gatherer would indicate the way in which information will be handled and the information provider would indicate the type of information that should be considered as private. A monitoring server would monitor the violation of privacy. Companies are suggested to wipe sensitive data of their clients before recycling hard drives, as formatting the hard drive alone does not ensure that data are irretrievable, as powerful investigation software programs such as Encase are capable of retrieving data. File systems can be made secure through encryption and by maintaining a short life-time for the keys. Steganographic file systems provide a high level of privacy as the existence of the file itself can only be known if the file name along with the password is known.

Proposed Forensic Model

The proposed forensic profiling system (FPS) builds profiles of cyber attacks as they occur. A forensic profile is a set of structured or unstructured alerts that define known and unknown attacks. Forensic profiles are built by continuously monitoring the activities and network traffic at all the participating entities in the network. The forensic profiling system is based on client-server architecture wherein each node in the network acts as a forensic client and sends an alert to the forensic server if a suspicious event takes place at the client's machine. A suspicious network activity is an event that poses a threat to the security of a network. This work refers to the suspicious activity as an alert initiated by the forensic client to the forensic server. Each alert is described in a predefined *when-subject-action-object* format and contains the supporting data. The forensic server correlates these alerts and subsequently builds the forensic profile. In case the series of alerts received by the server do not sufficiently match a profile, the server will pro-actively probe the clients for more details. Once all the necessary alerts and responses to probes are received, the server will create the profile. In case the server is not able to resolve the attack profile, it creates a profile with an unstructured set of alerts. Unstructured sets of alerts do not belong to a profile that is a part of the profile database.

In order to incorporate anonymity for the suspicious log entries logged on to the server the source address is hidden by the use of proxy servers. Each subnet in the organization has a subnet proxy. The number of proxies in the network is equal to the number of subnets. The traffic belonging to a particular subnet is sent to the allocated proxy. The proxy then either forwards the frame to another proxy in the network or to the final destination.

The logical architecture shown in Figure 1 is composed of the forensic server, the proxy servers that belong to each subnet, and all the different nodes in the network referred to as the forensic clients configured with security features and logging mechanisms. The components and their participation as forensic profiling entities is discussed in detail in the following subsections.

Figure 1. Logical architecture for the forensic profiling system

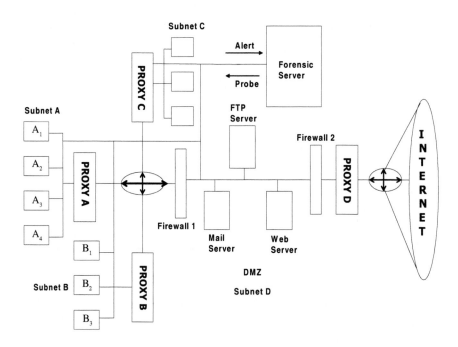

The forensic clients are composed of hosts, servers, firewalls and the router in the network. Communication signals exchanged between the forensic server and clients are alerts and probes. Subnet proxies A, B, C and D belong to their respective subnets.

Forensic Server

The forensic server is responsible for centrally monitoring and logging the malicious activities in the network that could eventually take the form of an attack. The suspicious activity is corroborated by the log entries that indicate it. To start with, the forensic server maintains a forensic profile database that contains the *forensic profiles* of the known attacks. Initially it is assumed that the network activity is composed of usual activities devoid of any security incidents. This state of the network is referred to as the *passive* state of the network. The forensic profile database maintains *passive profiles* that provide static information of individual attacks in terms of the events associated with each attack. *Passive profile* would become active if a forensic client detects an event that belongs to an attack. A *passive profile* is defined as a structure that provides known or investigated information about an attack in a succinct form. It would be a collection of alerts that provide an indication of the attack. An attack is composed of a series of interrelated events. A subset of these events might be common to several attacks. Thus, a stand-alone event does not give complete information about the attack. In order to ascertain that a particular attack has occurred, a certain minimum number of events must be detected. The profile would define an attack in terms of its related events (*alerts*).

The passive profile is partial because it provides static and general information about an attack. The detection of an event (malicious activity) would generate an alert and can eventually trigger a passive profile. The *passive profiles* which contain a match for the alert generated would become active. Figure 2 depicts the relationship between Alert X received from a forensic client with the forensic profile database which is required to shortlist the active profiles.

Figure 2. The forensic server scans for Alert X in the forensic profile database.

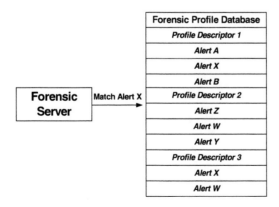

The scan results in transforming Profile Descriptors 1 and 3 as active.As Alert X is a subset of alerts associated with forensic profiles 1 and 3, the profile descriptors 1 and 3 are activated.

The alert generated by a forensic client hides the object by providing the address of one of the subnet proxies. The anonymity provided to the object through the subnet proxy accounts for the privacy issues related to the users of that particular object. The forensic server can traceback the original source by querying the subnet proxy for transaction entries associated with that particular request and time stamp. The transaction table maintained by each subnet proxy and its related significance in retrieving the original source involved in a security violation is discussed in a subsequent passage.

The forensic server builds the forensic profile of an attack with the help of information gathered by the forensic clients in the form of *alerts* and subsequent queries called *probes* generated by the server with the help of the profile database to the clients based on the received alerts. Probes A, B, and W are generated for the alert X shown in Figure 2.

Forensic Client

Different nodes in the network are capable of contributing to the security of the entire network if security features are configured and enabled. All forensic clients would participate in distributed intrusion detection and maintain logs. The forensic client can be a router, a signature analyzer, an IDS, a firewall, or a host in the network.

Each forensic client would be responsible for generating an *alert*. An alert depends on the detection of a *suspicious activity*. The detection process involves *active monitoring* and *active parsing*. Active monitoring is used to observe the performance parameters such as CPU utilization or event-log intensity, of the client and checking for discrepancies. Active parsing continuously scans the entries in the log files and history files and checks for suspicious keywords such as authentication failure, access denied, connection failure, and so forth.

The alerts generated by the forensic client to the forensic server have a dual purpose. An alert defines the type of suspicious activity and at the same time provides anonymity to the suspicious IP address. For instance, if a host in subnet A shown in Figure 1 sends a malicious request to the ftp server in DMZ then the alert generated by the ftp server to the forensic server would specify the source of the malicious request as one of the proxies. This in turn conceals the original source address and provides privacy to the users of that particular host. The anonymity is induced in the entire network by the use of subnet proxies.

Subnet Proxy

A subnet proxy, as the name suggests, works on behalf of the forensic client. An organization can be decomposed into different subnets. All the forensic clients that belong to a particular subnet are assigned a proxy server called the subnet proxy. A conventional proxy server acts as an intermediary between a client and a server. The main purpose of a conventional proxy is to serve requests from the cache in order to reduce the response time and can additionally be used for filtering requests. The subnet proxy however is used to propagate anonymity in the network and it does not analyze the frame.

Anonymity is accomplished by proxy chaining. All the packets destined for a particular destination are forwarded over a chain of subnet proxies. Consequently, when the frame reaches the destination the source would appear as one of the subnet proxies.

The working of the subnet proxy is similar to that of a FLOCK proxy (Olivier, 2004). All the forensic clients that belong to a particular subnet send frames to the subnet proxy. The subnet proxy would either forward the frame to the final destination or to one of the subnet proxies. As shown in Figure 1 the clients that belong to subnet A send frames to Proxy A. The subnet proxy can randomly decide to forward the frame to proxies B, C, or D or to the final destination itself. The subnet proxy associates each of its ports to a forensic client in the subnet. Thus, each forensic client is recognized by the subnet proxy by the port number. As the port number can be of 16 bits, the number of forensic clients associated with a particular subnet would be 65536. After excluding the reserved port numbers (1024) still a good number can be associated with each subnet. Each proxy maintains a port address translation table to identify each host in the subnet. A frame that originates from a particular subnet is sent to the subnet proxy.

Before a subnet proxy forwards the frame it registers an entry in the *transaction table* that indicates the time at which the request was made, the port number where the request originated, the final destination and the type of request made in the format (t,s,d,r). This approach is based on the model suggested by Olivier (2005). Each subnet proxy updates its *transaction table* each time it receives a frame. Eventually, when the packet reaches the final destination the source address would point towards one of the subnet proxies.

In case a *suspicious activity* is detected, the transaction table maintained by each subnet proxy can identify the original source. A sample cumulative *transaction table* associated with different proxies is shown in Table 1.

Table 1. Cumulative view of the transaction table entries maintained by different proxies (Based on the model presented by Olivier [2005])

Time	Proxy A	Proxy B	Proxy C	Proxy D
T_1	A_1D_2P		AD_2P	
T_2	A_2A_1Q	DA_1Q		AA_1Q
T_3	CIR	B_1IR	BIR	
T_4		B_1C_1S	D_1C_1S	BB_1S
T_5	CB_2T		DB_2T	D_2B_2T
T_6		CIR	C_1IR	
T_7		CD_1Q	C_1D_1Q	
T_7			BD_1Q	
T_8	A_1D_1R	DD_1R	BD_1R	AD_1R
T_9	BD_2P	B_3D_2P	AD_2P	
T_{10}		B_1D_3R		DD_3R

For simplicity, a forensic client that belongs to subnet A is designated as A_i where i is the index and is less than or equal to the total number of forensic clients associated with subnet A given by, n. A_i sends frames to proxy A, B_i sends frames to proxy B, so on and so forth. At time T_1, A_1 sends a frame to D_2, as A_1 belongs to subnet A, the frame is sent to proxy A, which in turn decides to forward to C, and C finally sends to D_1. In order to identify that the log entries in different subnet proxies belong to one particular communication sequence, the common parameters would be the destination, the request, and the time interval at which the communication occurs. It is essential that these events are temporally related.

The assumptions associated with the working of the subnet proxy are as follows:

- It is assumed that the communication between a source, destination, and the intermediary proxies takes place at approximately the same time. At the same time, the client that generates the alert is the victim and hiding the source address of the victim would be irrational.

- The purpose of the subnet proxy is to forward the packets and at the same time maintain a transaction entry for the packet. The subnet proxy does not interact with the forensic server and hence it is not a forensic client. However, to safeguard against a compromise, the log entries can be encrypted using symmetric keys.

- The alert generated by the forensic client is directed towards to the forensic server and it bypasses the proxies in the network. This is because an alert should be received by the forensic server as soon as a suspicious activity is detected. This would also help in generating prompt queries by the forensic server.

- In order to reduce the overhead associated with forwarding a packet, a limit can be set on the number of forwards. That is, the number of intermediary proxies can be fixed depending upon the size of the network. In order to avoid long trails the number of forwards is fixed.

- In order to reduce the overhead caused due to intermediary proxies, the path traversed by a source-destination pair can be preserved so that the same path can be used for subsequent communications.

- A subnet proxy is assumed to be repeated in the communication sequence if the subsequent forward occurs at approximately the same time. Thus, the path can be identified by time. This is depicted in T_7 in Table I where subnet proxy C is repeated for communication between C_1 and D_1.

Communication Signals between
Network Components: Alerts and Probes

The forensic client continuously looks for anomalous activity and listens to the server for probes simultaneously. In order to accomplish this, two different agents working independently of each other, agent alert and agent probe, are installed in each of the forensic clients. Agent_alert checks for any suspicious/unusual activity in the host by scanning logs, history files, and so on, and generates alerts. Agent_probe listens to the server for probes and sends the required information back to forensic server.

Agent_alert is responsible for generating alerts to the server. The alert depends upon the detection of suspicious activity. The detection process involves *active monitoring* and *active parsing*. Active monitoring involves observing the performance parameters such as CPU utilization or event-log intensity of the client and checking for discrepancies. Active parsing is continuous scanning of the entries in the log files and history files and check for suspicious entries (keywords) such as authentication failure, access denied, connection failure, and so forth.

The alerts generated by the forensic clients to the forensic server have a format that provides information about the time and the event that triggered it. The format is composed of *when-subject-object-action* fields. Subject is the forensic client that triggers the alert, object is the network element on which the action occurs and the action specifies the event.

Probes are the queries generated by the forensic server to the forensic clients. The forensic server stores logs that indicate some suspicious activities. The forensic server is capable of generating two kinds of probes, CheckProbe and GetLog Probe. Check Probe checks for suspicious activity in relation to an earlier alert that was received by the server. If the forensic client responds with a NULL packet to the Check Probe then the server will not send GetLog Probe. Otherwise, the forensic server sends GetLog Probe to receive the log entries for that particular event.

The Functioning of the
Forensic Profiling System

The *passive state* of the network is defined as the state wherein the network is involved in normal/usual (non-suspicious) activities that do not cause a threat to the security of the network. In the passive state the activity of the entire network would be monitored by the agents installed in each of the forensic clients. When an agent detects an event, it sends an alert to the forensic server along with log entries for that particular time. As an alert is a parameter of a profile, the forensic server would search for a match for the alert in the passive profiles and generate stack of active profiles. In order to select one particular profile, the forensic server would query the other forensic clients for complementary alerts associated with each active profile. If a forensic client responds with information pertinent to an active profile, the forensic server would analyze the active stack so as to reduce the number of active profiles. This would be a recursive process until the entire attack is detected. The forensic profile would thus be built from the detection of the first alert until the detection of the attack.

The alerts generated by the forensic client to the forensic server are such that they preserve the anonymity of the source. For instance if the Web server in the DMZ as shown in Figure 1 receives a malicious alert from one of the subnets then the alert sent by the Web server to the forensic server would specify last proxy that forwarded the request as the source. This is depicted in the log entry specified in T_9 where the forensic client B_3 sends a packet to D_2 (Web server). The path taken by the packet is $B_3 - B - A - D_2$. If we suppose that P is a malicious reque,st then the alert generated by the Web server to the forensic server would specify proxy A as the source. In order to identify the original client, the forensic server queries proxy A for the source associated with (time=T_9, destination=D_2, request=P). Based on the response received from proxy A, the forensic server either sends a query to another proxy (proxy B in this case) or retrieves the source address from the proxy. The proxy maintains an association table for the IP address of the forensic client and the port number and thus the original source can be traced.

Some concerns and limitations of the approach followed by the forensic profiling system are discussed in the following:

- Communication between the clients that are on the same LAN would incur a overhead because the frame would be forwarded to the subnet proxy and it would take a random path before it reaches the final destination and the packet would thus incur a large delay. The 80/20 Rule states that in any organization, 80 % of the connection requests are made to outside the organization (internet), and only 20% of the connections are established within the organization. Thus, only 20% of the packets would suffer the large delay.

- In case of retransmissions where error recovery is in place (particularly TCP connections), the overhead would increase. Maintaining a single path for the same source-destination pair can reduce the overhead. The path can be preserved and reused for subsequent communications.

- A packet can be forwarded to the same proxy more than once, as is depicted by T_7 in Table 1 where proxy C is repeated. This occurs because forwards are randomly decided by the proxies. This can be acceptable as long as a limit is set on the number of forwards.

- Identifying the original source responsible for the suspicious activity for the forensic server requires expenditure of more queries, and queries based on an IP address would be meaningless as the subnet proxies hide the original IP addresses. For instance, if we assume that A_1 is involved in some malicious activities specified by requests P and R at instances T_1 and T_8, the forensic server generates a different set of queries to get down to the same source. This process would involve a lot of exchange of queries and responses.

An unknown attack does not have a passive profile. But since attacks have common events that trigger them, the alerts generated would be used to save the log entries in the forensic server that can be later used for forensic evaluation in order to trace the attacker and corroborate evidence. Intrusion detection systems normally work based on a signature database and are unable to track illicit activity, if a new or unknown attack is performed. The signature database needs to be updated in order to prevent such attacks.

Forensic profiling system would deal with this problem by creating an unstructured profile. If a profile for some unsuspicious activity will not match with any of the known profiles, an unstructured profile would be built with all those alerts. This ensures that even if the attack was not stopped, the evidence related to the activity is collected and saved. The entire profile would be built depending on the alerts generated by the different forensic clients in the network and the response obtained from the clients for the probes generated by the forensic server. The complete profile would thus contain information about the attacker, type of attack, and a chronology of all the events that followed, along with the logs.

Evidence Collection Mechanism Using Privacy Enabled FPS: A Case Study

This section presents a case study that incorporates the privacy in a system that already has FPS installed. The case study includes the privacy model in the FPS system described by Kahai, Namuduri, and Pendse (2005). A brief overview of the FPS mechanism associated with the Washington University FTP Daemon (WU-FTPD) case study discussed by Mandia, Prosise, and Pepe (2003) is first presented and the functioning of the privacy components is later discussed.

Mechanism Employed by FPS Against WU-FTPD Attack

Before we discuss the progression of the attack, the network design of the company is presented. The DMZ consisted of all the standard set of network servers (Web, e-mail, DNS servers and also a dedicated FTP server, used to distribute hardware drivers for the company inventory). Two firewalls were used one separating the DMZ from the Internet and the other firewall separating the DMZ from the internal network (LAN). No connections were allowed from the DMZ to either the Internet or to the LAN. Also, no connection was allowed between the DMZ machines themselves. An outside machine could connect only to a single port of each of the DMZ hosts. The forensic server maintained a forensic file database and contained the forensic profile descriptor for WU-FTPD attack.

In the real case scenario analyzed by Chuvakin (2002), the forensic investigation was initiated after a customer was unable to connect to the company's FTP server. However, with the FPS installed in the system on the basis of the alert-probe mechanism adopted by the FPS would lead to a different chronology of events. The WU-FTPD attack was first detected by the IDS which acts as a forensic client, and therefore, generates an alert to the forensic server. The WU-FTPD profile is composed of the following components:

- Anonymous FTP Login
- Occurrence of Buffer Overflow in FTP server
- Process initiation by the root after the attacker acquires root privileges after buffer overflow is successful
- Installation of suspicious packages by the root (rootkit)

In response to the alert generated by the IDS, the forensic server launches probes in the entire network. The check probe queries for a specific alert that is a part of the forensic profile of the attack in question, that is, the WU-FTPD attack for this case. The check probes are generated simultaneously by the forensic server to different forensic clients. The check probe sent to FTP server sets the check flag to FTP login session for the time at which the IDS had generated the alert to the forensic server. If a NULL packet is sent by FTP server as a response to the query, it implies that no FTP login session is in progress. Otherwise, the FTP responds by providing the IP addresses of all the FTP sessions currently logged in. The forensic server maintains logs only for security incidents and a match obtained for the IP addresses retrieved from the FTP server and the logs residing in the forensic server indicates a suspicious IP address. Thus, the forensic server issues a get log probe to the FTP server demanding logs for the suspicious IP address. The log fragments that are indicative of a FTP login session through a suspicious IP address are as follows:

FTP System Logs:

Apr 1 00:08:25 ftp ftpd[27651]: ANONYMOUS FTP LOGIN FROM 192.1.2.3 [192.1.2.3], mozilla@

Apr 1 00:17:19 ftp ftpd[27649]: lost connection to 192.1.2.3 [192.1.2.3]

Apr 1 00:17:19 ftp ftpd[27649]: FTP session closed

Apr 1 02:21:57 ftp ftpd[27703]: ANONYMOUS FTP LOGIN FROM 192.1.2.3 [192.1.2.3], mozilla@

Apr 1 02:26:13 ftp ftpd[27722]: ANONYMOUS FTP LOGIN FROM 192.1.2.3 [192.1.2.3], mozilla@

Apr 1 02:29:45 ftp ftpd[27731]: ANONYMOUS FTP LOGIN FROM 192.1.2.3 [192.1.2.3], x@

From the logs it is inferred that the intruder was able to run an exploit to generate buffer overflow in the FTP server and was able to gain access to root privileges.

The check probe sent to the IDS by the forensic server checks for buffer overflow. On the other hand, the check probes that query for process execution under root privileges are sent to the FTP server.

The network access logs, given below, recovered from the FTP server show that the attacker spent sometime over the FTP server directories.

Network Access Logs:

Apr 1 00:17:23 ftp xinetd[921]: START: ftp pid=27672 from=192.1.2.3

Apr 1 02:20:18 ftp xinetd[921]: START: ftp pid=27692 from=192.1.2.3

Apr 1 02:20:38 ftp xinetd[921]: EXIT: ftp pid=27672 duration=195(sec)

Apr 1 02:21:57 ftp xinetd[921]: START: ftp pid=27703 from=192.1.2.3

Apr 1 02:21:59 ftp xinetd[921]: EXIT: ftp pid=27692 duration=101(sec)

Apr 1 02:26:12 ftp xinetd[921]: EXIT: ftp pid=27703 duration=255(sec)

Apr 1 02:26:13 ftp xinetd[921]: START: ftp pid=27722 from=192.1.2.3

Apr 1 02:29:40 ftp xinetd[921]: START: ftp pid=27731 from=192.1.2.3

Apr 1 02:30:07 ftp xinetd[921]: EXIT: ftp pid=27731 duration=27(sec)

Since, all the forensic clients in the network are responsible for detecting security incidents and generating corresponding alerts, any kind of unauthorized network connection would generate an alert. After gaining access to the FTP server, the attacker tried to connect to his machine, 192.1.2.3, which was not allowed. Also, the attacker attempted to connect to the mail server. This is implied by the following FTP connection logs.

FTP Connection Logs:

Apr 1 02:30:04 ftp ftpd[27731]: Can't connect to a mailserver.

Apr 1 02:30:07 ftp ftpd[27731]: FTP session closed

Thus, corresponding alerts indicative of unauthorized network access are generated by the FTP server and the firewall to the forensic server.

The attacker was able to gain root access upload file and later execute a script. This is inferred from the FTP transfer logs.

FTP Transfer Logs:

Mon Apr 1 02:30:04 2002 2 192.1.2.3 262924 /ftpdata/incoming/mount.tar.gz b i a x @ ftp 0 * c

Thus, depending upon the chronology of events, either the FTP server responds to check probes issued by the forensic server or sends an alert to the forensic server that is indicative of mounting of files by the root.

The privacy features incorporated in the FPS would hide the IP address 192.1.2.3 and the source address would be represented by a subnet proxy. Also the address would be hidden by the subnet proxies if it belongs to the company's network. Let us assume that D_1 is the FTP server and R is a malicious request. It can be seen from Table 1 that the time instant T_8 corresponds to the entire communication sequence that is comprised of $A_1 - A - D - B - C - D_1$. This sequence would be traced by the forensic server through queries to all the intermediary proxies.

Since the attacker was able to delete the operating system of the FTP server, the forensic server would not be able to receive response from the FTP server for any of its probes. Subsequently, the forensic server would contain a forensic profile that would contain all the alerts and the forensic evidence in the form of suspicious log entries.

Conclusions

We have proposed a forensic profiling system for real-time forensic evidence collection based on anonymity. A dedicated forensic server is capable of maintaining an audit trail embedded in the forensic profile. As the aim of the FPS is to keep track of the anomalous activities in the network, time spent in filtering the system log files during a forensic investigation can be drastically reduced. This would help an organization to resume normal functioning after a compromise has taken place. The logging mechanism adopted by the FPS is such that the source of any communication is hidden by a proxy. The source of a suspicious communication pattern is queried by the forensic server whenever an alert is generated. Thus the communication behavior of only the suspicious source is investigated, which helps in keeping privacy intact. Most of the hackers make sure that no logs are maintained while the attack is underway. FPS makes it easier to retrieve the logs of crashed hosts as the host is capable of sending log entries associated with an alert to the forensic server. Since all the attacks have a general commonality in them, unknown attacks can be tracked by the forensic sever on the basis of the alerts generated by the forensic clients. Later, the forensic profile so built can be used for improving the FPS itself. The incorporation of privacy by deploying proxies has its own drawbacks concerned mainly with the overhead associated with communication between a source-destination pair. But in order to automate the entire process of forensic investigation so that human intervention can be minimized, the proxies ensure that the privacy of the individuals is not compromised.

Future Work

The advantages offered by the FPS as opposed to the cost associated with its implementation require evaluation. Research in reducing the overhead sustained by the prototype FPS presented in this chapter is warranted.

Privacy is a fundamental attribute of the FPS. The component employed by the FPS to preserve privacy is the subnet proxy. Analysis regarding the scope of the overhead incurred by proxy chaining is required. The continuous process of active parsing and monitoring, which is a characteristic of each forensic client, imparts additional overhead. An absolute estimate in terms of the total overhead is essential.

The appropriate functioning of the FPS is largely dependent on the forensic profile database. The accuracy of the database is governed by the forensic profiles. Detailed investigation of the attacks is required to build the forensic profiles. In order to ensure the proper working of the FPS, keeping the profile database current is another challenge that needs to be addressed.

Acknowledgment

This work was done under the NSF DUE Grant 0313827.

References

Ashley, P., Hada, S., Karjoth, G., & Schunter, M. (2002). E-P3P privacy policies and privacy authorization. In *Proceedings of ACM Workshop on Privacy in the Electronic Society (WPES)* (pp. 103-109). ACM Press.

Barrus, J., & Rowe, N. (1998, June). Distributed autonomous-agent network-intrusion detection and response system. In *Proceedings of Command and Control Research and Technology Symposium* (pp. 577-586). Monterey, CA.

Cuppens, F. (2001). Managing alerts in a multi-intrusion detection environment. In *Proceedings of 17th Annual Computer Security Applications Conference (ACSAC).* New Orleans.

Cuppens, F., & Mi'ege, A. (2002). Alert correlation in a cooperative intrusion detection framework. In *Proceedings of the 2002 IEEE Symposium on Security and Privacy* (pp. 202-215). Oakland, CA.

Chuvakin, A. (2002). *FTP attack case study part I: The analysis.* Retrieved July 23, 2005, from http://www.linuxsecurity.com/content/view/117644/49/

Debar, H., & Wespi, A. (2001). Aggregation and correlation of intrusion-detection alerts. *4th Workshop on Recent Advances in Intrusion Detection (RAID)* (pp. 85-103). LNCS, Springer Verlag.

Huang, M., Jasper, R., & Wicks, T. (1999). A large-scale distributed intrusion detection framework based on attack strategy analysis. *Computer Networks.* Amsterdam, Netherlands.

Kahai, P., Namuduri, K., & Pendse, P. (2005, February). Forensics and privacy—Enhancing technologies—Logging and collecting evidence in FLOCKS. In *Proceedings of the 1st IFIP WG 11.9 International Conference on Digital Forensics National Center for Forensic Science,* Orlando, FL.

Kahn, C., Bolinger, D., & Schnackenberg, D. (1998). *Common intrusion detection framework.* Retrieved July 10, 2000, from http://www.isi.edu/gost/cidf/

Korba, L. (2002). Privacy in distributed electronic commerce. In *Proceedings of 35th International Conference on System Sciences.* IEEE Computer Society.

Mandia, K., Prosise, C., & Pepe, M. (2003). *Incident response.* Emeryville, CA: McGraw-Hill.

Michel, C., & M'e, L. (2001) An attack description language for knowledge-based intrustion detection. In *Proceedings of the 16th International Conference on Information Security* (pp. 353-368). Paris.

Ning, P., Cui, Y., & Reeves, D., (2002). Constructing attack scenarios through correlation of intrusion alerts. In *Proceedings of the 9th ACM Conference on Computer and Communications Security* (pp. 245-254).

Ning, P., Wang, X., & Jajodia, S., (2000, October). A query facility for common intrusion detection framework. In *Proceedings of the 23rd National Information Systems Security Conference* (pp. 317-328). Baltimore.

Ning, P., Wang, X., & Jajodia, S. (2001, November). Abstraction-based intrusion detection in distributed environments. *ACM Transactions on Information and System Security, 4*(4), 407-452.

Olivier, M. (2004). FLOCKS: Distributed proxies for browsing privacy. In *Proceedings of SAICSIT* (pp. 79-88). Stellenbosch, South Africa.

Olivier, M. (2005). Forensics and privacy—Enhancing technologies—Logging and collecting evidence in FLOCKS. In *Proceedings of the 1st IFIP WG 11.9 International Conference on Digital Forensics National Center for Forensic Science,* Orlando, FL.

Patzakis, J. (2003). *Digital privacy considerations with the introduction of encase enterprise, guidance software.* Retrieved January 16, 2005, from http://www.guidancesoftware.com/corporate/downloads/whitepapers/DigitalPrivacy.pdf

Porras, P., & Neumann, P. (1997). EMERALD: Event monitoring enabling responses to anomalous live disturbances. In *Proceedings of the 20th National Information Systems Security Conference* (pp. 353-365). Baltimore.

Shanmugasundaram, K., Memon, N., Savant, A., & Bronnimann, H., (2003). ForNet: A distributed forensics network. In *Proceedings of the Second International Workshop on Mathematical Methods, Models and Architectures for Computer Networks Security* (pp. 1-16). St. Petersburg, Russia.

Valdes, A., & Skinner, K. (2001). Probabilistic alert correlation. In *Proceedings of the Fourth International Workshop on the Recent Advances in Intrusion Detection (RAID)* (pp. 54-68). Davis, USA.

Yang, J., Ning, P., & Wang, X. (2000). CARDS: A distributed system for detecting coordinated attacks. *IFIP TC11 Sixteenth Annual Working Conference on Information Security* (pp. 171-180). Orlando, FL.

Chapter VIII

ASKARI: A Crime Text Mining Approach

Caroline Chibelushi, Staffordshire University, UK

Bernadette Sharp, Staffordshire University, UK

Hanifa Shah, Staffordshire University, UK

Abstract

The advancement of multimedia and communication systems has not only provided faster and better communication facilities but also facilitated easier means to organized crime. Concern about national security has increased significantly in the recent years due to the increase in organized crimes, leading to increasing amounts of data available for investigation by criminal analysts. The opportunity to analyze this data to determine patterns of criminal behavior, monitor, and predict criminal activities coexists with the threat of information overload. A large amount of information, which is stored in textual and unstructured form, contains a valuable untapped source of data. Data mining and text mining are two key technologies suited to the discovery of underlying patterns in large data sets. This chapter reviews the use of text mining techniques in crime detection projects and describes in detail the text mining approach used in the proposed ASKARI project.

Introduction

A recent report from the Home Office states that combating organized crime alone costs the United Kingdom (UK) about £40 billion a year (Sandford, 2004). This budget has been used by institutions like the security organizations, law enforcement agencies, and intelligence agencies such as CIA, FBI, and MI5 to dynamically collect and analyze information, and investigate organized crime activities in order to prevent future attacks. These institutions store large amounts of data; recent research has shown that almost 80% of most organizations' information is contained in text documents (Sullivan, 2001; Tan, 1999), whereas the amount of text/Web mining efforts do not exceed 7% (Drewes, 2002). The speed of security, without information lag, is necessary and requires organizations to make timely and effective decisions. Security organizations acknowledge the need for their textual-based tasks to be organized, managed, and deployed around a set of self-evolving processes, using newly emerging knowledge discovery and agent systems to identify, track, extract, classify, and discover patterns in their corporate databases so that they can be used to generate alerts or crime event notification in real-time. Therefore a clear challenge facing these institutions is how to make effective use of these emerging technologies to assist their intelligence analysts in detecting and anticipating organized crimes, and empower them with powerful tools that can identify patterns, monitor detectable clues across diverse document sources, build behavioral models, and thus improve decision making.

Despite the sudden increase in organized criminal activities in the recent years, there is still no generally accepted definition of organized crime. In order to fight it locally and internationally, we need to understand the common features that characterize the way in which organized criminals operate, as well as how to distinguish organized crimes from other crime. We define organized crime as a (structured or not structured) group of two or more people existing for a period of time and acting in concert with the aim of committing one or more serious crimes that are motivated by politics, religion, race, or financial gain (*Organised Crime in South Africa*, 1998). Organized crime can include terrorism, drug trafficking, fraud, gang robberies, and other group-oriented criminal activities. A terrorist incident is perceived to be significant if it results in loss of life, serious injury to persons, and/or major property damage. Terrorism activities in particular have risen rapidly for the past six years, as shown in Figure 1, which highlights two major incidents between 1998 and 2003. The highest number of casualties is the 1998 attacks in Africa; these attacks included the bombings of USA embassies in East Africa and other different attacks in the region. The second is the September 11, 2001 attacks in the USA. A number of recent attacks have followed namely the bombing of Madrid rail network in May 2004 and the attacks on London transport system in July 2005. These attacks have significantly raised many countries' concerns about national security.

This proliferation of organized crime and the threat of global terrorism have led to the ever-growing volume, variety, and complexity of data captured for analysis. Some intelligence data sources are growing at the rate of four petabytes per month now, and the rate of growth is increasing. The challenge of today lies no longer in the storage and retrieval of data, but in our ability to scan through huge amounts of information and extracting the right information for the right person at the right time.

Figure 1. A continental measure of total loss of lives caused by terrorist attacks (Patterns of Global Terrorism, 2003-2004)

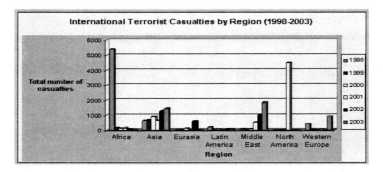

Source: http://www.globalsecurity.org/

Crime Prevention and Detection Approaches

The concern about national security and crime prevention has increased significantly over the last few years, and has led to the development of national and international funding initiatives, networks and research projects aimed at fighting organized crime. In the USA, the Defence Advanced Research Project Agency (DARPA) has initiated a homeland security program named Total Information Awareness (TIA), which incorporates a number of technologies such as data fusion, database searches, biometrics, and pattern recognition. This program seeks to develop a network of technologies to help security officers predict and prevent terrorism activity (Kenyon, 2003). In the UK, the Engineering and Physical Sciences Research Council, which claims that crime costs the economy 50 billion euro a year, has launched the Crime Technology Programme calling for research projects related to crime prevention and detection technologies. Security has been also considered as a priority research theme in the 7th Framework Programme for Research and Development of the European Union (EU). The AGIS framework program, named after a king of ancient Sparta, is one such a program aimed at promoting police and judicial cooperation in criminal matters, and covering a wide range of applications, such as the analysis of DNA and handwritten documents to solve fraud, identity theft, graffiti, and murder. While some projects are developing systems for tracking devices and people for crime prevention, other projects are focusing on improving chemical weapon and concealed material detection, image resolution, face recognition, and video processing.

To date, most national security organizations depend on data and text mining techniques to detect and predict criminal activities. While data mining refers to the exploration and analysis of large quantities of data to discover meaningful patterns and rules (Berry & Linoff, 1997), text mining (sometimes referred to as text data mining) is the process of analyzing naturally occurring text for the purpose of extracting interesting and nontrivial patterns or knowledge from unstructured texts (Hearst, 1997). Both data mining and text mining are often considered as subprocesses of the field of knowledge discovery. Until recently, the most significant applications of data mining have been used to predict consumer preferences and to profile prospects for products and services. In the aftermath of the recent terrorist attacks, data and text mining became one of the dominant approaches in an increasing number of research projects associated with organized crime and in particular with antiterrorist activities. The objective of many intelligence data analysis projects is to use data mining to find associations and/or discover relationships among suspect entities based on historical data. While data mining analyzes data from *structured* databases, there is a large volume of textual data (e.g., e-mails, telephone conversations, and text messages), which crime investigators have to examine, which are *unstructured*. Popp, Armour, Senator, and Numrych (2004) argue that intelligence analysts spend far more time on searching and preprocessing data for analysis, turning results into reports and briefings for the decision maker, and therefore less time analyzing the textual data. Advanced techniques to detect suspicious activities, discover relationships between materials, people, organization and events, and discover patterns of behavior can assist analysts in identifying unknown organized criminal activities from documents. In recent years, we have seen an impressive growth of data and text mining software systems, a list of some of these is provided in Table 1, which is by no means an exhaustive list of currently available tools on the market.

Text mining combines data mining techniques such as clustering, association rules, and neural networks, with methods used in information extraction and natural language processing techniques. There is a general consensus that the general knowledge discovery framework can apply to both data and text mining, and consists of three main stages: preprocessing, discovery, and post-processing (Ahonen, Heinonen, Klemettinen, & Verkamo, 1997; Fayyad, Piatetsky-Shapiro, & Smyth, 1996). Depending on the purpose of the text mining activity, the preprocessing stage may involve different levels of analysis: some projects may give prominence to lexical and syntactic analysis, others may also include semantic and domain knowledge analysis. In some research projects the last two stages are combined, as in the case of Tan's project (Tan, 1999) which proposes a text refinement stage that transforms raw text into an intermediate form, and a text distillation stage which analyzes the transformed text to discover patterns and semantic relationships among entities. Whilst clustering, categorization, and visualization are particularly relevant to the text refinement component, knowledge distillation deduces patterns from the intermediate form using familiar modelling techniques such as clustering, association rules, and classification. Different applications may require different levels of granularity when generating an intermediate form, so it may be sometimes necessary to undertake a deep semantic analysis to capture the relationships between the entities or concepts described in the texts. Domain knowledge plays an important role in the text refinement and distillation stages.

Though in the last few years there has been an increasing interest in deploying data mining in many applications including crime prevention and detection, text mining is a relatively young field which is gaining momentum in the domain of crime prevention and crime detection. In the following sections we review key text mining techniques and identify projects undertaken in the domain of organized crime.

Table 1. Data and text mining

Company name	Technology	Technique	Purpose	Country of application
HNC Falcon system	Neural networks	DM	A	USA UK Canada South Africa
DARPA	Agent technology and Sensors	DM TM	B	USA
ATAC	Association rules	Link Analysis	A	USA
Autonomy	Adaptive Probabilistic Concept Modelling (APCM), Neural networks, and Concept agents	TM	C	UK USA
DolphinSearch	Neural networks	DM	A	USA
Wolverhampton University and W. Midlands Police (UK)	Neural nets-Kohonen Maps (SOMs) – unsupervised learning	DM	S	UK (Police) USA
ChoicePoint (AutoTrackXP)	SQL	Link Analysis	D	USA
ALTA Analytics (NETMAP)	Vectorization	Link Analysis	A	USA
Bair Software Inc.	Neural networks	DM	G	USA
i2 Ltd.	Association rules	Link Analysis	G, P	UK USA
Crime Link	Association rules	Link Analysis	G	UK USA
Memex (Crime Workbench)	Database Intelligent management system.	Enhanced Search Engine	C	UK (Police) USA (Department of defence)
Clearforest	Categorisation	Categorisation	G	USA (FBI)
Copernic	Information/concept retrieval	Agents and TM	F	UK
Quenza (Xanalyst)	Pattern recognition and relationships	TM toolkit Link Analysis,	T and P	USA (Department of Homeland security)
COPLINK	Pattern/ data matching	Link Analysis TM	C	USA (Police)
FLINTS	Probability theories Previous Database-knowledge	Link Analysis	E and G	UK (Police)

A - Fraud and money laundering
B – Bio-terrorism
C - Clustering and categorisation of modus operandi and other criminal information in the databases
D - Drug enforcement, immigration and naturalisation
E – Extracting data and predict future attack
F - Forensic investigation
G - General linking analysis for visualising related crimes and crime networks
P – Paedophile Pornography related crimes
S – Sex and homicide related crimes
T – Tracking criminal gangs
O – Others (which can include feature extraction, searching, browsing, and visualisation)

Information Extraction

Information extraction (IE) occurs normally at the preprocessing stage. The aim is to extract meaningful terms from textual data which can then be further mined. However, most approaches using IE are intended to find a specific class of events. Mena (2003) suggests that IE can be used to combat bioterrorism by monitoring multiple online and wireless communication channels, scanning texts for keywords like *Anthrax* and the name of aliases of individual or group of people across documents. IE techniques are also used to automatically identify entities like suspect's address, vehicle, telephone number, and others from police narrative reports or e-mails. Chen et al. (2004) have developed a system to extract named entities from police narrative records, combining linguistic rules based on pattern matching and lexical lookup with neural networks. The text mining approach of Loh, Wives, and Oliveira, (2000) combines association rules with concepts extraction from large collections of texts, some of which are related to crimes and others related to elections and politicians. However, one of the complexities involved in analyzing criminal communications is that both the activities and individual's identities are often not explicitly stated in the documents.

Clustering

Clustering is the task of grouping similar entities into a number of homogeneous subgroups or clusters. For example, analysts may wish to identify crimes of similar characteristics, or to cluster police reports by type of events in order to investigate any useful associations about these events, or to visualize criminal incidents in relation to others. These techniques do not have a set of predefined classes for assigning entities. Sometimes clusters are viewed in the hierarchical fashion, in other words, when analyzing a set of documents for topical content one might first look for the two main topics, and then for subtopics in each of the two clusters, effectively "*drilling down*" into the clusters as warranted by the application (Drewes, 2002). Brown and Gunderson (2001) have applied sequential clustering to discover the preferences of computer criminals. Clustering techniques have also been used to associate person with organization and/ or vehicle in crime records (Chau, Xu, & Chen 2002).

Neural Networks

Neural networks are models of biological learning systems which learn from examples and can detect complex patterns. They have successfully been used to detect fraudulent transactions, computer intrusions, and other criminal activities from historical data. In recent years, neural networks have also been used on textual analysis. For example, the Concept Space for Intelligence Analysis (COPLINK) system allows the user to browse a map that classifies police incident cases narratives into categories by combining neural networks, Self Organizing Maps (SOM) in particular, with natural language processing (NLP) techniques such as extraction of noun phrase, entity extraction, and concept space

(Hauck, Atabakhsh, Angvasith, Gupta, & Chen, 2002). A case study of burglary offenses, which was carried out by the UK West Midland Police, illustrates how a multilayer perceptron, a radial basis function, and SOM can be applied to the building of special attributes of crimes to a network of offenders (Adderley & Musgrove, 1999).

Association Rule Mining

Introduced by Agrawal, Imielinski, and Swami (1993), association rule mining discovers frequently occurring item sets in a corpus, infers patterns and describes them as rules. The simplest definition of an association rule is a rule that implies a particular relationship amongst sets of objects within a data set, in the form of "if antecedent then consequent". Applications of association rules include fraud detection (Fawcett & Provost, 1997), investigation of profiles from forensic log files to databases, personal user files, and other documents (Abraham & Vel, 2002). In her paper, Gunderson (2002) describes the use of association rules to construct a predictive model of theft; these rules can predict from the location, time, and daily mean temperature the type of item stolen, and discovers the features that were salient to the choice of a target for these crimes.

ASKARI: A Crime Text Mining Approach

A variety of technologies have been used to analyze data and texts related to criminal offenses, some aimed at developing a descriptive model while others focused on predictive modelling. However most of the work carried out has focused on the analysis and modelling of data, and little emphasis is given into the building of an integrated environment to link these analyses across various databases and repositories thus assisting criminal analysts in their decision making. Our research project, ASKARI, is designed to facilitate the exploitation of structured and unstructured criminal textual data, including e-mails, text messages, telephone conversation transcripts and other textual related sources. The proposed approach combines agent technology with text mining techniques to dynamically extract criminal activity patterns, discover associations between criminal activities through detectable clues, and track them across multiple document sources. The goal of ASKARI is to support criminal investigators and intelligence analysts in their decision making by helping them anticipate and hopefully prevent future crimes from taking place.

Discovery Phase Using a Text Mining Approach

ASKARI is a multisource, multi-document, and content-based approach which seeks to analyze and discover hidden knowledge from textual crime data through understanding

Figure 2. Phases of the CRISP-DM reference model (Chapman et al., 2000).

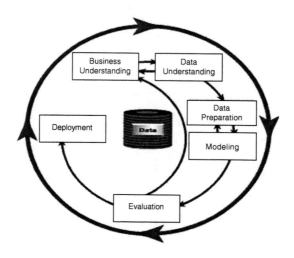

the meaning of data. This project extends the work carried out in a previous project called TRACKER (Chibelushi, Sharp, & Salter, 2004; Rayson et al., 2003) which used text mining to identify, track, extract, and relate different elements of decision making from transcripts and minutes of recorded meetings.

The ASKARI project proposes two phases: a discovery phase and a monitoring phase. The discovery phase is an adaptation of the Cross-Industry Standard Process for Data Mining (CRISP-DM) to text mining approach, as shown in Figure 2. This phase consists of two stages: a preprocessing stage and a modelling stage.

The preprocessing stage focuses on the goal of text mining, gathers and transforms the relevant corpus for analysis into an intermediate form for modelling. This will include the following tasks:

- **Understanding the investigation objectives:** In negotiation with criminal analysts, this phase focuses on understanding and identifying the requirements, objectives, and constraints of the intended application from the law enforcement perspective. The main task is to define and understand the type of crime to be analyzed, identify the important factors and assumptions that can influence the outcomes of the research, and hence determine the goals of text mining. This stage includes also the human and technical resources required to realize the project, and examines the risks and ethical issues associated with such a project.

- **Data understanding:** This involves the process of collecting all the textual data relevant to the study and a first approximation of its content, quality, relevance,

Figure 3. Text mining tasks

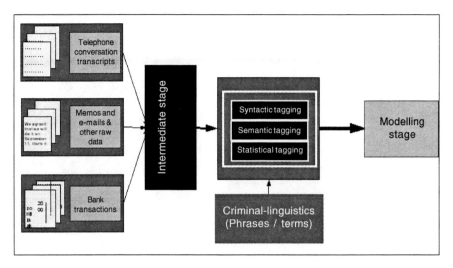

usability, and completeness. Initial exploration of the textual data is required using statistical analysis and visualization tools. As we are dealing with multiple sources, this phase ensures that appropriate textual data integration is achieved before proceeding to the next stage.

- **Data preparation:** This is a complex stage as it combines information extraction with natural language processing techniques to transform the text into an intermediate form, which can become the basis for further processing. The intermediate text will capture the important features extracted from the raw text for further analysis. Some data cleaning is involved consisting of the removal of ambiguous, redundant, and illegal characters, the removal of incorrect hyphenation, and the conversion of upper to lower case. In agreement with Hearst (1994) and Choi, Wiemer-Hastings, and Moore (2001) stemming is not applied as it has been shown to make no significant changes to the processing of the transcript and has led to some syntactically motivated inflections being placed in an incorrect equivalent class. Typical natural language processing tasks include lexical, syntactic, and semantic analysis (see Figure 3). Initially the textual data is syntactically and semantically tagged using online lexical dictionaries such as WORDNET (Fellbaum & Vossen, 1998) and part-of speech tagging tools, such as WMATRIX (Rayson, 2003) and WordStat (*WordStat 4.0*, 2004). WMATRIX can not only produce a list of significant concepts in this corpus and compute their frequency, but can also assign semantic categories to these concepts. WordStat, on the other hand, is a text analysis software used for automatic categorization of the corpus, and can uncover differences in word usage between subgroups of individuals, a very useful

Figure 4. An example of a conceptually tagged criminal conversation

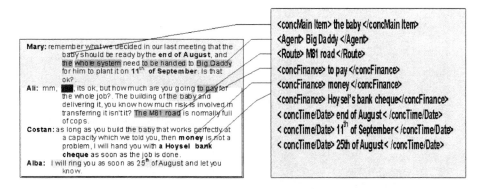

Figure 5. An example of terms used by criminals in their communication

Criminal term	Meaning
bucket, hotel	jail, prison
plastic	credit card
gatt	firearms
bull, cop, copper, fuzz, pig	uncomplimentary terms for a policeman
snitch	informant
send flowers to someone	killing someone
fishing	method used by burglars
collar, nail, apprehend, arrest, pick up, nab, cop	take into custody

feature for crime analysis. It includes a graphical tool which allows the exploration of relationships among concepts extracted from the corpus and different groups of individuals, as well as the measurement of similarity between different texts using hierarchical clustering and multidimensional scaling analysis.

The syntactic and semantic tagging help extract entities related to individuals, as well as noun phrases, which capture crime concept features, and verb phrases which represent actions and activities performed by individuals (see Figure 4). This can also capture linguistic relations such a synonymy (near synonymy, e.g., *stream* and *brook*, partial synonymy, e.g., *begin* and *start*), polysemy (a word or phrase with multiple meanings, e.g., *bank*, *bat*), hypernymy (*burglary* is a kind of *felony*), and meronymy (e.g., *No. 10* and *prime minister's office*). This tagging process is supported by the criminal linguistics glossary extracted from the corpus and semantically labelled with the help of criminal analysts, as illustrated in Figure 5.

The modelling stage applies a number of modelling techniques relevant to the project. It may include clustering techniques to classify concepts describing crime features such as event, instrument, method of working, location, time, individuals and organizations. Link analysis is used to identify specific crime concepts across document sources, and to investigate any common patterns and connections hidden in the textual data. The aim of this stage is to provide insights into the criminal activities and to discover any important associations among individuals and organizations through the analysis of crime features.

Monitoring Using an Intelligent Agent-Based System Framework

In addition to text mining, ASKARI proposes to use an intelligent agent system framework to track these patterns and connections across new incoming and existing textual data and alert analysts of potential suspicious activities. Intelligent agents can be defined as computing entities that perform user-delegated tasks autonomously. Agent-based applications have been used in a variety of applications, namely in manufacturing and telecommunications systems, air traffic control, traffic and transportation management systems, information filtering and gathering, electronic commerce, as well as in the entertainment and medical care domains (Jennings & Wooldridge, 1995). One of the most compelling applications of agent technology is their ability to assist users in coping with the information overload problem. Agent systems are a powerful medium to search, monitor and detect specific features across large corporate databases and texts on behalf of their users. As Popp et al. (2004) explain:

When doing traditional intelligence analysis, an analyst spends most of the time on the major processes broadly defined as research, analysis, and production... Analysts spend too much time doing research (searching, harvesting, reading, and preprocessing data for analysis), too much time doing production (turning analytical results into reports and briefings for the decision maker), and too little time doing analysis.

Agent technology can help improve the intelligence analysis by carrying out some of these basic activities of searching, preprocessing, and reporting. Agents can also enhance the text mining tasks, as they can perceive and react in an autonomous manner on behalf of analysts, can reason, and can communicate their observations to the analysts. In this project, the role of the agent is to make observations on a specific event or activity related to new and current textual sources, and based on these observations and its prior knowledge about specific features of a given criminal activity it is able to assess the status of this event or activity, and then determine the most appropriate action based on its belief and goal, such as whether to continue monitoring or to alert the analysts of a suspicious event, organization, or individual. As observations themselves can be often uncertain, ambiguous, vague, noisy, and/or unreliable, it is proposed to endow the agent with a Bayesian Networks model to update its hypothesis or belief as new evidence supporting a given observation emerge. The Bayesian Networks approach has found acceptance in part because of their ability to represent concisely a multivariate

Figure 6. ASKARI: Conceptual architecture

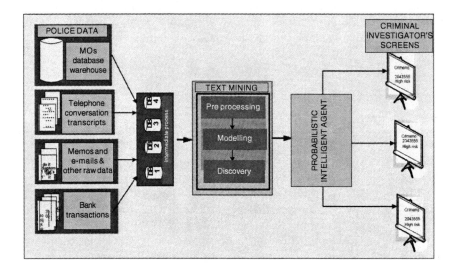

distribution by exploiting independent relations in the domain of interest. Bayesian Networks is also used as a concise graphical representation of a decision maker's probabilistic knowledge of uncertain domain. They are primarily used to update the belief of an agent when new evidence is received. This kind of probabilistic reasoning using Bayesian Networks is known as belief updating. Figure 6 describes the conceptual architecture of the ASKARI project.

The proposed approach uses patterns of human behavior to develop a model that can detect organized crime threats. These patterns originate from multisource information concept extracts, which assess the level of threat posed by a certain group of criminals. However, human behavior exhibits both systematic regularities and inherent unpredictability. In order to successfully draw on human behavior in applications such as crime prediction and alerting, a reasoning mechanism about the inherently uncertain properties of crime entities must be introduced. Tasks such as information fusion for organized crime detection and deterring require both reasoning under uncertainty and logical reasoning about discrete entities. Probability is the most applied logic for computational scientific reasoning under uncertainty (Fung, 2004). However, appropriate application of probability theory often requires logical reasoning about which variables to include and what the appropriate probabilities are, in order to maintain a semi- or a full-real-time predicting and alerting system (Sargunar, 2003). Such variables will be extracted from the text mining stages and refined after further discussions with the analysts.

Figure 7. A fictitious case scenario

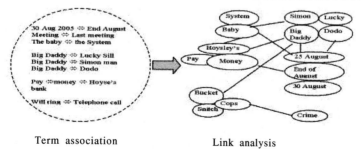

ACC. No. 018000-2020007-02			
Withdrawals Feb 05 – Sept 05	Date	Amount	Form
	12 Feb 05	5000	cash
	22 Feb 05	25000	cheque
	28 Feb 05	3000	cash
	2 May 05	35000	cheque
Deposits May 04 – Aug 05			
	19 May 04	26078	Transfer
	10 July 04	12000	cheque
	1 Sept 04	4300	cash
	11 May 05	26789	cheque
	30 Aug 05	17390	transfer
	13 Sept 05	2498	cash

Suspicious Bank Transaction

Email: *Lucky.sill@mayfair.com*

Are we meeting t'row then, the work is done, just waiting for the next action 25th August meeting We need not to fear, let work together to defeat the enemy. Clod bless

Email: *simon.man@azam.com*

25th August meeting depends very much on Dodo's telephone call otherwise it confirmed, to meet at Westend hotel. With t'row, not sure. I fear a snitch may be around and a bucket may follow

Suspicious e-mails

```
<ConcMain Item>Meeting </ConcMain Item>
<Agent>Simon Man</ Agent >
< Agent >Lucky Sill</ Agent >
< Agent >Dodo</ Agent >
< Location >Westend Hotel</ Location >
<ConcTime/Date >t'row</ ConcTime/Date >
< ConcTime/Date >25th August</ ConcTime/Date >
< ConcPhrase >Telephone call</ ConcPhrase >
< ConcPhrase >Snitch </ ConcPhrase >
< ConcPhrase >Bucket</ ConcPhrase >
< ConcURL >Email: simon.man@azam.com</ ConcURL >
< ConcURL >Email: Lucky.sill@mayfair.com</ ConcURL >
```

Mary:	remember what we decided in our last meeting that the baby should be ready by the end of August, and the whole system need to be handed to Big Daddy for him to plant it on 11th of September. Is that ok?
Ali:	mm, yes, its ok, but how much are you going to pay for the whole job? The building of the baby and delivering it, you know how much risk is involved in transferring it isn't it? The M81 road is normally full of cops.
Costan:	as long as you build the baby that works perfectly at a capacity which we told you, then money is not a problem, I will hand you with a Hoyse's bank cheque as soon as the job is done.
Alba:	I will ring you as soon as 25th of August and let you know.

Suspicious telephone coversations

```
<ConcMain Item>The baby </ConcMain Item>
<ConcActivity> Last meeting </ConcActivity>
<Agent Big Daddy</ Agent >
< Route >M81</ Route >
< ConcFinance >pay</ ConcFinance >
< ConcFinance >money</ ConcFinance >
< ConcFinance >Hoysley's Bank cheque</ ConcFinance >
< ConcTime/Date >end of August</ ConcTime/Date >
< ConcTime/Date >11th of September</ ConcTime/Date >
< ConcTime/Date >25th of August</ ConcTime/Date >
< ConcPhrase >will ring</ ConcPhrase >
< ConcPhrase >Cops</ ConcPhrase >
< ConcPhrase >whole system</ ConcPhrase >
```

30 Aug 2005 ⇔ End August
Meeting ⇔ Last meeting
The baby ⇔ the System

Big Daddy ⇔ Lucky Sill
Big Daddy ⇔ Simon man
Big Daddy ⇔ Dodo

Pay ⇔money ⇔ Hoyse's bank

Will ring ⇔ Telephone call

Term association

Link analysis

Fictitious Scenario

In this section we shall illustrate the proposed approach using a fictitious example scenario of a typical organized terrorist attack. In this example, the police and the bank are collaborating together and monitoring events of an individual. While the police are investigating its own records, the bank is monitoring suspicious financial transactions carried out by that individual over a specific period of time. What is particularly alarming in this case is the large amount of money withdrawn and deposited in this account given the modest profile of the account's owner. Communication between the bank and the police leads to further monitoring, and aided by independently received intelligence, the police are permitted to monitor telephone conversations and intercept e-mail communication involving that individual.

Text mining of transcriptions of telephone conversations, e-mails, and any other documents can lead to the discovery of correlations between various entities such as individuals, event and locations as shown in Figure 7.

Methodology

Identifying criminal behavior patterns is a complex problem. However the complexity is compounded when same criminals use different patterns for different crime activities. The mined entities can be used to produce a Bayesian Networks graphical structure (shown in Figure 8). By using these networks it is possible to identify qualitative structural relationships between entities, namely conditional, independence, cause and effect, and correlation.

The entities associated with the suspicious financial transactions in Figure 8a will be analyzed in relation to the entities extracted from the suspicious e-mail communication

Figure 8. Two Bayesian Networks fragments of suspicious activities

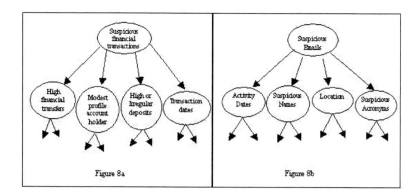

Figure 9. An example of spiral life cycle model

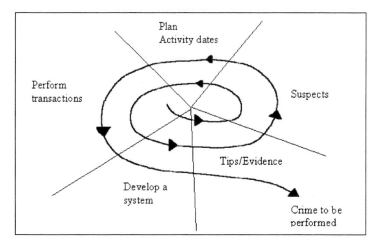

in Figure 8b revealing the various steps adopted for that particular criminal activity. Applying the well known spiral life cycle model (Pressman, 1987) on the two probability networks fragments (8a and 8b) will provide us with a systematic way of understanding the sequence of steps which describes that particular behavioural pattern (see Figure 9).

Multi-Entity Bayesian Networks (MEBN) Application

The application of traditional Bayesian Networks to crime detection and deterring may be hampered by the fact that utilizing massive amounts of evidence tends to produce arbitrarily large Bayesian Networks, which in turn generate computational complexities to analysts. Also Bayesian Networks are limited in that they are able to represent only a single fixed set of random variables, which has different evidence from problem to problem. A much more flexible representation capability is required to model human behavior in different situations. We propose the use of the MTheory developed by Laskey (Laskey, 2005) for Multi-Entity Bayesian Networks, and used in many different applications (AlGhamdi, Wright, Barbara, & Chang, 2005; Hudson, Ware, Mahoney, & Laskey, 2005; Laskey et al., 2004). An MTheory is a collection of *Bayesian Networks Fragments* that satisfy consistency criteria such that the collection specifies a probability distribution over attributes of and relationships among a collection of interrelated entities (AlGhamdi et al., 2005).

The model, we are proposing, consists of seven fragment patterns, which are used to distinguish normal patterns from criminal behaviour patterns that may pose a threat. The fragments we have identified are listed in Table 2.

Once the text mining process has extracted crime patterns from the textual data and identified clusters and associations between various crime patterns depicting criminal

Table 2. Fragment patterns

Fragment	Description
Crime Type	Nature of activity (e.g. bio-chemical attack, bomb threat, drug trafficking)
Criminal Profile	Representation of individual user profile - relevant attributes include name (and associated aliases), gender, race, residence and criminal records (e.g. type of felony and *modus operandi*)
Financial Status	Details of account (e.g. status, card number, expiry date, frequency of transactions, purchases and withdrawals)
Criminal Intention	Includes concepts that classify individual intentions as either normal or threat
Tips and key witness statements	Record tip-offs from individuals or key witness statements which can then be used to enhance the Bayesian Networks model
Target	Type of target (e.g. civilian, military, water source, livestock and crops)
Place	Geographical location of attack or likely locations of attack

behavior, these patterns can be then stored in a Bayesian Networks model which can then be used by a software agent to monitor and detect incoming and existing records. These patterns function as a trigger to the firing of a potentially suspicious node of activity as interpreted by the agent, which may then issue a warning message to the analyst. As new evidence emerges, the agent increases the probability of the corresponding suspicious node and when a certain threshold of suspicion is reached the agent sends a strong alert to the analysts.

Limitations and Future Research

Our approach has a number of limitations, which follow:

- **Differentiating suspicious e-mail from spam:** This is a complex problem, and is beyond the scope of this research. Our main goal is to advise and alert the security officials of suspicious acts, and support decision-making. There are many different technologies being developed in the area of spam filtering, the most common used and effective technology includes machine learning algorithms, namely naïve Bayes and neural network, which are able to block illegitimate lists and can improve the efficiency of challenge response systems (Goodman, 2003). There are a number of issues still needed to be addressed before a spam filter system becomes fully viable; these include aspects related to the effect of attribute-set size and feature selection, the training corpus size, stop lists, and lemmatization in particular

- **Data format and style:** This may hamper the performance of the system, for example with e-mail and text messages where people communicate using symbols like "@" to represent the preposition "*a*", or "u" to represent the pronoun "*yo*". This is a complex issue, as the data format and style are constantly evolving with time, and so future research would require a constant update of glossaries and dictionaries to store the new emerging styles and formats. Current systems rely on manually constructed patterns and styles, a system that could learn these patterns automatically would present significant advantages yet poses considerable challenges. There are ongoing systems developed to mine text messages (Eagle & Pentland, 2005) and e-mails (Marakami, Nagao, & Takeda, 2001), which could contribute to our project.

- **Data availability:** Our proposed system requires a large amount of training data, which is often difficult to access. Data from intelligence agencies and police authorities is confidential. Also, tapping individuals' telephone or e-mail conversations involve ethical issues, which need to be resolved. The difficulty in obtaining training data may limit the performance of the agent-based system to alert security officials on an imminent sensitive crime plot.

Conclusions

This chapter has provided an overview of the potential of the text mining technology in assisting law enforcement agencies in their monitoring and anticipation of criminal activities. Text mining is particularly suited to analyzing large volumes of textual data sources and can provide analysts with a valuable tool to sift through huge amounts of records and discover any useful patterns, any hidden clues, and any meaningful associations between individuals, organizations and crime incidents. The ASKARI project described here is an attempt at combining text mining with agent technology with the view to supporting analysts with new incoming textual data and also to provide a watchful eye on criminal activities.

References

Abraham, T., & Vel, O. (2002). Investigative profiling with computer forensic log data and association rules. In *Proceedings of the ICDM-2002 IEEE International Conference on Data Mining* (pp. 11-18). Maebashi City, Japan.

Adderley, R., & Musgrove, P. (1999). Data mining at the West Midlands police: A study of bogus official burglaries. In *Proceedings of BCS Special Group Expert Systems, ES99* (pp. 191-203). London: Springer-Verlag.

Agrawal, R., Imielinski, T., & Swami, A. (1993). Mining association rules between items in large databases. In *Proceedings of the International Conference on Management of Data (ACM SIGMOD'93)* (pp. 207-216). Washington, DC.

Ahonen, H., Heinonen, O., Klemettinen, M., & Verkamo, A. (1997). *Applying data mining techniques in text analysis.* Technical report. University of Helsinki, Department of Computer Science.

AlGhamdi, G., Wright, E., Barbara, D., & Chang, K. (2005). Modelling insider behavior using multi-entity bayesian networks. In *Proceedings of the 10th Annual Command and Control Research and Technology Symposium.*

Berry, M., & Linoff, G. (1997). *Data mining techniques: For marketing, sales, and customer support.* John Wiley & Sons.

Brown, D., & Gunderson, L. (2001). Using clustering to discover the preferences of computer criminals. *IEEE Transactions on Systems, Man and Cybernetics, Part A: Systems and Human, 31*(4), 311-318.

Chapman, P., Clinton, J., Kerber, R., Khabaza, T., Reinartz, T., Shearer, C., et al. (2003). *CRISP-DM 1.0 step-by-step data mining guide.* Retrieved August 10, 2003, from http://www.crisp-dm.org/

Chau, M., Xu, J., & Chen, H. (2002). Extracting meaningful entities from police narrative reports. In *Proceedings of the National Conference for Digital Government Research* (pp. 271-275). Los Angeles, California.

Chen, H., Chung, W., Xu, J., Wang, G., Qin, Y., & Chau, M. (2004). Crime data mining: A general framework and some examples. *IEEE Computer, 37*(4), 50-56.

Chibelushi, C., Sharp, B., & Salter, A. (2004). A text mining approach to tracking elements of decision making: A pilot study. In *Proceedings of 1st International Workshop on Natural Language Understanding and Cognitive Science* (pp. 51-63). Portugal.

Choi, F., Wiemer-Hastings, P., & Moore, J. (2001). Latent semantic analysis for text segmentation. In *Proceedings of the 6th Conference on Empirical Methods in Natural Language Processing(EMNLP)* (pp.109-117).

Drewes, B. (2002). Integration of text and data mining. In A. Zanasi, C. A. Brebbia, N.F.F. Ebecken, & P. Melli (Eds.), *Data mining III* (pp. 288-298). UK: WIT.

Eagle, N., & Pentland, A. (n.d.). *Reality mining: Sensing complex social systems.* Retrieved May 21, 2005, from http://reality.media.mit.edu/pdfs/realitymining.pdf

Fawcett, T., & Provost, F. (1997). Adaptive fraud detection. *Data Mining and Knowledge Discovery, 1*(3), 291-316.

Fayyad, U., Piatetsky-Shapiro, G., & Smyth, P. (1996). Knowledge discovery and data mining: Towards a unifying framework. In *Proceedings of the 2nd International Conference of Knowledge Discovery and Data Mining (KDD96)* (pp. 24-26). Portland, OR: AAI Press.

Fellbaum, C., & Vossen, P. (Eds.). (1998). *A lexical database of English: The mother of all Word Nets. Special issue of computers and the humanities* (pp. 209-220). Dordrecht, Holland: Kluwer.

Fung, F. (2004). *Predicate logic-based assembly of situation-specific.* Navy STTR FY2004. Retrieved February 26, 2005, from http://www.navysbir.com/04/65.htm

Goodman, J. (2003). *Spam filtering: Text classification with an adversary.* Invited Talk at Workshop on Operational Text Classification Systems, ACM KDD.

Gunderson, L. (2002). Using data mining and judgment analysis to construct a predictive model of crime. In *Proceedings of the IEEE International Conference on Systems, Man and Cybernetics* (p. 5).

Hauck, R., Atabakhsh, H., Angvasith, P., Gupta, H., & Chen, H. (2002). Using coplink to analyse criminal-justice data. *IEEE Computer, 35*(3), 30-37.

Hearst, M. (1994). Multi-paragraph segmentation of expository text. In Proceedings of *the 32nd Annual Meeting of the Association for Computational Linguistics* (pp. 9-16). Las Cruces, New Mexico.

Hearst, M. (1997, July). *Text mining: Issues, techniques, and the relationship to information access.* Presentation notes for UW/MS Workshop on Data Mining.

Hudson, L., Ware, B., Mahoney, S., & Laskey, K. (2005). *An application of bayesian networks to anti-terrorism risk management for military planners.* George Mason University Homeland Security and Military Transformation Laboratory. Retrieved May 12, 2005, from http://ite.gmu.edu/~klaskey/papers/Antiterrorism.pdf

Jennings, N., & Wooldridge, M. (1995). Applying agent technology. *Applied Artificial Intelligence, 9*(4), 351-361.

Kenyon, H. (2003). *Researchers leave terrorists nowhere to hide.* Retrieved October 20, 2004, from http://www.afcea.org/signal/articles/anmviewer.asp?a=113&z=31

Laskey, K. (2005). *First-order bayesian logic.* Retrieved May 11, 2005, from http://ite.gmu.edu/~klaskey/papers/Laskey_MEBN_Logic.pdf

Laskey, K., AlGhamdi, G., Wang, X., Barbara, D., Shackelford, T. Wright, E., et al. (2004). *Detecting threatening behaviour using bayesian networks.* BRIMS 04. Retrieved January 2005, from http://ite.gmu.edu/~klaskey/papers/BRIMS04_Insider Threat.pdf

Loh, S., Wives, I., & Oliveira, J. P. d. (2000). Concept-based knowledge discovery in text extracted from the Web. *ACM SIGKDD Explorations Newsletter, 2*(1), 29-39.

Marakami, A., Nagao, K., & Takeda, K. (2001). *Discussion mining: Knowledge discovery from online discussion records.* Retrieved May 5, 2005, from http://hal2001.itakura.toyo.ac.jp/~chiekon/nlpxml/murakami.pdf

Mena, J. (2003). *Investigative data mining for security and criminal detection.* USA: Butterworth-Heinemann.

Organised Crime in South Africa. (1998). Monograph 28, Retrieved July 7, 2004, from http://www.iss.org.za/Pubs/Monographs/No28/Definitions.html

Patterns of Global Terrorism-2003(2004). Retrieved July 7, 2004, from http://www.globalsecurity.org/

Popp, R., Armour, T., Senator, T., & Numrych, K. (2004). Countering terrorism through information technology. *ACM, 47*(3), 36-43.

Pressman, R. (1987). *Software engineering : A practitioner's approach* (2nd ed.). USA: McGraw-Hill.

Rayson, P. (2003). *Matrix: A statistical method and software tool for linguistic analysis through corpus comparison.* Ph.D. thesis, Lancaster University, UK.

Rayson, P., Sharp, B., Alderson, A., Cartmell, J., Chibelushi, C., Clarke, R., et al. (2003, April 23-26). Tracker: A framework to support reducing rework through decision management. In *Proceedings of 5th International Conference on Enterprise Information Systems ICEIS2003* (pp. 344-351). Angers, France.

Sandford, D. (2004). *Crime fighting for the 21st century.* Retrieved January 2005, from http://news.bbc.co.uk/1/hi/uk/3477261.stm

Sargunar, V. (2003). An introduction to bayesian networks for multi-agent systems. In *Proceedings of the Intelligent Systems Laboratory (ISLAB) Workshop.*

Sullivan, D. (2001). *Document warehousing and text mining.* John Wiley & Sons.

Tan, A. H. (1999). Text mining: The state of the art and the challenges. In *Proceedings of the Pacific Asia Conference on Knowledge Discovery and Data Mining PAKDD'99 Workshop on Knowledge Discovery from Advanced Databases* (pp. 65-70). Kyoto, Japan.

WordStat 4.0. (2004). Retrieved February 2, 2005, from http://www.kovcomp.co.uk/wordstart/

Chapter IX

Basic Steganalysis Techniques for the Digital Media Forensics Examiner

Sos S. Agaian, University of Texas, USA

Benjamin M. Rodriguez, Air Force Institute of Technology, USA

Abstract

This chapter focuses on the development of digital forensic steganalysis tools/methods through analysis and evaluation of the most popular "sample pair" steganalysis techniques—the key concept in cyber crime—for the digital media forensics examiner, specializing in the analysis, identification, and interpretation of concealed digital evidence. Success and proper implementation of a digital forensic steganalysis system is dependent of several necessary steps. The basic steps are to describe and implement a new generation of steganalysis systems applicable for various embedding methods in order to allow efficient, accurate, low-cost, and fast digital forensic analysis; and to make these methods applicable for automatic detection of steganographic information within noisy network environments while striving to provide a satisfactory performance in comparison with present technology. All efforts will allow the final goal to be reached which is the development of a digital forensic steganalysis system to aid law enforcement agencies involved in the field of cyber crime investigation. The presented techniques will be based on the statistics of sample pairs (the basic unit), rather than individual samples, which are very sensitive to least significant bit embedding. Particularly, in this chapter we discuss the process and necessary considerations inherent in the development of steganalysis methods applied for problems of reliable detection, estimation length, and localization of hidden data within various forms/ models of digital images.

Introduction

The ever-expanding growth of digital networks, the dwindling cost of computers, CDs, DVDs, digital cameras, digital devices, and the technological efficiency of digital transmission have made digital media an increasingly popular alternative to conventional analog media. Whether expensive stand-alone equipment or the economically manufactured units commonly incorporated into wireless devices, digital media/imaging is becoming prevalent throughout the Internet and data networks. The Internet has its positive sides. It is a commonplace containing billions of bits; the difficult challenge is discovering hidden information within these bits. The negatives are that the enormous onset of various digital media also gives rise to wide-ranging opportunities for mass piracy of copyrighted material, that is, "criminal communication/transmission" of information, and a multitude of windows facilitating malicious intent of ever-expanding technology.

New technologies and new applications bring the latest threats, and force us to invent new protection mechanisms. Developing digital technologies and then adapting them to benefit from forensic analysis techniques would be an irrational and unfruitful approach. Every few years, computer security has to re-invent itself. As a result of such, there is a critical necessity in law enforcement for an assurance in the reliability of available computer forensic tools. Law enforcement is in perpetual competition with criminals in the application of digital technologies, requiring constant development of new forensic tools to systematically search digital systems for pertinent evidence.

One area of *forensic science* specializes in the analysis, identification, and interpretation of concealed digital evidence. An annual report on high technology crime (The High Technology Crime Advisory Committee) "High Technology Crime in California" http://www.ocjp.ca.gov/publications/pub_htk1.pdf lists nine common types of computer crime: criminal communications, fraud, hacking, electronic payments, gambling and pornography, harassment, intellectual property offenses, viruses, and pedophilia.

In Johnson, Duric, and Jajodia (2000) and Johnson and Jajodia (1998a) computer forensic investigations is described as the analysis and investigation of digital information. There are numerous methods used to conceal the existence of malicious data that could pose a threat to digital forensic analysts. In the realm of cyber-warfare, the analyst must consider a much broader scope of information that includes activities of investigation and analysis on attacks and intrusions of systems. The forensic activities may include analyzing audit logs, intrusion detection in the computer and communication networks, locating relevant files and data to the investigation, obtaining data from encrypted or deleted files, and possibly even recovering systems after attacks. It is not enough that the investigator possess tools and techniques for handling password-protected files, but they must also be involved in locating and recovering data hidden within seemingly innocuous methods. There will always be a need for covert communications, therefore steganography will continue to develop and computer forensics must be able to meet the demand. With the vast amount of tools that are available to investigators for handling a broad range of data analysis, they must continually evolve to address the constant change used by criminals in their efforts to conceal or destroy information. The systems and steganalysis techniques used to recover seemingly destroyed information will be instrumental and essential for authorities engaged in computer forensics, digital traffic analysis, and cyber-warfare.

Digital forensics is a relatively new science, which has expanded to include forensics of all digital technologies. For example, it was stated in the *International Journal of Digital Evidence* (2002), "System challenges facing digital forensic analysts in a growing field of data secure transmission encompass the task of gathering evidentiary data when presented with volumes of digital files, a number of which may possibly contain hidden information." One of the basic parts of digital forensics is steganalysis.

Modern steganography (literally "covered writing" in Greek) is undetectable to an external observer: it is a secure communication of information by embedding a secret-message within a "cover" message. The primary goals of a digital steganographic system are: (a) to hide information in undetectable way both perceptually and statistically in a digital media and (b) to achieve high security and high capacity. The question arises, where can digital information be hidden? Digital data can be hidden almost anywhere on the Internet or any network. Digital steganography has evolved through theoretical study of secure communications and is currently an active research area. This science may provide some very useful and commercially important functions in the digital world. A specialized kind of steganography, digital watermarking, addresses copyright protection and intellectual property rights that ultimately may be used to identify or track digital media. Though both are used in information security, steganography and cryptography ("secret writing") are very distinct in nature. Steganography is used primarily when the very existence of a communication signal is to be kept covert. On the other hand, cryptography is used to hide the meaning of a message, not the fact that one is communicating. Ultimately, both concepts may be combined in order to simultaneously realize the benefits of both. With the use of the appropriate embedding tool, information can be secretly embedded into various digital media and sent secretly without exposing the hidden data. Figure 1 shows a basic method of steganographic system used in digital audio, imaging, and video.

Note that thorough understanding of steganography will add to the versatility and quality of the detection capabilities in the resultant forensic analysis system. The ability to actively detect and counter attack steganographic sources is an important goal in establishing the protection of various network infrastructures. One aspect of digital crime is the existence of computer warfare. In his thesis, Cochran (2000) investigates the feasibility of steganographic virus attacks. In his analysis, "The results indicate that steganography tools are not conducive to be sole attack weapons. However, the tools combined with other applications could be used to automatically extract the hidden information with minimal user intervention."

Recently Lathrop (2000) in his thesis investigated the possibility of virus attacks assisted through steganographic techniques. He finds that "The use of a separate engine

Figure 1. Basic steganography system

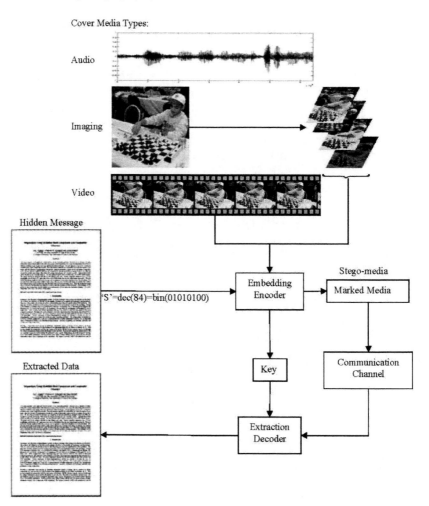

followed by an HTML-based electronic mail message containing a photographic image with a steganographic embedded virus or other payload is a vulnerable attack if implemented without the proper environment variables in place." It is impossible to know how widespread the use of steganography is by criminals and terrorists (Hosmer & Hyde, 2003). Today's knowledge of the widespread use of steganography, however, may not even matter. The use of steganography is certain to increase and will be a growing hurdle for law enforcement and counterterrorism activities. Ignoring the significance of steganography because of the lack of statistics is "security through denial" and not a viable defensive strategy. Therefore, forensic examiners must be provided with practical methods for identifying and recovering steganographic communications.

Steganalysis is the art of discovering hidden data in stego media which is contrary to steganography. In the following, we present an investigation of the process and necessary considerations inherent in the development of methods applied for the detection and localization of hidden data within various forms of digital media. In order to develop efficient steganalysis methods for detecting steganographic information, there must first be an immersive investigation and evaluation of existing steganography methods. One must take into consideration the effects on statistical characteristics and visual properties within the cover media both before and after a secret message has been inserted. It is clear, that the steganalysis techniques must receive derivation from a foundation of general detection and estimation theory, along with requiring a thorough understanding of statistical and visual properties of the digital media and creating the "signatures" to associate with individual embedding methods thus facilitating in the process of identifying the method applied when a stego bearing message is encountered by the detection process.

In Section 2, we describe the basic structure of a digital forensics steganalysis system used for the detection of steganographic content. In Section 3, we describe in detail the steganalysis system's individual components, primarily the steganography detection methods specifically applied for spatial domain, palette based and transform domain digital imagery.

Digital Forensic Steganalysis System

In Figure 2, a block diagram is presented showing the general structure of the first stage in digital forensic steganalysis. Stage 1, steganalysis, involves the thorough investigation of existing, emerging, and newly created steganography methods (see Figure 2). This understanding allows for a system of steganalysis implementations which may be constructed consisting of both universal detection methods and targeted methods. Universal detection methods are those which are formulated to detect over a broad range of steganography techniques. Targeted steganalysis techniques are specifically tailored to identify a specific steganographic approach; some of these methods are derived in the spatial domain and others in the transform domain. Stage 1 in summation is the overall detection process, identifying suspicious files. Once identified, the gathering of steganographic data takes place, preparing the media for further analysis.

The final goal involves the development and evaluation of a steganography detection system capable of implementing methods created in Stage 2 (see Figure 3). The system is to be compatible with existing hardware and software platforms, incorporating innovative solutions used to validate legal evidence in investigations of possible criminal activities for digital forensic analysts. This system is to be adaptive to continually changing technologies of steganographic tools used for maliciously intent. In addition, various well-known and newly emerging digital forensic steganalysis techniques may be incorporated with this system.

In combination with the gathered steganographic data from the first stage (see Figure 2), characteristics about the stego media, cover media, embedding procedure, or a combi-

Figure 2. Detection of concealed digital evidence

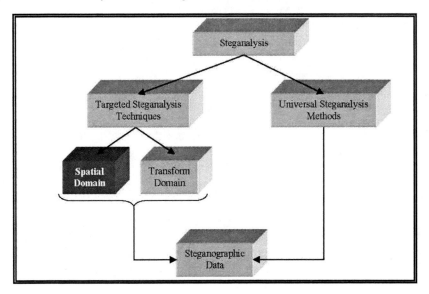

Stage I: Stego-only implies that there is no knowledge of the original carrier. Only the stego-carrier with hidden information is available for analysis.

Figure 3. Digital forensics block diagram

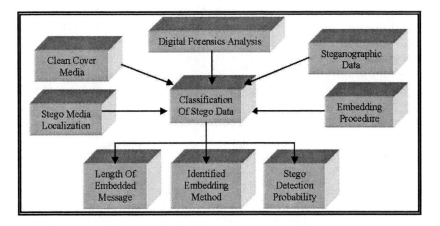

Stage II: Analysis, identification and interpretation of concealed digital evidence. (To determine the size of the stego message embedded, the steganographic method used to insert the information, and establish an overall probability of the accuracy of the conclusion)

nation of the three may be used for localization, identification, and interpretation of communication digital evidence (see Figure 3). Localization helps solve several problems for forensic science such as: (a) estimation of the embedded method signature and (b) minimization of the encryption time (see details in Stego Sensitivity Measure section). The steganography data inserted within cover media associated with each embedding procedure are used to impose a classification process on the suspected media. The classification refines the analysis into discerning an embedded message length, the embedding method used, and the probability of an accurate detection.

ILook Investigator© http://www.ilook-forensics.org/ "is a forensic analysis tool used by thousands of law enforcement labs and investigators around the world for the investigation of forensic images created by many different imaging utilities." Unfortunately, there is the lack of the ability to detect and localize the actual stego information.

As part of the digital forensic steganalysis system several detection methods are described in the following steganalysis section. We describe Raw Quick Pairs developed by Fridrich, Du, and Long (2000). A pixel comparison is shown which helps localize steganographic content by Agaian, Rodriguez, and Dietrich (2004). We also describe RS steganalysis developed by Fridrich, Goljan, and Du (2001b). A new stego sensitivity measure is presented for use for steganalysis, which focuses on the following problems: detection and localization of stego informative regions within digital clean and noisy images developed by Agaian et al. (2004). The new approach is based on a new sample pairs pixel comparison and a new complexity algorithm. The stego sensitivity measure shows that and image can be divided into ideal detection areas and ideal embedding areas.

Steganalysis

This section in steganalysis discusses the process and necessary considerations inherent in the development of methods applied for the detection and localization of hidden data within various forms/models of digital images. The section attempts to understand the two primary investigation techniques in digital forensics: to gain an understanding of detection methods and to investigate and develop new spatial domain techniques used to determine if an image contains hidden information, by using statistics gathered from the images.

Steganalysis has many challenging tasks with accuracy, efficiency, and destruction in detection. Destruction of the hidden information is the simpler of the tasks; this may be easily accomplished by introducing simple modifications into the cover media.

Steganalysis techniques can be classified in a similar way as cryptanalysis methods, largely based on how much prior information is known as follows (Curran & Bailey, 2003; Johnson & Jajodia, 1998b):

- **Steganography-only attack:** The steganography media is the only item available for analysis.

- **Known-carrier attack:** The carrier and steganography media are both available for analysis.

- **Known-message attack:** The hidden message is known.

- **Chosen-steganography attack:** The steganography media and algorithm are both known.

- **Known-steganography attack:** The carrier and steganography media, as well as the steganography algorithm, are known.

Steganography-only attacks involve the detection of hidden information based on observing some data transfer, while having no assumptions of the steganography algorithm applied. Steganography detection is generally sufficient if the purpose is evidence gathering related to a past crime, although destruction and/or alteration of the hidden information might also be legitimate law enforcement goals during an on-going investigation of criminal or terrorist groups. In order to be effective at steganalysis, the technique must not depend on prior knowledge of the embedding method, must not depend on having an original duplicate of the image and must have the ability to localize the hidden information in an effort to aid in the decryption process, but supplemental information can be used for a more accurate forensic analysis. In recent years, several different steganalysis techniques have been proposed in literature, addressing the forensic analyst's requirements. Many of these techniques involve a simple method of signature matching of common steganographic toolkit. More principled approaches applied towards steganalysis were presented in various publications. Most of them were based on *pixel comparison* approaches as well as color palette comparisons (Callinan & Kemick, 2005; Chandramouli, 2002; Farid, 2001; Farid & Lyu, 2003; Fridrich & Goljan, 2002a; Fridrich, 2001b; Johnson & Jajodia, 1998b; Provos & Honeyman, 2001; Westfeld & Pfitzman, 1999). They have provided considerable detection accuracy for specific embedding techniques as in Chandramouli and Memon (2001), Fridrich, Goljan, and Hogea (2002b), Fridrich (2003), Fridrich, Goljan, and Hogea (2002c), and Provos (2003). *Current limitations of these algorithms include the inability to localize the areas of steganographic content in an image, inability to increase the detection accuracy, difficulty in detection (in general) on grayscale images and processing time consumption problems.*

Targeted Methods: Spatial Domain

Targeted spatial domain methods have been designed for specific algorithms—good detection accuracy for the specific technique and ineffective for new techniques. This section presents several well-known and novel steganalysis techniques which are pixel-based comparisons. New methods have been developed with the ability to localize steganographic content while minimizing the likelihood of false detection. As a result of such, the new "steganalysis" techniques presented not only receive derivation from a foundation of general detection theory, but also incorporate a thorough understanding of the properties and statistical aspects of natural digital imagery.

Figure 4. Block diagram of detection methods on various image color models

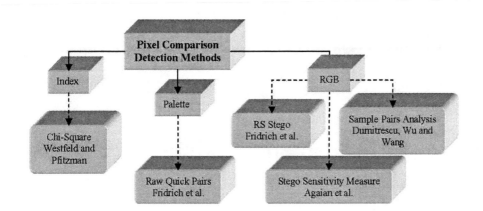

There are a wide variety of tools that are used to embed information using least significant bit algorithms. The large array of widely available tools has spawned the need for least significant bit-based steganalysis methods and algorithms. A site containing a list of many existing steganalysis programs may be found at www.StegoArchive.com (2003). Several steganalysis techniques which address compressed and uncompressed image detection have been developed, for example Chanramouli and Memon (2001), Dumitresctu, Wu, and Wang (2003), Fridrich et al. (2000), Fridrich, Golan, and Du (2001a), Johnson and Jajodia (1998b), and Westfeld and Pfitzman (1999) just to name a few. These approaches evaluate the entire digital image by comparing the adjacent pixels in a specific region, one pixel at a time, or by evaluating the color palette. In general the adjacent pixels comparison detection methods can be classified as shown in Figure 4.

The pixel comparison and color palette comparison approaches have provided remarkable detection accuracy for embedding methods. Existing problems of these implementations include the inability to localize areas of steganographic content in an image along with extensive process time problems.

Steganography localization as shown by Agaian et al. (2004) is making detection of hidden information in specific areas an important aspect of steganalysis leading to the following problem domains: detection, localization, fast disabling, extraction, and puzzlement of steganographic information within a digital cover media. Spatial domain detection methods will be used in this section to give an understanding of the detection process. The detection of steganographic content has many challenges with accuracy and efficiency in detection. The accuracy and efficiency in detection are the primary objectives in the majority of steganalysis implementations. With the general steganalysis method, as displayed in Figure 5, the question arises, "How does one develop a detection method that is both efficient and blind?", without targeting an embedding method.

Figure 5. General targeting steganalysis approach

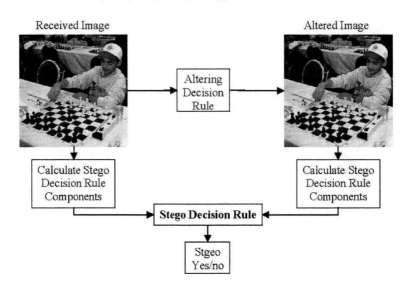

Raw Quick Pairs

In this section we present a steganalysis technique that detects the presence of a steganography message randomly spread in a color-image which has been developed by, Fridrich et al. (2000). The basic idea behind this algorithm is to inspect one or possibly more images for statistical artifacts due to message embedding in color images using the LSB method. This method presents a steganalysis technique based on analyzing the structure of the set of unique colors in the RGB color cube. It was observed that the number of unique colors for true-color images is typically significantly smaller than the number of pixels in the image. The ratio of the number of unique colors to the number of pixels ranges from roughly 1:2 for high quality scans in BMP format to 1:6 or even lower for JPEG images or for typical video grabs (Fridrich et al., 2000). In addition, they investigate the probability of both false detections and missing a secret message.

For presenting the method Raw Quick Pairs method we bring some necessary definitions. We will use the definitions and notation outlined by Fridrich et al. (2000) ensuring ease of understanding both materials for the reader.

Notations – Let:

- I be a color $M \times N$ image.
- U is the number of unique colors in the image I.

- P is the number of close color pairs between the unique colors within an image palette. For example, if is P the two sets of colors (R_1, G_1, B_1) and (R_2, G_2, B_2) then they are considered close if $|R_1\text{-}R_2| \leq 1$, $|G_1\text{-}G_2| \leq 1$, and $|B_1\text{-}B_2| \leq 1$.

- The number of all pairs of colors defined by : $\dbinom{U}{2} = \dfrac{U!}{2!(U-2)!}$ (3.2.1)

- R is the ratio between the number of closest pairs of colors and all pairs of colors:

$$R = \frac{P}{\dbinom{U}{2}},$$ (3.2.2)

It is easy to see that the ratio R is an estimation of the number of close colors within an image I.

- Denote the corresponding quantities for the new image after embedding the test message as U', P' and R'. Where, R' is the ratio of the number of closest pairs of colors and the number of all pairs of colors after embedding. The corresponding quantities for the new image after randomly altering pixel within the least significant bit are used to calculate the new ratio R':

$$R' = \frac{P'}{\dbinom{U'}{2}},$$ (3.2.3)

Figure 6. Raw quick pairs block diagram

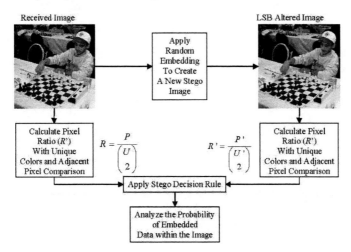

The basic block scheme of Raw Quick Pairs can be represented by Figure 6.

For comparison purposes another image is crated with the use of random least significant bit embedding. The number of bits to be altered are of size $\alpha 3MN$ ($\alpha = 0.01 - 0.5$) bits. Upon completion of embedding, the number of unique colors and the number of close pairs P' are calculated.

This observation leads to a relative comparison between the ratio R and R' as the decision rule as (see more details in [Fridrich et al., 2000]):

1.   The number of close color pairs relative to the number of all possible pairs of colors is smaller than an image containing an existing message.

2.   It has been noticed that the two ratios are approximately equal, $R \cong R'$, if the image contains a large hidden message. This means that if the image contains a large embedded message, embedding another message does not significantly modify the ratio R'.

3.   The secret message size is too small and the method will not be able to distinguish images with and without steganographic information.

4.   The ratio R' increases significantly if the image does not contain a secret message or they expect $R' > R$.

$$\text{Decision Rule} = \begin{cases} \text{if } R < R' \text{ then does not contain a secret message} \\ \text{if } R \cong R' \text{ image has a large message hidden inside} \end{cases}$$

Reliability of Decision: The reliability of decision means the estimation of the probability of falsely detecting a suspicious image. This subsection determines the probability of detecting a percentage of steganographic content within the image. The prediction is determined with a threshold that is derived for each percentage of embedded information within the LSB of an image. If, for example, image has been altered with 5% stego, thresholds are derived for the probability of each percentage of stego.

It is assumed the Gaussian peak $N(\mu,\sigma)$ with probability density $f_{\mu,\sigma}$ does not change with the message size. This corresponds with the probability density function of the ratio $\frac{R'}{R}$ for image set containing no messages. Assuming that a Gaussian distribution $N(\mu(s),\sigma(s))$ with a probability density $f_{\mu(s),\sigma(s)}$ corresponds to images with secret messages and it changes with the secret message sizes:

$$f_{\mu,\sigma} = \frac{1}{\sqrt{2\pi\sigma^2}} e^{-\frac{(x-\mu)^2}{2\sigma^2}} \tag{3.2.4}$$

The authors claim that:

$$f_{\mu(s),\sigma(s)} = \frac{1}{\sqrt{2\pi\sigma(s)^2}} e^{-\frac{(x-\mu(s))^2}{2\sigma(s)^2}} \qquad (3.2.5)$$

$\mu > \mu(s)$ for all s.

$$P(\mathrm{I}) = \int_{\infty}^{Th(s)} \frac{e^{-\frac{(x-\mu)^2}{2\sigma^2}}}{\sqrt{2\pi\sigma^2}} dx \quad : \text{The error of missing a secret message.} \qquad (3.2.6)$$

$$P(\mathrm{II}) = \int_{Th(s)}^{\infty} \frac{e^{-\frac{(x-\mu(s))^2}{2\sigma^2(s)}}}{\sqrt{2\pi\sigma(s)^2}} dx \quad : \text{The error of missing a secret message.} \qquad (3.2.7)$$

The threshold $Th(s)$ is defined by $P(\mathrm{I}) = P(\mathrm{II})$. Solving this equation, see Fridrich et al. (2000) for more details, the threshold was found as follows:

$$Th(s) = \left(\frac{\mu\sigma(s) + \mu(s)\sigma}{(\sigma + \sigma(s))} \right)$$

Computer Simulation: We performed numerical experimentation with an image database of 200 color images TIFF and RAW images taken with a Nikon D100 and Canon EOS Digital Rebel. The images were obtained using the two digital cameras and were stored as uncompressed TIFF. The detection method was written using Matlab.

Table 1. Results for test message size 5% (Fridrich, 2000)

Altered Bits within the LSB	Threshold $Th(s)$
1%	1.1606
5%	1.0935
10%	1.0506
20%	1.0206
50%	1.0059
100%	1.0028

Figure 7. The basic steps of Raw Quick Pairs

Algorithm for Raw Quick Pairs

Input: Digital color image.

Step 1: Generate a new image with randomly altered bit.

Step 2: Extract the unique colors from both images.

Step 3: Count the total number of unique colors and pixels that match for each image.

Step 4: Calculate the ratio between the unique colors and pixel comparison values is defined yielding the relative number of close colors within an image.

Step 5: Calculate the reliability estimation for each percentage.

Output: The probability of detected steganographic content.

Figure 8. Shows some images that have a ratio, R'/R, grater than or equal to 1: (a) jungle, (b) night view, (c) peppers, (d) pink flower, (e) rock

(a)   (b)   (c)   (d)   (e)

Figure 9. Shows some images that do not meet the ratio, R'/R, requirement of being grater than or equal to 1: (a) Blue Coast, (b) Chess Match, (c) Fisherman, (d) Golden Gate, (e) Trolley

(a)   (b)   (c)   (d)   (e)

Figures 8 and 9 present images with various ratio requirements.

Tables 2 through 6 show the reliability percentage of detection of a secret message within an image. The N/A (not applicable) corresponds to an image that does not have the required ratio greater than or equal to 1.

Table 2. Raw Quick Pairs detection of clean images

Cover Image	Reliability Estimation						
	0%	1%	5%	10%	20%	50%	100%
ChessMatch512x512	N/A	N/A	N/A	N/A	N/A	N/A	N/A
Fisherman512x512	N/A	N/A	N/A	N/A	N/A	N/A	N/A
GoldenGate512X512	N/A	N/A	N/A	N/A	N/A	N/A	N/A
Rock512X512	90%	9.7%	<1	<1	<1	0.0	0.0
Trolley512X512	N/A	N/A	N/A	N/A	N/A	N/A	N/A

Table 3. Raw Quick Pairs detection of added Gaussian Noise

Gaussian Variance	Cover Image	Reliability Estimation						
		0%	1%	5%	10%	20%	50%	100%
0.05	ChessMatch512x512	18.4	14.0	48.4	19.1	<1	<1	0.0
0.05	Fisherman512x512	4.8	1.6	<1	<1	7.0	87.0	<1
0.05	GoldenGate512X512	9.7	3.4	<1	<1	85.0	1.0	<1
0.05	Rock512X512	3.4	1.3	<1	<1	94.6	0.0	0.0
0.05	Trolley512X512	13.3	4.5	<1	<1	59.2	22.5	<1

Table 4. Raw Quick Pairs detection of added Salt & Pepper Noise

Salt & Pepper Percentage	Cover Image	Reliability Estimation						
		0%	1%	5%	10%	20%	50%	100%
5%	ChessMatch512x512	N/A	N/A	N/A	N/A	N/A	N/A	N/A
5%	Fisherman512x512	N/A	N/A	N/A	N/A	N/A	N/A	N/A
5%	GoldenGate512X512	N/A	N/A	N/A	N/A	N/A	N/A	N/A
5%	Rock512X512	73.4	26.6	0.0	0.0	0.0	0.0	0.0
5%	Trolley512X512	N/A	N/A	N/A	N/A	N/A	N/A	N/A

Table 5. Raw Quick Pairs detection of 5% embedded information

Cover Image	Reliability Estimation						
	0%	1%	5%	10%	20%	50%	100%
ChessMatch512x512	N/A	N/A	N/A	N/A	N/A	N/A	N/A
Fisherman512x512	N/A	N/A	N/A	N/A	N/A	N/A	N/A
GoldenGate512X512	N/A	N/A	N/A	N/A	N/A	N/A	N/A
Rock512X512	15.5%	7.8%	4.2%	72.0%	<1%	<1%	0.0%
Trolley512X512	N/A	N/A	N/A	N/A	N/A	N/A	N/A

Table 6. Raw Quick Pairs detection of clean images from Figure 2

Cover Image	Reliability Estimation						
	0%	1%	5%	10%	20%	50%	100%
Jungle 512x512	30.6%	8.7%	<1%	<1%	1.1%	59.3%	1.0%
Night View 512x512	7.2%	2.1%	<1%	<1%	1.0%	90.0%	<1%
Peppers 512X512	5.9%	2.0%	<1%	<1%	90.0.%	<1%	0.0%
Pink Flower 512X512	6.8%	2.2%	<1%	<1%	12.9%	77.9%	6.8%
Rock 512X512	90%	9.7%	<1%	<1%	<1%	0.0%	0.0%

Through experimental results it was suggested that reliable detection of a secret message is possible when the hidden message is embedded within the LSB of the image. The number of unique colors increases and/or decreases the reliability of detection. The experimentation written in Fridrich et al. (2000) stated that some of the high quality scans stored as lossless images may contain an extremely high number of unique colors resulting in detection technique becoming unreliable. This problem occurs when the number of unique colors is more than one half of the number of pixels.

The main limitations are: (1) If the size of the embedded message on the digital image is significantly small the Raw Quick Pairs algorithm is unable to detect a hidden message; (2) The method is applied to digital color images with unique colors in the image less than 30% and greater than 50% of the number of pixels within the image; (3) The method cannot be applied to grayscale images due to non-existing unique colors.

Problems for the investigator are classifying the images based on the size of the class of color images with $R > R'$.

Localized Pairs Method

The previous section presented Raw Quick Pairs which is based on comparisons of unique colors. Going back to Tables 2 through 6, one may see that the number of unique colors is not sufficient to satisfy the condition. This method does not analyze pairs of adjacent pixels. How to get around this problem along with localizing the detected information? In this section, we present a technique that virtually solved these problems. We will introduce a so-called *localized pixel pairs analysis* scheme. The basic idea of *localized pairs*, concentrates on several problems within RQP. The basic differences between the new method and Raw Quick Pairs are: (a) it directly works with RGB (Red Green and Blue) image model individually while Raw Quick Pairs is working with (comparing pairs of colors with the image) palette; (b) the probability of detection is based on the detection of embedding types; (c) it can reliably detect images with secret messages that are embedded in both consecutive pixels such as (wbStego and SecurEngine), and randomly scattered within the image (such as S_Tools and J-Steg); and (d) it doesn't depend of the unique colors in the image (Westfeld & Pfitzman, 1999). In addition, the new method can be applied to grayscale images with analysis yielding a rough estimation of the hidden information size.

Figure 10. Shows current steganalysis techniques

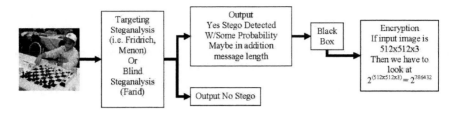

Figure 11. Shows why one needs the localization techniques

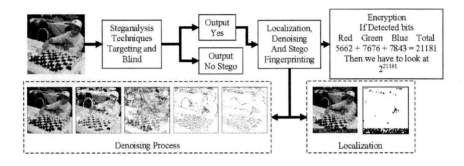

One of the advantages of localization method is the minimization of time during the encryption procedure as shown in Figure 10 and Figure 11. The *localized pairs* scheme is based on statistical analysis of sampled pixel pair comparisons on various structures (masks) to further expand and improve the ability to detect smaller concentrated areas of hidden information within stego images. By modifying the masks, the number of adjacent pixel pairs in the new method is able to detect information on a variety of images not just digital color image. The mask sizes trigger various sensitivities in detection which are an advantage for various digital image types. The new detection method uses an initial estimation of altered bits to determine if information is indeed contained on the stego-image. Initial results dictate if hidden information is probable within the image for further investigation and a close estimation of hidden data is determined.

Notations – Let:

- I be an M by N image

- β is an incremental count of matched adjacent pairs of pixels

- β_{max} is the maximum number of adjacent pairs of pixel comparisons

- R is the ratio between the matched adjacent pairs of pixels and the maximum number of adjacent pairs of pixel comparisons:

$$R = \frac{\text{\# of Matched Pixel Pairs}}{\text{Total \# of Possible Pixel Pairs}} = \frac{\text{Match}}{\text{Max}} = \frac{\beta}{\beta_{max}} \qquad (3.3.1)$$

The definition of β and β_{max} is defined in detail in (Agaian, 2004).

- The corresponding quantities for the new altered images after embedding random messages of various percentages are denoted as β'_k, β'_{max} and R'_k, where k is the image containing the random message of $1\%, 2\%, ..., n\%$.

$$R'_k = \frac{(\text{Match})_k}{\text{Max}} = \frac{\beta'_k}{\beta'_{max}} \qquad (3.3.2)$$

The relationship between R and R'_k can be used as a relative comparison for determining if a secret message exists. The following decision rule will be used:

$$\text{Decision Rule} = \begin{cases} \text{if } R < R'_k \text{ then does not contain a secrete message} \\ \text{if } R > R'_k \text{ use other methods} \\ \text{if } R \cong R'_k \text{ it could be case 1,2,...} \end{cases}$$

The various cases correspond with the classification of the embedding methods. The basic block diagram for the localize pairs scheme is represented Figure 12.

Reliability of Decision: Using test of statistical hypotheses, Type I error, Type II error, and normal distribution for reliability of decision, we are able to determine the probability of detecting steganographic content. Similar reliability of decision was used by Callinan and Kemick (2005), Fridrich et al. (2000), Provos and Honeyman (2001), and Westfeld and Pfitzman (1999). For our case of Improved Raw Quick Pairs, we will define Type I error as testing for possible rejection of the presence of steganographic content and Type II testing for the possibility of accepting the detection of steganographic content when in fact no steganographic content exists.

Figure 12. The block diagram bellow shows the steps necessary in analyzing an input image to determine if steganographic content exists within the suspected image.

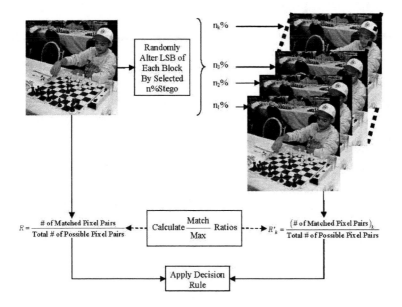

The Gaussian (Normal) distribution functions for Type I and Type II errors:

$$P(\mathrm{I}) = \int_{\infty}^{Th(s)} \frac{e^{-\frac{\left(\frac{R'}{R}-\mu\right)^2}{2\sigma^2}}}{\sqrt{2\pi\sigma^2}} \, d\frac{R'}{R} \tag{3.3.3}$$

$$P(\mathrm{II}) = \int_{Th(s)}^{\infty} \frac{e^{-\frac{\left(\frac{R'}{R}-\mu(s)\right)^2}{2\sigma^2(s)}}}{\sqrt{2\pi\sigma(s)^2}} \, d\frac{R'}{R} \tag{3.3.4}$$

One may define the threshold $Th(s)$ from the following reliability:

P(Detecting a false message) = P(Missing a secret message). OR...

$$P(I) = P(II)$$

Solving this equation, $P(I) = P(II)$ we obtain (Fridrich et al., 2000):

$$Th(s) = \left(\frac{\mu\sigma(s) + \mu(s)\sigma}{(\sigma + \sigma(s))} \right)$$

(3.3.5)

The user should have to adjust the threshold $Th(s)$ to adjust for the importance of not missing an image with a secret message at the expense of making more errors of Type I for different sizes of the secret message ranging from $s = 0, \ldots, 50\%$. The color channels contain a message bit and different sizes of the test message.

Note that the threshold value Th is calculated as follows, i.e., for 1% probability of the prediction:

$$Th(s) = \frac{\mu\sigma(s) + \mu(s)\sigma}{(\sigma + \sigma(s))} = \frac{(1.1798)(0.0642) + (1.1444)(0.0801)}{(0.0801 + 0.0642)}$$

$$= \frac{0.07574 + 0.09166}{0.1443} = \frac{0.16741}{0.1443}$$

$$= 1.1601$$

The reliability of decision can be estimated by using the following:

$$P(I) > 90\% \text{ and } P(II) > 90\%$$

Table 7. Was generated with the use of randomly embedding 200 images with 5% to calculate the 0% mean and variance then embedding once again with the percentage shown and generating the mean and variances.

Altered Bits within the LSB	Threshold $Th(s)$	Mean $\mu(s)$	Variance $\sigma(s)$
0%		$\mu = 1.1798$	$\sigma = 0.0801$
1%	1.1601	1.1444	0.0642
5%	1.0929	1.0689	0.0221
10%	1.0582	1.0420	0.0107
20%	1.0227	1.0101	0.0064
50%	1.0126	1.0068	0.0028
100%	1.0031	1.0014	0.0008

Determining the accepted decision, we set thresholds: (a) we determine the acceptable decision with a 90% or greater reliability for detecting a message; and (b) 90% reliability for no stego. These reliabilities are determined for the percentage of detected steganographic content along with the embedding method used.

Computer Simulation: We performed numerical experimentation with an image database of 200 color TIFF and RAW images taken with a Nikon D100 and Canon EOS Digital Rebel.

The basic steps for the localize pairs scheme block diagram in Figure 12 are listed in Figure 13.

Tables 8 through 12 show the reliability of detection on the type of embedding alterations, such as selective and random embedding. If the reliability does not meet the requirement of 90% it is considered as no detection or unreliable so it is marked by (-). The reliability estimation tables for random embedding were generated using images that contained randomly embedded information for the calculations of R and R'_k. For selective embedding, the analysis was generated by using the images that contained selectively embedded information for the calculations of R and R'_k.

Figure 13. Basic steps for the localize pairs scheme

Algorithm for Localize Pairs Method

Input: A digital image.

Step 1: Divide the input image into its three layers followed by a division of n by m blocks.

Step 2: Calculate the ratio of adjacent pixels using equation 3.3.1.

Step 3: Generate k new images by randomly inserting percentages of hidden data within the image's least significant bits.

Step 4: Calculate the ratio using equation 3.3.2

Step 5: Apply the decision rule for the embedding type and the percentage of stego information.

Step 6: Determine the message length of the detected stego by calculating the number of blocks, the estimated pixels and the summing the results.

Output: Detection probability and estimation length of hidden information.

Table 8. Localize pairs method detection of clean images with random embedding reliability

Cover Image	Reliability Estimation (Random Embedding)					
	0%	1%	5%	10%	20%	50%
ChessMatch512x512	-	91.5%	-	-	-	-
Fisherman512x512	90.8%	-	-	-	-	-
GoldenGate512X512	-	94.6%	-	-	-	-
Rock512X512	-	91.1%	-	-	-	-
Trolley512X512	96.2%	-	-	-	-	-

Table 9. Localize pairs method detection of clean images with selective embedding reliability

Cover Image	Reliability Estimation (Selective Embedding)					
	0%	1%	5%	10%	20%	50%
ChessMatch512x512	-	94.4%	-	-	-	-
Fisherman512x512	92.7%	-	-	-	-	-
GoldenGate512X512	-	-	93.2%	-	-	-
Rock512X512	92.2%	-	-	-	-	-
Trolley512X512	98.1%	-	-	-	-	-

Table 10. Localize pairs method detection of added Gaussian Noise with random embedding reliability

Gaussian Variance	Cover Image	Reliability Estimation (Gaussian Noise Embedding)					
		0%	1%	5%	10%	20%	50%
0.05	ChessMatch512x512	-	-	-	93.3%	-	-
0.05	Fisherman512x512	-	-	92.6%	-	-	-
0.05	GoldenGate512X512	-	-	-	-	92.1%	-
0.05	Rock512X512	-	-	92.7%	-	-	-
0.05	Trolley512X512	-	-	-	90.2%	-	-

Table 11. Localize pairs method detection of added Salt & Pepper Noise with selective embedding

Salt & Pepper Percentage	Cover Image	Reliability Estimation (Salt & Pepper Embedding)					
		0%	1%	5%	10%	20%	50%
5%	ChessMatch512x512	-	-	-	90.5%	-	-
5%	Fisherman512x512	-	94.7%	-	-	-	-
5%	GoldenGate512X512	-	-	-	92.8%	-	-
5%	Rock512X512	-	-	90.8%	-	-	-
5%	Trolley512X512	-	-	96.1%	-	-	-

Table 12. Localize pairs method detection of 5% randomly embedded information

Cover Image	Reliability Estimation					
	0%	1%	5%	10%	20%	50%
ChessMatch512x512	-	-	-	90.4%	-	-
Fisherman512x512	-	-	96.6%	-	-	-
GoldenGate512X512	-	-	-	91.0%	-	-
Rock512X512	-	-	-	95.1%	-	-
Trolley512X512	-	-	91.7%	-	-	-

Figure 14. Shows the detection in black blocks which meet the reliability requirement and the white blocks are areas which do not contain steganographic content

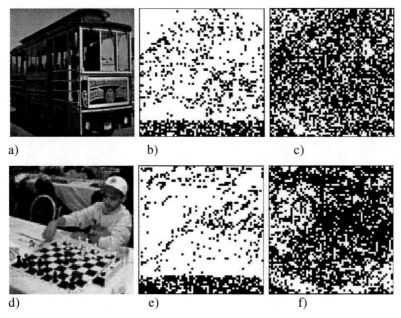

a)   b)   c)

d)   e)   f)

(a) Original Image, (b) image embedded with 5k file using wbStego, (c) image embedded with 5k file using S-Tools, (d) Original Image,(e) image embedded with 5k file using wbStego, and (f) image embedded with 5k file using S-Tools.

The test in Figure 14 shows the ability of this method to localize steganographic content.

The main advantages of this *Localize Pairs* Method are:

- The ability to detect on color images with unique colors within the image of less than 30% of the number of pixels.
- The ability to detect steganographic content on gray scale images.

Figure 15. Classification block diagram of different embedding methods (StegoArchive, 2003)

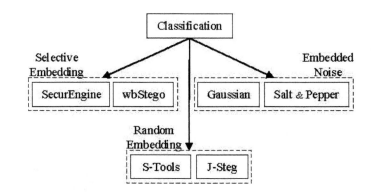

- The ability to localize steganographic content.
- The ability to "some how" classify the embedding method.

Regular Singular Steganalysis (RS Steganalysis)

In this section we present RS steganalysis concept which was developed by (Fridrich, 2001) and focuses on detection of least significant bit embedding within digital images. This method is based on the statistics of sample pair (the basic unit) rather than individual samples which are very sensitive to least significant bit embedding (Fridrich, 2003; Fridrich et al., 2000). Another method using sample pairs analysis for LSB detection method which uses sample pairs and estimates the message length was developed by Dumitrescu et al. (2003). The statistical analysis of Pairs of Values was introduced by Westfeld and Pfitzman (1999) which analyzes pairs that have been exchanged during message embedding. In Fridrich (2001) Fridrich stated that:

1. Pairs of Values method provides very reliable results when the message placement is known and
2. Only randomly scattered messages can be detected with this method when the message length becomes comparable with the number of pixels in the image.

Another method which is also based on the comparison of Pair of Values is Raw Quick Pairs detection method which was developed by Fridrich et al. (2000). We will use the terminology and definitions presented by Fridrich et al. (2000). We let the input cover image, for example the Chess Match Figure 3.4.1, be of size $M{\times}N$ pixels with pixel values from the set P, for an 8-bit color layer, $P = \{0,\dots, 255\}$.

Figure 16. Block diagram of RS Steganalysis

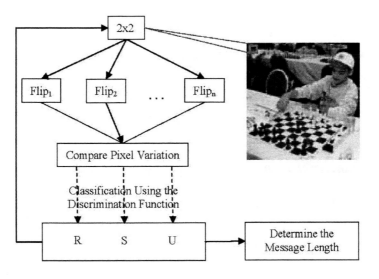

The image is divided into 2×2 blocks and mapped into a vector,

$$\begin{bmatrix} x_1 & x_2 \\ x_3 & x_4 \end{bmatrix} \Rightarrow \begin{bmatrix} x_1 & x_2 & x_3 & x_4 \end{bmatrix}.$$

The meaning of mapping a block into one dimension is that one can easily measure statistically the changes before and after the least significant bit embedding. We define a flipping operation $F(x)$ as a mapping of pixel values from the set P to $[0,1]$ with properties (Fridrich, 2001):

a.   Is an invertible operation

b. $F_1(x) = x$, 0 plus 1,

c. $F_0(x) = x$, identity permutation $F(x) = x$ for all $x \in P$

d. $F_{\{-1\}}(x) = F_1(x+1) - 1$ for all x this means that the flipping operation F_{-1} is the same as applying F_1 to an image whose colors have been shifted by one.

For example the flipping operation can be applied to a set of pixels from image I denoted as $G = [x_1,...,x_n]$ and M is a mask $M = [m_1,...,m_n]$, where m_i becomes $\{-1, 0, 1\}$ for $i = 1,...,$ n. It can be shown that the following operation:

$$F(G) = G \oplus M = [x_1 \oplus m_1, ..., x_n \oplus m_n] \qquad (3.4.1)$$

where $\oplus$, is a modulus 2 operator on least significant bit of m_i and x_i, $i = 1, 2, ..., n$.

The flipped group $F(G)$ is denoted as the set:

$$F_M(G) = \{F_{M(1)}(G) \quad F_{M(2)}(G) \quad \cdots \quad F_{M(n)}(G)\}, \qquad (3.4.2)$$

which specifies where and how pixel values are to be modified.

We will define and use the flipping function F_1 by permutation values: $0 \leftrightarrow 1, 2 \leftrightarrow 3, ...,$ $254 \leftrightarrow 255$ ($00000000 \leftrightarrow 00000001, 00000010 \leftrightarrow 00000011, ..., 11111110 \leftrightarrow 11111111$) which corresponds to flipping the least significant bits of each gray level/ color layer. Using logical operation the uniquely defined permutations can be shown as follows:

$$F(x) \Rightarrow 0 \leftrightarrow 1 \Rightarrow \dfrac{\begin{array}{r}00000000 \\ + \qquad\qquad 1\end{array}}{00000001} \qquad\qquad 2 \leftrightarrow 3 \Rightarrow \dfrac{\begin{array}{r}00000010 \\ + \qquad\qquad 1\end{array}}{00000011}$$

$$F(F(x)) \Rightarrow 0 \leftrightarrow 1 \Rightarrow \dfrac{\begin{array}{r}+ \qquad\qquad 1\end{array}}{00000000} \qquad\qquad 2 \leftrightarrow 3 \Rightarrow \dfrac{\begin{array}{r}+ \qquad\qquad 1\end{array}}{00000010}$$

The shifted least significant bit is defined as flipping F_{-1} as "$1 \leftrightarrow 0, 1 \leftrightarrow 2, 3 \leftrightarrow 4, ..., 253$ $\leftrightarrow 254, 255 \leftrightarrow 256$ (tow's complement for $-1 = 11111111 \leftrightarrow 00000000, 0000000 \leftrightarrow 00000010,$ $00000011 \leftrightarrow 00000100, ..., 11111111 \leftrightarrow 100000000$). This operation is similar to applying positive or negative masks using simple addition and subtraction operations (see following example).

Let G be a set of n pixels and M is a set of k masks. Applying these masks to G we may map:

$$\begin{bmatrix} x_{i,j} & x_{i,j+1} \\ x_{i+1,j} & x_{i+1,j+1} \end{bmatrix} \Rightarrow \begin{bmatrix} x_{i,j} & x_{i,j+1} & x_{i+1,j} & x_{i+1,j+1} \end{bmatrix} = G \Rightarrow F_{M_k}(G) = \begin{cases} F_{M_1}(G) \\ F_{M_2}(G) \\ \vdots \\ F_{M_n}(G) \end{cases}$$

Example: Let $P = \begin{bmatrix} 15 & 18 \\ 19 & 20 \end{bmatrix} \Rightarrow G = [15, 18, 19, 20]$, and masks are:

$M_1 = [0\,1\,1\,0]$, $-M_1 = [0\,-1\,-1\,0]$, $M_2 = [1\,-1\,-1\,1]$ and $-M_2 = [-1\,1\,1\,-1]$

then

$F_{M_1}(G) = [15+0, 18+1, 19+1, 20+0] = [15, 19, 20, 20]$,

Similarly,

$F_{\{-M_1\}}(G) = [15, 17, 18, 20]$, $F_{M_2}(G) = [16, 17, 18, 21]$ and $F_{\{-M_2\}}(G) = [14, 19, 20, 19]$.

So, after the flipping operations one may have:

$$P = \begin{bmatrix} 15 & 18 \\ 19 & 20 \end{bmatrix} \Rightarrow G = [15, 18, 19, 20] \Rightarrow F_{M_4}(G) = \begin{cases} F_{M_1}(G) = [15, 19, 20, 20] \\ F_{\{-M_1\}}(G) = [15, 17, 18, 20] \\ F_{M_2}(G) = [16, 17, 18, 21] \\ F_{\{-M_2\}}(G) = [14, 19, 20, 19] \end{cases}$$

Next, let's classify the set $F_M(G) = \{F_{M(1)}(G)\ \ F_{M(2)}(G)\ \ \cdots\ \ F_{M(n)}(G)\}$ (the example case $F_{M_4}(G)$) into three groups smooth (singular), regular and unusable with the use of the so called discrimination function f:

$$f(F_M(G)) = f(x_1, x_2, ..., x_n) = \sum_{i=1}^{n-1} |x_{i+1} - x_i|, \quad f \in \mathbb{R} \tag{3.4.3}$$

as a rule:

Regular group: $G \in R \Leftrightarrow f(F_M(G)) > f(G)$

Singular group: $G \in S \Leftrightarrow f(F_M(G)) < f(G)$

Unusable group: $G \in U \Leftrightarrow f(F_M(G)) = f(G)$.

Note, that the function f is a real function of each pixel group $G = (x_1, x_2, ..., x_n)$ and it based on some statistical measure of sample pairs $[x_i, x_{i+1}]$, $i = 1, ..., $ n-1, that are sensitive to least significant bit embedding operations. The authors (Fridrich, 2001) also stated that because in typical images randomly adding small amount of noise will lead to an increase in f.

For example, the larger the pixel variation of the pixels $f(F_M(G))$ the larger the values of the discrimination function becomes. Using the results from the previous example we may have:

$$f(F_M(G)) = |15 - 18| + |18 - 19| + |19 - 20| = 5$$

$$f(F_{M_1}(G)) = 7, \ f(F_{\{-M_1\}}(G)) = 5, \ f(F_{M_2}(G)) = 5, \ f(F_{\{-M_2\}}(G)) = 7$$

Or, the results might be put into a classification diagram as seen in Figure 17.

The total number of regular groups is larger than the total number of singular groups (Fridrich, 2001). We will do this procedure for each 2 by 2 block within the input image.

Now we will introduce the estimation length of the embedded message.

During the development of RS steganalysis algorithm several quantities distinguishing statistics and assumptions are introduced.

Let us denote the quantities by:

Figure 17. RS steganalysis classification diagram

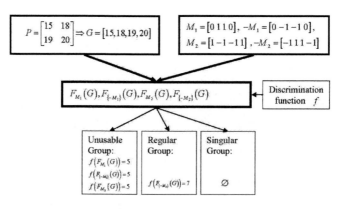

- $R_M(p)$ the relative number of regular groups for a non-negative mask M.
- $R_{-M}(p)$ the relative number of regular groups for a negative mask $-M$.
- $S_M(p)$ the relative number of singular groups for a non-negative mask M.
- $S_{-M}(p)$ the relative number of singular groups for a negative mask $-M$.

where, p is the number of embedded samples divided by the total number of pixels. In Fridrich (2001), the authors make the following assumptions:

a. $R_M(p) + S_M(p) \leq 1$ and $R_{-M}(p) + S_{-M}(p) \leq 1$, for the negative mask.

b. The expected value of $R_M = R_M(p)$ is equal to that of $R_{-M} = R_{-M}(p)$, and the same is true for $S_M = S_M(p)$ and $S_{-M} = S_{-M}(p)$ assume that:

$$E\{|R_M|\} \cong E\{|R_{-M}|\} \text{ and } E\{|S_M|\} \cong E\{|S_{-M}|\}$$

Or, the authors also stated that for images taken with a digital camera for both lossy and lossless formats the following equations hold true.

$$|R_M| \cong |R_{-M}| \text{ and } |S_M| \cong |S_{-M}|$$

c. The distance between $R_M(100 - p/2)$ and $S_M(100 - p/2)$ approaches zero as the embedded message length increases and the opposite occurs as the message length increases the distance between $R_{-M}(100 - p/2)$ and $S_{-M}(100 - p/2)$ increases.

d. $R_M \cong S_M$ after flipping 50% of the LSB pixels. R_M at 50% flipped least significant bits and S_M at 50% flipped least significant bits are equal, which is what would happen after embedding a random message bit into every pixel. They have experimentally verified that this assumption for a large database of images with unprocessed Raw, BMP, and JPEG processed images.

e. $R_M(0) = R_{-M}(0)$ and $SM(0) = S_{-M}(0)$ which means that the number of Regular group R_M for a mask M and number of Regular group R_{-M} of the mask $-M$ are the same if no message has been embedded, similarly this is true with $S_M(p)$.

The following assumptions are also used in RS steganalysis:

$R_M(p) = a_1 p^2 + b_1 p + c_1$ and $S_M(p) = a_2 p^2 + b_2 p + c_2$ are quadratic functions and

$R_{-M}(p) = b_3 p + c_3$ and $S_{-M}(p) = b_4 p + c_4$ are linear functions of the embedded message length p_o, where a_i, b_i and c_i, $i = 1,2,3$ and 4, are undetermined constants. To avoid the computation time the authors are using eight points needed to described the lines and polynomials for $R_M(p/2)$, $R_{-M}(p/2)$, $S_M(p/2)$, $S_{-M}(p/2)$, $R_M(100-p/2)$, $R_{-M}(100-p/2)$, $S_M(100-p/2)$ and $S_{-M}(100-p/2)$.

From Fridrich (2001) it is stated that the curves created from $R_{-M}(p)$ and $S_{-M}(p)$ are well-modeled with straight lines, while second-degree polynomial scan approximate the "inner" curves R_M and S_M reasonably well. The points from Figure 18 are used to estimate the parameters of the four curves.

Note that using the substitution:

$$z = \frac{x - p/2}{100 - p/2}$$
(3.4.4)

the x axis is rescaled so that $p/2$ becomes 0 and $10 - p/2$ becomes 1.

The constants a_i, b_i, and c_i ($i = 1, 2, 3$ and 4) can be calculated using the information that these functions/curves are passing through to following points:

$$\{0, R_M(0); 1/2, R_M(1/2); 1, R_M(1)\} \qquad \{0, S_M(0); 1/2, S_M(1/2); 1, S_M(1)\}$$

$$\{0, R_{-M}(0); 1, R_{-M}(1)\} \qquad \{0, S_M(0); 1, S_{-M}(1)\}$$

The message length p_o can be calculated using a combination of these functions we obtain:

$$2(d_1 + d_0) x^2 + (d_{-0} - d_{-1} - d_1 - 3d_0) x + d_0 - d_{-0} = 0,$$
(3.4.5)

where:

$$d_0 = R_M(p/2) - S_M(p/2), \quad d_1 = R_M(100-p/2) - S_M(100-p/2),$$
$$d_{-0} = R_{-M}(p/2) - S_{-M}(p/2), \quad d_{-1} = R_{-M}(100-p/2) - S_{-M}(100-p/2).$$
(3.4.6)

The message length p_0 can be calculated from the root x whose absolute value is smaller by:

$$p_0 = x/(x - 1/2)$$
(3.4.7)

We have tested 190 color TIFF and RAW images taken with a Nikon D100 and Canon EOS Digital Rebel. The images obtained using the two digital cameras and were stored as uncompressed TIFF. Note that Fridrich (2001) used unprocessed RAW, BMPs, JPEG and processed BMP images for testing. Tables 13 through 16 show the RS steganalysis on the clean, Gaussian, salt & pepper noise, and 5% stego embedded images.

Estimation error $\hat{p} - p$ (Dumitrescu et al., 2003). The average error magnitude is 0.023 and it stays almost the same for different p values and the false alarm rate when $p = 0$ is 13.79%. The false alarm rate drops to 11.03% when $p = 3\%$ and drops to 0% when the embedded message length $p > 3\%$ (Dumitrescu et al., 2003).

The false alarm rate for RS steganalysis at $p = 0$ is 2.8% when clean images have shown detection values when a database of 200 images are analyzed. The false alarm rate increases as the embedding message size increases, i.e., when $p = 5\%$ the false alarm rate is 4.5%.

Noise (Fridrich, 2001): For very noisy images, the difference between the number of regular and singular pixels in the cover image is small. Consequently, the lines in the RS diagram intersect at a small angle and the accuracy of the RS steganalysis decreases.

Message placement (Fridrich, 2001): RS steganalysis is more accurate for messages that are randomly scattered than for messages concentrated in a localized area of the stego image.

Figure 18. RS-diagram of the chess match image taken by a digital camera. The x-axis represents the percentage of pixels with flipped least significant bits while the y-axis is the relative number of regular and singular groups with masks M = [0 1 1 0] and -M = [0 -1 -1 0].

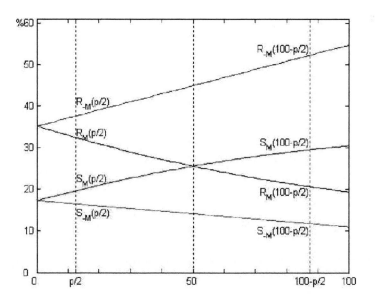

Figure 19. Computer simulation: Representation of the basic steps of RS steganalysis

---

Algorithm for RS Steganalysis

Input: Image to be analyzed.

Step 1: Create masks for flipping pixels.

Step 2: Generate class of regular, singular and unusable groups.

Step 3: Using the discrimination function, classify these groups.

Step 4: Calculate the quantities at the points, $p = 50$ and.

Step 5: Generate the first and second order polynomials.

Step 6: Calculate the coefficients d_1, d_0, d_{-1} and d_{-0}.

Step 7: Solve the equations (3.4.5) and take the minimum absolute value of the two solutions from the second order polynomial.

Step 8: Calculate the message length p using equation (3.4.7).

Output: The estimated amount of steganographic content per color channel and the estimated message length of the color channels.

Table 13. RS steganalysis detection within clean images

Cover Image	Percent of Detection per channel		
	Red (%)	Green (%)	Blue (%)
ChessMatch(Sarkis)512x512	29.1	5.2	11.4
Fisherman512x512	7.9	1.7	0
GoldenGate512X512	0	0	0
Rock512X512	0.2	2.5	0
Trolley512X512	0.8	1.3	0.0

Table 14. RS steganalysis detection of added Gaussian noise

Gaussian Variance	Cover Image	Percent of Detection per channel		
		Red (%)	Green (%)	Blue (%)
0.05	ChessMatch(Sarkis)512x512	49.9	33.9	42.3
0.05	Fisherman512x512	27.6	21.4	23.9
0.05	GoldenGate512X512	19.8	15.2	17
0.05	Rock512X512	43.0	41.7	41.2
0.05	Trolley512X512	20.5	17.4	18.4

Table 15. RS Steganalysis detection of added Salt & Pepper Noise

Salt & Pepper Percentage	Cover Image	Percent of Detection per channel		
		Red (%)	Green (%)	Blue (%)
5%	ChessMatch(Sarkis)512x512	49.9	33.5	41.5
5%	Fisherman512x512	27.5	21.6	24.2
5%	GoldenGate512X512	20.5	15.9	17.6
5%	Rock512X512	43.0	40.7	39.8
5%	Trolley512X512	20.5	7.4	8.4

Table 16. RS steganalysis detection of 5% stego embedded with stools

Embedded Percentage STools	Cover Image	Percent of Detection per channel		
		Red (%)	Green (%)	Blue (%)
5%	ChessMatch(Sarkis)512x512	36.3	14.9	20.5
5%	Fisherman512x512	17.3	11.8	9.8
5%	GoldenGate512X512	9.8	9.0	8.5
5%	Rock512X512	10.2	12.2	8.4
5%	Trolley512X512	10.8	11.4	10.3

Experimental Results have shown the following advantages and disadvantages.

The main advantages of RS steganalysis which detected least significant bit embedding in continuous-time images (Fridrich, 2001):

- The size of the embedded data can be estimated.
- It depicted vulnerabilities on detection on the Windows base embedding software Steganos, Windstorm, S-Tool, and Hide4PGP (StegoArchive, 2003).
- It can used for both grayscale and color digital images.
- It works well if the least significant bit embedding is done randomly used in the spatial domain.

The main limitations of this method are:

- If the amount of hidden data onto the digital covered image is small the probability of detecting the hidden data is reduced significantly.

- It does not work well if one uses least significant bit sequential pixel embedding techniques, for example wbStego and Encrypt Pic, which reduce the detection by RS steganalysis (Fridrich, 2001).

- The false detection for non compressed images is very high.

- It cannot distinguish noise from stego causing RS steganalysis to detect noise.

- It does not work for steganography.

- The method does not show the estimation error.

- It does not localize the stego regions

Stego Sensitivity Measure

A complexity based measure to determine informative regions of images, for the purposes of image compression, has been developed by Kawaguchi and Niimi (1998). This measure identifies the informative and noise-like regions of an image, with the objective of image compression by saving informative regions and discarding portions of noise-like areas. It was used for embedding stego data. From this measure the question arises, *can the complexity measure be used to identify the informative stego region?* Unfortunately, this method cannot be directly used to detect hidden information. Another problem exists which is related with the detection and localization of stego informative regions, along with the complexity of the algorithms.

This section presents a new stego sensitivity measure used for steganalysis approach. Modifying the pixel comparison method and combining a new complexity measure algorithm has yielded results which address several key issues including the ability to localize the steganographic content. The stego sensitivity measure shows that an image can be divided into ideal detection areas and ideal embedding areas.

Notations – Let:

- I be an M by N image

- $M_{R,C} = [\;]$ be any mask at R, C pixel location (see Figure 20)

- R and C the number of adjacent pixels surrounding a center pixel

- A is a threshold for the bit plane that is being analyzed for stego information

- β is an incremental count of matched adjacent pairs of pixels that meet a given threshold A

- β_{max} is the maximum number of all adjacent pixel comparisons meeting the threshold within a block size and a moving mask

The pixels are compared with $\left| P_{R,C} - P_{R-1,C} \right| \leq A$, $A = 0, 1, 2, 3$, by the mask used and block size. Where the different masks used are: Masks contain a block of adjacent pixels that are to be compared, for example, horizontal mask $\begin{bmatrix} P_{R,C-1} & P_{R,C} & P_{R,C+1} \end{bmatrix}$.

Figure 20. Mask structures; (a) Mask$_{Square}$, (b) Mask$_{Cross}$, (c) Mask$_{X}$, (d) Mask$_{V}$

$$
\begin{bmatrix} P_{R-1,C-1} & P_{R-1,C} & P_{R-1,C+1} \\ P_{R,C-1} & P_{R,C} & P_{R,C+1} \\ P_{R+1,C-1} & P_{R+1,C} & P_{R+1,C+1} \end{bmatrix}
\quad
\begin{bmatrix} & P_{R-1,C} & \\ P_{R,C-1} & P_{R,C} & P_{R,C+1} \\ & P_{R+1,C} & \end{bmatrix}
\quad
\begin{bmatrix} P_{R-1,C-1} & & P_{R-1,C+1} \\ & P_{R,C} & \\ P_{R+1,C-1} & & P_{R+1,C+1} \end{bmatrix}
\quad
\begin{bmatrix} P_{R-1,C} \\ P_{R,C} \\ P_{R+1,C} \end{bmatrix}
$$

(a)	*(b)*	*(c)*	*(d)*

The pixel comparison based complexity measure is defined as:

$$\gamma(m,n) = \frac{\beta}{\beta_{max}} \tag{3.5.1}$$

where n and m are the block locations being analyzed.

Stego sensitivity measure for an image is defined by:

$$\Gamma = \frac{1}{\hat{M}\hat{N}} \sum_{m=1}^{M} \sum_{n=1}^{N} \gamma(m,n) \tag{3.5.2}$$

where $\gamma(m, n)$ are the block values containing all of the complexity values within the image, $\hat{M}$ is the number of rows in Γ and $\hat{N}$ is the number of columns in Γ.

In Agaian et al. (2004) we show that the definition, Γ, is used for calculation of the ideal threshold for γ. Stego sensitivity measure Γ is dependent of the following parameters:

a.   The input image;

b.   The threshold set for the comparison of pixels, A;

c.   The structure of the masks used;

d.   The blocking size of an image.

Tables 17 through 20 show the analysis of the stego sensitivity measure on the clean, Gaussian, salt & pepper noise, and 5% stego embedded images.

In this section of the chapter, we have presented stego sensitivity measure as a new steganalysis method. The new approach has the following advantages:

Figure 21. Computer simulation: Representation of the basic steps of stego sensitivity measure

---

Algorithm for local stego sensitivity measure

Input: Input an image of any size to be analyzed for stego information.

Step 1: Determine the block size to use.

Step 2: Divide the image into sections to be analyzed.

Step 3: Add rows and columns to the individual blocks being analyzed.

Step 4: Determine the mask size to use.

Step 5: Calculate the value offor each block ensuring the blocks overlap.

Step 6: Calculate the initial value for the threshold of.

Step 7: Determine ifmeets the threshold and categorizeinto stego or non-stego.

Step 8: Create a new altered image from the received image.

Step 9: Repeat steps 1 through 7 for the new image.

Output 1: An image showing the texture areas and non-texture areas.

Output 2: An image showing the stego locations from the received image Figure 3.5.2 and 3.5.3.

- Detection and localization of stego informative regions within digital images.
- Detection and separation of stego information within edges.

Conclusions

In this chapter, we have presented pixels pair comparisons based steganalysis methods used for digital forensics. The primary focus was on the spatial domain based steganalysis algorithms. We described two commonly used methods such as Raw Quick Pairs and RS steganalysis. In addition, we have presented computer simulations of these methods which show the advantages and limitations of the methods.

Also in this chapter, we have also introduced two new steganalysis algorithms: Localized Pairs Method and stego sensitivity measure. In addition, we have also shown improved detection rates over existing methods by employing a modified reliability decision process, adjacent pixel comparisons, and a new stego complexity measure. One of the main advantages of the new methods is to detect the steganographic content within the multiple layers of the bit planes of digital image. This leads to the competence of the new

Figure 22. Trolley image used to show detectable regions (white) and the hard detectable regions (black): (a) Original Image, (b) comparative image, (c) detected image when embedded with 5k file using wbStego, (d) detected image when embedded with 5k file using S-Tools (Table 20)

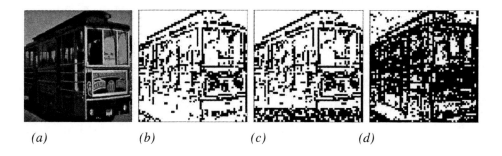

(a)   *(b)*   *(c)*   *(d)*

Figure 23. Chess match (Sarkis) image used to show detectable regions (white) and the hard detectable regions (black): (a) Original image, (b) comparative image, (c) detected image when embedded with 5k file using wbStego, (d) detected image when embedded with 5k file using S-Tools (Table 20)

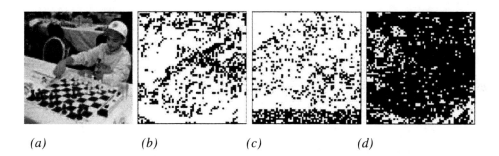

(a)   *(b)*   *(c)*   *(d)*

Table 17. Stego sensitivity measure detection of clean images

Cover Image	Percent of Detection per channel		
	Red (%)	Green (%)	Blue (%)
ChessMatch(Sarkis)512x512	2.45	3.19	2.70
Fisherman512x512	1.01	1.60	1.42
GoldenGate512X512	2.82	2.27	2.30
Rock512X512	2.79	2.11	3.37
Trolley512X512	1.61	1.01	1.19

Table 18. Stego sensitivity measure detection of added Gaussian Noise

Gaussian Variance	Cover Image	Percent of Detection per channel		
		Red (%)	Green (%)	Blue (%)
0.05	ChessMatch(Sarkis)512x512	4.79	4.74	5.68
0.05	Fisherman512x512	4.92	5.44	5.30
0.05	GoldenGate512X512	9.73	9.93	10.54
0.05	Rock512X512	10.17	9.46	10.15
0.05	Trolley512X512	2.40	2.41	2.69

Table 19. Stego sensitivity measure detection of added Salt & Pepper Noise

Salt & Pepper Percentage	Cover Image	Percent of Detection per Channel		
		Red (%)	Green (%)	Blue (%)
5%	ChessMatch(Sarkis)512x512	6.93	7.84	6.37
5%	Fisherman512x512	5.91	6.53	5.86
5%	GoldenGate512X512	10.41	10.2	10.85
5%	Rock512X512	10.89	9.67	8.59
5%	Trolley512X512	6.05	5.83	5.49

Table 20. Stego sensitivity measure detection of 5% randomly embedded information

Embedded Percentage STools	Cover Image	Percent of Detection per Channel		
		Red (%)	Green (%)	Blue (%)
5%	ChessMatch(Sarkis)512x512	7.35	7.02	6.89
5%	Fisherman512x512	6.81	668	6.82
5%	GoldenGate512X512	8.01	7.37	7.64
5%	Rock512X512	9.96	6.28	7.40
5%	Trolley512X512	7.2	6.5	6.66

methods to localize the hidden data, and the ability to separate the vital data from the noise-like content from the transmitted digital image. Comparisons of the newly developed methods with existing detection algorithms have shown improved detection rates, even in the presence of added noise. One of the basic advantages of the new methods is the localization of steganographic information in digital images. This is the next step for forensic science. Because these methods are able to localize hidden data steganography signatures of the embedding method are possible and minimization of the encryption time when extracting the hidden data.

Acknowledgments

This research was partially funded by the Centre for Infrastructure Assurance and Security and the U.S. Air Force. The views expressed in this chapter are those of the authors and do not reflect the official policy or position of the Air Force, Department of Defense, or the U.S. Government. We would additionally like to express our appreciation to June Rodriguez for the contribution of a multitude of digital images for analytical support.

References

Agaian, S., Rodriguez, B., & Dietrich, G. (2004). Steganalysis using modified pixel comparison and complexity measure. *IS&T/SPIE's 16th Annual Symposium, Electronic Imaging 2004, Science and Technology, Proceedings of the SPIE Security and Watermarking of Multimedia Conents IV* (Vol. 5306, pp. 46-57).

Callinan, J., & Kemick, D. (2005). *Detecting steganographic content in images found on the Internet.* Department of Business Management, University of Pittsburgh at Bradford. Retrieved December 11, 2003, from http://www.chromesplash.com/jcallinan.com/publications/steg.pdf

Chandramouli, R. (2002). Mathematical approach to steganalysis. *Proceedings of the SPIE Security and Watermarking of Multimedia Contents IV* (pp. 14-25). International Society for Optical Engineering.

Chandramouli, R., & Memon, N. (2001). Analysis of LSB based image steganography techniques. *Proceedings 2001 International Conference on Image Processing,* (Vol. 3, pp. 1019-1022).

Cochran, J. T, & Captain, R. (2000). *Steganographic computer warfare.* Master's thesis, AFIT/GCS/ENG/00M-03 School of Engineering and Management, Air Force Institute of Technology (AU), Wright Patterson AFB, OH. Retrieved July 29, 2005, from http://research.airuniv.edu/papers/ay2000/afit/afit-gcs-eng-00m-03.pdf

Curran, K., & Bailey, K. (2003, Fall). An evaluation of image-based steganography methods. *International Journal of Digital Evidence, 2*(2), 1-40. Retrieved December 29, 2003, from http://www.ijde.org/docs/03_fall_steganography.pdf

Dumitrescu, S., Wu, X., & Wang, Z. (2003). Detection of LSB steganography via sample pair analysis. *IEEE Transactions on Signal Processing, 51*(7), 1995-2007.

Farid, H. (2001). *Detecting steganographic messages in digital images.* Technical Report TR2001-412, Dartmouth College, Computer Science Department, Retrieved April 8, 2005, from http://www.cs.dartmouth.edu/~farid/publications/tr01.pdf

Farid, H., & Lyu, S. (2003). Higher-order wavelet statistics and their application to digital forensics. *IEEE Workshop on Statistical Analysis in Computer Vision* (pp. 1-8).

Fridrich, J., Du, R., & Long, M. (2000). Steganalysis of LSB encoding in color images. *IEEE ICME 2000* (pp. 1279-1282).

Fridrich, J., & Goljan, M. (2002a). Practical steganalysis of digital images: State of the art. *IS&T/SPIE's, Electronic Imaging 2002, Science and Technology, Proceedings of the SPIE Security and Watermarking of Multimedia Contents IV* (Vol. 4675, pp. 1-13).

Fridrich, J., & Goljan, M. (2004). On estimation of secret message length in LSB steganography in spatial domain. *IS&T/SPIE's 16th Annual Symposium, Electronic Imaging 2004, Science and Technology, Proceedings of the SPIE Security and Watermarking of Multimedia Contents VI* (Vol. 5306, pp. 23-34).

Fridrich, J., Goljan, M., & Du, R. (2001a). Steganalysis based on JPEG compatibility. *IS&T/SPIE's Symposium, Photonics West 2001, Electronic Imaging, Science and Technology, Proceedings of the SPIE Multimedia Systems and Applications IV, Special Session on Theoretical and Practical Issues in Digital Watermarking and Data Hiding* (Vol. 4518, pp. 275-280).

Fridrich, J., Goljan, M., & Du, R. (2001b). Detecting LSB steganography in color and grayscale images. *Magazine of IEEE Multimedia Special Issue on Security*, 22-28.

Fridrich, J., Goljan, M., & Hogea, D. (2002b). Attacking the OutGuess. *Multimedia and Security Workshop at ACM Multimedia 2002, Proceedings of the ACM Workshop on Multimedia and Security 2002*, Juan-les-Pin, France (pp. 1-4).

Fridrich, J., Goljan, M., & Hogea, D. (2002c). Steganalysis of JPEG images: Breaking the F5 algorithm. *5th Information Hiding Workshop*, Noordwijkerhout, The Netherlands (pp. 310-323).

Fridrich, J., Goljan, M., & Hogea, D. (2003). New methodology for breaking steganographic techniques for JPEGs. *IS&T/SPIE's 15th Annual Symposium, Electronic Imaging 2003, Science and Technology, Proceedings of the SPIE Security and Watermarking of Multimedia Contents V* (Vol. 5020, pp. 143-155).

Fridrich, J., Goljan, M., Hogea, D., & Soukal, D. (2003). Quantitative steganalysis of digital images: Estimating the secret message length. *ACM Multimedia Systems Journal, Special issue on Multimedia Security, 9*(3), 288-302.

Fridrich, J., Goljan, M., & Soukal, D. (2003). Higher-order statistical steganalysis of palette images. *IS&T/SPIE's 15th Annual Symposium, Electronic Imaging 2003, Science and Technology, Proceedings of the SPIE Security and Watermarking of Multimedia Contents V* (Vol. 5020, pp. 178-190).

Hosmer, C., & Hyde, C. (2003). Discovering covert digital evidence. *Digital Forensic Research Workshop (DFRWS)*. Retrieved January 4, 2004, from http://www.dfrws.org/2003/presentations/dfrws2003presentations.html

International Journal of Digital Evidence. (n.d.). Retrieved from http://www.utica.edu/academic/institutes/ecii/ijde/index.cfm

Johnson, N. F., Duric, Z., & Jajodia, S. (2000). *Information hiding: Steganography and watermarking: Attacks and countermeasures.* Norwell, MA: Kluwer Academic.

Johnson, N. F., & Jajodia, S. (1998a). *Exploring steganography: Seeing the unseen.* Retrieved May, 28, 2005, from http://www.jjtc.com/pub/r2026.pdf

Johnson, N. F., & Jajodia, S. (1998b). Steganalysis of images created using current steganography software. *Lecture Notes in Computer Science, Volume 1525* (pp.273-289). Springer-Verlag.

Kawaguchi, E., & Niimi, M. (1998). Modeling digital image into informative and noise-like regions by complexity measure. *Information Modeling and Knowledge Bases IX* (pp. 255-265). IOS Press.

Lathrop, D. A. (2000). *Viral computer warfare via activation engine employing steganography.* Master's thesis, AFIT/GCS/ENG/00M-14. School of Engineering and Management, Air Force Institute of Technology (AU), Wright Patterson AFB, OH. Retrieved July 29, 2005, from http://www.books-on-line.com/bol/BookDisplay.cfm?BookNum=23269

Provos, N., (2003). *Steganography detection with stegdetect.* Retrieved December 29, 2003, from http://www.outguess.org/detection.php

Provos, N., & Honeyman, P. (2001). *Detecting steganographic content on the Internet.* Center for Information Technology Integration, University of Michigan, CITI Technical Report 01-11. Retrieved November 12, 2004, from http://www.citi.umich.edu/techreports/reports/citi-tr-01-11.pdf

Rodriguez, B., Agaian, S., & Collins, J. (2003). An improved Raw Quick Pairs. *DFRWS 2003 Presentations.* Retrieved December 7, 2003, from http://www.dfrws.org/2003/presentations/dfrws2003presentations.html

StegoArchive.com. (2003). Retrieved December 30, 2003, from http://www.stegoarchive.com/

Westfeld, A., & Pfitzman, A. (1999). Attacks in steganographic systems. In *Proceedings 3rd Info* (pp. 61-75). Dresden, Germany: Hiding Workshop.

Section III:
Incident Response

Chapter X

Incident Preparedness and Response: Developing a Security Policy

Warren Wylupski, University of New Mexico, USA

David R. Champion, Slippery Rock University, USA

Zachary Grant, New Mexico Mounted Patrol, USA

Abstract

One of the emerging issues in the field of digital crime and digital forensics is corporate preparedness in dealing with attacks on computer network security. Security attacks and breaches of an organization's computer network can result in the compromise of confidential data, loss of customer confidence, poor public relations, disruption of business, and severe financial loss. Furthermore, loss of organizational data can present a number of criminal threats, including extortion, blackmail, identity theft, technology theft, and even hazards to national security. This chapter first examines the preparedness and response of three southwestern companies to their own specific threats to corporate cyber-security. Secondly, this chapter suggests that by developing an effective security policy focusing on incident detection and response, a company can minimize the damage caused by these attacks, while simultaneously strengthening the existing system and forensic processes against future attacks. Advances in digital forensics and its supporting technology, including intrusion detection, intrusion prevention, and application control, will be imperative to maintain network security in the future.

Introduction

On 12 April 2005, LexisNexis acknowledged that personal information on as many as 310,000 U.S. residents may have been stolen from its databases. The company had announced in March that information on approximately 30,000 persons had been stolen, but an internal investigation increased the estimate. LexisNexis is informing affected individuals by mail that they may be at risk of identity theft from unknown persons who illegally accessed the passwords and identity information of legitimate customers of Seisint, which LexisNexis bought in September 2004. (Litan, 2005)

Information is crucial. Those armed with information have the ability to do great good or cause great harm. Corporations and organizations that harbor personal, sensitive, or proprietary information can no longer take a passive approach to computer network and data security. Even while companies strive to apply the evolving field of digital forensics to their overall network security, external and internal threats to corporate cyber-security have grown tremendously. External threats consist of *malware* such as *viruses* and *Trojan horses*, *spyware*, and *adware*. Malware is malicious software that designed to disrupt or damage systems. Other external threats include, *script kiddies*, *social engineering*, *spam*, and *hacking*. (See Table 1 for definitions of these terms.) Internal threats stem from disgruntled employees and non-compliant (non-malicious) employees. These activities can lead to a loss of network integrity and loss of data. Worse, criminals can use proprietary organizational data for a number of dangerous or illegal activities, including extortion, fraud, theft or national security threats.

Attempted computer intrusion has become a common occurrence for businesses, regardless of their size or nature of their industry. Even the familiar and ubiquitous e-mail venue has become a thoroughfare for malicious entry into organizations. One southwestern healthcare company receives over 70,000 e-mail messages a month, of which 17,000 are legitimate messages, while the others are spam. Another southwest organization estimated that 70% to 75% of the incoming e-mail was unwanted. While most of these e-mail messages cause no harm, the cost to prevent a breach in computer security from this and other methods increases every year, according to Ware (2004).

Additional security challenges can come from the installation of wireless routers, unauthorized downloads and installation of software, and the loss and theft of computer desktops, laptops, and portable storage media. Loss of hardware or storage media can cause considerable damage to an organization's reputation. In 2005, Bank of America disclosed that in late December 2004 it lost unencrypted computer backup tapes containing Social Security numbers and other personal data belonging to government employees based on 1.2 million federally issued credit cards. At the time of the announcement, there was no evidence that any fraudulent activity had occurred due to information that existed on those tapes. In 2001, the Federal Bureau of Investigation announced that it was missing 184 laptop computers; three computers held information considered sensitive, and one computer held confidential information (Weyden, 2001).

Given the increase in intensity and severity of system intrusion attempts, most organizations today are without sophisticated protection systems or an effective security

Table 1. Definition of key terms

Term	Definition
Malware	Short for malicious software. Malware is designed to disrupt computers and systems. Examples of Malware include viruses or Trojan horses. (Webopedia, n.d.)
Virus	A program that is easily reproducible, which spreads quickly within and across networks. Viruses can be disguised as or embedded within legitimate programs. Viruses quickly multiply and cause systems to slow down and stop functioning. (Webopedia, n.d.)
Trojan Horse	A program that is in the form of a non-malicious program. Trojan horses act as a shell for malicious payloads such as a virus or spyware. (Webopedia, n.d.)
Spyware	A program that becomes hidden on a system that captures the user's activities such as email and credit card numbers, and logs websites visited. This spyware then relays this information back to another unauthorized individual. (Webopedia, n.d.)
Adware	This program displays unwanted advertisements to the user based on user's web-browsing activity. (Webopedia, n.d.)
Script Kiddies	A person who is not technologically sophisticated, such as a "kiddie", who randomly seeks out a specific weakness over the Internet. (Webopedia, n.d.)
Social Engineering	Collecting private information by using tricks in order to gain the trust of victims. Social security numbers are often by convincing the victim that something is wrong with their account, and they need verification in order to correct the problem. (Webopedia, n.d.)
Spam	"Electronic junk mail or junk newsgroup postings" (Webopedia, n.d., para. 1).
Hacking	"Unauthorized access to or use of data, systems, server or networks, including any attempt to probe, scan or test the vulnerability of a system, server or network or to breach security or authentication measures without express authorization of the owner of the system, server or network" (Terms of Use Agreement, n.d., para. 20).

policy or process that addresses prevention, detection, and response to attempted network intrusion (Strahija, 2003).

Among the key findings of a Congressional report prepared by the Office of National Counterintelligence Executive was the integral role of digital forensics in combating economic and industrial espionage. The report notes that the vulnerability of technological and business secrets constitutes a threat to national security, as foreign governments or other individuals delve into corporate structures in order to secure sensitive technologies, collect profiles on potential human sources, and exploit industry conferences and seminars (Office of the National Counterintelligence Executive, 2005). Moreover, the exposure of medical, financial, legal, and other personnel data due to security breaches leaves corporations open to blackmail, theft or fraud. The threats associated with the loss of sensitive or proprietary corporate data are limited only by the imagination of the perpetrator. Furthermore, much of the nation's infrastructure hinges upon the effectiveness of both private and public institutions, such as those in the transportation, information and technology, chemical and hazardous materials, finance, energy, and telecommunications industries, to name a few. Criminal or terrorist breaches into these systems represent a potentially devastating threat to national security (The National Strategy to Secure Cyberspace, 2003). Therefore, not only is an effective preparedness and response plan integral to the network security policy of any company or organization, it is also important to the national infrastructure.

The loss of sensitive or proprietary data to criminal or otherwise illegitimate parties should be a primary concern for any organization. *Network intrusion*, *security breach,* and *security incidents* all relate to unauthorized access to computer data and systems. Security incidents are broken into three distinct types of activities:

1. Any breach or unauthorized access of corporate data which may or may not result in losses or damage. Individual computer hardware (such as laptops and desk top machines), storage media, or entire network systems are all potential targets.

2. Any use of corporate computer systems for malicious activity by internal or external forces.

3. Any event, malicious or accidental, which results in damages or losses to the company such as a virus or worm (*CIO Magazine*, 2004).

Examples of network threats include external and internal hacking and unauthorized entry, malicious code, and denial of service (DOS). The effects of network intrusion attempts can include the slowing or disrupting of network and software applications, hijacking of systems to send out unauthorized Spam, and damage or erasure of operating systems and computer files. The financial cost to an organization of responding to a one-time computer intrusion and its damage typically exceeds the organization's annual security budget, in some cases these costs exceeding $500,000 (*CIO Magazine*, 2004). These threats are no longer a petty annoyance. They are potentially disastrous and costly, and organizations should take steps to prevent and minimize their effects. The forensic process to collect, examine, analyze, and report intrusion attempts should be embedded within a company's network security policy through intrusion detection, intrusion prevention and application control.

This chapter focuses on three organizations' existing preparedness and responses to computer and network security incidents. The identity of these organizations has been obscured, so that the material presented will not be used in an attempt to access their systems. These three organizations shall be referred to in this work as follows: the health care company will be referred to as *Healthcare Company*; the school district will be referred to as *School District*; and the county government as *The County*. This analysis is provided in order for the reader to understanding the challenges to providing a secure network. Through the discussion of breach prevention and detection, as well as appropriate incident response, our intent is to (a) provide information about the real challenges involved in defending against system compromises, (b) to provide a foundation for the reader, and an ideal security policy against which his or her own network security policy can be compared. Lastly, (c) we look to future trends in the area of network security.

Issues, Controversies, Problems

The amount of money that organizations choose to spend on network security, and its corresponding complexity, varies greatly among organizations. Some companies believe in a comprehensive system for breach prevention and detection, with a physical separation of systems including utilizing a Demilitarized Zone (or DMZ) for access to the Internet, while others rely on their hardware for multiple purposes and systems with a direct connection to the outside world. There is also significant variability in organizations' security policy and planned response/ data collection. Some of the reasons for this variability include the organization's size, industry, and exposure to the internet companies that prevent external e-mail and Web-surfing have lower chance of intrusion attempt than a company that allows those activities. Other reasons for variability in network security are the requirement to comply with certain regulatory legislation such HIPAA or Sarbanes-Oxley; risk of catastrophe—will the impact of a successful intrusion attempt be extreme or minimal; does the organization have a disaster recovery systems in place, and how quickly will the organization be able to recover; and the history of severe intrusion attempts.

Breach Prevention/Detection

Organizations aiming to maximize their protection against computer breaches should first do self-assessments to determine their attractiveness as targets, and to identify their primary assets. Companies must determine "What kind of a target am I?" Financial, government, or government support agencies would take different approaches to security, than would smaller, local business such as a mom and pop bagel shop. In the same way, organizations must understand their assets that they are trying to protect. Is an operational network used for normal data-collection and processing most important, or is it protection of the already existing data? Answering this question should help the company to determine where they should allocate their resources. This analysis includes actual breaches as well as detecting/recording of blocked attempts. This collected information helps organizations understand the actual threats and detect patterns. For example, in 2003 experts were able to forecast the blaster worm by patterns they had seen of intrusions blocked.

In reference to the security breach at LexisNexis presented earlier in the chapter, Avivah Litan from the Gartner Group (2005) suggests three specific actions that should be implemented immediately by companies that possess sensitive customer information:

- Implement two-factor authentication for access for systems and databases. This will deter unauthorized sharing of simple user IDs and passwords in organizations that have access to such data.
- Implement activity-monitoring tools, at the application or database level, to detect patterns of unusual activity that may indicate fraud.

- Consider security practices as a key criterion when selecting information services providers.

The Security Policy

Dancho Danchev is a security consultant focusing on the implementation of security solutions, research and development of marketing concepts. Danchev (2003) stated that at a minimum, an organization's security policy should at a minimum address some of these following elements:

- How sensitive information must be handled.
- How to properly maintain user ID(s) and password(s), as well as any other accounting data.
- How to respond to a potential intrusion attempt.
- How to use workstations and Internet connectivity in a secure manner.
- How to properly use the corporate e-mail system. (p. 4)

Cisco Systems, a provider of Internet protocol-based (IP) networking solutions, identify three types of policy statements that should cover all network systems and data within an organization—the usage policy statement, partner acceptable use statement, and administrator acceptable use statement (Network Security Policy: Best Practices White Paper, 2003). They suggest that the usage policy statement should describe the users' roles and responsibilities and provide for punitive or disciplinary actions against an employee. The partner acceptable use statement should describe the use of data and appropriate conduct as well as what constitutes a security intrusion attempt and what actions will be taken should that occur. The administrator "acceptable use" statement should describe network administration, privilege review, and policy enforcement. Each of these policy statements should complement the other, without conflict or ambiguity. An aid in developing these statements and the underlying network security policy document is being able to draw upon the experiences of other organizations. In the remainder of this section we share successes and ongoing challenges faced by organizations trying to maintain their network security.

Planned Response/Data Collection

Larger companies should have certified forensic specialists on staff, to capture the appropriate information. Smaller organizations can use software such as EnCase Forensic Software by Guidance Software to preserve the electronic evidence, analyze it, and report on it. Companies specializing in forensic analysis can be found in most major US cities, and often they will assist in litigations. Each organization should make every attempt to prosecute these intrusions; however, these decisions are often made at the federal level. Because of legislation such as the HIPAA, Gramm-Leach-Bliley Act, and Sarbanes-Oxley require data collection, documentation and reporting, most organizations are mandated to collect this information and act on it regardless of prosecution.

The following section provides a brief description of how three different organizations had prepared for, and subsequently dealt with their own security breaches. The first, Healthcare Company, is a fairly detailed case study. The second two cases, School District and County, are shorter and are based on the limited information available at the time of this writing. However, all three of these cases demonstrate integral aspects of incident preparedness in digital forensics.

Case I: Healthcare Company

In early 2005, Healthcare Company was alerted to an outage on an internal firewall. The firewall bridged the companies "remote network" from their core campus network. The internal firewall had stopped responding to all management requests and any type of electronic communication.

The initial troubleshooting steps indicated that there may be hardware failure on the firewall itself. Engineers from the company worked with their hardware vendor and after several hours of troubleshooting, it was decided that there was a flood of data packets that caused the firewall to utilize 100% of its resources. The utilization was so high that utilities such as packet dumps or management analysis were not possible. A physical disconnect of the interfaces was required to determine where the traffic utilization was originating from. It was later found to be a single host sending an extremely large number of very small packets, and in effect caused a denial of service attack on the firewall. The attack was not directed at the firewall, but as the firewall inspected each packet, it overloaded its capabilities. Though the bandwidth capabilities of the firewall were not affected, the interrupt process utilization was at 100%.

The network service was degraded for three days. It was later found that the single host had connected to the network via a dialup connection into a remote access server. Further analysis determined that the host was not foreign, but actually was a company asset that was assigned to a field employee. Further investigation of the host found a great amount of unwanted software that may have caused the network interruption, but it was unknown which software was actually malicious. After comparing data to firewall logs and other key security devices, the most suspicious application was called "view toolbar".

Company staff researched the view toolbar and found it to be a somewhat harmless application that came with the standard adware features. The company set up a laboratory environment to download the application to test their research. The results from a Google search with the verbiage "view toolbar download" were a page full of Web sites from which the toolbar could be downloaded. The first Google result appeared to be a page to download the toolbar. Within three to eight seconds of launching that Web site and opening the Web page, the computer hung, that is its processing ceased, and the lab firewall went down. Immediately the staff realized they were dealing with a malicious Web site, not a malicious toolbar. Later, through trial and error, it was determined that the first five results from their Google search were all malicious sites.

The company contacted the major security companies such as Symantec, Microsoft, and Checkpoint to discover if what they had found was a known vulnerability. None had seen this new type of exploit.

Healthcare Company contacted SecureWave, a Luxembourg company. SecureWave advertised a product that gave administrators complete control of both hardware and software. In late January 2005, SecureWave gave a demonstration of their software capabilities to the management of Healthcare Company. Though impressed, the engineers from the healthcare organization wanted to truly test the product. They advised the SecureWave representative of their latest security exploit and asked if SecureWave would be willing to install their product in a lab environment and visit the malicious Website. SecureWave agreed; their representative stated, "If there is vulnerability on an operating system that our product can't stop, we want to know about it."

The laboratory was set up and SecureWave software installed on a host provided by the healthcare company. The host was pointed to the known malicious Web site. The results were astounding. SecureWave not only stopped the vulnerability, but gave the onlookers a peek into how the malicious site worked. SecureWave logs detailed exact steps of how the Web site operated, including the files is placed on the host and registry changes it tried to make. Initially a java script was run that disabled all ActiveX security that was on the browser. An ActiveX session was then started and nine DLL application files were loaded to miscellaneous directories on the host. Multiple registry changes were attempted, but stopped by SecureWave. "View Tool Bar" replica appeared, but turned out to be nothing more than a Java IFrame posing as a toolbar.

Once again the major security companies were given the information found in the SecureWave logs. Three weeks later, Microsoft released nine critical operating system and explorer patches that are believed to be linked to the type of exploit stopped by SecureWave.

Though Healthcare Company experienced a network impact, the story is still a success. They were able to find a true zero day protection software for their host and server assets along with additional benefits to assist them in safeguarding their patient information and exceed their HIPAA requirements for electronic security.

Security Policy

In addition to their published security policy, Healthcare Company uses six techniques for breach prevention and detection: (1) *Firewalls* are deployed throughout the network to interface between the private network and the public Internet. All traffic and breach attempts are logged and stored on a security server for historical evaluation. All computers that can be taken off of the network, such as laptops, should also have firewall software installed, which blocks and logs intrusion attempts. Traffic auditing should also be enabled on the firewalls to capture what traffic is being allowed through and what traffic is being blocked as well as determining if the firewall settings have changed. Healthcare Company uses information gained by auditing firewall traffic to gather information about employees' network habits and bandwidth utilization. This information is reviewed on a monthly basis looking at from which it is determined what sites should be blocked based on amount of traffic and subsequent bandwidth utilization. (2) *Intrusion Detection Systems (IDS)* are strategically placed throughout the network. IDS systems watch for signatures of vulnerabilities, and their databases of intrusion patterns are updated periodically to insure networks against the latest intrusion attempts. (3) *IDS Reporting* records the data in the historical logs and prepares daily/weekly/monthly reports. These reports are analyzed and for traffic patterns or policy violations. (4) *Router / Switch fail Attempt Alerts* are used to notify security staff when a router or switch has three or more failed attempts at login. Notification is logged and sent to the security staff via e-mail. (5) *Network Filters* are put in place on the majority of remote Wide Area Network devices. These devices have filters that limit network traffic. For example, Internet Control Message Protocol (ICMP) or PING is often used by support staff. The ICMP is allowed from the support staff subnet, but is not allowed from any other network. Hackers often use ICMP to assist in network discovery and denial of service attacks. There is a vulnerability of *Teardrop attack* on computers running Windows NT 4.0, among other operating systems. In a Teardrop attack, the receiving network is unable to handle certain erroneous packets causing the network to crash. This vulnerability has been closed years ago as most systems have migrated to Windows 2000 or Windows XP. The ongoing problem with PING is that an outside person is able to guess the company's network topology. Using PING using tools such as traceroute or tracert for windows an individual can determine how many hops (such firewalls and routers) are present, and name of the company's ISP. Although organizations are able to block external ICMP, internal ICMPs can still be accomplished by an organization's guests if the individuals are given access to the network for print, Internet, e-mail or file access. (6) *Operating System Hardware/Software lockdown* is a key in securing a network. SecureWave is an IO control software that can lock down any IO device so physical security breaches can be prevented. SecureWave also allows software control, so that only approved files can be loaded to memory. This prevents Trojan horses, viruses, spyware, and other malicious vulnerabilities from being launched on a computer.

As a proactive intrusion detection tool, Healthcare Company uses *honey pots* in an unsecured area of the Internet. A *honey pot* (also spelled honeypot) is a host computer that is purposely left vulnerable, but with some minimum security in order to entice an intruder. The techniques of hackers and activities of viruses are monitored and adjustments to the network are made in response. Spernow (2000) has identified how Microsoft uses the honeypot as an important aspect of intrusion detection and prevention.

The honeypot-network approach to intrusion detection has recently emerged as one of the most important trends in enterprise information security. In setting up a honeypot network, security administrators design a section of an enterprise's network to make it attractive to intruders. This section will contain false information that appears to be, for example, application source code or future marketing plans. Once an intruder enters this area—which no authorized user would have reason to enter—the system automatically alerts security staff, who begin tracking the intruder's activities and may even feed him disinformation for the purpose of learning more about his identity and location.

Understanding the nature and motivation of intrusion attempts is critical to enhancing information security procedures. A hack by a teenager hoping to impress his friends can have serious consequences for an enterprise but usually poses less of problem—and almost always calls for a different degree and type of response—than corporate espionage or politically motivated "information terrorism." The honeypot network offers enterprises the most important element they need in identifying intruders and their motives: time. Time is especially critical when—as perhaps with the Microsoft hack— the intruders work in foreign countries, where identifying and apprehending intruders may require high-level cooperation between governments. (para. 5&6)

Only the larger companies typically use honeypots, although only a few companies in fact actually need them—the others are able to use the information gathered by the hosts of the honeypots. The following section addresses what to do in the event of intrusion detection.

Planned Response/Data Collection

The key to network security is the response plan. Though each breach is different, simple yet comprehensive plans can keep a breach minimized or contained.

As a part of its planned response and data collection activities, Healthcare Company considers reporting authority and reporting formats. The kind of breach and data accessed must be reviewed to determine the nature of incident reporting required. Reporting is encouraged, if not mandated, to internal company legal, risk management and compliance designees, law enforcement, and federal government. Patients are to be notified if protected information is disclosed due to HIPAA, and finally notification should be made to customers, if their personal information has been exposed.

Prosecution of intrusion is encouraged, although cost is often a barrier for small companies. Forensic analysis and even the data capture and imaging of the affected hardware can become costly. While many organizations cannot afford proper analysis needed for prosecution, they prefer to patch the hole and move on. Prosecution in general is a complex problem due to multiple jurisdictions and the nature of the crime. These types of crimes often occur from a distance, either across state lines or internationally. The collection of credible evidence is therefore an important task for any criminal investigation of network breaching. We will look at specific steps to be taken to preserve evidence in the discussion of Data Collection below.

1. **Planned Response.** Healthcare Company has an emergency response team (ERT) consisting of information technology staff that respond to security breaches. Because each breach is different, the team analyzes the effect and severity of the breach to help them determine the appropriate response. General guidelines are set within the team to know how to respond in general. One guideline is "if the attack is a denial of service, but the security and data of a host system is intact, filtering countermeasures should be employed to prevent the attacker's source address from getting through." Another such guideline is "to isolate and disconnect infected systems, and disable ports if necessary. Test your system to determine if the virus is still spreading."

   The ERT team has the endorsement from upper management to shut down any and all systems necessary to prevent protected health information (PHI) or financial information from being accessed. Normally, any planned outage must have executive authority, but during such crises the ERT has full authority to stop any vulnerability to save critical information.

2. **Data Collection.** Data collection is an important piece in vulnerability assessment and recovery. Any time a system is suspected of being breached, the machine is secluded and a bit for bit replica is created. The replica is created so IT staff or investigators can go through the information without damaging evidence of the breach. Network logs from firewalls and IDS systems are captured and copied for examination.

Data is examined with the following intent:

- Method of the breach.

- What information was revealed?

- Is there still vulnerability on a different system?

- What was left behind, such as a *rootkit* or a Trojan horse? A rootkit is a set of tools allowing an intruder to collect user IDs and passwords.

These findings would be used for determining the next step. For example, if a violation of federal law occurred, federal law enforcement would be notified. If patient information was breached, the appropriate patients would be notified immediately.

Documenting incidents is very important, not only as an aid for solving the intrusion problem, but also to develop an audit trail that may be used in criminal proceedings. It is critical to capture as much information as possible and create forms enabling users who are not ID specialists to provide as much information as possible. Some of the important elements of incident reporting forms are:

1. Contact information for person(s) discovering problem and/or responsible parties.

2. Target systems and/or networks. Know all about the systems under attack, including operating system versions, IP addresses and so on.

3. Purpose of systems under attack. What are the systems used for (Payroll, Research and Design, Patient Records, and so on), as well as some kind of a ranking of the importance of the system.

4. Evidence of intrusion. Discover anything that is known about the intrusion.

    a.   Method of attacks used

    b.   Source IP address of attacker

    c.   Network contact information for this address

5. List of parties notified. This can include the technical contacts, internal legal contacts and possibly the legal authorities.

Healthcare Company had its computer network infected with the Nimda-D virus in 2002, which cause a full network outage for five days. The cost to repair the damage caused by the virus, excluding lost productivity and revenue, was in excess of $150,000. The cost to repair the damage from this virus was 2.5 times the amount the organization budgeted for security for all of 2002. This organization plans to spend approximately $1.8 million over two years 2004 and 2005, due to the requirements of Sarbanes-Oxley Act and Health Insurance Portability and Accountability Act (HIPAA). The current year annual budget for security in 2005 is approximately $700,000, more than a ten-fold increase over their 2002 security budget.

Case II: School District

In its current state, network security at the School District is heavily slanted toward the end user and decentralized site management. Each site is able to purchase equipment and software and establish e-mail and Web presence autonomously with little mandate to follow guidelines provided by the technology department. One school installed its own e-mail system, which was hacked into and taken over as an e-mail forwarding service for illegitimate e-mail. Since spam is blocked by the IP Address from which it is sent, using the school district's IP address gave the hacker the ability to temporarily bypass e-mail filtering software. Once the e-mail forwarding was realized and shut down by the School District's technology department, the hacker was then able to use the e-mail system as a proxy to deliver pornography. If the technology department had been involved in setting up the e-mail system, it would have been standardized to another, more secure system.

Security Policy

School District does not have an official computer and network security policy. Their informal policies are driven by funding and legality. As their federal funding mandates content filtering, School District is obligated to comply. Likewise, illegal peer-to-peer file sharing such as the old Napster and Kaaza, are also prevented. While the technology department manager wrote and submitted a formal security policy to the administration for approval, it was subsequently returned for clarification. After additional rewrites and resubmission attempts, which were met with additional and requests for clarification by the administration, the policy was abandoned by the technology manager.

School District's management staff identified that ideally, their security policy would include a number of aspects including (1) an override to the existing site-based IT management, (2) establishing a DMZ, (3) centralized purchasing and standardization on applications and hardware, (4) control of wireless access points, and (5) limit network access to School District owned equipment only.

Planned Response/Data Collection

School District has not considered a planned response to network intrusion, or how data are to be collected. In contrast to Healthcare, School District (with over 100 schools) spends only a little more per year on network security than the salary of their security manager. The answer to why one organization's security is more inclusive than another's can be demonstrated in four areas. These are: (1) *liability* (HIPAA, Sarbanes-Oxley), (2) *risk of catastrophe*—impact of intrusion attempt, (3) *existence of disaster recovery*, and (4) *history of severe intrusion attempt,* or loss. Should their network become affected and unusable, the schools can continue to function until they can activate their disaster recovery plan, using tape backups at an offsite location. Therefore, while School District has yet to experience a network intrusion, their risk of catastrophe is minimal. These schools also have little exposure with regard to Sarbanes-Oxley due to their non-for-profit organizational structure. HIPAA liability, while present due to student medical information, remains relatively minimal in contrast to a typical medical provider.

Case III: The County

Due to heightened security concerns, the County divulged comparatively few details about their intrusion event. What is known is that the County gave little attention to the importance of their network security, until they had a major security incident in which their 600 employees' and seven councilors' payroll and personal information were lost. A data storage device was stolen from an office, and this device held the payroll and personnel information.

Security Policy

At the time that this theft occurred, the county did not have an effective, written policy in place. The County implemented their security policy two months after their security breach.

Planned Response/ Data Collection

The County did not have a planned response or data collection plan. They did however pay for credit monitoring for these individuals for one year, at considerable cost. The presence of an effective security policy may have helped prevent the loss and subsequent liability incurred by the County.

We will now look at existing security policies, and the challenges faced in developing effective policies.

Lessons Learned

From the descriptions of how three different organizations prepared for and responded to security threats, three clear lessons emerge: have a clear policy, engage in continuous reassessment, and learn from past mistakes.

Clear Policy

A lucid and effective policy that is widely disseminated and familiar to employees is essential. Healthcare Company's clearly defined policy enabled it to respond effectively to network intrusion. Their policy is as follows:

1. User IDs and passwords must be kept confidential and cannot be displayed.

2. Employees cannot connect company equipment to other networks or to wireless networks without IT involvement.

3. The loading of any software without IT involvement on company computer systems or on the network can cause network disruptions and the loss of productivity or data. Such unauthorized action is unlawful and subject to monetary penalties.

4. Personal software, unauthorized software or unlicensed software cannot be loaded on company equipment.

5. Copies of company owned software cannot be made or loaded on personal computers.

6. The IT User Administrator form must be completed for all terminated employees.

7. If an employee has patient health information, company proprietary information or employee ID information on a mobile device, such as a laptop, PDA or USB drive, or on any form of media, such as a CD or floppy drive, the file must be password protected or encrypted.

8. Patient health information, company proprietary information or employee ID information should not be maintained on personal computer systems (non-company-owned systems).

9. Employees may not disable virus protection or any other software running on company equipment without IT involvement.

10. Computer or system hardware and software must be purchased through IT.

11. Managers are responsible for ensuring their employees adhere to this policy.

However, although they have a written policy that is specific in nature and covers many of the aspects that should be included, there are few repercussions for employees that are in non-compliance with the standards provided. A written policy that can be ignored is as ineffective as no policy at all, as we shall see later in the chapter, in the Attacks and Outcomes section.

Continuous Reassessment

As threats evolve to overcome defenses, cybersecurity demands an ongoing testing and evaluation of existing systems. School District surprisingly reported only the one security incident involving the takeover of an unsecured e-mail server. Their liability so far has been minimal, given their absence of a written security policy, and ineffective topology. While continuing their existing site based IT management and decentralized purchasing of software and hardware, School District moves forward integrating their systems. As their systems become more easily accessible, with connectivity through the Internet, we expect this to drastically increase their number and severity of intrusion attempts, both internally and externally generated. Even while they seek to improve their topology by adding a DMZ and additional intrusion detection systems, the absence of a security policy will probably lead to additional, more serious security breaches.

After their system became impacted due to an employee downloading unauthorized and malicious software, Healthcare Company was able to respond quickly, identify the problem, and identify and report a new type of exploitation. Reassessments of network security are an ongoing effort.

Learn from Past Mistakes

As an ongoing practice, Healthcare Company examines network breaches and case studies from other companies to insure their network is secure. They also write a detailed report of any system intrusion and use the information to find ways to improve the long-term security of the network. Their goal is to learn from their mistakes and find ways to patch the holes. The employee that downloaded an unauthorized program that was unknowingly malicious was not sanctioned, which exposes a large gap in Healthcare Company's policy. Healthcare Company is aware that threat of sanctions and punishment for non-compliance of their security policy, is not followed up with imposed sanctions and penalties, such as reprimands and suspension from work. While they acknowledge that their policy is ineffective as a threat of sanctions or punishment to employees for non-compliance, they have no plans to fix this problem. As non-compliance with the security policy continues to be tolerated, lapses in security and intrusions will continue as a result.

The County's security incident, a lost laptop computer containing employee personal data, was extremely costly in terms of both dollars and reputation. In response, the county implemented their 21-page security policy. Their policy provides specifics relating to physical security and asset management, account access and control, prohibited and personal use, as well as specific enforcement and sanctions. There have been no further employee causes security lapses since this policy was enacted.

Solutions and Recommendations

Effective intrusion preparedness and response relies on a combination of policies and processes, organizational commitment, and employee accountability. An Ideal Security Policy and an Ideal Security Topology are presented as the ideal model of organizational security.

Ideal Security Policy

There are many challenges to formulating a comprehensive and effective computer and network security policy. External customers, internal customers and employees, organizational goals, and emerging security threats must all be considered. Organizations must weigh the cost of protecting the network against the possibility of a serious security incident. Internal political considerations must be taken into account. For example, Healthcare Company had to overcome the disparity between its executive's needs and wishes, and operational security. Executives demanded Web-based e-mail such as HotMail or Yahoo Mail, although these e-mail pathways are unprotected by the organization's e-mail filters. Other political considerations must also be weighed, such as how to spend the limited IT budget; should the organization purchase new desktop computers, or upgrade their virus protection. As a network becomes breached by a hacker, the IT department may decide to shut down access to other applications or systems, in order to observe the ongoing intrusion to learn how to make the network more secure in the future. This exploration is often necessary, especially when dealing with an unknown or new threat, although the organization's executives might disapprove. The following is a framework or model of an ideal security policy.

Purpose /Goal

According to Robert J. Shimonski (2004), the purpose of the security policy is to formally state the "objectives, goals, rules and formal procedures that help to define the overall security posture and architecture for said organization" (para. 5). In addition to that basic framework, Shimonski goes on to say that security policies must address seven important functions: (1) it must be understandable; (2) it must be realistic; (3) it must be consistent; (4) it must be enforceable; (5) it must be documented, distributed, and communicated properly; (6) it must be flexible; and (7) it must be reviewed periodically (2004).

Customization

Security policy should be customized to the organization's unique characteristics. A policy should provide reasonable expectations of privacy for employees. List procedures used by IT to review security especially when it impacts the productivity or privacy of employees. It should, for instance, include the people who need to be notified when reviewing an employee workstation (the employee's manager, and others in the chain of command) or shared file system.

Asset Defining/Risk Analysis

Danchev (2003) suggests a strategy for asset definition and risk analysis. He suggests identification of company assets and determination of potential risks and an ongoing process. Assets must be defined to ensure that they are properly protected.   Consider who the assets are protected from, and then identify the potential risks. Set up a process for continuous or at a minimum, periodic review to identify new assets.

List and prioritize the organization's critical assets (categories, systems, processes). Hardware, networks and software, should all be included in the risk analysis process. In reviewing hardware, all servers, desk top and laptop machines, and removable media such as CD's and USB drives should be considered.

Networks provide outside access for employees, vendors, and clients. Security of the point of entry, whether it is via VPN or dialup, should be considered. Restriction of access to specific applications or systems, and setting limits to the duration which a password will be active.

Outdated software and patches may lead to vulnerabilities, and should be identified. Unencrypted software and file sharing applications (Kazaa, Sharereactor, E-Donkey, etc.) also represent potential vulnerabilities, as do Instant Message (chat) software, entertainment or freeware software coming from unknown and untrustworthy sources.

Threat Management

The organization must perform a risk analysis, identifying company assets and determining who should access them using the principal of *least privilege*, or minimum access necessary to perform required activities. Assets could include proprietary information, customer data, intellectual property, or simply access to e-mail or access to the Internet. These assets may be used by employees, partners (for instance, an extranet), vendors (servicing large-scale mainframe or storage), customers (registered users to receive service information or upgrades), or general Internet users. The access policy should define these groups, and define roles within these groups; for instance an employee can be an accountant, manager, or administrator roles. Access to the assets should be defined for each role, including access to the Internet and e-mail. Third-party policy enforcement tools Netegrity's eTrust Identity and Access Management tools look at (1) Who are you? (authentication), (2) What do you want? (authorization), and (3) Why do you want it? (role—defines reading/writing/executing policies).

Threat management is separated between on-site physical security threats, and Internet threats. Physical security threats exploit passwords, virus protection, removable media, and incident handling. Creation of passwords is an important task that often is given little thought, due to the increasing of systems and accounts that requiring password protection. Care should be taken so an individual's login consists of a password unique to only one account. The same password should not be used across systems, as once that password is compromised, complete access is available. Do not use common or familiar words as passwords, such as a child's name or birthday, or social security number. As a rule, passwords should be no longer than seven characters, and should contain some numbers and symbols. New passwords should not consist of a previous password with a "1" added to the end, i.e. the old password is FL&3RX and the new password then becomes FLY&3RX1.

Automatic aging of passwords should be turned on for every application or system. Users are encouraged to change their password prior to the aging expiration, at which time they are forced to change it. Users should only be allowed to reuse a password after the fifth time they change passwords. The new password should following the creation process listed above. When practical, organizations should consider using two-factor authentication mechanisms such as RSA's SecurID to secure VPNs, and requiring public-key signatures for authenticating the source of e-mail.

Danchev (2003) suggests that organizations structure their security policy to explicitly instructing employees how to work on the computer and in the cyber world, in order to avoid exposure to computer viruses. He suggests never opening files and programs received from unknown sources. At a minimum, all file and program should be scanned with an updated virus scanner before they are opened, regardless of the file extension (.exe, .bat, .com, .doc, etc.). Full system scans should be scheduled to run at least once a week using updated virus signatures. Virus protection should never be deactivated, unless it is done so temporarily by the IT or security department.

Removable media (CD's, floppies, tapes, USB drives, etc.) should be controlled so that their use is restricted to only company owned machines. Media brought in from outside the organization should never be accessed. If it is required that this media be used, care must be taken to ensure that no malicious programs are present in them. A process for conducting periodic system backup and testing as well as system maintenance should be included in the security policy.

Since every situation of security intrusion will vary, organizations should predefine and implement an intrusion response plan that provides general overview of how to respond to vulnerabilities. Within the response plan should exist prior authorization to shut down systems if necessary to protect critical data and systems. The organization should have at the ready, trained personnel with the ability to user forensic technology to track the steps of an exploit. The organization should use security incidents as a training tool, refocusing policy or topology as necessary.

Danchev (2003) identified Internet-based threats to security that include Web browsing, e-mail, instant messaging (IM), and downloading software and opening files. He suggests that organizations determine acceptable use for each of these activities that could lead to a security breach. Companies need to define when and how individuals are allowed to browse the Web, download and open files, and communicate using e-mail and IM. The potential threats posed by each of these activities should be clearly communicated, in addition that their activities monitored for inappropriate or illegal activity.

Additional Internet-based threats include Web conferencing tools, remote computing, and employee owned equipment. Web conferencing tools and their access remote control tools also expose organizations to vulnerability. Networks should default to prevent access to conferencing and remote control applications such as WebEx. Then networks are configured to allow for Web conferencing, it provides vulnerability for hackers to come in and take over using the remote control tools.

Remote access can take the form of Virtual Private Network (VPN) or wireless Internet access. VPN solutions are good for productivity, but without control of what is done allow for network vulnerability. Systems using VPN are still connected to the Internet, and Internet activities should be regulated with this in mind. Systems using VPN must be protected with an updated firewall; without a firewall, the system and network is vulnerable to intrusion attempt.

By using Wi-Fi, laptop users are vulnerable to hackers who could steal data, introduce viruses, launch spam or attacks other computers. This type of vulnerability is easily exploited in public hotspot locations. In January 2005, the total number of public hotspots exceeded 50,000 internationally, with approximately 25,500 of these locations in the U.S. (Worldwide WiFi Hotspots Reach 50,000 Milestone, 2005). With the total number of hotspots is expected to double in 2005, Wi-Fi vulnerability will continue to grow (ibid).

And finally, employee owned equipment should never be used to gain access the network.

Balance

Organizational security must be balanced against external customer needs, internal customer requirements, and employee privacy issues. At the same time, organizations must determine their risk for a security breach versus how much they should expend to prevent and detect such intrusions. Balancing the need to allow software vendors access to perform maintenance against keeping the network and attached systems secured is not an easy decision, nor are the other balancing questions. The decisions of access by customers, employees, and internal customers must be carefully weighed in favor of organizational security. These decisions will not be popular, and will often require further and frequent review.

Implementation/Distribution

Post the security policy centrally, so that it is available to all employees both electronically and in paper form. The policy should be reviewed on a regular basis, with changes made as necessary. Send out important changes, additions, and deletions when warranted. Other notification of changes can be made via e-mail, memo, or voicemail.

Distribute policy to employees, having then sign and return their promise to comply with the policy. Annually thereafter, employees should review the entire policy and sign that they promise to comply. Definitions of terms should be included in the policy's glossary.

Enforcement and Sanctions

List and enforce disciplinary action for lapses in the security policy. Appropriate use, prohibited use, and personal use should all be defined, in addition to listing types of activities requiring management approval, and approval hierarchy. Define disciplinary action up to and including termination, for violations of the security policy. In addition, contractors may be liable to damages and penalties allowed under law. Illegal activity should be reported to the appropriate legal authorities.

Supervisors are responsible for ensuring employee's compliance with the security policy. Employee's usage can be monitored based on request by the employee's supervisor, department head, or Human Resources. An account can be immediately suspended with reasonable suspicion of a security breach or misuse. The employee's supervisor and Human Resources will be notified, and analysis of the account and records completed. Disciplinary action should result if warranted.

Revisions

Set a goal, perhaps annually, to revise the security policies. Understand and know where vulnerabilities exist. Set goals to correct them vulnerabilities, neutralizing as many of them as possible. Learn from each incident and response. Create and implement audit and test policies, including these in the revised versions of the security policy.

Ideal Security Topology

Every network will be unique, but core techniques can be utilized to minimize vulnerabilities. Hackers and scripted vulnerabilities use many techniques to not only penetrate the network, but gather information that could be used to infiltrate a network. There are basic measures that can be implemented, which would enhance network protection and force malicious attackers to move on to their next victim. If a company does not have the resources to employee network security staff, they should hire an outside company or service provider that would help to secure their network. The following is a comprehensive list of basic protective measures included in an ideal security topology.

1.   **Edge Network**
   a.   Service Provider—Many Internet service providers provide denial of service (DOS) attacks and pattern alerts. Though a firewall is designed to fend of DOS attacks, this option allows the firewall to operate with out the additional load of DOS attacks. Limiting any unnecessary traffic to the network equipment will enhance your quality of service to the organization and its customers. Receiving alerts from the service provider about possible vulnerabilities and traffic patterns can assist in foreseeing large scale vulnerabilities.

b. Perimeter Equipment—Separate the firewall function from the perimeter routers. A perimeter router should have a minimal number of services. Services such as FTP, TFTP, Telnet, should only be utilized if absolutely necessary. Console access is the most secure way to manage a network device, allowing all IP access to be minimized. Applications such as IP-Reach by Raritan, allow management of an access point that must be physically connected to the router.

   i. Security—Perimeter routers should contain access lists or filters to only allow management from a small range of IP's, preferably from the organization's private network. If remote access is needed encrypted communications should be utilized such as SSH. Filters should shut down top vulnerabilities ports that are not used. For example, few companies actually utilize TCP and UDP ports 135 – 139 to the Internet. Filters should shut these ports down. ICMP should also be used only if mandatory. Shutting ICMP down will further assist in hiding the network from some of the basic intrusion attempts.

c. Firewall—A firewall should be capable of stateful packet inspection, tracking each connection traversing all interfaces of the firewall and makes sure they are valid. This allows packet inspection for vulnerabilities and exploits.

   i. The network between the firewalls and perimeter routers should be as minimized as possible. If there is only one single router and a single firewall, a 30 bit mask (255.255.255.252) should be used to minimize the available network space within that zone.

   ii. Security—Outbound ports should be limited. Many companies secure inbound connections, but open most outbound ports. This topology can empower exploits and open gaps within security. Only outbound ports needed for legitimate business purposes should be opened. Auditing and logging of the traffic will also help identify patterns and possible exploits.

d. Traffic Monitors / IDS / IPS

   i. Services such as Websense should monitor and report Web traffic and block known malicious Websites that deliver code to computers via Web surfing. Spyware and adware can have an adverse affect on operating systems and provide information useful for potential hackers. Generated reports can also be used by administrators to enforce company policies regarding Web surfing and in return provide a better quality of service to their customers and employees.

   ii. IDS and IPS systems are an integral piece in network security. Never rely solely on a firewall for protection. Placing IDS & IPS systems strategically within the network will allow enable the organization to see what vulnerabilities are getting past the firewall. Free IDS systems are available, such as Snort (www.snort.org) to allow real-time monitoring of data. LanCope offers a StealthWatch product that offers excellent functionality for quick monitoring of vulnerabilities and network analyzation.

2.   **DMZ**

    a.   A DMZ is recommended. A zone that has a physical or virtual separate assignment with a structured topology to limit its communications to other company assets. DMZ or exposed hosts should be monitored very closely. Any server or computer that has a Static Public IP, NATed or not, should have all unnecessary services shut off. The host should have minimal purpose. Limit the amount of allowed traffic to this host.

    b.   Inbound and outbound e-mail should utilize two different hosts. Allowing a single host to act as inbound and outbound gateways, single use servers allow for the possibility that it will be used as a gateway for unwanted e-mail.

3.   **Internet Network Hosts & Network Topology**

    a.   Servers and PC's cannot be ignored. Updated security patches and correct configuration is an important step in securing the network. Having a firewall in and IDS in place is only a piece of the puzzle. A poorly configured computer can have all the security bypassed and expose the network to malicious intrusion attempts.

        i.   Patch Management—Keeping Servers and PC's up to date with the current patches can help alleviate the possibility of a vulnerability being exploited. Unfortunately, many patches from the OS vendor are released weeks or months after vulnerability is discovered.

        ii.   Install Lockdown—Normal users should not be administrators on hosts. Administrator level functions should be handled by IT personnel. In addition, unauthorized applications and I/O devices should be controlled. Many companies have paper policies but no enforcement actions.

            1.   SecureWave has a product that allows full I/O and Application control. This allows administrators to deny items such as thumb drives, CD-ROMs, and floppy drives. SecureWave allows encryption of certain I/O devices and also allows only certain types or brands to be utilized. SecureWave also allows application control. No files can be loaded to memory, unless it is approved on a white list. This allows complete protection from spyware, adware, Trojans, and unwanted applications from being installed on company hosts. The *white list* concept is a paradigm shift in administration theories. Many products offer control and will have a list of unapproved applications or files. A white list is a list of approved applications or files. This provides a smaller more comprehendible list to manage.

        iii.   File Encryption—Encryption on hard drives of servers and hosts of important or proprietary information can prevent information from being stolen if a computer is ever stolen. This information can be easily accessed, without a system password. Even bios passwords cannot protect the data, as the hard drive.

    b.   Internal Protocols and network management should be limited as much as possible. For example, only allow ICMP from a subnet designated to IT staff.

ICMP is used in many Trojans as a discovery to pass vulnerabilities on a mass scale.

Alternative Solutions

One example of trying a variety of approaches is the *New Mexico Mounted Patrol*. This organization is an unfunded law enforcement agency that utilizes officers with a range of experience from the private sector. All of their officers volunteer on a part-time basis to provide the state of New Mexico with thousands of hours of policing with no cost to New Mexico taxpayers.

One of the focuses in the recent years is digital crime. Each year statistics of digital crime increases and the resources for law enforcement are limited. The New Mexico Mounted Patrol has been working with several companies in the private sector to help understand and defeat intruders of digital crime.

During an evaluation of software, officers from the New Mexico Mounted Patrol were able to test an effective product from LanCope called StealthWatch. StealthWatch is a utility that monitors network traffic and alerts to any vulnerabilities or anomaly within a network. "The demo was setup within a ten minute period, and shortly after an intruder was found on the test environment" explained Chief Erwin. "The demonstration was meant to give an overview of the product; we didn't expect to actually find an intruder on the test network that we thought was secure!"

This software demonstration provided law enforcement with a good example of the tools that the private industry uses for protection. It is critical that law enforcement understand these types of tools so they may partner with the private industry to defeat system intruders.

Future Trends

There is no end in sight to the increasing number and varieties of computer network intrusions taking place. While the awareness of computer based crime increases, the complexity of prosecuting offenders across jurisdictions or internationally does little to deter these types of crime. Fortunately, technology continues to advance with regard to intrusion prevention, detection, and response.

Adaptive Behavioral Intrusion Detection

The concept of behavioral intrusion detection is comparing activity across a network to a pre-established baseline. The organization establishes some access points in the network, such as at the firewall, and determines a normal level of activity, around which ongoing activity is compared. The baseline is set during a designated learning period, after which the system only then evaluates ongoing system data. By this comparison of ongoing activity to the static baseline, deviations from the baseline would be investigated for potential security threats. The limitation of the one-time learning period is that the baseline becomes quickly obsolete due to business changes, network updates, and emergent security threats. Resetting the baseline can remediate the problem, until the next internal or environmental change.

Adaptive behavioral intrusion detection collects data from the network to sets its baseline continuously, rather than a one-time basis. Using real-time network data provides a higher level of security. The system continuously analyzes network data, which allows it to "identify previously unknown threats, covert channel attacks and sophisticated evasion techniques" (Paly, 2004, para. 29). Using this methodology allows the system to respond to changes in network traffic and evolving security threats. The system monitors both inside and outside of the firewall, so that attempted intrusions as well as actual intrusions can be monitored.

Network Cloaking

Network cloaking prevents network intrusions by making protected networks invisible to malicious external users. It does so by responding to an intrusion attempt while the attack is in progress. This occurs as the technology recognizes the intrusion attempt and stops it before any malicious packets penetrate the network. Hiding the ports prevents unauthorized users from discovering other potentially damaging information about the protected network such as applications. It is believed that the use of cloaking eliminates the risk of port service attacks from unauthenticated users.

Application Control

While most organizations work off a prohibited or *black list*, it is now possible for these same organizations to restrict unauthorized and malicious programs using application control via a *white list* of centrally approved program files. Only those programs appearing on the white list are enabled for execution. By restricting which programs are authorized for execution, it is possible to eliminate the launching of games, shareware, malicious programs, and any other unauthorized and unwanted programs. Each allowed program is assigned a signature algorithm, which is verified prior to its execution. Should a program not be approved or is approved but contains any type of modification, it will be prevented from running unless it receives specific approval.

These three security advancements within intrusion detection, intrusion prevention, and application control continue the fight for network security. We expect to see more complex and effective developments in the area as a direct response to the number and severity of network intrusions increase.

Conclusions

One integral component of digital forensics is the safeguarding of corporate and organizational data that can lead to identity theft, technology theft, monetary larceny, fraud, blackmail, extortion, and even threats to national security if it falls into the wrong hands. Continuous organizational vigilance is required in order to maintain security against network intrusion. A business owner, manager, and network security administrator has many tools that allow him or her to adequately protect their vital computer systems and databases. Unfortunately, as we have shown above, organizations and the people within them do not always act as they should. Companies fail to develop, implement, and enforce their policy. Employees circumvent established procedures and processes, and equipment frequently becomes lost or stolen. We discussed these and other challenges to network security, and provide guidance as to creating an effective network topology and security policy. Finally, we reviewed newer and emerging technologies, which companies can now employ to prevent data loss and network intrusion. Safeguarding organizational data is a key component in the forensic application of cyber technology, given the risks to personal, corporate, and even national security.

References

Danchev, D. (2003). *Building and implementing a successful information security policy*. Retrieved April 15, 2005, from http://www.windowsecurity.com/articles/Building_Implementing_Security_Policy.html

Litan, A. (2005). *Latest security breach shows need to tighten data access.* Retrieved April 19, 2005, from http://www.gartner.com/DisplayDocument?doc_cd=127287

National strategy to secure cyberspace. (2003). Retrieved July 25, 2005 from http://www.whitehouse.gov/pcipb/

Network security policy: Best practices white paper. (2003). Retrieved April 18 2005, from http://www.cisco.com/warp/public/126/secpol.html

Office of the National Counter Intelligence Executive. (2005). *Annual report to Congress on foreign economic collection and industrial espionage.* Retrieved July 26, 2005, from http://www.nacic.gov/publications/reports_speeches/reports/fecie_all/fecie_2004/FecieAnnual%20report_2004_NoCoverPages.pdf

Paly, S. (2004). *Adaptive and behavioral approach to new threats.*

Global DataGuard, Inc., Retrieved April 18, 2005, from http://www.net-security.org/article.php?id=751

Shimonski, R. (2004). *Defining a security policy.* Retrieved April 29, 2005, from http://www.windowsecurity.com/articles/Defining_a_Security_Policy.html

Spernow, W. (2000). *Microsoft hack may really be a sweet success for honeypot networks.* Retrieved April 19, 2005, from http://www.gartner.com/DisplayDocument?ref=g_search&id=316940

Strahija, N. (2003). *Lack of security policy in companies*. Retrieved April 18, 2005, from http://www.xatrix.org/article2891.html

Terms of use agreement (n.d.). Retrieved April 27, 2005, from http://takeaction.worldwildlife.org/terms.html

Ware, L.C. (2004). *State of information security*. Retrieved April 25, 2005, from http://www2.cio.com/research/surveyreport.cfm?id=75

Webopedia. (n.d.). Retrieved April 27, 2005, from http://www.webopedia.com/TERM/

Weyden, J. (2001). *FBI 'loses' hundreds of laptops and guns*. Retrieved April 27, 2005, from http://www.theregister.co.uk/2001/07/18/fbi_loses_hundreds_of_laptops/

Worldwide WiFi hotspots reach 50,000 milestone. (2005). Retrieved April 28, 2005, from http://www.jiwire.com/press-50k-milestone.htm

Chapter XI

The Relationship Between Digital Forensics, Corporate Governance, IT Governance and IS Governance

SH (Basie) von Solms, University of Johannesburg, South Africa

CP (Buks) Louwrens, University of Johannesburg, South Africa

Abstract

The purpose of this chapter is twofold: Firstly, we want to determine the relationships, if any, between the discipline of digital forensics and the peer disciplines of corporate governance, information technology governance, and information security governance. Secondly, after we have determined such relationships between these disciplines, we want to determine if there is an overlap between these disciplines, and if so, investigate the content of the overlap between information technology governance and digital forensics.Therefore, we want to position the discipline of digital forensics in relation to corporate governance, information technology governance, and information security governance, and describe in detail the relationship between information technology governance and digital forensics.

Introduction

It is widely accepted today that the increasing and ubiquitous use of computers and Information Technology (IT)-based systems, in all spheres of life, and specifically in the corporate world, had led to companies becoming more and more dependent on their IT systems. Such systems, with all the corporate data and information stored in such systems, had become strategically important for the success or failure of the company.

This increasing use of and dependence on IT systems, had of course created other risks —such as risks of unauthorized access to and use of corporate electronic resources (software, data, and information) which could again result in major problems for the company, including computer crime and fraud.

The challenge to companies therefore is to put measures and processes in place to ensure that the confidentiality, integrity, and availability of all electronic resources are protected, and to ensure that any such crime and fraud are prevented, or when they are committed, to be able to identify and prosecute the culprits.

Two very important disciplines resulted from this challenge. The first is that of information security, which can seen as the discipline to protect the confidentiality, integrity, and availability of all electronic resources, and the other is digital forensics which can be seen as the discipline to ensure that if a crime, involving the confidentiality, integrity, and/or availability of these electronic resources had been committed, the culprits can be identified and prosecuted.

Even from these high-level definitions of information security and digital forensics, it is already intuitively clear that some relationship exists between these two disciplines.

However, information security is a component of information technology (IT) governance, which in itself is again a component of corporate governance.

If a relationship does exist between information security and digital forensics as claimed above, and information security is related to IT and corporate governance, it seems logical that some relationship must also exist between digital forensics, IT governance, and corporate governance.

For any company who wants to create an effective digital forensics environment, it seems prudent to precisely know the relationships between digital forensics, information security, IT governance, and corporate governance. The reason is that if a digital forensics environment is created, and any of the relationships mentioned above are ignored, it may result in an environment which will not operate optimally.

Imagine for example that a digital forensics environment is created with no interface to an existing information security environment in the company. A lot of duplication will result, including the creation of policies and procedures overlapping with information security policies and procedures. A prime example is the backup and archiving of data and information. This is essential for digital forensics, but is most probably already included in the policies and procedures existing within the information security environment. It is therefore important for the company to take this relationship into account to avoid duplication and inconsistencies.

The objective of the remainder of this chapter is twofold. Firstly, we want to investigate, identify and formalize the relationships which exist between the disciplines of corporate governance, IT governance, information security, and digital forensics. Secondly, we desire to determine how information technology governance and digital forensics overlap, and then identify the contents of this overlap.

Having a thorough understanding of these relationships, overlaps and contents, will add a lot of value in creating and running an optimal digital forensics environment, by preventing unnecessary duplication and inconsistencies.

Relationship vs. Overlap and Content

As indicated previously, we now want to:

- investigate, identify, and formalize the relationships which exist between the disciplines of corporate governance, IT governance, information security, and digital forensics, and
- determine how information technology governance and digital forensics overlap, and where they do overlap, identify the contents of such overlap.

Determining the relationships is quite easy. We will investigate different definitions of these disciplines appearing in the subject literature, and from these, it should be straightforward to establish the relationships where they do exist.

To identify where these disciplines overlap, and to determine what the content of these overlaps consist of, is more difficult. Merely defining overlap and content without good motivation is not acceptable, because that will result in ad hoc and subjective reasoning. In order to properly determine overlap and content, we will need two reference frameworks. Firstly we need some internationally acceptable reference framework for IT governance containing specific content. Furthermore, we need a framework representing digital forensics. Guided by these two reference frameworks, we can then properly motivate our decisions as far as content of overlap is concerned.

The internationally acceptable reference framework for IT governance we have selected, is COBIT (COBIT—Control Objectives for Information and Related Technologies, 2000).

This chapter is organized as follows: In the section "Digital Forensics and Information Security", we will investigate the relationship between information security and digital forensics, while in the section "Corporate Governance, IT Governance, and Information Security", we will investigate the relationship between corporate governance, information technology (IT) governance, and information security governance. In the section "Corporate Governance, IT Governance, Information Security, and Digital forensics", we will provide a diagram depicting our hypothesis concerning the relevant overlaps. The section "COBIT – The Information Technology Governance Reference Framework used for determining the content of overlaps", will introduce our reference framework COBIT.

The reason for selecting COBIT will also be discussed in this paragraph. The section "Defining a Digital Forensics Reference Framework", introduces our framework for digital forensics. In the section "Mapping of Digital Forensic Control Objectives to COBIT", we use the COBIT framework and the digital forensics framework to determine the content of the hypothesized overlap between information technology governance and digital forensics. The "Conclusions" section provides some conclusions about the content of this chapter. In the next section, we will start our more detailed investigation by looking at digital forensics and information security.

Digital Forensics and Information Security

Information security can be defined in many ways, and a representative definition for information security is:

...information security is protecting the interests of those relying on information, and the systems and communications that deliver the information, from harm resulting from failures of availability, confidentiality and integrity. (Information Security Governance: Guidance for Boards of Directors and Executive Management, 2001)

Digital forensics can be defined in different ways, and a representative definition for digital forensics is the one used by the authors in Louwrens and Von Solms (2005):

Digital forensics is the analytical and investigative techniques used for the preservation, identification, extraction, documentation, analysis, and interpretation of computer media which is digitally stored or encoded for evidentiary and/ or root cause analysis.

Intuitively, it seems obvious that there should be some close relationship between digital forensics and information security. In theory, one can reason that to commit a computer crime or computer fraud, (unauthorized) access to and (unauthorized) transactions on the electronic resources of the company are needed. If however, the company's information security is 100% effective, computer crime and fraud would be impossible, because any such unauthorized access and unauthorized transactions would be impossible.

In reality, information security can never be 100% effective, therefore, such unauthorized access and unauthorized transactions do take place, and therefore the discipline of digital forensics is essential to investigate such unauthorized access and unauthorized transactions.

Some references to such relationships do appear in the subject literature, for example:

... a company must realize that in support of the security policies and various security technologies they have in place, computer forensics provides the means of investigation when these plans and tools are compromised in some way. (Armstrong, 2002)

This implies that the necessary information security policies and technologies must be in place (pro-active), and computer forensics will investigate the compromise of such policies and technologies (reactive).

Web forensics has become a vital Internet security component. (Armstrong, 2002)

In Brancik (2003), the following intensity of the relationship between information security and digital forensics are formulated as starting from a worst case where:

Information security policies and practices are critically deficient ... As a result of woefully inadequate information security controls, the potential computer crime and need for computer forensics is extremely high

...to a best case where:

Information security policies and practices are strong ... As a result of strong information security controls, the potential computer crime and need for computer forensics is reduced.

From the reasoning above, we can therefore characterize the relationship between information security and digital forensics as both information security and digital forensics having a proactive and a reactive mode.

The proactive mode of information security ensures that all the policies, procedures, and technical mechanisms are in place to prevent damage to the electronic resources of the company. The reactive mode of information security ensures that if damage does occur to such electronic resources, the damage can be repaired. Good backups and disaster recovery techniques are examples of this reactive mode.

The proactive mode of digital forensics ensures that all necessary process, procedures and technologies are in place to be able to act when required. The reactive mode of digital forensics ensures that when required, the necessary actions can be performed to support the specified analytical and investigative techniques required by digital forensics.

In an oversimplified way, it may be stated that the main emphasis of information security (the real action) should be on its proactive mode, while the main emphasis of digital forensics (the real action) should be on its reactive mode.

From the discussion above, we can postulate that there is not only a relationship between digital forensics and information security, but that there is actually an overlap in the processes and procedures between the two disciplines.

In the next section, we will investigate the relationship between corporate governance, IT governance, and information security.

Corporate Governance, IT Governance, and Information Security

In this section, we start off with definitions of corporate governance, IT governance, and information security governance. This is followed by a discussion of the relationship between them.

Definitions

Corporate Governance consists of the set of policies and internal controls by which organizations, irrespective of size or form, are directed and managed. (Information Security Governance – A Call to Action, 2004)

IT Governance is the responsibility of the board of directors and executive management. It is an integral part of enterprise (corporate) governance and consists of the leadership and organizational structures and processes that ensure that the organization's IT supports and extends the organizations strategies and objectives. (Board Briefing on IT Governance, 2003)

Adapting the definition for IT governance given above, we can define information security governance as:

Information security governance consists of the leadership and organizational structures and processes that ensure that the organization's information, and the systems and communications that deliver the information, are protected from any risks which may harm the availability, confidentiality and integrity of such information and systems.

Having now established an understanding of these disciplines, we will now highlight the relationship between them, by making reference to established subject literature.

Relationships

The definition for IT governance above clearly makes IT governance an integral part of corporate or enterprise governance. Information Security Governance again, is a component of IT governance.

Within IT governance, information security governance becomes a very focused activity.... Hence, information security should become an important and integral part of IT governance. (Information Security Governance – Guidance for Boards of Directors and Executive Management, 2001)

Transitively, it is therefore clear that information security governance is an integral part of corporate governance. This is however, lately, emphasized more directly:

... boards of directors will increasingly be expected to make information security an intrinsic part of governance, preferably integrated with the processes they have in place to govern IT. (Information Security Governance – Guidance for Boards of Directors and Executive Management, 2003)

An information security program is a risk mitigation method like other control and governance actions and should therefore clearly fit into overall enterprise governance. (Information Security Governance – Guidance for Boards of Directors and Executive Management, 2003)

It should therefore now be clear that information security governance is part of IT governance, which again is part of corporate governance. They are therefore part of the same family, and they overlap to a significant extent.

Hypothesis

The sections "Digital Forensics and Information Security" and "Corporate Governance, IT Governance, and Information Security" therefore clearly bring digital forensics into the family of corporate, IT ,and information security governance.

We now hypothesize that there exist overlaps between these disciplines. We further hypothesize that there may be aspects of digital forensics that are not included in our current definition of information technology governance.

The next section depicts the hypothesis based on the discussion in the previous two sections, that there are overlaps between digital forensics, corporate governance, information technology governance, and information security governance. By definition we accept that digital forensics is fully included in corporate governance. In the rest of

Figure 1. Corporate governance, IT governance, information security, and digital forensics

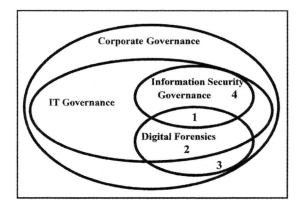

this chapter we will more precisely investigate the overlap between information technology governance and digital forensics.

Corporate Governance, IT Governance, Information Security and Digital Forensics

The discussions in the previous two sections are illustrated in Figure 1.

From Figure 1, the following features of the relationship between corporate governance, IT governance, information security, and digital forensics can be distinguished as seen in Table 1.

Table 1. List of overlapping features as depicted in Figure 1

No	Relationship
1	Overlap between Digital Forensics and Information Security
1, 2	Overlap between Digital Forensics and Information Technology (IT) Governance
3	Aspects of Digital Forensics not included in IT Governance
4	Overlap between IT Governance and Information Security Governance

Now that we have determined a relationship between these disciplines, and have identified certain overlaps, we will investigate the content of the overlap (1,2) indicated above, in other words, the one between information technology governance and digital forensics. We do this by using our internationally accepted reference framework for information technology governance, COBIT, as well as the created reference framework for digital forensics.

COBIT: Information Technology Governance Reference Framework Used for Determining the Content of Overlaps

Rationale for Using COBIT as Reference Framework

Of course, the content determined will be influenced by the "wider" reference framework used for Information Technology (IT) Governance. Different reference frameworks may result in different results. For this exercise, the reference framework chosen for information technology governance is COBIT (COBIT - Control Objectives for Information and Related Technologies, 2000).

COBIT, Control Objectives for Information and Related Technology, is a set of documents made available by ISACA, the Information Systems Audit and Control Association.

Several IT internal control frameworks exist in addition to COBIT, like ISO17799 (ISO/IEC 17799, Information Security – Code of Practice for Information Security Management, 2000) and the Information Technology Infrastructure Library (ITIL, IT Infrastructure Library). However, COBIT is considered particularly useful as an open framework. COBIT is an IT governance model that provides both company-level and activity-level objectives along with associated controls. COBIT therefore provides a good basis for comparison of aspects related to COBIT and aspects related to digital forensics.

Should any aspects of digital forensics have "relevance" to COBIT, it can be safely assumed that an intersection exists between IT governance and digital forensics. Further comparisons of digital forensics with other IT control frameworks would therefore serve no purpose in the context of this document, as the existence of the intersection would already have been established. On the other hand, should there not be relevance indicated, digital forensics should be mapped against other IT control frameworks to prove or disprove exclusivity.

COBIT is seen as a good practice for information technology governance. Because of the way in which COBIT was drafted, and evolved over time, it can be seen as the "consensus of experts", because many people provided input. COBIT is also seen by many, including the authors of COBIT themselves, as *the* information technology governance guide, and used in more than 100 countries.

We are confident that by using COBIT to determine overlap content, we will get a very representative result.

The Structure of COBIT

COBIT can be viewed and interpreted from different angles and dimensions. For purposes of this paragraph, we approach COBIT from a specific angle, as discussed.

The basic idea behind COBIT, for purposes of this paragraph, is that COBIT divides information technology governance into 34 high-level processes, also referred to as COBIT Control Objectives (C-COs). The idea therefore is that if these 34 processes, or COBIT Control Objectives, are managed properly, the relevant risks are mediated, and good information technology governance is the result.

Each of the 34 high-level processes is again divided into a set of supporting COBIT Detailed Control Objectives (C-DCOs). These C-DCOs are the more detailed "actions" which must be managed to comply to the relevant high level C-CO. In total there are 318 C-DCOs supporting the 34 C-COs (COBIT – Control Objectives for Information and Related Technologies, 2000).

The Use of COBIT in a Company

COBIT can be introduced in a company from different viewpoints. The viewpoint we use in this chapter is that of an information technology governance tool. If COBIT is introduced and viewed in this way, as a broader information technology governance tool, then it can be used to determine the "completeness" of the company's IT governance approach.

A company may decide to see which of the 34 high-level processes are actually being implemented in the company, and who are the owners of those processes. If one or more of these 34 processes are not implemented, they should investigate reasons why it is not, and make the necessary corrections.

In this way a company can determine if they are doing the "right things", where the "right things" are accepted as prescribed by good or best practice, in this case COBIT. This way of using COBIT therefore provides a best practice reference framework, against which a company can compare its own IT management approach.

The 34 C-COs or High-Level Processes of COBIT

The 34 high-level processes are indicated in Table 2. The 34 processes are divided into four groups: Planning and Organization (PO), Acquisition and Implementation (AI), Delivery and Support (DS), and Monitoring and Evaluation (M).

As stated above, every C-CO is subdivided into a number of C-DCOs, for example C-CO DS 5 in Group 3 above is subdivided into 21 C-DCOs.

Table 2. COBIT control objectives

COBIT Control Objectives	
PO	**Planning and Organization (Group 1 – 11 C-COs)**
PO1	Define a Strategic IT Plan
PO2	Define the Information Architecture
PO3	Determine Technological Direction
PO4	Define the IT Organization and Relationships
PO5	Manage the IT Investment
PO6	Communicate Management Aims and Direction
PO7	Manage Human Resources
PO8	Ensure Compliance with External Requirements
PO9	Assess Risks
PO10	Manage Projects
PO11	Manage Quality
AI	**Acquisition and Implementation (Group 2 – 6 C-COs)**
AI1	Identify Automated Solutions
AI2	Acquire and Maintain Application Software
AI3	Acquire and Maintain Technology Infrastructure
AI4	Develop and Maintain Procedures
AI5	Install and Accredit Systems
AI6	Manage Changes
DS	**Delivery and Support (Group 3 – 13 C-COs)**
DS1	Define and Manage Service Levels
DS2	Manage Third-Party Services
DS3	Manage Performance and Capacity
DS4	Ensure Continuous Service
DS5	Ensure Systems Security
DS6	Identify and Allocate Costs
DS7	Educate and Train Users
DS8	Assist and Advise Customers
DS9	Manage the Configuration
DS10	Manage Problems and Incidents
DS11	Manage Data
DS12	Manage Facilities
DS13	Manage Operations
M	**Monitor and Evaluate (Group 4 – 4 C-COs)**
M1	Monitor the Processes
M2	Assess Internal Control Adequacy
M3	Obtain Independent Assurance
M4	Provide for Independent Audit

Now that we have become familiar with COBIT, let's investigate the way we will use COBIT for our content-determining exercise.

Using COBIT as a Content Determining Framework

The methodology in which we will use COBIT for the positioning exercise is as follows:

- We investigate the 318 COBIT Detailed Control Objectives (C-DCOs).
- A subset of these C-DCOs is related to information security (COBIT Mapping: Mapping of ISO/IEC 17799:2000 with COBIT, 2004). This document provides a

mapping from COBIT to ISO 17799 (ISO/IEC 17799 – Information Security – A Code of Practice for Information Security Management, 2000). ISO 17799 is a widely accepted international standard for information security management. This subset therefore defines the "overlap" between information technology governance, as defined by COBIT, and information security governance as defined by ISO 17799, and is indicated by 4 in Figure 1. This makes information security governance a proper subset of information technology governance.[1]

- Another subset of these 318 C-DCOs is related to digital forensics. This subset, indicated by 1 and 2 in Figure 1 above, will be identified and discussed. This subset of C-DCOs identified for digital forensics then defines the "overlap" between information technology governance and digital forensics.

- Of course, in using this approach, we also need some reference framework for digital forensics. We cannot determine those COBIT C-DCOs relevant to digital forensics if we have no reference framework to specify what a Digital Forensic DCO should consist of. Such a reference framework for digital forensics is established in the following section.

- Using the COBIT framework, and the established digital forensics Framework, the content of the overlap between information technology governance and digital forensics can then be determined (in the section "Mapping of Digital Forensic Control Objectives to COBIT").

- Lastly, using the content of the overlap between information technology governance and digital forensics determined in the section "Mapping of Digital Forensic Control Objectives to COBIT", and the COBIT mapping between COBIT and ISO 17799 (COBIT Mapping: Mapping of ISO/IEC 17799:2000 with COBIT, 2004), the content of the overlap between information security governance and digital forensics, indicated by 1 in Figure 1, can be determined. This intersection will clearly indicate the overlap between digital forensics and information security governance, according to COBIT, ISO 17799 and our established digital forensics framework. This will however, not be done in this chapter, but is fully discussed in Reekie, von Solms, and Louwrens (2005).

Defining a Digital Forensics Reference Framework

Introduction

First, a basis for comparison of digital forensics needed to be established. As no digital forensics framework currently exists, it had to be defined using digital forensics literature and practical experience. Literature on digital forensics, computer forensics, computer crime investigation, digital evidence, and incident response was researched to formulate both digital forensics control objectives (DF-COs) and digital forensics detailed control objectives (DF-DCOs).

A Proposed Taxonomy of Digital Forensics

In order to be able to provide a proposed taxonomy to the digital forensics control objectives, it was classified into the different phases of the digital forensics process. Carrier (2005), defines three phases of crime scene investigation:

- system preservation phase,
- evidence searching phase, and
- event reconstruction phase.

Rowlingson (2004), believes that considerable effort should be put into what he calls "Forensic Readiness" to serve as an enabler to the subsequent incident response and Investigation phases. This clearly involves the activities of planning and preparation.

According to Kruse and Heiser (2004) one of the major goals for digital forensics is successful criminal prosecution. Therefore the investigator's job does not end when the investigation has been completed, but it also requires the presentation of the evidence in a clear, understandable, and professional way. Figure 2 shows the phases of the digital forensics process.

Digital Forensics Reference Framework

Using the phases of the digital forensics process (see Figure 2) as taxonomical basis, the following five digital forensic control groupings had been identified. (seeTable 3)

These five digital forensic control groupings were then refined into 22 digital forensics control objectives (DF-COs) and these 22 DF-COs were again refined into 66 digital forensics detailed control objectives (DF-DCOs).

Several of the DF-DCOs relate to "forensically sound processes"[iii] and need to be executed in sequence or in conjunction with each other.

Figure 2. The phases of the digital forensics process[ii] (Louwrens & Von Solms, 2005)

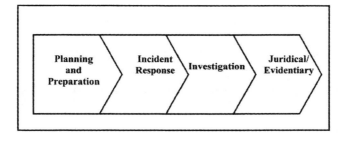

Table 3. Mapping digital forensics control objectives to the phases of the digital forensics process (Louwrens & Von Solms, 2005)

Phases of the Digital Forensics Process	Digital Forensics Control Groupings
Planning and Preparation Phase	I. Digital Forensic Readiness
Incident Response Phase	II. Evidence Preservation
Investigation Phase	III. Forensic Acquisition
	IV. Forensic Analysis
Juridical / Evidentiary Phase	V. Evidence Presentation

The full digital forensics reference framework, resulting from this exercise, is presented in Tables 4 to 8.

Digital Forensics Governance

The detailed digital forensic control objectives identified in Tables 4 through 8 thus constitutes the framework for a new discipline, which we shall call "Digital Forensic Governance". This forms the basis for further mapping of digital forensic governance requirements to COBIT. The details of mapping and examples are discussed in the following paragraph.

Mapping of Digital Forensic Control Objectives to COBIT

Mapping Methodology

These 66 digital forensic detailed control objectives (DF-DCOs) were mapped to each of the 318 COBIT detailed control objectives (C-DCOs), using the following criteria:

- Does the specific C-DCO fulfill all the requirements of the DF-DCO?
- Is the C-DCO relevant to the requirements of the DF-DCO?
- The results were expressed as a percentage of the relevant number of DF-DCOs in terms of the total number of C-DCOs per DF-CO.

Table 4. Digital forensic readiness (Louwrens & Von Solms, 2005)

Digital Forensic Readiness (DFR)—Group I
(4 DF-COs with 21 DF-DCOs)

DFR1	Retaining Information
DFR1.1	Define the business scenarios that require digital evidence;
DFR1.2	Identify available sources and different types of potential evidence;
DFR1.3	Determine the evidence collection requirement;
DFR1.4	Establish a policy for secure storage and handling of potential evidence;
DFR1.5	Establish a capability for securely gathering legally admissible evidence to meet the requirement;
DFR1.6	Time synchronization of all relevant devices and systems;
DFR1.7	Systematic gathering of potential evidence;
DFR1.8	Preventing Anonymous Activities.
DFR2	**Planning the Response**
DFR2.1	Ensure monitoring is targeted to detect and deter major incidents;
DFR2.2	Implement Intrusion Detection Systems (IDS);
DFR2.3	Specify circumstances when escalation to a full formal investigation (which may use the digital evidence) should be launched;
DFR2.4	Establish a Computer Emergency Response Team (CERT);
DFR2.5	Establish capabilities and response times for external Digital Forensic Investigation (DFI) professionals.
DFR3	**Digital Forensic Training**
DFR3.1	Train staff in incident awareness, so that all those involved understand their role in the digital evidence process and the legal sensitivities of evidence;
DFR3.2	Develop an in-house DFI capability, if required;
DFR3.3	Enhance capability for evidence retrieval.
DFR4	**Accelerating the Digital Forensic Investigation**
DFR4.1	Document and validate a DFI protocol against best-practice;
DFR4.2	Acquire appropriate DF tools and systems;
DFR4.3	Ensure legal review to facilitate action in response to the incident;
DFR4.4	Clear definition of responsibilities and authority for the CERT and DFI teams;
DFR4.5	Define circumstances when to engage professional DFI services should the need arise.

Table 5. Evidence preservation (Louwrens & Von Solms, 2005)

Evidence Preservation (EVP)—Group II
(4 DF-COs with 13 DF-DCOs)

EPV1	Incident Response
EPV1.1	Initiate Incident Response plan
EPV1.2	Activate the CERT
EPV2	Secure Evidence
EPV2.1	Secure the physical environment of the crime scene
EPV2.2	Secure all relevant Logs and Data
EPV2.3	Secure **Volatile** evidence, including Laptops
EPV2.4	Secure Hardware
EPV2.5	Label and seal all exhibits
EPV2.6	Preserve **chain of evidence**
EPV3	Transport Evidence
EPV3.1	Securely transport evidence
EPV3.2	Preserve **chain of custody**
EPV4	Store evidence
EPV4.1	Store evidence in safe custody room
EPV4.2	Control access to evidence
EPV4.3	Preserve **chain of custody**

Table 6. Forensic acquisition (Louwrens & Von Solms, 2005)

Forensic Acquisition (FACQ)—Group III
(5 DF-COs with 8 DF-DCOs)

FACQ1	Ensure Integrity of evidence
FACQ1.1	Follow established **Digital Forensic Investigation protocol**
FACQ1.2	Write-protect all evidence source media
FACQ2	Acquire evidence
FACQ2.1	Acquire evidence in order of volatility
FACQ2.2	Acquire **non-volatile** evidence
FACQ3	Copy Evidence
FACQ3.1	Make **forensic copies** of all evidence
FACQ4	Authenticate evidence
FACQ4.1	Authenticate all evidence to be identical to original
FACQ4.2	Time stamp all copies of the authenticated evidence
FACQ5	Document Acquisition process
FACQ5.1	Document all actions

Table 7. Forensic analysis (Louwrens & Von Solms, 2005)

Forensic Analysis (FAN)—Group IV
(6 DF-COs with 14 DF-DCOs)

FAN1	Plan Investigation
FAN1.1	Review all available information regarding the incident
FAN1.2	Identify expertise required
FAN1.3	Identify most suitable DF tools to be utilized
FAN2	Develop Hypothesis
FAN2.1	Develop hypothesis to cover most likely scenarios
FAN2.2	Define criteria to prove / disprove hypothesis
FAN3	Acquire the evidence
FAN3.1	Acquire the evidence by means of the most suitable DF tool available
FAN3.2	Analyze evidence by means of the most suitable DF tool available
FAN3.3	Conform to the requirements of the "Best evidence rule"[i]
FAN4	Test Hypothesis
FAN4.1	Reconstruct sequence of events
FAN4.2	Compare evidence with other known facts
FAN5	Make finding
FAN5.1	Make a finding that is consistent with all the evidence
FAN5.2	Document finding
FAN6	Document the case
FAN6.1	Document all aspects of the case
FAN6.2	Enter documentation into safe custody

Table 8. Evidence presentation (Louwrens & Von Solms, 2005)

Evidence Presentation (EP)—Group V
(3 DF-COs with 10 DF-DCOs)

EP1	Prepare case
EP1.1	Determine target audience (Court, Disciplinary hearing, Incident inquiry)
EP1.2	Assemble all evidence required for presentation
EP1.3	Prepare expert witnesses
EP1.4	Prepare exhibits
EP1.5	Prepare presentation aids like graphics, slides, hardware
EP1.6	Preserve chain of custody
EP2	Present case
EP2.1	Present evidence in a logical, understandable way to ensure that the court can critically assess every bit of information and understand the relevance to the case at hand.
EP2.2	If needed, make use of graphics and/or physical examples to illustrate difficult or critical concepts
EP2.3	Ensure that a Digital Forensic specialist is at hand to assist in providing expert evidence.
EP3	Preserve evidence
EP3.1	Preserve the evidence after the case has been presented, as it may be needed again in case of appeal, or where new evidence becomes known.

"Relevance" Defined

In the context of this mapping exercise, a C-DCO was deemed relevant if it:

- Fulfills the DF-CO requirement,
- Partly fulfills the DF-CO requirement,
- Could fulfill the DF-CO requirement if applied in a Digital forensics context.

Mapping DFCOs against COBIT DCOs

The 66 DF-DCOs were mapped to the 318 C-DCOs using the criteria as set out in the section "Mapping Methodology". The three categories of relevance, introduced in the previous section, were identified and grouped to obtain the total score per C-DCO. The scores were then converted to a percentage of relevance against the total number of potential C-DCOs. Refer to Tables 9 and 10 for examples.

In Table 9, five of the 17 C-DCOs of the C-CO AI2 "Acquire and Maintain Application Software" had relevance to some DF-DCOs.

In Table 10, two of the eight C-DCOs of the C-CO DS 9 "Manage the Configuration" had relevance to some DF-DCOs, and two of the five C-DCOs of the C-CO DS 10 "Manage Problems and Incidents" had relevance to some DF-DCOs.

Mapping Results

From the methodology described above, we have determined that at least 58 of the 318 COBIT DCOs are relevant to digital forensics and by implication thus relevant to digital forensic governance. The detailed mapping results are depicted in Tables 11 through 14.

Interpretation of the Results

We can thus conclude that the set of the DF-DCOs overlap with the set of C-DCOs, specifying the content of the overlap between information technology governance and digital forensics governance, using the two reference frameworks we selected. From the analysis, it is also clear that the aspects relating to jurisprudence[iv] and forensically-sound processes are not represented in the identified intersection with IT governance. Our hypothesis, that there are aspects related to digital forensics which are not included in IT governance, is thus confirmed.

It is also interesting to note that the percentage proactive versus reactive relevant control objectives are almost evenly balanced: 55.4% of the control objectives relevant to digital forensics can be deemed proactive (plan and organize, acquire and implement), while

Table 9. Example of DF mapping to acquire and implement

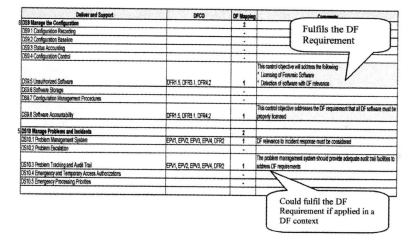

Acquire and Implement	DFCO	DF Mapping	Comments
AI2 Acquire and Maintain Application Software		5	
AI2.1 Design Methods		.	
AI2.2 Major Changes to Existing Systems		.	
AI2.3 Design Approval		.	
AI2.4 File Requirements Definition and Documentation		.	
AI2.5 Program Specifications	DFR1.3, DFR1.4	1	DF requirements and logs in applications
AI2.6 Source Data Collection Design		.	
AI2.7 Input Requirements Definition and Documentation		.	
AI2.8 Definition of Interfaces		.	
AI2.9 User-machine Interface		.	
AI2.10 Processing Requirements Definition and Documentation			
AI2.11 Output Requirements Definition and Documentation	DFR1.3, DFR1.4, DFR1.5, DFR1.6	1	DF requirements and logs in applications
AI2.12 Controlability	DFR1.1, DFR1.2, DFR1.3, DFR1.4	1	DF requirements to be included in the internal control aspects of system development
AI2.13 Availability as a Key Design Factor	DFR1.5, DFR1.7	1	Availability of DF requirement information within applications files and archives must be considered
AI2.14 IT Integrity Provisions in Application Program Software	DFR1.3, DFR1.4, DFR1.5, DFR1.6	1	Integrity of systems must be adequate to be allow presentation of data for evidence
AI2.15 Application Software Testing		.	
AI2.16 User Reference and Support Materials		.	
AI2.17 Reassessment of System Design		.	

> Partly fulfils the DF Requirement

Table 10. Example of DF mapping to deliver and support

Deliver and Support	DFCO	DF Mapping	Comments
8 DS9 Manage the Configuration		2	
DS9.1 Configuration Recording		.	
DS9.2 Configuration Baseline		.	
DS9.3 Status Accounting		.	
DS9.4 Configuration Control		.	
DS9.5 Unauthorized Software	DFR1.5, DFR3.1, DFR4.2	1	This control objective will address the following * Licensing of Forensic Software * Detection of software with DF relevance
DS9.6 Software Storage		.	
DS9.7 Configuration Management Procedures		.	
DS9.8 Software Accountability	DFR1.5, DFR3.1, DFR4.2	1	This control objective addresses the DF requirement that all DF software must be properly licensed
5 DS10 Manage Problems and Incidents		2	
DS10.1 Problem Management System	EPV1, EPV2, EPV3, EPV4, DFR2	1	DF relevance to incident response must be considered
DS10.2 Problem Escalation		.	
DS10.3 Problem Tracking and Audit Trail	EPV1, EPV2, EPV3, EPV4, DFR2	1	The problem management system should provide adequate audit trail facilities to address DF requirements
DS10.4 Emergency and Temporary Access Authorizations		.	
DS10.5 Emergency Processing Priorities		.	

> Fulfils the DF Requirement

> Could fulfil the DF Requirement if applied in a DF context

44.6% of the control objectives could be classified as reactive (deliver and support, monitor and evaluate). Please refer to Figure 3 for a graphical representation of this relationship.

Conclusions

At the beginning of this chapter, we set ourselves two objectives:

Table 11. Mapping results: DF-DCOs to the COBIT group "Plan and Organise"

COBIT Detailed Control Objective	DF-DCO	Relevant	Total	%
Plan and Organise				**25.01%**
PO1 Define a Strategic IT Plan	DFR1.1, DFR1.2, DFR1.4 , DFR4.3	5	8	62.50%
PO2 Define the Information Architecture	DFR1.1, DFR1.4, DFR1.5, DFR1.8	2	4	50.00%
PO3 Determine Technological Direction	DFR1.3, DFR1.4, DFR1.5, DFR1.7, DFR2.1, DFR2.4, DFR2.5, DFR4.1	4	5	80.00%
PO4 Define the IT Organisation and Relationships	DFR1.4, DFR1.5, DFR2.4, DFR2.5, DFR3.2, DFR4.3, DFR4.4	2	15	13.33%
PO5 Manage the IT Investment		0	3	0.00%
PO6 Communicate Management Aims and Direction	DFR1.4, DFR2.1, DFR2.2	2	11	18.18%
PO7 Manage Human Resources		0	8	0.00%
PO8 Ensure Compliance with External Requirements	DFR1.4, DFR4.3	2	6	33.33%
PO9 Assess Risks	DFR2.4, DFR2.5, DFR4.3	1	8	12.50%
PO10 Manage Projects		0	13	0.00%
PO11 Manage Quality	DFR1.4, DFR2.1, DFR4.1	1	19	5.26%

Table 12. Mapping results: DF-DCOs to the COBIT group "Acquire and Implement"

COBIT Detailed Control Objective	DF-DCO	Relevant	Total	%
Acquire and Implement				**10.92%**
AI1 Identify Automated Solutions	DFR1.1, DFR1.3, DFR1.5, DFR2.2	2	18	11.11%
AI2 Acquire and Maintain Application	DFR1.1, DFR1.2, DFR1.3, DFR1.4, DFR1.5, DFR1.6, DFR1.7	5	17	29.41%
AI3 Deliver and Maintain Technology		0	7	0.00%
AI4 Deliver and Maintain procedures	DFR4.1	1	4	25.00%
AI5 Install and Accredit Systems		0	14	0.00%
AI6 Manage Changes		0	8	0.00%

Table 13. Mapping results: DF-DCOs to COBIT group "Deliver and Support"

COBIT Detailed Control Objective	DF-DCO	Relevant	Total	%
Deliver and Support				**16.47%**
DS1 Define and Manage Service Levels		0	7	0.00%
DS2 Manage Third-party Services	DFR1.4, DFR1.8, DFR2.5, DFR4.3	3	8	37.50%
DS3 Manage Performance and Capacity	DFR1.5, DFR1.7	1	9	11.11%
DS4 Ensure Continuous Service		0	13	0.00%
DS5 Ensure Systems Security	DFR1, DFR2, DFR3, DFR4, EPV1, EPV2, EPV3, EPV4, FACQ1, FACQ,2, FACQ3, FACQ4, FACQ5, FAN1, FAN2, FAN3, FAN4, FAN5, FAN6, EP1, EP2, EP3	5	21	23.81%
DS6 Identify and Allocate Costs		0	3	0.00%
DS7 Educate and Train Users	DFR3.1	1	3	33.33%
DS8 Assist and Advise Customers		0	5	0.00%
DS9 Manage the Configuration	DFR1.5, DFR3.1, DFR4.2	2	8	25.00%
DS10 Manage Problems and Incidents	DFR2, EPV1, EPV2, EPV3, EPV4	2	5	40.00%
DS11 Manage Data	DFR1, EPV2, EPV3, EPV4, FACQ4	13	30	43.33%
DS12 Manage Facilities		0	6	0.00%
DS13 Manage Operations		0	8	0.00%

Table 14. Mapping results: DF-DCOs to COBIT group "Monitor and Evaluate"

COBIT Detailed Control Objective	DF-DCO	Relevant	Total	%
Monitor and Evaluate				12.50%
M1 Monitor the Process		0	4	0.00%
M2 Assess Internal control Adequacy		0	4	0.00%
M3 Obtain Independent Assurance	DFR2.5, DFR4.1, DFR4.3, FACQ1.1, FACQ4	3	8	37.50%
M4 Provide for Independent Audit	FACQ1.1	1	8	12.50%

Figure 3. Digital forensic control objectives mapped to COBIT, with special reference to proactive and reactive components

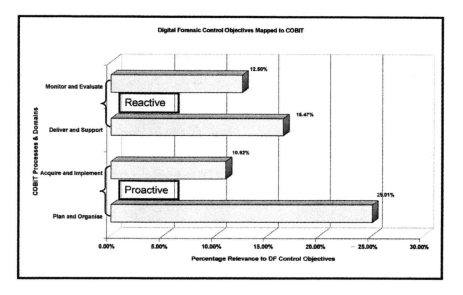

- First, to determine the relationships, if any, between the discipline of digital forensics and the peer governance frameworks.

- Second, to determine if there is an overlap in content and if so, determine the detail of the overlap between IT governance and digital forensics.

From the outset, it was clear that digital forensics should form part of corporate governance, IT governance and information security governance.

When compared with the proposed digital forensics framework, the overlaps between these disciplines became evident. We have determined that at least 58 of the 318 COBIT detailed control objectives are relevant to digital forensics and by implication thus relevant to DF governance. These objectives are both proactive and reactive in nature, and define the overlap between digital forensic governance and IT governance, using the COBIT reference framework for IT governance, and our proposed framework for digital forensics governance.

We can thus conclude that digital forensics governance forms part of the disciplines of IT governance and information security governance, and also as stated before, by definition part of corporate governance.

From the analysis of the contents of the overlap, it was clear that the digital forensics aspects relating to jurisprudence and forensically sound processes were not represented in the identified intersection with IT governance. Thus we can conclude that digital forensic governance is not a proper subset of IT governance.

References

Armstrong, I. (2002). Computer forensics: Detecting the imprint. *SC Online*. Retrieved March 2006, from http://www.tlsi.net/articles/scmagazine0802.pdf

Board Briefing on IT Governance (2nd ed.). (2003). USA: IT Governance Institute. Retrieved March 2006, from http://www.cisecurity.org/document/26904_board_breifing_final.pdf

Brancik, K. (2003). The computer forensics and cybersecurity governance model. *Information Systems Control Journal, 2*, 41-47.

Carrier, B. (2005). *File system forensic analysis*. Upper Saddle River, NJ: Addison-Wesley.

COBIT: Control Objectives for Information and related technologies (COBIT) (3rd ed.). (2000). USA: IT Governance Institute. Retrieved from http//:www.itgi.org

COBIT Mapping: Mapping of ISO/IEC 17799:2000 with COBIT. (2004). USA: IT Governance Institute. Retrieved from http//:www.itgi.org

Information Security Governance: A Call to Action, National Cyber Security Summit Task Force. (2004). USA. Retrieved from http://www.technet.org/resources/InfoSecGov4_04.pdf

Information Security Governance: Guidance for Boards of Directors and Executive Management. (2001). USA: IT Governance Institute. Retrieved from http//:www.itgi.org

ISO/IEC 17799, Information Security—Code of Practice for Information Security Management, International Organization for Standardization (ISO). (2000). Switzerland.

ITIL, IT Infrastructure Library, Office of Government Commerce. UK. Retrieved from http/:www.itil.co.uk

Kruse, W., & Heiser, J. (2004). *Computer forensics, incident response essentials*. New York: Addison-Wesley.

Louwrens, C., & Von Solms, S. (2005). A control framework for digital forensics. *Internal Report, Academy for Information Technology*, 1-22. University of Johannesburg, South Africa. Available from basie@rau.ac.za, buksl@nedbank.co.za

Oxford Dictionary. (1998). *Oxford Dictionary* 347. New York: Oxford University Press.

Reekie, C., von Solms, S., & Louwrens, C. (2005). The relationship between information security governance and digital forensic governance. *Internal Report, Academy for Information Technology,* 1-18. University of Johannesburg, South Africa. Retrieved from basie@rau.ac.za, buksl@nedbank.co.za

Rowlingson, R. (2004, Winter). A ten step process for forensic readiness: QinetiQ Ltd. *International Journal of Digital Evidence, 2*(3), 1-24.

Endnotes

i   The authors' view is that this is not completely true. There are some aspects related to Information Security Governance which do not directly fall within IT Governance. These aspects relate to audit and legal requirements. It must be stated that these aspects are a small component of Information Security Governance, and that the major part of Information Security Governance is included in IT Governance. This view does not really impact on the theme of this book, and is of course open for debate.

ii   "Juridical" defined : *Judicial proceedings, relating to the law*. Oxford Dictionary (1998)

iii "Forensically sound processes" are defined as: "Processes that maintain the integrity of evidence, ensuring that the chain of custody remains unbroken and that collected evidence will be admissible in a court of law." Louwrens and Von Solms (2005).

iv   According to the Oxford Dictionary (1998) "Jurisprudence" means "*science or philosophy of law*" and includes juridical and evidentiary aspects.

Section IV:
Cyber Investigation
and Training

Chapter XII

Law, Cyber Crime and Digital Forensics: Trailing Digital Suspects[1]

Andreas Mitrakas,
European Network and Information Security Agency, Greece

Damián Zaitch, Erasmus University, The Netherlands

Abstract

The steep increase of cyber crime has rendered digital forensics an area of paramount importance to keep cyber threats in check and invoke legal safety and security in electronic transactions. This chapter reviews certain legal aspects of forensic investigation, the overall legal framework in the EU and U.S. and additional self-regulatory measures that can be leveraged upon to investigate cyber crime in forensic investigations. This chapter claims that while full-scale harmonisation of forensic investigation processes across the EU and beyond is unlikely to happen in the foreseeable future, cross-border investigations can be greatly facilitated by initiatives aiming at mutual assistance arrangements based on a common understanding of threats and shared processes. Involving the users through self-regulation and accountability frameworks might also contribute to reducing risks in electronic communications that emanate from cyber criminal threats.

Introduction

Relying on information technology in transactions has led to the steep rise of criminal acts that are carried out through the use of Information and Communication Technologies (ICT) or target information technology resources for malicious purposes. Although information security measures strive to protect information systems users and service providers alike, electronic crime marks a growing trend. The opportunity to access vast interconnected information resources through open electronic networks multiplies exponentially the level of potential benefit that criminals can reap if they attack successfully information systems and their users. Cyber crime has already been subjected to regulation and is a matter of concern for public and private parties involved in electronic transactions. Forensic investigation of cyber crime emerges as a necessary link between evidence that is left behind at a crime scene and its potential use in criminal proceedings. Forensic investigations aim at following the trail that alleged criminals leave behind and connecting the various elements discovered with a view to obtaining an integrated view of the situation at hand.

The legal framework associated with forensic investigation nurtures concerns related to protecting fundamental rights such as privacy and data protection, data confidentiality, trade secrets, and intellectual property rights. Beyond the emerging legal framework voluntary frameworks for handling, retaining, and archiving systems and data set the stage for greater end user involvement in digital forensics. Methods and practices to conduct digital investigations are of particular importance especially in areas where rights might be at stake or sensitive information is risking disclosure. The approach to accessing and managing information is also critical for the admissibility of that information as evidence in a trial or other proceedings. Information security practices safeguard the quality and reliability of collected information. Additional attention must also be paid to cooperation across law enforcement agencies as well as the initiatives of the EU to counter cyber crime by safeguarding network and information security.

This chapter kicks off with an overview of digital forensics from a criminology viewpoint prior to reviewing some pertinent legal aspects. A criminological overview brings in the social and behavioural elements that are critical in assessing criminal acts. Pursuant to the criminological typology of cyber crime, some definitions and specific features of cyber crime, this chapter addresses the procedural framework to investigate cyber crime. This chapter also presents certain legal aspects of forensic evidence investigation in the EU and the U.S., the overall legal framework associated with information security safeguards and the institutional framework that can contribute to investigating and keeping cyber crime at bay. Finally some self-regulatory aspects are presented as well as some pertinent future trends.

Background

Forensics or forensic science is the application of science to questions, which are of interest to the legal system. Computer forensics is the analysis of data processing equipment such as a computer, a network, and others to determine whether that equipment has been used for illegal or unauthorized purposes. In spite of the criminological debate regarding concept and scope, most authors and policy makers interchangeably use concepts such as high-tech crime, digital crime, e-crime, computer-facilitated crime, cyber crime or computer-related crime as mere synonyms. Cyber crime involves attacking information systems or data for malicious purposes that often include a wide variety of crimes against persons, property, or public interest. In these instances information systems are used to facilitate criminal activity. In other cases cyber criminals might directly target such information systems. Collecting electronic evidence through forensics is essential in order to investigate crimes and to assure that appropriate support is afforded to evidence that is introduced in criminal or other legal proceedings. Crime investigation involves examining electronic evidence, using information technology to carry out forensic investigations, as well as collecting, archiving, and managing digital evidence in a way that renders it admissible in proceedings.

Law enforcement response to electronic evidence requires that officers, investigators, forensic examiners, and managers get involved in recognizing, collecting, preserving, transporting, and archiving electronic evidence. Digital forensics is the concern of law enforcement professionals who come across cyber crime in their day-to-day duties, investigators who collect electronic evidence, and forensic examiners who provide assistance at crime scenes and examinations of evidence. Additionally implicated parties include system administrators, internal investigators, and support staff who are often required to produce directly or indirectly evidence in support of investigations. The acts of the implicated law enforcement and support parties must safeguard, collect, and preserve volatile electronic evidence according to established principles and procedures. While evidence must be carefully treated when collected and sorted, the courts closely scrutinize actions that allow altering, damaging, or destroying evidence in order for it to become admissible.

In recent years, digital forensics has gained in importance due to the growth of cyber crime that threatens the legal safety and security of electronic transactions to the detriment of the legitimate interests of the end users. Enabling law enforcement agencies to access data by using standard police processes and without resorting to potentially extreme measures is a matter than can be given further attention. Consideration also merits the disclosure of evidence under certain circumstances and especially with regard to the delivery of high quality forensic recovery and examination of digital evidence.

Cyber Crime Typology

To address digital forensics, a first general distinction is made between computers as targets of crime and computer-facilitated crime. While the former refers to crimes targeting computers or other electronic channels as such and include acts like unauthorized entry into computer systems, vandalism, virus attacks, or warfare offensives, so called computer-facilitated crimes are in fact "traditional crimes that can be or have been committed by using other means of perpetration which are now carried out through an Internet based computer-related venue (e.g. e-mail, newsgroups, other networks) or other technological computing advancement"; or, to put in other words, crimes that use the computer as a medium to commit crimes (Transcrime, 2002). The distinction is, however, not nearly as clear as it first appears, for example, in cases of theft, computer cracking, or espionage.

Computer-facilitated crime can be more systematically classified under three main traditional categories of crime: against persons, against property, and against public order and public interest. With the explosion in electronic- or computer-facilitated communications it is highly unlikely that even traditional forms of crime do not leave some sort of digital trace behind. Again, criminal schemes often include acts belonging to more than one of the above-mentioned categories. Computer crime against persons includes:

- Breach of privacy (spamming, use of cookies, customer profiling, database trade, stalking, or harassment)

- Identity theft (creation, marketing, and selling of high quality false identification, link capture, or site cloning for copying personal data)

- Hate crime (racial hatred, xenophobia, anti-Semitism, hooliganism)

- Defamation (by e-mail, message boards, or Web sites)

- Blackmail (e.g., threatening to publish photos)

- Cyber-stalking (e.g., via chat rooms)

- Prostitution (actually cyber-pimping, sexual exploitation, and pornography, since prostitution as such is not a crime in many countries)

- Human, and especially women, trafficking (recruitment, arranged marriages, advertisement of fake employment opportunities)

- Child exploitation (luring, pornography)

The most common forms of computer-facilitated crime against property is:

- Violation of intellectual property (piracy, downloading of films, music or other work, plagiarism, publishing work without author's permission)

- Violation of patent and trademark (copyrights and design rights, copying, distributing, or selling of unlicensed computer software or trade secrets)

- Fraud (business or financial institution fraud such as credit card fraud or e-payment systems fraud, investment fraud, customer fraud such as online auction fraud, forgery, and counterfeiting, etc.)

- Economic espionage

- Theft and embezzlement

Finally, a growing number of criminal violations committed through or facilitated by computers and the Internet can be regarded as crime against public order and public interest:

- Trafficking of a variety of illicit or protected goods, including: illicit drugs (all levels from import-export to retail), weapons, human organs, firework, protected animal species, stolen art, prescription drugs, etc.

- Gambling (internet casinos, game-boys)

- Money laundering (false documents, placement, layering, integration)

- Government espionage (theft of national defence information or data)

- Terrorism (recruiting, organization, virus attacks, *info wars*, bomb-making instructions, money transfers, etc.)

It is clear that this vast range of illicit or unethical acts cannot be explained by one set type of factors, causes or offender's individual motivations. "*Hacktivist*" for example, hackers pursuing in their intrusions a political aim or statement, are rather different than fraudsters misusing credit cards or paedophile networks distributing child pornography. However, most cyber crimes can be explained by the conjunction of three factors: motivation, opportunity, and the lack of capable guardianship or formal control (Grabosky, 2000; Grabosky & Smith, 1998). Motivation can be individual or collective and can range from greed, lust, revenge, political commitment, respect-seeking, challenge, or adventure.

Criminal opportunities rapidly grow at the speed of change and innovation in technology arising from the convergence of communications and information technology. Enhancing the conditions that nurture crime, ICT has become available globally and at a high speed because under certain conditions it can ensure anonymity at technical and legal level, it is prevalently inexpensive and is easy to use if compared with other technologies that seek to achieve similar goals (Savona & Mignone, 2004).

Several factors account for a weak control from private, national, or international agencies on those crimes. Firstly, victims themselves whether corporate or individual are often incapable or unwilling to react due to a lack of technical resources and know-how, vested interests, or unclear codes of conduct. Although market and technological solutions, self-help prevention, self-regulation, and compliance are pivotal in effectively tackling computer crime, they often involve a degree of awareness and commitment that is not always present. Secondly, the global reach and multi-jurisdictional nature of computed-related crime poses great challenges to detect, investigate, and prosecute cyber offenders by law enforcement agencies. Essential questions about which law applies, for which acts, by whom and how to do it, are all still open in the field of computer crime. As Grabosky aptly notes, the policing of computer crime often has prohibitive costs, it requires concerted international cooperation, which only exists infrequently (beyond issues such as child pornography or serious fraud) and has to cope with problems such as corruption, lack of resources, and lack of expertise (Grabosky, 2000).

Forensic Process

Forensics is closely related with electronic evidence. Electronic evidence is information and data of investigative value that is stored on or transmitted by an electronic device. Such evidence is acquired when data or physical items are collected and stored for examination purposes (Rathmell & Valeri, 2002). A forensics investigation requires the use of disciplined investigative techniques to discover and analyze traces of evidence left behind after an information security breach (Department of Justice, 2001). The main focus of a forensics investigation is to determine the source and full extent of a breach. Starting from an on-site investigation, the existing network, application infrastructure, and flows of pertinent information are analyzed to discover where the breach occurred or originated from (Caelli, Longley, & Shain, 1991). In digital forensics it is necessary to associate common information security objectives with the acts at hand and strive to associate evidence in the field with the implementation of the following information security principles (eEurope Smart Cards TB2, 2002):

- Confidentiality ensuring that information is accessible only to those authorized to have access, according to the International Standards Organization (ISO). Confidentiality is typically ensured through encryption.

- Integrity is the condition that exists when data is unchanged from its source and has not been modified, altered, or destroyed at any operation according to an expectation of data quality.

- Availability of data is the degree to which a system is operable and in a committable state at the start of an assignment.

- Accountability of parties involved for acts performed being held to account, scrutinized, and being required to give an account. Especially in white-collar crime, accountability is often associated with governance.

As the above-mentioned principles might only be observed within highly organized environments that operate on the basis of audited security policies and practices (e.g., in white collar crime investigated in a corporation) more mundane methods have to be employed to ensure that odd data is equally retrieved and exploited for the purpose of gaining access to critical information for the crime under investigation.

Additional measures include the setting up of the social context of the data environment by conducting interviews with key personnel that can additionally offer a more whole-some understanding of the facts of the case at hand and identify sources of forensics data. Data becomes more valuable once the operational framework is established. On-site investigation is followed by a comprehensive analysis of case evidence. Data and facts collected can be stored in a secure and controlled manner, meeting stringent chain-of-custody requirements. Incident response and forensics investigation teams are capable of providing subject matter expert testimony to assist with prosecution or litigation support requirements. Digital evidence collection includes four phases being collection, examination, reporting, and analysis.

The collection phase involves the search for, recognition, collection, and documentation of electronic evidence. Collection addresses aspects of real-time information that may be lost unless precautions are taken early enough in the investigation process. Additionally, archived information is also critical, especially if there is risk of it being perished or deteriorating due to circumstances or poor storage conditions.

The examination process allows presenting evidence, determining its provenance, and designating its significance with reference to the specific crime under investigation, as it might be necessary. The examination process comprises of the following:

- Documenting the content and state of the evidence in order to allow all parties discover what is contained therein and includes the search for information that may be hidden or obscured.

- Analyzing the product of investigation for its significance and evidential value to the case.

- Examining from a technical viewpoint through a forensic practitioner and an investigative team that may need to testify the conduct of the examination, the validity of the procedure, and qualifications to carry out an examination.

When dealing with electronic evidence, general forensic and procedural principles are applied:

- Actions are taken to secure and collect electronic evidence in a way that cannot be changed.

- Examiners of electronic evidence are appropriately trained for the purpose.

- Activities relating to the seizure, examination, storage, or transfer of electronic evidence are fully documented, preserved, and made available for review.

Digital forensics methodologies recognize that digital media examinations do not resemble one another and although a generic process model may be recommended, the situation on the ground will ultimately determine the quality of the collected results. Circumstances might significantly influence the outcome and examiners may sometimes need to adjust to evolving conditions on the ground.

Digital investigations usually involve actors across a number of countries that render cross-border and international cooperation inevitable. Multiple agencies across several jurisdictions might have to be involved in order to investigate and analyze suspicious activities. The various procedures implemented by each implicated agency have to be somehow reconciled in terms of formal as well as substantive features they have to allow for the seamless cooperation of the parties involved. Digital devices and media can be used as evidence much like any other piece of evidence can be used in support of a case. Documentation and evidence handling is, therefore, important in collecting, handling, and temporarily storing these items. A computer system for example must be physically examined and an inventory of hardware components be compiled. Supporting documentation should include a physical description and detailed notation of features of the components in question.

In forensics investigations it is critical to gain sufficient understanding of the level of sophistication of the suspect and possibly of its behavioural pattern. Suspects must be considered experts and should be presumed to have installed countermeasures against eavesdropping or forensic techniques. Forensic drills must appear as normal as possible and quite indistinguishable from any other activity in and around the system. The purpose of this requirement is to avoid that valuable data be rendered unusable in an effort to destroy evidence such as by modifying drives, deleting files, and so forth.

When examining a computer system, time information should be collected, preferably from the BIOS set-up while effort must be made to cross check time with other dependable sources (e.g. timestamps or other remote computers that might have been accessed). The date and time should be compared to a reliable time source and any differences be noted as appropriate. It is desirable that for critical applications time stamping or time marking be used to differentiate high reliance requirements from generic application environments. If networked, the computers under examination can be checked for log traces that might have been left on remote machines to piece their activity together.

Examination of media should be conducted in a sound examination environment according to a prescribed methodology. Admittedly, a critical element of media that relates to volatile memory is still missing. This is quite important due to the variety of personal identifiable information or other critical information that is may be stored in volatile memory. In terms of process, examining original evidence media should be avoided and examinations of copies should be conducted instead. Special care must be reserved for special compartments that are hidden or encrypted. The use of strong encryption on data under scrutiny might significantly slow down forensic investigation and require the breaking of encryption keys prior to accessing recovered data.

Appropriate documentation must describe employed procedures and processes as well as detailed notation of any known variations thereof (Ford & Baum, 2001). Additionally, establishing the chain of custody through appropriate policy frameworks can be used in order to assess the quality of the collected data. Chain of custody investigations may also help in establishing the hierarchical structure that prevailed at the time that the acts under investigation were committed. Policy for forensics may address the practices of forensics agents and labs in investigating cyber crime.

In some cases the forensic process can be greatly facilitated through the use of intelligent agents. Intelligent agents are software elements that work without the assistance of physical users by making choices independently from them. Choices are based on rules that have been identified and built into the software system that controls the agents (Luck, Macburney, & Preist, 2003). Operational frameworks can be set up to ensure adherence to prevailing rules by autonomous agents. Basic duty of care must also be exercised to observe accountability. Intelligent agents can be used to carry out various tasks, for example, automated tasks for the user through user agents such as sorting out e-mails according to the user's order of preference, assemble customized news reports, and so on. In forensics, user agents can be exploited to reveal habits and patterns of behavior in investigating criminal acts. Predictive agents are used to carry out monitoring and surveillance tasks like observing and reporting on information systems. Such agents contribute to tracking company inventory, observing directories for competitor prices, follow patterns of behavior for stock manipulation by insider trading and rumors, and more. Data mining agents use information technology to find trends and patterns in a heap of information that originates from several sources. Data mining agents detect market conditions and changes and relay them back to the decision maker. Launching intelligent agents for the purpose of collecting forensic evidence from on line sites can reduce significantly the repetitive manual tasks that are usually associated with forensic investigations. Limitations in the use of intelligent agents include their relative incapacity to investigate data held in encrypted or otherwise stealth form.

With a view to combating serious crimes like financial crime, money laundering, and terrorism, investigations have gained in importance especially when dealing with known individuals who may be suspects. In the first instance, as comprehensive a financial profile as possible is built. Such profile is then projected as far back in the past as it is possible, seeking traces of information in connected databases, the accounts of other individuals, and so forth. Additional input is leveraged through connecting communication records to also validate a sequence of events and possibly set up a chronology. Raw data might include bank account details, credit card transactions, dialed numbers, network addresses, corporate registries, charity records, as well as data from electoral rolls and police records. The goal of such an investigation is to reconstruct the social context of the alleged criminals and reveal the spider's web of connections between the perpetrators and their financiers, trainers, and supporters.

Considerations on Law and Law Enforcement

In Europe, in spite of progress made, there are still important gaps and differences across the EU member state laws that address cyber crime. While some countries have preferred to reform their criminal code, others have decided to pass specific laws on computer-related crime, which were eventually included in the criminal code. Still some other countries do not have any legal provisions regarding cyber crime whatsoever (Savona & Mignone, 2004). At European level, efforts are aimed to regulate the most pressing and critical issues. The Council of Europe Convention on Cyber Crime (2001) and the Council Framework Decision on Attacks against Information Systems (2003) are both attempts to categorize and regulate the problem and they are closely connected and their definitions overlap, offenses being defined as follows: illegal access, illegal interception, data interference, system interference, and misuse of devices.

Article 15 of the Convention on Cyber crime of the Council of Europe stipulates that investigative powers and procedures are subject to conditions and safeguards provided for under domestic law in a way that provides for adequate protection of human rights and liberties. The protection afforded to citizens must be commensurate with the procedure or power concerned. Currently, this Convention is nonbinding pending ratification by member states' parliaments (CoE, 2001a; CoE, 2001b). However this Convention makes significant steps towards defining crimes related to computer systems.

The EU has also launched a number of initiatives to tackle computer-related crime including the EU Action Plan for eEurope 2005 (eEurope Smart Cards TB2, 2002), the Communication Network and Information Security: Proposal for a European Policy Approach (COM, 2001), and Creating a Safer Information Society by improving the Security of Information Infrastructures and combating computer-related crime (COM, 2000). Next to the output of the Council of Europe and the European Commission, legislation originating from the OECD can also be highlighted (OECD, 1997). This legislative activity in the form of Action Plans and communications aim at preventing the exploitation of children on the Internet (child pornography), attacks against computers, economic crimes related to unauthorized access such as sabotage, intellectual property offenses and privacy offenses, computed-related fraud, and to a lesser extent cover issues such as racist acts and computer-related forgery. Cyber crime law protects certain rights and assets such as privacy by rendering illegal the interception and unauthorized access thereto. To investigate cyber crime and crimes carried out with the help or by information technology, law enforcement agencies seek access to the content of communications, data in transit, stored data, and authentication data.

While information society is vulnerable from coordinated attacks against information systems, shortcomings in Internet security can compromise the unfettered use of network resources. Legislative measures have raised the stakes for computer intrusions that put life or limb at risk by curbing so-called terrorist and criminal cyber attacks in line with the Proposal for a Council Framework Decision on Attacks against Information Systems (2002/C 203 E/16). Mandating security on critical network infrastructures is of paramount importance to meet security requirements and protect critical infrastructures. The approved proposal creates a new criminal offense of "illegally accessing an information system" and recommends prison sentences in serious cases. Although this decision is not directly binding because it must be ratified by member states' parliaments, it can still be a very important instrument to confront growing threats on communication networks and information systems. To combat cyber crime, greater cooperation is required among the law-enforcing agencies across national borders. Often valuable data that can be used in criminal proceedings might be stored by service providers that are remotely located; such providers can be accessed and investigated by their home country authorities that respond on a request of the one that investigates the crime in question. The influence of the EU policy and legal framework are of paramount importance in this regard.

At a European level, policy initiatives associated with information security include the set up of the European Network and Information Security Agency (ENISA) through regulation 460/2004 that marks the priority of the EU with regard to building a culture of network and information security. From a policy perspective, the primary aim of ENISA is to contribute to the better functioning of the internal market while other purposes might be served in the future. ENISA assists the Commission, the member states and, consequently, the business community in meeting the requirements of network and information security, including present and future EU legislation. The tasks of ENISA include advising and assisting the Commission and the member states on information security and in their dialogue with industry to address security-related problems in hardware and software products. ENISA also collects and analyzes data on security incidents in Europe and emerging risks as well as it promotes risk assessment and risk management methods to enhance our capability to deal with information security threats. Finally, awareness raising and cooperation between different actors in the information security field, notably by developing public and private partnerships with the industry in this field. It is generally expected that ENISA will also contribute to bridging the differences across member states in combating cyber crime associated with the internal market and in developing practices for the investigation of cyber crime.

Beyond procedural and organizational matters, the legal aspects of forensics involve legal ways to seize digital evidence, constraints implied by law, types of digital evidence accepted in courts, investigative and testimonial challenges, and so forth. A broader legal framework associated with the regulation of electronic transactions and information security also sets the scene for both investigators and end users with regard to cyber crime investigation.

In Europe, information security policy requirements gained new impetus through the Bonn Ministerial Declaration of July 8, 1997. The Bonn Declaration resulted in broad consensus among ministers, the industry and end users on key issues regarding the development of global information networks. The protection of the fundamental right to privacy as well as personal and business data was also put high on the agenda. The adopted approach opted for voluntary industry self-regulation. It was also highlighted that strong encryption technology is necessary for the successful development of electronic commerce, within the limits of applicable law for cryptographic products (COM, 2001). The demand for information security that has been voiced by private companies, consumers and the public administration highlights the dependencies of end users and service providers on ICT. Information security is an essential element to contain and combat cyber crime and to establish appropriate practices and procedures to ensure the confidentiality, availability and integrity of electronic services. Information security is also the link that connects a committed act with *ex post* investigation due to the quality assurance and meticulous recording of actions and actors that it entails.

In the EU, information technology can also be seen from the view point of national security for the member states since much of the technology needed to ensure the security of information, can only be developed within the private domain. The increased EU cooperation within the Third Pillar for police cooperation, or even the Second Pillar for a Common EU-wide defence policy might additionally contribute to this area. Combating cyber terrorism requires that technologies are developed and tested first before any significant results are noted in practice.

In the U.S. policy developments have largely been instigated by the response to the threat of terrorism. In November 25, 2002 at the U.S. executive level, the Department of Homeland Security was established through the Homeland Security Act. The primary missions of the department include preventing terrorist attacks within the U.S., reducing the vulnerability of the United States to terrorism, minimizing any potential damage, and assisting in the recovery from any attacks that might occur. The Department's role is critical because it coordinates activities *inter alia* in terms of information analysis and infrastructure protection as well as emergency preparedness and response. The response of the U.S. Congress to terrorism has also been enshrined in the Uniting and Strengthening America by Providing Appropriate Tools Required to Intercept and Obstruct Terrorism (USA PATRIOT) Act (P. L. 107-56). The act gives law enforcement and intelligence agencies greater authority, albeit temporarily, to gather and share evidence particularly with respect to wire and electronic communications. The act also amends money-laundering laws with emphasis on overseas financial transactions and facilitating background investigations of suspicious parties. The Patriot Act enhances the ability of law enforcement to access, collect, and investigate evidence that relates to terrorist acts. The act specifically permits the monitoring of electronic communications traffic the sharing of grand jury information with intelligence and immigration officers, and imposing new accountancy requirements on financial institutions. Although these provisions have all been criticized as intrusive the act creates certain judicial safeguards for e-mail monitoring and grand jury disclosures. The act also authorizes organizations that oversee financial institutions to enforce money-laundering requirements.

Prior to the Patriot Act, law enforcement agencies could subpoena electronic communications or services providers for personal identifiable information associated with the users of an information system. To bypass the hurdle created by erroneous or deliberately false identity information, the Patriot Act permits the collection of contextual information in order to establish the identity of an individual. Permitting investigators to obtain credit card and other payment information by a subpoena, along with subscriber information that can already be obtained under law, helps forensic investigations in establishing the identity of natural persons. Service providers may have to disclose to law enforcement agencies customer identifying information without necessarily notifying their customers in advance. Creating a duty for the service provider, subscriber data can be disclosed if the provider reasonably believes that an emergency involving immediate danger of death or physical injury is imminent. Such action can support forward-looking investigations that seek to scout for evidence ahead of a suspected act. In the absence of any hard-coded assessment criteria to determine what constitutes a suspicious act, it is necessary for authorities to make available guidance to service providers. Procedural safeguards are also required to ensure due process for suspects and fines against overly active law enforcement agencies might avert potential cases of false accusation against suspects.

In the U.S., law enforcement agencies are also permitted to secretly access physical or information resources in order to carry out a search, or download or transmit computer files without leaving any notice of their presence. After the execution of a federal search, a copy of the warrant and an inventory of seized items must be lodged with the court issuing the warrant. Cyber attacks that could be associated with terrorist or criminal actions may be subjected to interceptions when authorized by the victims, under limited circumstances. The Patriot Act adds to the definitions the terms protected computer and computer trespasser that mean a person who is accessing a protected computer without authorization and thus has no reasonable expectation of privacy in any communication transmitted to, through, or from the protected computer.

Other U.S. initiatives that can facilitate forensic investigations associate with the requirements for greater transparency and accountability in corporate governance and health care services. These initiatives aim at containing corporate crime that has severe repercussions to investment and the market. Since 2002, the Sarbanes-Oxley Act holds executives liable for information security by mandating internal information security controls within the organization. While information security controls must be adequate, auditors have started to include information security in the threats that require specific measures and monitoring to keep organizations clear from potential liability. Banks and other financial-services organizations face similar obligations under the Gramm-Leach-Bliley Act of 1999. Health-care service providers will have to ensure by April 2005 that electronic patient data is stored in a confidential and secure manner, under the Health Insurance Portability and Accountability Act of 1996.

In an international context, the Organization for the Economic Cooperation and Development (OECD) has been active in the areas of privacy, encryption and security by issuing guidelines and setting up awareness programs. Public awareness on cyber security for example has been elevated through the "OECD Guidelines for the Security of Information Systems and Networks: Towards a Culture of Security". The objective of this set of guidelines is to assist economies, industry, and consumers to develop the necessary culture of security for information networks.

The Regulation of Encryption and Dual-Use Technology

Signing data at the point of collection for logging purposes is a good practice that can enforce accountability at the user level. Other practices such as data time stamping and time marking can invoke certainty in establishing certain events (Koops, 1998). Encrypting and storing data for audit purposes is also a practice that has yet to be exploited at large scale to serve commercial purposes.

In the past, encryption had been in the centre of a bitter dispute between governments and the private enterprise. In spite of the early-day differences, it has been acknowledged that encryption contributes to security and prevention of crime more than in facilitating it, as it had been previously feared. This conclusion, however, has not been always self-evident. With regard to the regulation of cryptography, an important policy objective at a EU level is to observe the principles of nondiscrimination and abolition of all barriers to the internal markets in the legislation of the member states concerning cryptography. The current export regime permits the commercial use of encryption without any significant limitations (See The Wassenaar Arrangement on Export Controls for Conventional Arms and Dual-Use Goods and Technologies Initial Elements, and Council Regulation No 1334/2000 of June 22, 2000 setting up a Community regime for the control of exports of dual-use items and technology. See also Council Regulation 3381/94 which establishes a Community regime for the export of all dual use goods and the Council Decision of June 22, 2000 repealing Decision 94/942/CFSP on the joint action concerning the control of exports of dual-use goods). Prior efforts to limit the publication of cryptoanalytical material led to the ruling in the case of Bernstein v. U.S. Dept. of Justice (No. C-95-0582 MHP). In this case, while an academic defended his right to teach about cryptography, and collaborate with his peers around the world a major issue had been whether he could publish source code that foreigners can access, or speak about such source code with foreign individuals. This case has been based on established First Amendment law and relies on the fact that computer source code is human-to-human communication protected by the First Amendment.

National legislation limiting the use of cryptography in the fight against crime and terrorism has not necessarily plausibly proved its usefulness and has therefore, been subject to reviewing and amendments. Such regulation could potentially have an adverse impact on the economy and privacy. The only efficient way to tackle risks of criminality related to the use of cryptographic techniques is increased cross-border cooperation among the law enforcement agencies of the member states. The protection of copyright and related rights has also been emphasized in the EU. Data security regulation relating to the protection of copyright has, to date, largely focused on criminalizing unlawful decoding of protected services otherwise known as encrypted services.

The role and effectiveness of technology in fighting crime has been debated, with little consensus on where exactly the balance might be found between conflicting require-ments. Technology has been seen as a necessary but insufficient condition to protect information. Even if strong cryptography was used, it was recognized that other weak points in the process of composing, sending or receiving messages would remain. The use of cryptography ensures a certain level of security and provides safeguards for the confidentiality, integrity, and authenticity of messages, but does not necessarily remove entirely the risk of unauthorized access gained to valuable resources. As security is not a product but a process, the use of cryptography alone might not be sufficient to solve the security issues of the Internet. The OECD Guidelines of 1997 have removed regulatory uncertainty prevailing until then and supported the availability of encryption for commercial purposes and several countries have since then loosen up or out rightly eliminated any restrictions to it (OECD, 1997). The OECD Guidelines contributed significantly to the distinction among the various functions of cryptography being authentication, non-repudiation, and encryption. In what appears to be a reincarnation of the dual-use concept of technology that has originally been a military concept, criminals might also leverage the techniques used to protect the confidentiality of messages to maintain the secrecy of their operations. The use of routine surveillance techniques by law enforcement agencies may result in adopting encryption and other similar technologies by criminals that eventually hampers investigations. A technology race shrinks citizen rights, such as privacy that remain at a high and often prescriptive level. To their protection of rights, the selective use of efficient technologies must be employed on suspect situations like in the case of Privacy Enhancing Technologies (PET) that also seek to strengthen citizen's rights in automated environments. Interest-ingly, the lines, which have divided the various views in the debate, have been drawn, not according to the various national jurisdictions or cultures, but on the basis of the professional competencies represented by law enforcement, technology, and privacy proponents. Technology, however, is the indispensable instrument to safeguard rights and support law and law enforcement agencies in combating crime (Mitrakas, 1997).

From a forensics perspective, while cryptography might at times be considered as a facilitator to crime due to the protective mantel it might at times afford to criminal communications, its value is undisputed to protecting the rights of individuals and organizations that carry out electronic communications. The widespread use of SSL (Secure Socket layer) encryption, for example has led to the pick up of secure and dependable electronic communications in an array of application areas (e.g., e-commerce, e-banking, etc.) while often the use of encryption for criminal purposes has successfully been kept at bay. In view of developments with regard to personal data and confidentiality, consideration could be given to enhancing the use of encryption for personal and business purposes. The immediate repercussion for digital forensics is the need to increase the capacity of law enforcing agents to gain access to data that has been signed for the purpose of encryption, which could be pertinent in the course of investigations. Alongside that, organizations could be held responsible for the purposes that data encryption is used for, which in any case should be assessed on the basis of security and other corporate policies.

The EU framework for telecommunications services contains several provisions with respect to "security of network operations", which gets the meaning of "availability of networks" in case of emergency as well as "network integrity", which receives the meaning of ensuring the normal operation of interconnected networks (see Commission Liberalisation Directive 90/388/EC, Interconnection Directive 97/33/EC, Voice Telephony Directive 98/10/EC). The framework for electronic communication services restates the existing provisions as regards network security and integrity. Data security provisions arising from the regulation of the telecommunications sector are related to the principle of quality of the telecommunication networks and services, which however stretches beyond mere data security requirements. In assuring sufficient quality of telecommunications network and service providers must meet certain requirements that include:

- The security of network operations also in the event of catastrophic network breakdown or in exceptional cases of *force majeure*, such as extreme weather, earthquakes, flood, lightning, or fire.
- Network integrity with the objective to identify as much as possible actors that have access to and data that is trafficked in a specific network.

Data Protection Considerations

According to Article 10 of Directive 97/33/EC (June 30, 1997) on interconnection in telecommunications with regard to ensuring universal service and interoperability through application of the principles of Open Network Provision (ONP) protection of data is afforded "to the extent necessary to ensure compliance with relevant regulatory provisions on the protection of data including protection of personal data, the confidentiality of information processed, transmitted or stored, and the protection of privacy" (Scholz, 2003). Regarding the protection of data, a European Parliament and Council Directive concerning the processing of personal data and the protection of privacy in the telecommunications sector is being elaborated within the EU. Building on the directive on the free flow of personal data, the European Directive 02/58/EC has introduced new rules for an array of issues associated with information security in electronic communications. The objective of the directive is to ensure an equivalent level of protection of fundamental rights and freedoms and to ensure the free movement of such data and of telecommunications equipment and services in the community as well as to provide for protection of legitimate interests of subscribers who are legal persons. This directive includes provisions on such aspects as General security, confidentiality, cookies, traffic and location data, directories, unsolicited mail, and data retention. This directive addresses the principle of confidentiality of communications and the related traffic data by taking specific measures. The directive therefore prohibits listening, tapping, storing, or any other kind of interception or surveillance without ensuring the prior consent of the users concerned. An exception is made here for legally authorized interceptions only. With the exception of evidence of a commercial transaction or of other business communications the Directive prevents technical storage, which is necessary to convey a communication.

While cookies can reveal user behavior, the directive stipulates that member states must ensure that the use of electronic communications networks to store information or to gain access to information stored in the terminal equipment of a subscriber or user, is only allowed on condition that the subscriber or user concerned is provided with clear and comprehensive information and is offered the right to refuse such processing by the data controller. A data-protection policy or subscriber agreement is an appropriate way to convey such information to the end user. Exceptions are permitted for technical storage or access for the sole purpose of carrying out or facilitating the transmission of a communication over an electronic communications network. Such permissions may only be allowed for as long as it is strictly necessary in order to make available a service explicitly requested by the subscriber or user. Using cookies is permitted for transaction tracking for a service initiated by the end user. The ability to treat cookies remotely ensures that if cookies are used as tracking devices the end user might have exclusive control over them.

The directive mandates that traffic data relating to subscribers and users that is processed and stored by a service provider be erased or made anonymous when it is no longer needed for the purpose of the transmission of a communication. However, traffic data necessary for subscriber billing and interconnection can be further processed until the end of the period during which the bill may lawfully be challenged or payment pursued. While this period should be equal to the time required to raise an invoice in a member state, storage of information should not exceed the period mandated for document archival for audit purposes. An exception is made here with regard to the direct marketing of communication services, which require the consent of the user. While following the money trail is an age-old practice in order to chase criminals, it is very much useful a method in the electronic age as well due to the multiple possibilities to follow the transfer of funds across the globe.

In the U.S., the Health Insurance Portability and Accountability Act (HIPAA) of 1996, addresses the issue of security and privacy of health data and encourages the use of secure electronic data interchange in health care. This Act adopts standards for the security of electronic protected health information to be implemented by health plans, health care clearinghouses, and certain health care providers. The use of information security measures is expected to improve federal and private health care programs. An additional objective is the improvement of the effectiveness and efficiency of the health care sector as a whole by establishing a level of protection for certain electronic health information. The National Institute for Standards and Technology (NIST) has drafted a Resource Guide for Implementing the HIPAA Security Rule (NIST SP 800-66, Draft May 2004). This guide summarizes the HIPAA security standards and explains the structure and organization of HIPAA.

Electronic Signatures

Electronic signatures are but a means to safeguard the transaction against, for example, unauthorized access, non-repudiation, and so on. The EU Directive 99/93/EC on electronic signatures grants legal status to the technical use that electronic signatures have had (Mitrakas, 2003). Directive 99/93/EC on a common framework for electronic signatures has impact digital forensics because electronic signatures are the means to ensure the authentication of a certain actor and distinguish her from others. Perpetrators of criminal acts can be authenticated and in some cases linked to an act. Directive 99/93/EC introduces three classes of electronic signatures, namely:

- A general class of electronic signatures
- Advanced electronic signatures
- Advanced electronic signatures based on qualified certificates and created by a secure signature creation device

Electronic signatures are significant also in identity management that can be leveraged upon to authenticate end users. Electronic signatures have in some cases epitomised the security requirements mandated for certain eGovernment applications in the EU member states (Reed, 2000). The reason is that electronic signatures ensure already the non-repudiation of the transaction, the authentication of the transacting parties, the confidentiality of the communication and integrity of the exchanged data (Pfleeger, 1998). The use of electronic signatures provides reasonable assurance irrefutable evidence with regard to data and signatory. An additional aspect concerns the use of cryptographic keys that are used in specific sessions that are only stored on the volatile memory of the computer of the end user.

In the U.S., the E-SIGN Bill (S.761) as the Millennium Digital Commerce Act (2000) has been known contains certain exclusions and a framework for inquiries into compliance of state law and international law. The Act provides for the validity of electronic signatures and contracts and contains exceptions, restrictions, and qualifying provisions. Electronic signatures and electronic contracts used in interstate commerce shall not be denied validity because they are in electronic form. To corroborate accountability and the use of electronic signatures the Act provides that any statute, regulation, or other rule of law with respect to any transaction in or affecting interstate or foreign commerce (a) a signature, contract, or other record relating to such transaction may not be denied legal effect, validity, or enforceability solely because it is in electronic form and (b) a contract relating to such transaction may not be denied legal effect, validity, or enforceability solely because an electronic signature or electronic record was used in its formation.

The Role of Service Providers

The Directive 00/31/EC on electronic commerce considers the liability of the information society service providers. As long as the service provider plays the role of a mere bit pipeline in transmitting data and it refrains from talking any decision with regard to the content, it can benefit from a limitation of liability to simple transit (*mere conduit*). While the Directive permits member states to require from the service provider to contain or stop illegal activities, the general approach to information society service providers is very similar to telecommunications service providers. Due to the content they feature, electronic communications networks have a substantially different performance than voice telephony networks (Mitrakas, 2004).

Risks from electronic communications such as spam, cyber crime, and so forth, might be more easily kept in check should an enhanced duty of care of service providers be introduced. Routine controls of transit and stored data can be used to detect undesired activities such as patterns of crime, control of viruses, spamming, and others. Such controls can be invoked by industry code of practices possibly supported through standards. An enhanced level or responsibility for service providers in practice would mean that transit data must be analyzed *ex ante* a situation that would have a positive influence on forensic data investigations. Prolonging the time limits for which data can be held is also an additional positive requirement that can have a positive impact.

Admissibility of Electronic Evidence

The admissibility of electronic evidence greatly depends on the meticulousness of the collection of that material. Sensitive information must also be subject to additional safeguards in terms of handling and storing it due to repercussions on third parties that might unintentionally be tangled. In the past, concerns associated with the admissibility of electronic evidence have been instigated by ambiguities on the admission of electronic documents as evidence. The admission of electronic documents must be based upon harmonized requirements with respect to form. The law has developed criteria on the admission of electronic evidence that can reinforce the position of digital evidence collected in a crime scene.

Evidence assumes two major components: the formal requirements and the material requirements. The formal requirements are drawn up in the civil procedure legislation and they refer to the means of evidence that are admissible. The material requirements concern the credibility of evidence submitted in a case. Security measures can be used to safeguard and evaluate the evidential value of electronic messages in open e-commerce (Poullet & Vanderberghe, 1998). With respect to the admissibility of electronic documents as evidence, it is of paramount importance to invoke the credibility of electronic evidence methods. Admissibility requirements must relate to network and information security requirements and address also third parties such as insurers, the administration, customs, and so on are not necessarily part of the crime under investigation, which may, however, provide appropriate evidence in support of an investigation. In Europe, continental legal systems provide that all means of evidence, irrespectively of the form they assume, can be admitted in legal proceedings. A general framework has been drawn up which can accommodate all means, unless it is deemed otherwise. The court assesses the value in each case of the produced piece of evidence. Within this context any kind of computer-generated evidence can be admissible, provided that specific requirements with regard to collection constraints are respected. These constraints are individually introduced in each member state under question (Poullet & Vanderberghe, 1988). Few countries in Europe lists the acceptable means of evidence (e.g. Greek Civil Procedure), but even in those cases the clear trend has been marked towards the conditional acceptance of electronic evidence in court, typically effected through the interpretation of the existing statutes.

Regarding the valuing if electronic evidence it can be argued that in cases where evidence of natural persons is available like for example closed circuit television evidence, juries might be inclined to value it more that stale log files and the like. In this regard consideration can be given to associating the social context of a criminal act and identification data that might become available through the forensics process, witnesses, and so forth.

Self-Imposed Requirements

On top of the described legal framework, voluntary frameworks imposed by the private partners themselves foresee information security measures as a means to ensure data. These frameworks can be leveraged upon in a forensics investigation and they include policies and agreements that aim at setting up the conditions for information security safeguards within an organization, or in transaction frameworks. At a bilateral level, the parties use service level agreements to specify the quality service they seek from their provider and ensure availability rates for their applications. Quite often, however, parties might set up security frameworks, which are activated by means of subscriber agreements executed individually. In this latter example, the service can be a generic one that does not necessarily often a high degree of customization.

Voluntary frameworks (e.g. security policies based on ISO 17799, etc.) and accreditation schemes (audits of policies and practices) aim at safeguarding private security goals for the purpose, *inter alia*, of corroborating evidence if needed in proceedings. Setting up private security frameworks addresses on one hand the needs of trade parties, but if needed they may also provide sufficient support to, for example, collected data, and others. Information security can be assured by supporting policies through appropriate international standards (ISO/IEC 17799:2000, 2000). Regardless of the form that information takes, or means by which it is shared or stored, it should always be appropriately protected. The standard ISO 17799 gives recommendations for information security management for use by those who are responsible for initiating, implementing or maintaining security in their organization. It is intended to provide a common basis for developing organizational security standards and effective security management practice and to provide confidence in inter-organizational dealings.

A typical example of a self-imposed framework includes best practices in the banking sector known as Basel II. Basel II aims at reducing the exposure of banks with regard to information security shortcomings of their systems. The Basel II Capital Accord is an amended regulatory framework that has been developed by the Bank of International Settlements. Basel II requires all internationally active banks to adopt similar or consistent risk-management practices for tracking and publicly reporting exposure to operational, credit, and market risks (Basel Committee on Banking Supervision, 2001). Banks need to implement comprehensive risk management programs to build business systems that are available and secure from cyber threats. Voluntary frameworks ensure the uniformity in applying security safeguards and they ensure data and user information that set the stage for effective forensics research. It is necessary, however, that end users become aware of forensic investigation requirements on their systems in order to prepare appropriately resources that could be scrutinized and investigated.

Future Directions

To make sure that cyber threats do not go undetected and that cyber crime is properly investigated, digital forensics require additional attention from a research as well as implementation viewpoint. Accelerating cyber crime investigation will result in a speedier turnover of cases while broadening the success rate of successfully arresting and prosecuting cyber criminals. Future priorities in digital forensics may include measures such as the ones presented in the following paragraphs.

Forensic methodologies can be developed in such a way as to provide a holistic answer to digital forensics. Currently available methodologies suffer from a compartmentalized approach that addresses specific high priority areas; however special attention must be paid to a generic model that addresses all aspects of the problem.

It is necessary to enhance the ability to pinpoint the origin of cyber attacks regardless of the form they assume (e.g., a virus outbreak, serious crime, etc.). This might require enhancing the ability of law enforcement agencies to manage and process encrypted data as well as to rely on data stored by service providers. Putting the service provider in the position of the safe keeper of collected data, until such time as it might be come necessary to process, might also be a valuable extension in the current set of requirements emanating from Directive 00/31/EC on electronic commerce. Additionally, enhancing the ability to collect evidence in volatile environments and tracing stolen information (e.g., identity theft). Identity management systems can be of help by storing and safekeeping information for longer periods of time. Also, the ability to gain access to damaged memory chips including smart cards is an additional requirement. Collecting data in unfriendly or otherwise uncooperative environments especially to investigate cases of cyber terrorism or other serious crimes is an additional matter of concern. Greater cross-border cooperation would also enhance the ability of law enforcement agencies to gain access to records kept beyond their jurisdiction.

Raising the profile of reporting of incidents as collected by appropriate authorities (e.g., computer emergency response teams) and linking them up with digital forensics investigations. Public policy in this area has quite a lot to contribute and the expectations are high especially with regard to the European agency ENISA in terms of coordinating pertinent activities. Greater cooperation among competent agencies and government departments such as ENISA, Homeland Security, and others across borders is also likely to enhance the expected results.

The risk, in case of fraud, is that the spiraling influence of cyber crime will erode public trust on electronic communications and compromise the use of electronic communication means as a valid way to carry out dependable communications. This assertion has been vividly illustrated by experts in the U.S. and it also covers transactions that are carried out by electronic means that eventually might cover the full realm of economic activity (PITAC President's Information Technology Advisory Committee, 2005).

The harmonization of penalties and legislation with regard to specific cyber crimes, such as denial of service, hacking, and so forth across EU member states may help, but is just a part of a larger picture. As economic crime and terrorism mark the trend for the crime to combat in the future, legislation might result in the bending of civil liberties and guaranties afforded to citizens. The selective or superficial application of such rights might erode the confidence of citizens to the ability of law enforcement agencies to appropriately safeguard their rights and carry out the anticrime fight effectively, that both can have a significant content as well as a symbolic component for the society. The fight against cyber crime must take into account the effective protection of civil liberties; forensic processes must also reflect this assertion when a suspected crime is under investigation.

Finally connecting forensic investigation with technology means might additionally yield good results in supporting the application of law and assisting the operations of law enforcement agencies. Especially the areas of identity management, privacy enhancing technologies, and so on, can help linking actions to specific actors for the purpose of crime investigation.

Conclusions

To enhance the conditions under which cyber crime can be investigated, certain technical and organizational measures are necessary in an effort to detail further support the legal framework. More effective cooperation across jurisdictional boundaries must be marked, as well as a need to involve service providers more closely. Full-scale harmonization of criminal law and legal processes across the EU or even beyond is unlikely to occur in the foreseeable future. Possible actions in the future could include the synchronization of high-level policies across borders. Additionally safe havens where criminals could operate from could also be suppressed. Moreover, legislation should avoid shifting costs of crime fighting directly to businesses operating on the Internet since the adverse impact of such a move might hamper the growth of small and medium sized companies. Most importantly the application of civil liberties should not be put under question in the advent of forensic investigations.

Cross-border investigations can, however, be greatly facilitated by initiatives aiming at effective mutual assistance arrangements, which have to go beyond the EU, since crime does not stop at the outer EU boundaries. It is difficult to think of effective prevention strategies without more cooperation among national authorities and between them and industry players.

Additionally, forensics can become sensitive to lateral requirements in information technology including identity management techniques and privacy enhancing technologies that can help link actions to specific actors for the purpose of crime investigation. Evidence can be gathered to support one's own defense in case of litigation. Additionally, evidence can be used as a way to invoke better corporate procedures and accountability while deterring insider threat. Forensic readiness that complements the security setup of an organization can improve security posture and provide coverage from cyber crime.

References

Basel Committee on Banking Supervision. (2001, May). *Overview of the new basel capital accord*. Report to the Bank for International Settlements.

Caelli, W., Longley, D., & Shain, M. (1991). *Information security handbook*. New York: Macmillan Publishers.

CoE. (2001a). *Convention on cybercrime explanatory report* (adopted on November 8, 2001). Strasbourg: Council of Europe.

CoE. (2001b). *Convention on cybercrime and explanatory memorandum*. Strasbourg: Council of Europe.

COM. (2001). *Network and information security: Proposal for a European policy approach*. Brussels: European Commission.

Department of Justice (DOJ). (2001) *Electronic crime scene investigation: A guide for first responders*. Washington, DC: United States Department of Justice.

eEurope Smart Cards TB2. (2002). *White paper: Identification and authentication in eGovernment*. Leuven: Ubizen.

Ford, W., & Baum, M. (2001). *Secure electronic commerce* (2nd ed.). London: Prentice-Hall.

Grabosky, P. (2000). *Computer crime: A criminological overview.* Paper for the Tenth United Nations Congress on the Prevention of Crime and the Treatment of Offenders, Vienna. Canberra: Australian Institute of Criminology.

Grabosky, P., & Smith, R. (1998). *Crime in the digital age: Controlling telecommunications and cyberspace illegalities.* Sydney: The Federation Press.

ISO/IEC 17799:2000. (2000) *Information technology: Code of practice for information security management.* Retrieved from htttp//:www.iso17799.net

Koops, B. (1998). *The crypto controversy: A key conflict in the information society.* The Hague: Kluwer Law International.

Lindup, K., & Lindup, H. (2002). The legal duty of care—A justification for information security. *Information Security Bulletin, 8*(1).

Lodder, A., & Kaspersen, H. (2002). *eDirectives: Guide to European union law on e-commerce.* The Hague: Kluwer Law International.

Luck, A., Macburney, P., & Preist, C. (2003). *Agent technology: enabling next generation computing.* Southampton: AgentLink.

Mitrakas, A. (1997). *Open EDI and law in Europe: A regulatory framework.* The Hague: Kluwer Law International.

Mitrakas, A. (2003). Electronic signatures in European and Greek law: Application issues in banking transactions. *Hellenic Bankers Association Bulletin.* Athens.

Mitrakas, A. (2004). Spam is here to stay. In S. Paulus, N. Pohlmann, & H. Reimer (Eds.), *Information security & business processes (Highlights of the Information Security Solutions Conference 2004).* Wiesbaden: Vieweg Verlag.

OECD (1997, March). *Recommendation of the council concerning guidelines for cryptography policy* (Ver. 27). Paris: Organization for Economic Co-operation and Development.

Pfleeger, C. (2000). *Security in computing.* London: Prentice-Hall.

PITAC President's Information Technology Advisory Committee. (2005). *Cyber security: A crisis in prioritisation.* Arlington: COITRD.

Poullet, Y., & Vanderberghe, G. (Eds.). (1988). *Telebanking, teleshopping and the law.* Deventer: Kluwer.

Rathmell, A., & Valeri, L. (2002). *Handbook of legislative procedures of computer and network misuse in EU countries,* Study for the European Commission Directorate-General Information Society. Cambridge: Rand Europe.

Reed, C. (2000). *Internet law: Text and materials.* London: Butterworths.

Savona, E., & Mignone, M. (2004). The fox and the hunters: How IC technologies change the crime race. *European Journal on Criminal Policy and Research, 10*(1), 3-26.

Scholz, P. (2003). *Datenschutz beim internet einkauf.* Baden-Baden: Nomos.

Transcrime. (2002). *Transatlantic agenda EU/US co-operation for preventing computer related crime— Final report.* Trento: Transcrime Research Centre, University of Trento.

Ward, J. (2003, February). Towards a culture of security. *Information Security Bulletin.*

Endnote

[1]   This article represents the authors' personal views and not those of any organization whatsoever including the authors' employers.

Chapter XIII

Forensic Computing: The Problem of Developing a Multidisciplinary University Course

Bernd Carsten Stahl, De Montfort University, UK

Moira Carroll-Mayer, De Montfort University, UK

Peter Norris, De Montfort University, UK

Abstract

In order to be able to address issues of digital crime and forensic science in cyberspace, there is a need for specifically skilled individuals. These need to have a high level of competence in technical matters, but they must also be able to evaluate technical issues with regards to the legal environment. Digital evidence is worth nothing if it is not presented professionally to a court of law. This chapter describes the process of designing a university course (a full undergraduate BSc degree) in forensic computing. The aim of the chapter is to present the underlying rationale and the design of the course. It will emphasise the problem of interdisciplinary agreement on necessary content and the importance of the different aspects. It is hoped that the chapter will stimulate debate between individuals tasked with designing similar academic endeavours and that this debate will help us come to an agreement what the skills requirement for forensic computing professionals should be.

Introduction

The fact that cyberspace increasingly is turning into a place where criminal acts are committed requires law enforcement agencies, businesses and other organizations to develop new competences. This means that either existing personnel will have to develop new skills or that new personnel with specific skills will have to be employed. These alternatives require facilities that allow people to learn the skills required for dealing with computer crime and digital evidence. The evolving sophistication of computer crime, together with the methods and tools required to detect and deal with it, demand the timely development of new university programs. It is the purpose of this chapter to recount the development of a new undergraduate course[1] in forensic computing in the School of Computing of De Montfort University, Leicester, UK (DMU). The chapter will start by providing a general background of the rationale for starting the course. It will go on to describe the requirements and organizational constraints that shaped the outline of the course. The chapter will then overview the topics to which students must be exposed in order to discharge their professional responsibilities. Finally the chapter will discuss the implementation of the forensic computing course and reflect upon the problems arising due to its complex and multi-disciplinary nature.

The chapter should prove interesting to readers of the book for several reasons. Among these is the fact that the chapter moves beyond the theoretical and academic discussion to deal with the important question of how forensic computing can be taught with requisite emphasis upon the practical, legal, and ethical issues to which it gives rise. The chapter raises the problem of where those professionals with the skills necessary to address the issues of forensic computing will come from and of how a university can deal with the challenge of setting up and teaching degree courses in the field. More importantly, the chapter reflects upon the interdisciplinary nature of forensic computing and the problems to which this gives rise in the design and delivery of forensic computing courses. Competition for resources between the technical, legal, and professional components of the degree is generated by the complexities of forensic computing. Which skills and to what degree are these needed by a high-technology crime investigator? How much technological knowledge is necessary and how much knowledge of the law does a forensic computer scientist need? Who can count as an expert witness in a court of law? These questions lead to greater questions: What is the role of computers in society, the function and purpose of the law, and ultimately to the deep question of how may we, as societies, design our collective lives. While we cannot answer these questions comprehensively here, it is important to stress the role they must play in the development of a successful forensic computing course.

Rationale of Introducing Forensic Computing at De Montfort University

Since the end of the dot.com boom, student interest in computing and related disciplines has noticeably declined. One answer to this problem is to recruit students to innovative and more exciting courses. The current attempt to design a course in forensic computing is one example of this drive to diversify the teaching portfolio of the DMU School of Computing.

Forensic computing, in the imagination at least, carries the promise of excitement redolent of TV series and thrillers. Whatever the reality, the enthusiasm thus engendered, no less than that derived from intellectual propensity, should be harnessed by universities in both their own and society's interests. Several universities in the UK have set up courses related to forensics in the last few years. The School of Computing at De Montfort University is running a course in forensic science, which has managed to attract students against the general tide of disinterest in and lack of recruitment to science studies noted nationally.

Given the ubiquity of computing and other forms of information and communication technologies in modern societies, it is not surprising that these technologies are used for criminal purposes. Consequently, the police need to be able to investigate ICT and they need to be able to present their findings as evidence in courts of law. Since the DMU School of Computing has substantial experience teaching and researching various aspects of ICT, it seems a sensible choice to offer a course that will specifically satisfy these demands.

Moreover, DMU as a new university (that is one of the UK universities that were polytechnics and were elevated to university status in 1992) prides itself in being professional, creative, and vocational. Accordingly the teaching portfolio aims to be applied and practical, unswervingly directed towards the provision of graduates with the skills required by employers.

In the case of forensic computing, there are two main areas of possible employment. Firstly, the police force with its need to develop high technology crime units[ii], and then the private companies that wish to deal with a variety of illegal behavior involving their technology. Both areas are predicted to grow quickly in the coming years and it is expected that the job market for graduates skilled in forensic computing will grow concomitantly. These predictions are corroborated by the local high-technology crime unit of the police as well as by market research conducted by the marketing department of De Montfort University. Most importantly, the marketing department predicted that there would be ample interest by students in the course. These reasons were sufficient to persuade the university to start designing the course and to offer it to students.

Competitor Analysis

In order to be sure that the course would be viable and would be able to cater to a market that exists but is not already saturated, the course team undertook a competitor analysis. At undergraduate level for UK 2005 entry, UCAS (the UK Colleges Admission Service) listed three competitors in July 2004 when detailed course design was initiated. At the point of preparation of this document (April 2005), this had risen to four with the addition of Sunderland. None of these institutions is geographically close to DMU and so offered minimal direct competition for applicants who want to stay close to home. On a content level, the planned course was set apart by a strong presence of digital evidence handling within the professional context of forensic investigation. A brief overview of the competing courses can be found in Table 1.

There is thus a small but growing market for forensic computing in the UK. We did not consider the international competition for several of reasons. Firstly, most of our students are UK students and, at least initially, we expect that students will make a rather ad hoc decision to enter the course. Such a decision in our experience tends to be rather

Table 1. Other university courses in forensic computing offered in the UK

Institution	Award	Summary (*edited from web site*)
Huddersfield	BSc(Hons) Secure and Forensic Computing. G603 3yr FT 4yr SW 20 places	This course is a 4 year sandwich (or 3 year full time) programme designed to produce computer professionals with the skills required to design and develop computer systems secure against unauthorized access and criminal manipulation, evaluate existing computer systems in terms of their security, and investigate computer based crime presenting evidence to a standard required of a criminal court.
Staffordshire University	Forensic Computing BSc/BSc Hons FG44 (4yr SW) FGK4 (MEng 5yrSW) also joint with various others	This award attempts to give you the knowledge and skills to enable you to prevent, repair and detect the causes of data corruption, loss or theft.
University of Central Lancashire	BSc(Hons) Computing (Forensics) GF44 3yrFT	Forensic computing is about detecting, preserving and presenting evidence of computer crime.
University of Sunderland	Forensic Computing 3 year full-time Degree, 4 year sandwich Degree	BSc (Hons) Forensic Computing is designed for those wanting to study and develop skills in forensic data computing. The degree provides an understanding of criminology, types of forensic data and appropriate analysis techniques, and how to operationalise findings in decision support software based upon advanced artificial intelligence technologies and 'industry entrance level' computer programming skills.

local than international. Secondly, forensic computing is closely linked to the legal and regulatory system and we can only claim expertise in areas of forensic computing in the UK. Questions of the legal framework, including requirements for the handling and presentation of evidence may be different in other jurisdictions, which means that professionals active in the UK need to know the UK model. We realize that this may turn out to be a problematic assumption in the light of the international nature of ICT and related misuse and crime. We may have to revisit this problem but it did not influence our initial design of the course.

A possible alternative to a full three to four year BSc course might have been a one or two year postgraduate degree. There are a number of such top-up options available in the UK and elsewhere. We did not choose to follow this route because we believe that the amount of material—technical, legal, and professional, that needs to be mastered in order to be a successful professional in forensic computing is such that it deserves to be taught in a full first degree course. However, if our BSc turns out to be a success and attracts a large number of students, then we will consider offering a follow-up postgraduate option.

Requirements

In order to perform a useful requirements analysis for the course we concentrated on the potential employers of our students and asked what they would wish their employees to know. The two main employers are expected to be the police and security/IT departments in commercial organizations. These have distinct but partially overlapping needs and interests and it is therefore important to distinguish between the different sets of requirements.

The police require expertise in forensic computing for the purpose of identifying, trying, and convicting criminals. This refers to specific computer crime but also to general crime that is committed with the involvement of ICT. Today nearly every crime that is investigated by[3] the police involves digital media (Janes, 2005). Computer crime includes matters such as hacking into systems, online fraud, etc. (Tavani, 2001). The advent of broadband has attracted unprecedented numbers of hackers and botnet herders involved in the commission of increasingly sophisticated crimes (Deats, 2005). In general crime ICT is used for many purposes. These include for example the storing of drug dealers' customer data on mobile telephones and the e-mailing of threats by murderers to their victims. While the use of technology for the purposes of finding evidence is indispensable to the police force, and while it is increasingly involved in the commission of crime, computer-based evidence is useless unless it is collected and presented in court in such a way that it will not contravene the rules of admissibility and will lead to the successful conviction of criminals. The collection and presentation of computer evidence is therefore a technical matter that must nonetheless be undertaken in strict compliance with legal rules. This duality in the purpose and nature of computer forensics means that experts, especially those involved with law enforcement, must be trained to quite literally look both ways simultaneously.

The goals of business organisations in employing forensic computing experts often differ from those of the police. Businesses incline to the quiet detection and prevention of outside attacks as well as internal misuse. Forensic computing can be helpful in detecting and following up attacks and in determining and documenting the misuse of systems for future reference. Issues of risk management, avoidance of legal liability (Straub & Collins, 1990) and issues of productivity loom large in the annals of computer forensics in the commercial field. Research indicates that the main threat to business originates from employees and that the use of ICT for non work-related purposes is very problematic. A number of terms have been developed by businesses to describe these unauthorised activities, "cyber-slacking" (Block, 2001, p. 225), "cyberslouching" (Urbaczewski & Jessup, 2002, p. 80), or "cyberloafing" (Tapia, 2004, p. 581). The investigation of employee misuse of ICT by employers is often satisfied employing lower standards of evidence collection and presentation than that required by the police force. This is because employers are often content to dismiss recalcitrant workers and in any case prefer not to attract attention to adverse behaviour in the workforce. This does not mean however that computer forensics conducted in the workplace should be with a blind eye to legal requirements; a wrongful dismissal suit may be grounded on a lack of respect for privacy, avoidable had the legal rules of forensic computing been observed. Figures released for the first time by the National High Tech Crime Unit (UK) show that the value of losses suffered as a result of commercial e-crime in 2004 alone stand at 2.4bn pounds. For this reason alone, forensic computing within the commercial context will have to be increasingly tailored to take account of the law.

This brief résumé of the requirements of the two main groups of potential employees indicates that it is otiose to tailor the course specifically for computer forensics in either one or the other group. Students of computer forensics, regardless of their destination should be equally well-versed in technical and legal matters.

Given the fast pace of change in the field of computer forensics, one can safely assume that the technologies we teach to our students in the first year will be outdated and forgotten (at least by criminals) by the time they graduate. Students should therefore be able to continuously educate themselves as to changes in the technology and in the procedural and substantive law relevant to their field. It is clear that students must be taken to the wide horizon of computer forensics to understand the technical, legal, ethical, and societal aspects of their role as experts in forensic computing. This leads us to the question of how the different skills can be implemented.

Implementation of the Course

This section will explain how we planned the delivery and structure of the course in order to address the skills requirements indicated above. It will therefore explain the content and purpose of the course structure that can be found in the appendix. As can be seen from the appendix, all of the modules to be taught in the first two years of the course are 30-credit modules. That means that they are taught over a whole year and typically have a contact time of three or four hours per week. The assumption is that students should spend about ten hours per week on each module. The modules are assessed by a mix of coursework and examination, depending on the specific outcomes being assessed. All students will be expected to do a placement year during their third year of study. Placements consist of work in a company or other organisation in an area close to the subject. Placements are standard in all courses offered by the School of Computing and our experiences with them have been very encouraging. They allow students to apply their theoretical knowledge and expose them to the organizational environment in which most of them will eventually go to work. The third year placement within a forensic computing environment is important from the recruitment point of view since employers prefer recruits with practical experience (Janes, 2005). While placements are spent in an organisational environment, they are still supervised by academics and students' have to write an assignment in order to get their placement recognized. During their final year, students are required to undertake a major project, which can be directed towards research or the creation of a system. They have a choice of two smaller (15 credit) modules and have two more compulsory modules. The content of their modules will now be described in two sections technical/legal and professional/ethical.

The evaluation of the different modules will depend on their content. Traditionally, the technical modules that require hands-on activity are assessed by practical tests in labs. Modules that have a theoretical and practical content will usually have one-part coursework assessment and an exam paper at the end of the module. Other modules with a more theoretical content, such as the legal and professional modules, will require students to submit coursework, usually in the form of essays and presentations. This mix of different assessment modes will also help students develop a range of different skills and will thereby support the interdisciplinary education of the students.

One common source of tension in obtaining, presenting, and understanding technical evidence is the difference in mindset between the technical and normative worlds. If code works, background study and documented analysis is generally irrelevant. But lawyers depend increasingly upon the advance preparation of reports compulsorily required in the discovery process. Answers are useless unless the reasoning, background, and process are properly chronicled and legally obtained (Slade, 2004). From the outset students whose propensity is for either the technical or normative side of the course will be encouraged to work to see the other's point of view.

Technical Content

As can be seen from the appendix, half of the teaching time during the first two years will be allocated to purely technical topics. Students will in the first year learn the fundamentals of computer science as well as an introduction to programming in C. It was felt that, in order to be able to work successfully in forensic computing, students would need a broad general understanding of computing and ICT. This includes an understanding of modern programming as well as a general overview of hardware, software, and related concepts. These basic skills will be taught in the two first year modules, "Programming in C" and "Foundations of Computer Science". During the second year students will build on these foundations and be introduced to more advanced topics in the modules "Internet Software Development" and "Systems Programming".

For a student to become an effective investigator, it is our belief that they need to have spent some time approaching the technical material from a creative, rather than an analytical, point of view, in effect, creating digital evidence. These technical modules in the first two years therefore develop, albeit in a somewhat limited extent, the mindset of the conventional applied computer scientist. In particular, deep understanding of the way that data is stored on, or communicated between, computer systems is clearly critical to the ability to perform a digital investigation.

It was perceived that it would be useful to tailor the technical modules to the specific needs of forensic computing. Students might have been exposed to hardware and software tools used by the police force or they could have learned about issues of interest in criminal investigations such as encryption or specific technical platforms. However, for economic reasons it was considered to be impossible to create such new modules. If the number of students on the course becomes sufficiently large, the modules will be customized for the needs of the students.

In the final year, students have some choice regarding their specialization. They can choose further technical topics such as compilers and network protocols but they are also free to look in more depth at organizational or social issues such as privacy and data protection. Their final year project can also be of a technical or a research-oriented nature, depending on their interests.

Legal, Professional, and Ethical Content

As indicated earlier, our requirements analysis led us to believe that nontechnical skills are at least as important to forensic computing scientists as technical ones. We therefore dedicated the same amount of time to nontechnical issues that are specific to forensic computing. In the first year, this includes a module that describes the "Essentials of Forensic Investigations". This module was developed for a forensic science course and includes the basic problems and questions of forensic science in a general way.

The final first year module, called "Normative Foundations of Forensic Computing" is divided into four main themes and will be delivered over the course of the year. The four main themes are,

1. **Ethical and moral questions in forensic computing:** This will provide students with an introduction to ethics and morality. They will be encouraged to understand morality as an expression of social preference/need and to recognize manifestations of this in several areas associated with computer forensics. These include intellectual property rights issues, privacy/ surveillance issues, access to data issues and issues of human-computer interaction. The theme will also provide an overview of ethical theories and explain these as reflections of morality. Building upon this, students will be encouraged to apply ethical reasoning to moral cases.

2. **Foundations of the law:** This theme will provide students with an essential understanding of what law is and with the ability to relate their understanding of it to forensic computing scenarios. The part played by ethics and morality in the

development of the law will be overviewed and students will be introduced to the common law, case law, and legislative sources. Probably one of the most important functions of this theme will be to equip students with the "know-how" to undertake research in legal issues relevant to forensic computing. This will be accomplished by careful *in situ* explanation of the law library so that students will be able to navigate and utilize its contents independently. Additionally, students will be familiarized with online sources of legal information. The theme will also be directed at elucidating legal language so that students can move confidently through legal texts.

Such skills are indispensable to a main aim of the module that of developing critical competence. Students will be asked to critically reflect, taking account of the current legal situation, on the role of forensic computing professionals and to discuss ethical and legal issues they may face.

3.   **Substantive law in computing:** This theme will provide students with an understanding of the principles that the courts apply in their approach to cases involving computer crime. This will be accomplished by examining examples provided in case law and by scrutinizing the relevant legislation. Students will then be provided with hypothetical scenes of computer crime including evidential scenarios that they will be expected to relate to the relevant law and for which they will be expected to assess likely outcomes. Areas of computer crime to be studied include computer fraud, unauthorized access to computer materials, unauthorized modifications to computer data, piracy, and computer pornography and harassment. The theme will also cover instances where technology is involved in "traditional" crimes such as murder.

4.   **Forensic issues in computer crime:** This theme will introduce students to the practical issues that arise in relation to forensic issues and computer crime. Students will be made aware of the importance of recognizing when in the course of their investigation they are about to take an action upon which legislation and case law impacts. The main areas to be covered in this part of the course are the search and seizure of evidence of computer crime, the interception of computer crime, and the preservation of evidence of computer crime. It will be necessary also to ensure that students are familiarized with the international approach to computer forensics.

The second year will be linked to the content of the first year. Students will attend a module on "Forensic Data Analysis" where specific forensic issues of databases will be taught. In parallel they will be taught "Issues in Criminal Justice", to be delivered by the Law School, which will build on the legal knowledge they acquired in the first year.

The third year of the course will comprise students either in placements with the police or with a commercial organization. It is expected that the knowledge they will have gained in the first and second years of the course will have provided students with a sufficient level of understanding to be able to follow the daily routine of a forensic computing professional and, where it is appropriate, to work independently.

The fourth and final year of the course is designed to prepare the students for their emergence as qualified professionals in computer forensics. The two main modules, next to the final year project and the electives, are designed to simulate the environment in which the students will work after graduation. The "Digital Evidence" module will provide a number of case studies that will use real-life problems and data and show students the current tools, technologies, and techniques used by high-tech crime units. The design of this module, has of itself produced huge ethical challenges. How do we provide students with data to investigate which has been ethically obtained yet is sufficiently large in quantity and representative in quality to give them a realistic challenge? Similarly, do we explicitly teach students to hack systems so they can recognize the patterns of hacking? Further, how do we protect the University's IT infrastructure from the various malevolent things (viruses or password cracking tools for example) that they will be studying? Substantial effort continues to be expended developing the tools, working practices, and physical and logical investigative environment so we provide safe educational experiences. Parallel to this, students will follow the module "Professionalism in Forensic Computing". This module will build on the professional and ethical foundations of the first year module. It will continue to link the technical knowledge the student will have at this stage with their legal and professional experience. An important part of the module will consist of mock trials or "moots" where students will take the role of expert witnesses, for the prosecution or the defense, and where they will be asked to present evidence in the manner of policemen or expert witnesses in a court of law. The two modules will be closely related and the presentation of the evidence will be based on the technical case studies of the "Digital Evidence" module.

Problems of the Course

We hope that the above description of the rationale, requirements, and implementation of the forensic computing course will have convinced the reader that we have managed to create a viable, worthwhile, and interesting course. We should admit, however, that this set up contains several problems. Some of these are probably generic to all university courses, some specific to the university, while others would seem to be typical of interdisciplinary courses.

The general problems include questions of resources and economic viability. Ideally, we would have designed all new modules for the course but that would have required large student numbers, which we are not likely to obtain, at least not at the start of the course. Another general problem is the question of the limits that students need to know. It is always desirable for students (and anybody else, for that matter) to know more than they do. The technological knowledge could be extended to other technical platforms, such as handheld or mobile devices, to more than one programming language, to more software tools, and so on. Similarly, on the legal side, it would be desirable for students to have a good understanding of all legal matters related to forensic computing and maybe even be solicitors or barristers. There is thus the difficult problem of drawing the line between the knowledge that will be essential and that which they cannot be taught. A related problem is that of the evolution of knowledge and the resulting fact that universities must teach students how to learn independently to keep up to date, rather than given them material knowledge that becomes outdated quickly. This is true for most subjects, and it is certainly true for something developing as quickly as information technology and its possible criminal applications. Our endeavour to ensure student competency in the handling of legal materials and familiarity with forensic tools, it is hoped, will go a considerable way towards assuaging this problem. Apart from such general problems that all university courses face, the interdisciplinary nature of forensic computing posed several unique challenges. The main problem is that the individuals who are knowledgeable in one field usually do not have expertise in the other fields. In our case, the two big groups of disciplines can be called the technical and the normative. The first includes all of the technical issues from hardware to software, networks, and so forth. The normative knowledge refers to the legal but also to the ethical and professional issues involved. While the individuals within the two groups may not always be aware of all the details in their own group (a hardware specialist may not be a specialist in programming; a legal scholar may not be an ethical expert), they are usually sufficiently similar in their knowledge and worldviews to be able to communicate. The same cannot be said for members of the different groups. Legal scholars do not have to be computer literate and an expert programmer may not have the first clue of the law. This is partly a result of the disciplinary division of academia and often produces no problems. This changes, however, when the different individuals need to agree on the set up of a course and when they have to collaborate to make it successful. For the nontechnical legal expert it is very difficult to assess the level of technical knowledge required to competently present digital evidence in a court of law. Similarly, the technical expert will find it hard to assess which legal or ethical constraints apply in their approach to possible evidence. To have it otherwise requires individuals who are experts in both fields and these are rare beings. They are also unlikely to be found in universities where, lip service withstanding, scholars are encouraged to stay within their disciplinary boundaries.

Another resource issue is that of the provision of specific equipment for such a course. Some of the modules can be taught in traditional labs which allow access for all our students. However, it is clear that the most interesting part of the course will necessitate specific equipment in the form of hardware, software, and regulations, which will only be accessible to students of the course. Examples are viruses and worms and other malicious software that students have to learn to deal with. They will furthermore be required to undertake actions, albeit under strict supervision, that will normally be prohibited for students. They will learn to tinker with security mechanisms and to access data that users do not want to be accessed. These considerations led the management of the school to the decision to create a new laboratory which is to be used exclusively by forensic computing students and staff.

A final set of problems has to do with the question of critical reflection and the role of forensic computing professionals in society. The above outline of the course shows that our students will be quite busy learning the material presented to them. Critical reflection, which universities tend to see as a desirable skill to be taught to students, can easily be forgotten in the rush. Or, if it is actually addressed, it may be applied to limited areas, such as in a critique of certain tools or legal precedents. This is problematic because the work of a forensic computing professional is likely to involve activities which are located at some of the major fault-lines of societal discourses. It will have to do with fundamental ethical and social issues. Obvious examples are issues of privacy or intellectual property. Businesses who employ our graduates are likely to use employee surveillance and the graduates' skills will be well-suited to the identification of employees who misuse company equipment for personal purposes. At the same time, one must be aware that the very idea of employee surveillance is highly contentious (Stahl, Prior, Wilford, & Collins, 2005) and that the role of the computing expert is anything but neutral. A similar case can also be made regarding possible uses of the students' skills in public service in the police force. Forensic computing can be used to identify the illegal use or duplication of copyright material. There have been a number of high profile court cases in the last few years in which major holders of intellectual property (music labels, film studios, software companies) have controversially asserted their rights by suing individuals. The very issue of intellectual property is contested (Stahl, 2005) and the forensic computing scientist needs to be aware of the influence he or she may have on social debates. Clearly there is great scope for critical reflection upon the role of forensic computing in society. It is highly desirable that students be capable of taking a coherent stance on these matters and that they are able to defend it, but it is open to debate whether students will in fact have the time or be prepared to undertake critical analysis sufficient for the consideration of other stakeholders' views.

Conclusions

This chapter set out to describe the challenges encountered by the School of Computing of De Montfort University in establishing a course in forensic computing. The course started in the autumn of 2005 because of great student demand. This chapter is more a reflective account of the creation of the course than a classical academic paper. We hope nevertheless that it will be of interest to the audience of the book because it highlights some of the problems that will have to be addressed if forensic computing is to become a recognized profession. The chapter has given an authentic account of the history and intended structure of the course. It has also outlined some of the problems we have had and that we foresee for the future. We do not claim to have found all the right answers. Instead, we hope that the chapter will work as a basis of discussion for people and institutions with similar questions.

References

Block, W. (2001). Cyberslacking, business ethics and managerial economics. *Journal of Business Ethics, 33*(3), 225-231.

Deats, M. (2005, April 28). Digital detectives. Quoted by Clint Witchalls in *The Guardian*, 19.

Janes, S. (2005, April 28). Digital detectives. Quoted by Clint Withcalls in *The Guardian*, 19.

Slade, R. (2004). *Software forensics*. McGraw Hill.

Stahl, B. (2005). The impact of open source development on the social construction of intellectual property. In S. Koch (Ed.), *Free/open source software development* (pp. 259-272). Hershey, PA: Idea Group Publishing.

Stahl, B., Prior, M., Wilford, S., & Collins, D. (2005). Electronic monitoring in the workplace: If people don't care, then what is the relevance? In J. Weckert (Ed.), *Electronic monitoring in the workplace: Controversies and solutions* (pp. 50-78). Hershey, PA: Idea-Group Publishing.

Straub, D., & Collins, R. (1990). Key information liability issues facing managers: Software piracy, proprietary databases, and individual rights to privacy. *MIS Quarterly, 14*(2), 143-156.

Tapia, A. (2004). Resistance of deviance? A high-tech workplace during the bursting of the dot-com bubble. In B. Kaplan, D. Truex, D. Wastell, A. Wood-Harper, & J. DeGross (Eds.), *Information systems research: Relevant theory and informed practice* (pp. 577-596) (IFIP 8.2 Proceedings). Dordrecht: Kluwer.

Tavani, H. (2001). Defining the boundaries of computer crime: Piracy, break-ins, and sabotage in cyberspace. In R. Spinello & H. Tavani (Eds.), *Readings in cyberethics* (pp. 451-462). Sudbury, MA: Jones and Bartlett.

Urbaczewski, A., & Jessup, L. (2002). Does electronic monitoring of employee internet usage work? *Communications of the ACM, 45*(1), 80-83.

Witchalls, C. (2005, April 28). Digital detectives. *The Guardian*.

Appendix A:
Draft Course Structure of
the BSc Forensic Computing

Year 1	CSCI1401 Programming in C (30 credit) Existing module	CSCI1408 Foundations of Computer Science (30 credit) Existing module	CHEM1050 Essentials of Forensic Investigations (30 credit) Existing module from Applied Sciences	INFO1412 Normative Foundations of Forensic Computing (30 credit) **New Module** *Establishes the ethical and regulatory framework within which an investigator must operate*
Year 2	CSCI2404 Internet Software Development (30 credit) Existing module	CSCI2410 Systems Programming (30 credit) Existing module	INFO2425 Forensic Data Analysis (30 credit) **New Module**	LAWG2003 Issues in Criminal Justice (30 credit) Existing module from Law Dept
	Placement year			
Year 4	CPRJ3451 Computing Double project (30 credit) Existing module	Option 1 (15 credit) Existing module Option 2 (15 credit) Existing module	CSCI3427 Digital Evidence (30 credit) **New module** *Series of case studies, using tools and techniques to detect, preserve, analyse and present digital evidence from a variety of devices.*	INFO3427 Professionalism in Forensic Computing (30 credit) **New module**

BSc Hons Forensic Computing – Draft Course Structure – I

Example final year options include:

CSCI3401 – Broadband Networks

CSCI3402 – Network Protocols

CSCI3405 – Genetic Algorithms and Artificial Neural Networks

CSCI3406 – Fuzzy Logic and Knowledge-based Systems

CSCI3412 – Compilers

CSCI3426 – Telematics

INFO3406 – Privacy and Data protection

INFO3421 – Database Management Systems

Appendix B:
Syllabi of New Modules
to be Developed for the Course

Appendix B1:
Normative Foundations of Forensic Computing

1. **Ethical and moral questions in forensic computing**

- Introduction to ethics and morality
- Morality as an expression of social preferences
- Examples of moral problems in computing
  - intellectual property
  - privacy / surveillance
  - access
  - human - computer interaction
  - ...
- Ethics as the theoretical reflection of morality
- An overview of ethical theory
  - classical Greek ethics
  - virtue ethics
  - deontology
  - teleology
  - ethical scepticism
  - modern approaches to ethics
  - ...
- Application of ethical reasoning to moral cases
- Reading and understanding ethical texts

2. **Foundation of the law**

- Historical development of legal systems
- ethics, morality, and the law
- sources of law (civil law, case law traditions, influence of the EU on UK law)

- understanding legal language
- doing research in legal issues

3.   **Substantive Law in Computing**

- Introduction to computer crime
- Computer fraud
- Hacking— unauthorised access to computer materials
- Unauthorised modifications to computer data
- Piracy and related offences
- Computer pornography and harassment

4.   **Procedural Law in Forensic Computing**

- Introduction to forensic issues and computer crime
- The search and seizure of evidence of computer crime
- The interception of evidence of computer crime
- The preservation of evidence of computer crime
- International harmonization and assistance in computer forensics
- Review of legislative issues in computer forensics

B2: Forensic Data Analysis

The following represents a broad range of topics that can be addressed within this module. The actual emphasis and topics covered each year will depend on the availability of expert speakers and changes in the subject.

Indicative Content:

Intro to Module: content & assessment

Introduction to Literature Review, Writing Academic Papers and Presenting the Results

Intro to Forensic Data Analysis

Role of data and data management in forensic IT

Data analysis, normalisation and determinacy

Database design, implementation, interrogation and management

Using databases to facilitate forensic investigations

Forensic Computing and Forensic Data Analysis

The use of IT in criminal activities

- E-crime
- E-terrorism
- Credit card fraud
- Internet abuse

Computer Security

Incident response—preserving forensic data as admissible evidence; strategies, techniques and challenges

Incident response strategies for specific types of cases

Data hiding strategies

Data discovery and analysis strategies

E-mail investigations and data analysis

Image file investigations and data analysis

Forensic Software, FRED and other data analysis software

Use of data in the judicial system

Modern and developing forensic data analysis technologies, i.e.:

- Image analysis, enhancement and facial reconstruction
- DNA databases, human genome project and fingerprint comparison
- AI and forensic data analysis

B3: Digital Evidence

Tools

- low-level tools to examine blocks on disks, partition tables, file dumps, network packets, etc.
- specific tools for particular tasks / device types
- tool capabilities and limitations
- specialist forensic toolsets (such as EnCase)

Working Practice

- ACPO Good Practice Guide for Computer based Electronic Evidence
- RIPA—Regulation and Investigatory Powers Act
- Maintenance of evidence audit trail.

Detection

- security (logging, port monitoring, traffic monitoring),

Preservation

- data volatility—order of volatility—order of recovery
- duplication (bit copy) of original data to two locations prior to analysis
- verification of copy via hash value(s)
- Hard Disc Drive / boot disc preservation

Analysis

- Reconstructing fragments of data
- determining significance
- drawing conclusions based on evidence
- hypothesis generation and confirmation

Presentation *(it is probable that this aspect will operate in conjunction with INFO3427)*

- audience, assumptions about prior knowledge, especially expert vv lay person
- technical report
- oral cross examination such as would be expected in court

B4: Professionalism in Forensic Computing

1. **Framework of Professionalism in Forensic Computing** (1ˢᵗ half)

- Introduction to legal philosophy (positivism vs. conventionalism)
- Ethics and Human Rights
- Critical Analysis of the role of law enforcement and its agents in society.

2. **Professional Conduct in Forensic Computing** (1ˢᵗ half)

- Code of Conduct for police officers
- Ethical reflection of this code of conduct
- Stakeholder analysis in investigative work
- Discussion of conflicts of interest
- Application to case studies
- The first half of the module (semester 1) will be assessed through an essay.

3. **Professional Presentation of Evidence (2ⁿᵈ half)**

- Gathering evidence
- Legal interpretation and presentation of technical evidence
- Court room presentation scenarios (moot)
- This module will be closely related to the Digital Evidence module in order to develop the technical skills acquired there for use in the preparation and presentation of evidence
- The module will involve "real life" preparation and presentation of evidence and will be conducted in close collaboration with the police

- This half of the module will be marked through examination of the skills displayed during the court room presentation scenario (moot)

Endnotes

[1]   We should clarify at this stage what we mean by "course". A university course in the UK stands for the totality of teaching that a student is exposed to in order to receive a degree. It is thus what might be called a "program" in the U.S. and elsewhere. A single unit in such a course, which typically lasts a semester, or a year in the case of DMU, is called a module.

[2]   According to Simon Janes international operations director for the computer security firm Ibis less that 1% of the UK police force is trained to gather computer evidence and there are estimated to be less than 100 experts in the UK capable of analyzing computer evidence to the standard of the court. Janes was interviewed by Clint Witchalls for an article entitled "Digital Detectives", The Guardian, April 28th, 2005, page19.

[3]   Botnets consist of thousands of compromised computers working together. The combined processing power is harnessed in a "herding" process and used to send massive quantities of spam or to carry out denial of service attacks.

Chapter XIV

Training the Cyber Investigator

Christopher Malinowski, Long Island University, USA

Abstract

This chapter considers and presents training possibilities for computer forensic investigators. The author differentiates between civil service and industry needs for training, as well as cites differences in considerations for providing such training. While each organization has its own requirements, different paradigms and forums for training are offered allowing the reader to develop a training plan which may be unique to his/her organization. Those common subject matter areas which are felt critical to all organizations and needs are identified as well, providing a "core" knowledge and skill base around which to plan a training strategy.

Overview

Maintaining operations in an investigative environment is a time-consuming task. The process is exacerbated with the addition of technology, either in performing the investigations, or when technology is the subject of the investigation. When one considers the rate at which technology is constantly advancing, the burden is exponentially aggravated.

The issues concerned in this chapter fall into the realm of training, and affect staffing and budgeting. These issues, particularly in a civil service environment, are tightly bound. The manager of any unit, and the administration structure of the organization in which that unit is embodied, determines the likelihood at every level of such a cyber unit's success. This chapter applies therefore not solely to the manager of the unit itself, but also to those administrative managers involved in any decision-making process affecting the budgeting, training, and staffing of any cyber unit.

While this author's experience deals with the command structure of the NYPD (New York City Police Department), many of the issues will apply to both public agencies as well as many private institutions.

The reasons for training properly are obvious: efficient and adequate job performance depends on training levels commensurate with the tasks to be performed. A failure to provide adequate training will leave individuals and organizations vulnerable to court actions (either civil or criminal). The failure to process electronic evidence may result in a failure to exculpate an individual, or may result in failure to protect an organization in the event of a dispute. This impact will affect the individuals who are the subjects of the investigation as well the organizations for which they work.

Budgeting concerns are not part of this chapter other than to state that equipping and training on an ongoing basis are required. The justification for budgeting is rarely demonstrated in the public sector as a return on investment (ROI); instead, the justification is a negative one. The negative justification of risk avoidance and mitigation includes the cost of training individuals and properly maintaining the digital investigative environment.

The intended purpose of this chapter therefore, is to consider training paradigms and determine the applicability of any training models which meet job performance requirements.

Examination of typical tasks (as well as those not-so-typical tasks) can indicate the range of knowledge, skills, and abilities (KSA) required fulfilling cyber investigative roles. If possible, the categorization of these functional roles may allow a manager to better compartmentalize training requirements to a particular role (eventually assigned to a staff member), and thereby better plan training needs.

An alternate method of determining training possibilities is to survey training programs currently in place: the caveat here is that current offerings are designed to fit a "common" need, which may in fact not suit a unit's specific needs.

Still another technique of finding training topics is to examine course offerings in formal education institutes, both on the undergraduate as well as the graduate level. The distinction between the two should be the level and depth of expertise as well as the quality of research requirements in a course of study.

Roles

If we ignore the budgeting issues, the staffing and training requirements revolve around the critical question,

"What tasks will be performed for which we require training?"

A very broad description states that the computer forensic specialists *acquire*, *archive*, *analyze*, and *attest to* computer-related evidence.

A "macro level" method of determining training needs is to categorize the required, as well as desired, skills and knowledge according to the levels of sophistication and prerequisite knowledge which the trainee must possess. Yasinsac, Erbacher, Marks, Pollitt, & Sommer (2003), recommended a Computer/Network Forensics (CNF) matrix based on levels of sophistication mapped against the tasks required of the practitioner. This author suggested using the matrix as a possible basis for the establishment of a computer and network forensics curriculum on the university level (Malinowski, 2004). If examined, the CNF matrix suggested by Yasinsac et al. may be appropriate for many of the functions required by a computer forensic practitioner.

According to the Yasinsac's CNF matrix, a progression of skills exists for the various roles which include *technician*, *professional*, *policy maker*, and finally *researcher*. While I suggest this as a basis for a formal educational curriculum, it is possible that a similar model can be applied toward training efforts of any unit dealing with cyber investigations. The matrix is role-based and therefore allows a manger to determine the appropriate levels of training or education for each functional role in the unit.

Table 1. CNF Matrix (© [2003] IEEE), Reprinted with permission.

Role	Education	Training
CNF Technician	Introductory level: Computer Science, Hardware, Operating Systems, Forensic Science, Civil and Criminal law	Professional certification training for hardware, network (e.g., A+, Net+), "bag-and-tag", basic data recovery and duplication
CNF Policy Maker	Information Management, Forensic Science, Information Assurance, Knowledge Management, Enterprise Architecture	Survey / seminar courses in Information Assurance, legal, and CNF techniques
CNF Professional	CNF Technician items, upper level courses in IS, Networks, Architecture, and law (civil, criminal and procedural)	CNF Technician training, Advanced data recovery and courtroom training
CNF Researcher	Doctorate level education or master's degree, extensive experience in computer forensics	Hands-on training for specific research areas being pursued

CNF technicians are capable of acting as "incident first responders" and performing "bag-and-tag" (seizure), duplication, and recovery of digital evidence. It should be noted that much of the knowledge for this role can be acquired through an educational institution, perhaps opening up a pool of candidates for staffing purposes.

A CNF policy maker possesses knowledge of a "broader" nature enabling him to function as a manager. While the matrix is focused on the technical breadth, I would argue that this role requires managerial skills in order to manage a technical staff (a job often likened to "herding cats").

The CNF professional has a greater depth of knowledge and skills than the technician in the areas of computer science, information systems, and the legal concerns involved in the field. Should the CNF technician encounter difficulties in data recovery, it is expected that the CNF Professional has more developed skills and knowledge allowing for a successful data recovery. It should be noted that Dr. Yasinsac cites that the legal knowledge at this level should incorporate criminal, civil, and *procedural* law.

Finally, a CNF researcher extends the body of knowledge in the field. This person is knowledgeable in the arena of computer forensics. It should be noted that there is no specific training other than that required in order to pursue a particular line of research.

Consideration must be given in order to encompass the entire range of skills and knowledge for which training might be necessary. Even though tasks routinely performed by a "forensic specialist" (technician) might include only one facet of the "acquire, archive, analyze, and attest" characteristics of cyber forensics, often a failure to fully appreciate the nature of the technology may render the cyber investigation incomplete or erroneous.

In many of the incidents to which the author has responded, full knowledge of the system(s) was not known until actually walking into a site. Once the subject system is encountered, circumstances may require additional personnel or expertise in order to perform tasks. The contention is, therefore, more knowledge (training) brought by a responder to the incident allows for a more appropriate response to that incident.

A microscopic, or more granular, view of skills will focus on the discrete tasks involved in any given role of the CNF matrix. A listing of considerations and tasks for a *"computer forensics specialist"* as provided by Judd Robbins (Robbins, 2004) is paraphrased below:

1.   Protect the subject computer from alteration, damage, data corruption, or virus introduction.

2.   Discover all files on the subject system including normal files, deleted files, hidden files, system files, password-protected files, and encrypted files.

3.   Recover discovered deleted files (total or partial).

4.   Reveal contents of hidden files, swap, and temp files.

5.   Access (if possible and legally appropriate) contents of encrypted or protected files.

6.   Access data in "special" areas of the disk, including unallocated space and slack space.

7.   Provide an analysis report of the subject system, listing all relevant files and discovered file data. Provide opinion of system layout, file structures discovered and discovered data. Provide authorship and ownership information. Provide opinion of efforts to hide, delete, alter, protect, or encrypt data. Include any other relevant information discovered during the computer system evaluation.

8.   Provide expert testimony or consultation as required.

Hal Berghel indicates that we should be aware of the differentiation between *computer* and *network* forensics (Berghel, 2003). This difference may have implications in providing the required training, as neglecting one component might leave a deficiency in field personnel's training. Perhaps a better term to use would be *cyberforensics* as the nature of the systems encountered in the field often include both computers and the networks they comprise; data might reside on individual computer systems, or may be distributed over several systems linked together in a network. Indeed, data might reside on a wide variety of devices. Some of these devices may or may not be within one organization, or even a single legal jurisdiction. A keen appreciation of legal issues is therefore required in order to pursue any cyber investigation. This is one of the reasons by which it can be argued that cyberforensics is in many respects an interdisciplinary field.

Selection of Personnel

Quite obviously, a manager seeks to fill a role with people having the proper qualifications. Part of this consideration must take into account those prerequisite skills which the trainee should already possess prior to starting any course of training.

Staffing a cyber unit is problematic: either the prime directive of the unit is to investigate and prosecute cyber incidents, or these investigative tasks are incidental to an already established job description. In either case, evaluation of the knowledge and abilities of staff must be performed in order to determine what, if any, deficiencies exist according to the roles to be performed in order to plan training.

In the corporate world often these tasks fall upon the network or system administrator. In the civil service world (law enforcement in particular) the possibilities are much more limited. Due to the laws and regulations governing personnel titles and tasks performed, often matching the title with the required skills is an impossible one.

The dilemma that exists is investigators who are traditionally trained in investigations may not have basic computer skills. This trend is changing however as younger investigators, having grown up in the computer era, are becoming a larger part of the work force. The level of these skills however is generally basic: for example, an investigator might have those skills required in order to navigate the Internet, read e-mail, and produce basic office documentation.

In many instances, a manager will not have the luxury of selecting personnel from a pool of skilled forensic specialists. Having stated that, a manager is then left with the option of locating persons with the best aptitude for the tasks to be performed.

Managers may prefer staffing with persons having certifications or field experience as technicians. The immediate benefits may be in obtaining a specific skill set for a subset of tasks required in the role to be filled.

Candidates having a degree in either information systems or computer science have an advantage insofar as they understand to some degree the underlying technology, despite the specific curriculum taught at different university systems. This education serves as a foundation for the task-specific courses or training which need to supplement the basic education. In either case, there will generally be some kind of deficiency in training which requires remediation.

In civil service, those who are versed in computer technology usually will be titled personnel in the information systems section, and oftentimes will be civilian personnel. In the event that some IS personnel *are* uniformed personnel (sworn members qualified to enforce criminal statutes), generally they may not have investigatory titles or the background to conduct a real world investigation. It is for this reason that in many respects staffing a unit is similar to the "chicken-or-the-egg" question in determining which comes first when staffing a unit. A manager needs to determine which skills are immediately required in order to commence a cyber investigation and find the most appropriate person to fill that role, and then provide the training.

In my experiences with criminal investigations, generally an actual incident occurred leading to a cyber trail. In the private sector however, an investigation may initiate with a cyber incident such as intrusion attempts, a DoS (*denial of service*) attack, information security violations, unauthorized usage of a system, or some other such incident.

Selecting personnel (and subsequently training these people) depends on the prime impetus of investigations: criminal investigations require standard investigative techniques at the onset in many cases, whereas cyber investigations may *never* require personnel to venture outside the cyber world.

In cyber investigations an initial "lead" or occurrence may be either technology-based in nature or may be a "traditional" lead. For example, a threat conducted via telephone may be traditionally dealt with, as opposed to an e-mailed threat. The understanding of the entire telephone system is not required in order to further develop information regarding the source of a telephone call. In contrast, an e-mail requires knowledge of how e-mail is processed both as a protocol as well as physical and electronically.

To emphasize how a cyber investigative lead may turn into a "real world" lead, the uncovering of an e-mail user on a server may lead to locating a real person or a location. Investigators need to be careful however in making assumptions from these uncovered facts. The mere understanding that an e-mail might be "spoofed" (falsified to misrepresent the sender's identity) will not provide the investigator with the capability of determining the "*how* and *where* and *who*" of the spoofing. A deeper knowledge of the underlying protocols is required in order to determine what *possibly* occurred. Failure to recognize how cyber leads can be spoofed may result in pursuing a false trail or coming to wrong conclusions.

As seen in the simplified Figure 1, specialized leads or evidence require specialized knowledge in order to develop further information. As a result, an iterative IPO (input-process-output) process takes place which builds on the developed information until

Figure 1. Blending of cyber and real-world skills

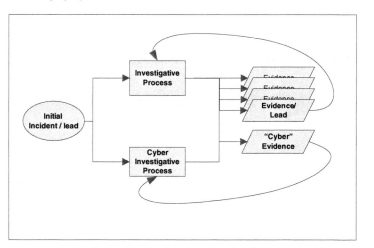

enough information develops to form a conclusion. The ultimate goal is finding the pattern which points to a real-world cause or culprit. As depicted in Figure 1 it is hoped that uncovering a "cyber lead" as an input to the cyber investigative process will eventually lead to a "real-world" output.

The investigator's role is to take the disparate pieces of information and link them demonstrating a chain of causality. As investigations tend to overlap between the real and digital world, the leads must be followed, documented, and validated in order to provide a basis for a prosecution of a criminal, or to support the dismissal of an employee.

Difficulties are encountered when the additional burden of investigating incidents is imposed onto the tasklist. Real-world investigative techniques eventually will join cyber investigative techniques and become additional training requirements. The role of the cyber investigator is to uncover traces indicating the "*how*" and the "*who*" of a cyber incident. In many instances however, the traces found by a cyber investigator only indicate *possibilities* of the "*who*". While a cyber investigator may posses the skills to elicit and develop information from cyber sources, technology issues must be thoroughly understood so as not to exclude possible causes of an incident.

For example, an investigator may find network messages being delivered to a specific physical address (MAC) on a network and base further actions focused on that specific network node. Failing to take into account the manner in which MAC addresses can be spoofed will direct an investigator's attention to the false target (i.e., not recognizing unsolicited ARP messages which update volatile ARP tables).

Adversely a cyber investigator may follow a lead which ultimately results in real-world investigations, such as tracing telephone records, or financial records of subjects. Experienced network administrators well versed in locating network anomalies would be hard pressed to pursue real world leads.

Due to the nature of investigations, training of personnel will require supplementing the skills of prospective investigators available in a staff pool, as it will be unlikely that investigators possess both real-world as well as cyber-world investigative abilities.

Staffing plays a major role, both in identifying the immediate skills available (immediate capabilities of the unit), as well as in projecting the future needs for training of personnel. The next step is how the determination of these appropriate skills occurs. If we revisit the CNF roles, we might develop an understanding of how training may not necessarily be a clear-cut decision.

The CNF technician will be responding to a location and will be responsible for securing any evidence. The requirements are a basic understanding of the storage technologies currently available. While this may sound trivial, by no means is it necessarily a trivial task for many reasons. Technicians need to be trained for forensic data recovery, documentation, and "digital situational awareness".

Ideally the technician will walk into a location and the simplest task might be to make a "bit-for-bit" forensically sound copy of the data on a machine. This could be as simple as backing up a hard drive. Needless to say, the investigator requires the training in order to properly secure the evidence without altering the original data he wishes to capture. In a Windows environment, it is possible to utilize a device and connect it to an IDE drive. This device will read the contents of the drive without writing to the device. The training for this operation is minimal, and a basic understanding of the technology is required.

Notwithstanding this simple scenario, at times it may be impractical to utilize a turnkey or simple system in order to obtain a forensic copy. Nonstandard devices, or technology that is either too new, or even too old, may prove difficult to process. The technician will need the appropriate training in order to secure the data as best possible. Part of this training will include forensic training: appropriately documenting the site, the target environment, the equipment used to perform the forensic image, the evidence acquisition results, and the protocol used to perform the forensic imaging.

If the technician is not proficient with the equipment or in the operating systems involved, the task of acquiring digital evidence will be made more complex. In fact, the process may result in obtaining the wrong data as evidence, missing evidence, or in having the results contaminated. Knowledge of operating systems standard tools and protocols and their limitations is required.

A "situational awareness" will enable the technician, in the role of a first responder, to determine the possible locations and nature of any evidence. An example of this would be the discovery of networked locations of data. Through the examination of documents (logs, procedures, etc.), or through interviews a responder might develop information indicating the possibility of data existing off-site, or on other systems at that location. Furthermore, a detailed notation of the system environment may provide insight to investigator as to the possibility of something having happened at a particular location; in effect the "means" and the "opportunity" aspects of the "means, motive, and opportunity" axiom may be overlooked. The argument to be made is that there is no clear delineation of tasks encountered in the real world.

Playing the devil's advocate can be beneficial in determining the level of training required for any of the roles in the CNF matrix. The manager must decide the balance between functionality of personnel and the cost incurred to provide the training of these personnel. Not evident in risk mitigation is the fear that any investment would result in the increased possibility of personnel loss. In the private sector, this may not be an overriding concern as salaries and benefits can be matched. Conversely, in the public sector training of personnel can lead to eventual loss of personnel as they become marketable commodities and the agency proves incapable of matching competitor compensation. Many administrators exercise care in personnel selection, as training personnel on either end of their career life expectancy can result in employee loss: those with little time invested may feel little compunction against leaving for better pay and those at the end of their service will finish out their minimum required time to achieve a pension and depart for more monetarily rewarding positions.

In considering the training, once again we should compare the knowledge and skills to the role or function of our first responders and investigators. The investigators may be field or lab investigators, or in fact may conduct the entire investigative effort. The CNF matrix holds, for the most part, for the corporate world. The responders roughly equate to the "technician" in Dr. Yasinsac's matrix and the investigators or analysts roughly correspond to the "professional". We should not forget the "policy maker", which would be incorporated into the cyberforensics manager or supervisor.

My personal opinion is that any technician or investigator, whether he is called a "security specialist", "legal compliance associate", "forensic technician" or "computer crimes detective" requires a basic legal understanding as provided by the CNF matrix. In other words, those aspects of the training required by a "policy maker" (manager) need to be incorporated at least to *some* degree in subordinates or the other CNF matrix roles. One simple reason is risk reduction: the technician or the investigator is required to have an understanding of the legalities in order to ensure the forensic integrity of any results in an investigation. In many instances the ability to defer to another person (such as a manager) who does have that knowledge may be impractical or impossible at the time. The risk exposure is in producing a product that is forensically inadmissible, or in being subjected to a lawsuit at some later point in time.

The one role neglected so far in this chapter is that of the "CNF Researcher". The basic definition is a person possessing the skills and knowledge of the CNF professional having the additional capability of extending the body of knowledge in the field.

While it might be desirable to have someone of this expertise on staff, unless the mission of the unit or organization includes extending the body of knowledge, training for this role should be considered carefully. One example would be a unit member developing software to provide new one-way hash codes, or to write new software or modify a software suite which processes data forensically. The considerations against training such a member would include the training cost, as well as the time which may be taken away from other mission objectives (e.g., analysis of forensic product).

Scope of Functions (Roles)

Unfortunately the nature of cyber investigations does not always confine itself to one narrow aspect of an investigation. Should a manager be fortunate enough to have a staff of reasonable size, then a division of labor might be established which allows for performance of discrete tasks which would not rely on other (seemingly unrelated) components of an investigation.

For example in the event that data seems to be encrypted, a technician may be qualified to process the data. Ideally, a trained analyst should be qualified to recognize the possible presence of hidden data (encryption, steganography, etc.). The analyst should also be trained in the methods in how such encryption might be cracked, rather than turn this facet of the investigation over to yet another staff member.

For various reasons it is not desirable to introduce more individuals into the investigation of any incident. One reason is that additional links are forged into the "chain of custody", as well as unnecessarily introducing another human factor into the investigation. This may lead to documentation problems, as well as introducing new tasks and resources in the investigative project life cycle. The author's contention is that the manager should ensure appropriate training levels of staff so as not to create a scenario in which many persons are responsible for the end result of an investigation. The ideal state of any investigative unit would be to have a cross-trained staff so as to respond more efficiently and with better effect to any cyber incidents or investigations. If one considers that any investigator/analyst might be testifying, the potential "downtime" of those staff members might well justify any training costs.

Training Modalities

At least three different learning paradigms exist: a formal education model, real world experience (on-the-job-training), and professional training. Until recently, it is my belief that the formal education model has been lacking in many respects as universities are just beginning to offer courses in computer forensics and security. Additionally, in the subject matter areas which are covered, for the most part the students are not practitioners.

Real-world experience often surpasses the level of detail of a formal education setting. While invaluable, the breadth of knowledge may be sporadic, and requires passage of time as well as the opportunities of circumstances in order to gain knowledge in this fashion.

The professional training model also focuses on specific subject matter areas and often does not delve into the underlying principles or theories. For example, the professional training model may offers classes or seminars by a software provider or professional training service for a specific product. General principles may be covered insofar as they underlie the proper application of a particular software product, however a vendor may assume certain knowledge on the part of the participant. This is not to say however, that all such trainers neglect underlying theory.

One training solution may be that skills may be mapped against courses offered in a formal educational setting. The gaps in those skills are the areas for which training must be provided. As mentioned earlier, those skills of the CNF technician map out rather nicely against a formal educational background.

Traditional computer science and information systems curricula have provided students with backgrounds and skills in coding, analysis, database fundamentals, networking, and other knowledge areas in order to cope with working in an industrial or technical setting. One of the more common complaints often heard of educational institutions is the lack of "training" that is provided. Essentially many corporations develop training programs in order to supplement the basic skills provided by a formal educational institution. The dilemma revolves around the "training versus education" mode of instruction. Many formal education systems seem to disdain *training* citing that those classes belong in "continuing education" courses, or in a professional training forum. Rather, formal education is concerned with underlying theory, and providing basic knowledge and skills, as well as the ability for a student to extend his own knowledge. Curriculum growth or changes may often be hampered by organizational inertia, or the regulatory concerns required in adopting educational program changes, making it difficult to locate the appropriate degree program in which to enroll.

For many reasons, rarely are staff equipped to cope with the tasks required in a forensic (legal) setting which transcends the traditional IS model of class instruction. Only recently have universities started offering instruction in computer and network security, as well as forensics.

This means that while members who *have* had formal instruction may be familiar with the fundamentals of networking, they have no experience in security issues past the rudiments. Additionally the approach of a formal education is based on business-oriented goals, and students have little or no training in the investigative side of the industry. In many cases these skills are developed during on-the-job training or apprenticeships. Indeed, the nearest that such institutions have come to handling these issues are during instruction in the configuration of operating system services or router configurations. One skill which is definitely not in a college brochure is that of interviewing: investigators need to elicit information from sources other than digital ones! The fine art of finessing, cajoling, and social engineering responses from interviewees is a developed skill (in which I have personally observed the NYPD detectives excel).

Depending on the role required, training may be supplemented by a formal education, or may be satisfied by a course of study covering specific, technical courses. My suggestion is to "overtrain", that is to say, train beyond the limitations of the immediate functions (associated with the role) to be performed.

Traditional Education

An examination of a "traditional" curriculum in a computer science program may include some of the skills or knowledge areas required within a computer forensics discipline. They knowledge areas at a minimum should encompass a *basic* understanding of the technology in order to provide the investigator with skills of a "first responder" or "investigator". Some of the courses might include the following:

- **Computer literacy** and "office suite productivity tools" which allow the trainee to manipulate standard documents using OTS (off-the-shelf) software suites. Additionally, the trainee should be versed in using typical network client applications such as e-mail, Web browsers, file transfer, news readers as well as be aware of other client-server or peer-to-peer (P2P) applications.

- **Operating systems** provide a survey of available operating systems, as well as the command sets available to perform user and administrator level tasks. Additionally the trainee can gain an understanding of the system-level data structures (partition tables, file tables, and directories, etc.) as well as any security related structures (system, group, and user tables).

- With the proliferation of graphical user interfaces (GUI) allowing users to invoke system functions, many users are no longer familiar with command line interactions. In many instances, the **command line interface** may be the sole secure method of acquiring forensic data from a target system making this a critical skill to master.

- **Introductory programming and graphical interface (GUI) programming** provide an appreciation for understanding coding as well as allow the trainee to develop "home grown" solutions when investigations require solutions that are not yet addressed by OTS software suites.

- **Data structures and algorithms** bolster the user's ability to provide software solutions, as well as increase the analyst's awareness of possible evidentiary structures which may be encountered during an investigation.

- **Database fundamentals** allow an investigator to manipulate data in order to develop correlations of evidence, or to develop "in-house" custom databases to support investigative efforts.

- **Networking and data communications** assist the investigator in developing a situational awareness at cyber incident scenes, as well as provide an understanding of possible mechanisms employed during a cyber incident. Additionally investigators need to understand how technology may be leveraged against them during any interactive phase of an investigation (sting operation, online chats, or other communications, etc.).

Formal education curricula, for varying reasons, are often deficient in knowledge areas specific to cyberforensics. Selection of additional coursework can supplement the basic computer science/information systems curriculum in supplying that specific knowledge to the student.

The most obvious courses to add to this study program would be those addressing aspects of computer and network forensics. Oftentimes the subject matter of these courses consist of utilities, which together may constitute a course in recovery, incident response, intrusion detection, or a similar subject area. These courses are normally not offered as part of a "general" computer science curriculum. Rather, they are often found in a specific niche (if offered), or as a special topics elective. More often than not, these courses are found in industrial training settings addressing specific topic areas, such as a SANS training course or a vendor supplied training series of courses.

Computer security and network security may fill part of the "gap"; however courses in educational institutions tend to be general and not focused on any particular technology, or solely on one technology. In addition, they tend to address broad underlying issues and may never include skills on addressing these issues.

Instruction in the security related aspects of a networked computer environment will assist the responder or investigator in determining which possible means were utilized in mounting an attack, or assist in locating possible sources of information in determining the severity and source of any attacks. For example, a network security course may spend time on encryption, but may never explore techniques on breaking or cracking that encryption (such as *John the Ripper* or *l0pht*). Likewise a great deal may be made of WEP (Wired Equivalent Privacy) and the ability to crack it, however very seldom in a college will assignments include using AirSnort and WEPcrack to illustrate the point and develop those skills.

For technicians as well as investigator/analysts, an understanding of servers, client-server technology, as well as the technologies and associated devices allowing the logical and physical network connections, is critical in the response to a cyber incident.

Topics such as these are not consistently delivered via the traditional syllabus in universities, nor is the thrust of the course necessarily intended to support investigations and security, but rather they may be based on general theory. In short, an alternate means of training may be required.

In some cases, educational institutions seem to be reticent to provide instruction in subject matter in which they feel that the institution may incur a liability: that is to say, students will abuse the knowledge and cause monetary damage or commit criminal acts. For this reason, you will rarely see a "Hacking 101" offering in the syllabus of a college. This attitude also applies in some degree to industrial/professional training, as several courses are restricted to law enforcement. Indeed, several products are available solely to law enforcement and governmental agencies.

In many cases, the components which are most often neglected are applications and systems coding. While an investigator can appreciate that server-side scripting is a vulnerability, he might be sorely challenged in *finding* the actual vulnerability in a particular piece of code.

One case in which I participated dealt with the degradation of a predictive model by a disgruntled employee. The code employed was designed to gradually erode the value of trading commodities displayed to a client base over time. Fortunately the "error" was caught by another coder who by chance noticed the discrepancy. If left to an investigator to locate the offending code, perhaps it would have gone unnoticed. The challenge to the investigators was to prove that the coder *intentionally* eroded the value displayed, as opposed to a mistake in coding (the difference resulting in criminal charges). To illustrate the nature of investigations, the intent was proven using traditional investigative methods (eavesdropping) rather than an analysis of the coding.

Instruction in the legal and ethical aspects of computer/network forensics will provide a legal backdrop as well as a context against which the science in "computer science" has relevance. The methodologies and protocols as well as demonstrations of performing forensic activities using built-in system tools will be taught. An introduction of forensic toolkit usage will demonstrate the forensically sound advantages gained in using such toolkits. Perhaps more importantly, when taken into account with the computer science knowledge, the limitations of toolkits will also be brought to a student's attention. Much of the training is designed to support standard operations, toolkits, and so forth; however education and training should also be pursued to surmount any limitations of the currently available tools.

John R. Vacca contends that the [United States] practitioner should apply the federal protocols and be cognizant of U.S. Code in performing forensic acquisitions and analyses (Vacca, 2005). The implication is that the practitioner should apply the more stringent protocols applicable in his/her judicial system. My advice to industry specialists has been to follow *legal* requirements, even though their investigation might be an internal investigation to a corporation, as the investigation has potential to result in uncovering criminal actions and ultimately be prosecuted in a criminal court setting.

Note that not all subject matter topics are required for the responder (technician), or for the investigator (professional). If the two roles can be separated, then the training can be limited for each role. In the case of a smaller unit, however, that may rarely be the case. A manager needs to determine the nature of the tasks which the "technician/responder" and the "professional/investigator" will encounter and provide those necessary training modules. Managers (policy makers) themselves require training in order to oversee operations of a team.

Professional Training

Two general routes exist by which skills for the actual acquisition, archival and analysis are learned. One route involves learning the methodologies and protocols for cyber forensics in general. The second method concentrates on a specific product, such as Guidance Software's EnCase®.

General courses provide the investigator with the general needs and current methodologies and protocols of the industry. The course should present examples of tools which can be utilized, as well as reference their capabilities as well as limitations. Essentially, the trainee should have an idea of which tools to use dependent upon the circumstances at hand. In these cases, the investigator is left to his own devices to document the case and maintain the chain of evidence and custody.

In the event that investigations will be conducted with a specific product, such as EnCase, ILook, FTK, SMART, or some other such tool, the training desired should probably be delivered by the product vendor, or an authorized provider. In many instances these training courses result in obtaining certification in the usage of the product which may be advantageous for the investigating agency.

For several reasons, many managers prefer industry/professional training courses. One of the reasons is that in many instances the coursework is narrowly focused on a particular subject matter area. It may also be possible, in some civil service agencies, that managers are precluded from sending personnel to university for training, or that training in not permissible without the trainee becoming a matriculated student in a degree study program.

While this is not an endorsement of any one particular organization, the listings below are offered as examples of courses currently being offered to industry professionals.

SANS Institute (SANS Institute, 2005):

- SEC401: SANS Security Essentials Bootcamp
- SEC502: Firewalls, Perimeter Protection, and VPNs
- SEC503: Intrusion Detection In-Depth
- SEC504: Hacker Techniques, Exploits and Incident Handling
- SEC505: Securing Windows
- SEC506: Securing Unix/Linux
- AUD507: Auditing Networks, Perimeters & Systems
- SEC508: System Forensics, Investigation and Response
- SEC309: Intro to Information Security
- AUD410: IT Security Audit Essentials
- MGT512: SANS Security Leadership Essentials For Managers
- MGT414: SANS® +S™ Training Program for the CISSP® Certification Exam
- SEC616: .NET Security
- SEC616: Linux Administration Bootcamp

As seen, coursework is more focused on specific areas. Courses such as these have the benefits of narrowing the scope of topic, as well as may introduce tools or skills specific to that topic.

Notwithstanding gaining specific knowledge in a product's usage, investigators are still responsible for understanding the general principles and procedures accepted by industry practitioners, including the less glamorous task of documenting the case.

Training Shortcuts and Supplements

If the intent of alternatives to educational courses or industry training is to "fast-track" productivity, then such alternatives *do* exist. Practitioners can avail themselves of software "all-in-one" tools, seminars, and professional organizations.

Software suites or toolkits have been developed in recent years which take remove much of the burden from the cyber investigator; unfortunately, the responsibility and accountability of the investigator remains. EnCase® is one example of such a forensic tool. As other toolkits do, EnCase can acquire, archive, and analyze evidence data. The work of documenting various processes is incorporated into the toolkit, so as to better ensure inclusion of analysis results.

Tools work within parameters: that is to say, a tool is written with a set of available functions which can be used in order to examine data, within constraints. As the nature of the operating environment or the underlying technology changes the tool may be rendered ineffective. Worse still, the tool may be deficient in which case the results of any investigation may be voided. In the worst instance, the procedure may be suspect, bringing into question all of the other investigations performed using either that procedure or software tool to examine evidence.

Reliance upon a software suite or a tool is no substitute for training. While the immediacy of the result might be better served, the lack of training may not determine when the tool is deficient, or in those known cases of a deficiency may not allow an investigator to justify any results obtained.

Training of individuals will allow for recognition of potential problems, or provide for the development of alternate means of obtaining the required data from an evidence source. While the investigator is relieved of detailed knowledge of specific tools to utilize and their operations, the investigator still requires a fundamental understanding of the process, its limitations and the evidence being examined by this process.

Organizations sometimes provide lectures or seminars on specific topics which may be of interest to practitioners. The purpose of these seminars is not to explore any topic in depth, but rather to introduce an area of interest, or to pursue one particular topic. Conferences are often the forum for such seminars, in which lecturers provide information, in some cases showcasing their product or services. Each lecture may be brief in duration, and conferences may be arranged in "tracks", allowing practitioners to select a track which follows a specific interest, such as networking or forensics.

Professional organizations and associations offer forums for meeting other practitioners and exchanging information. One such organization is the HTCIA (High Technology Crime Investigative Association). The HTCIA is an international association with members from both law enforcement as well as corporate security tasked with the investigation of cyber incidents. Some of the excerpts of the 2005 HTCIA conference (HTCIA, 2005) in Monterey, California are listed below:

- Physically locating IP addresses on the Internet
- ILook (toolkit developed by/for Federal agencies)

- FTK for the Internet
- FTK Imager and the Basics of FTK
- Computer Forensics in the 21st Century
- Capturing Digital Forensic Evidence with SnagIt and Camtasia Studio
- Steganography: Investigator Overview
- Network 101: The Basics
- Computer Forensics : Best Practices
- Who is the CyberSex offender?
- WhiteHat / BlackHat toolkit 2005

Certifications

One of the questions often asked is whether or not an investigator should be certified. Certifications are granted by professional associations or corporations and either are specific to a product or service, or in fact, may be general. The benefits of certification can be determined by examining the acceptance of the industrial acceptance of certifications as a "stamp of approval"; essentially providing a shortcut in validating a person's body of knowledge within a subject matter area. Not having certification, per se, does not preclude acceptance of someone's expertise; however without having certification expertise must be established by some other means in order to allow expert testimony, and is in fact routinely done.

Certifications are generally not incorporated into a formal educational setting, but can be issued in training settings such as in a "professional institute" or in a "continuing education class". Managers need to be aware that training may be derived from both formal education classes as well as training-based classes and adjust policy accordingly, as policies may often preclude formal education classes.

A caveat is that certification in a product may be *too* specific to a particular product. The hidden negative aspect may be that the "expertise" may not extend to other products dealing with the technology, or not include expertise in newer versions of the product, or may not include expertise in the underlying technology itself.

While the author formerly did not subscribe to the notion of certification as a necessity, in recent years the industry has changed, becoming more aligned with protocols of forensic sciences with methodologies and toolkits becoming widely accepted as industry standards and practice. Certification currently demonstrates that the practitioner shares accepted and common core knowledge with other professionals in the industry and helps establish an expertise.

The CISSP (certified information systems security professional) certification (CISSP, 2005) currently spans 10 knowledge areas, and demonstrates that the practitioner has basic knowledge in those areas. The 10 areas are listed next:

- Access control systems and methodology
- Applications and systems development
- Business continuity planning
- Cryptography
- Law, investigation, and ethics
- Operations security
- Physical security
- Security architecture and models
- Security management practices
- Telecommunications, network and internet security

Several organizations offer training and certifications for the CISSP which culminates in a 250 question exam lasting six hours.

Whereas the CISSP is a *general* certification of knowledge, the GIAC (global information assurance certification) series of certifications (SANS, 2005) demonstrates a proficiency in specific areas (such as firewalls). The SANS Institute established the GIAC and offers training and certification in the GIAC series.

Training Coverage

This aspect of training relies on the level of staff support at any given time. It is a reasonable assumption that no one single person can embody all of the knowledge, skills, and abilities of a digital investigator in the full sense of the term. Likewise, the KSA for any single facet or aspect of the work to be performed cannot be embodied solely in one individual.

While on the face of it, any unit can demonstrate that the required skillsets are encompassed by unit members; due to absences a skill may not be available when needed. An additional consideration is that during "routine" performance of any job, an awareness of another separate knowledge area may be required. For example, a "first responder" whose responsibility is securing and retrieving data at a scene may come across a technology which affects the manner in which his job is performed, or that indicates additional measures need to be taken. In many of the incidents to which the author has responded full knowledge of the system(s) was not known until actually walking onto the site. Once the subject system is encountered, circumstances may require additional personnel or expertise in order to perform tasks.

A second issue is that university models are based on an *education* model rather than the *training* model. The difference is that education focuses on theory and in understanding the underlying principles, and often leaves students incapable of functioning in a real-world environment: employers often need to supplement education with training. The benefits of an education however *do* enable the student to extend bodies of knowledge. The implication is that a manager cannot rely on selecting available personnel with the most qualifications; both educational as well as professional training modes have knowledge and skills gaps as far as cyberforensics are concerned.

Typically, systems or network administrators are tasked with following up incidents on their systems. In many instances their breadth of knowledge is narrowly constrained to their particular system. Additionally, for many reasons, the simple act of safeguarding and retrieving data which constitutes evidence is compounded by technology and legal constraints.

This essentially means is that a unit which is designed to deal with cyber incidents, or deal with corporate policy enforcement, rarely has personnel available to deal with the problem from the onset. This argues once again for cross-training of personnel, as well as supplementing current training of personnel.

Identifying Training Needs

While the focus of this chapter is on the training of technical personnel, we need to maintain a perspective on *when* in the investigative lifecycle this one function occurs. Figure 2 places the planning of training in an iterative cycle allowing for ongoing training. Essentially a manager needs to recognize the fact that training is necessarily an ongoing process if *any* element in the environment changes. Staffing changes, new technologies, new procedures or laws, or an increase in the volume of work demanded may each lead to training requirements.

In determining the level of training, consider the role to be performed. Other factors, which may not be obvious at first glance, require consideration in any decisions. Some of these factors deal with staffing issues, such as staffing levels and coverage of roles which may require cross-training of personnel. Also bear in mind that a unit may experience attrition of personnel which will develop into training needs.

Figure 2. Iterative training process

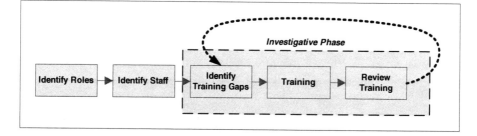

Considerations

Budgeting decisions must be reviewed in order to allow for ongoing training. Many organizations require budgeting to be projected for "multi-year plans". It is impractical to forecast budgeting for technologies which currently do not exist. Despite that, a manager is still required to project a budget.

Staff selection ideally would be based on matching skills and knowledge to the roles to be performed. In many instances, managers cannot expect to have personnel already trained, therefore managers must expect to select persons with either education or job experience and supplement training. Care needs to be exercised in determining which gaps exist in a member's knowledge base. It is conceivable that both the educationally as well as professionally trained person has such gaps in knowledge or skills.

If a formal educational track is considered, the manager should be aware that not all of the curriculum may apply to the immediate tasks to be performed. Unfortunately, many institutions will not allow a student to participate in a plan of study unless he is matriculated into a program; consequently many organizations will not reimburse a trainee for those non-related courses in the plan of study.

Professional training is a better "fit" for this reason, as it is more specific to the tasks required, as well as does not incur additional time or cost for the trainee. Managers need to examine the training in order to determine whether it addresses the needs of the trainee. Additionally, if training is specific to a product, training cannot neglect general protocols and methodologies as these provide professionally accepted background knowledge.

Technical issues need to be addressed. While the role of the first responder (technician) is to "identify, safeguard, and acquire evidence", oftentimes the skills to do so will require someone to utilize operating system commands, write or execute scripts, or to extract data from a "data store" (such as a database) or device. If the expectation is that the responder will not have the luxury of waiting for the arrival of appropriate expertise, consider incorporating some of the CNF professional skills which would be performed by a forensic investigator or analyst into the responder role.

The skills required by an investigator may be refined or narrowed in focus if that investigator is not required to perform that actual forensic analysis of data. The decision to "specialize" these roles may be contractually based, or policy based. The consequences of this specialization will not be addressed in this chapter, however.

Finally, other training venues must be explored. Personnel should be encouraged to join professional associations and network with other professionals in these organizations. These interactions often provide leads for training opportunities, offer forums for discussions on current industry topics, and provide a means of establishing contacts for future questions and referrals. One such organization is the HTCIA (High Tech Computer Investigators' Association).

Managers need to understand the limitations of certain training opportunities: while seminars provide information, the goal of training is to obtain *knowledge* and skills. Selection of training opportunities should be based with this goal in mind. One factor in choosing training is the content to be delivered, and how broad or specific (firewalls in general, or a specific vendor's product) that content is, as well as certifications derived. If appropriate, ensure that the instructor has the appropriate experience or credentials for delivering that content.

In many instances a certification can demonstrate knowledge and skills possessed by the trainee in order to obtain that certification, hence the desirability of a certification.

For those law enforcement agencies in the United States, training opportunities may be found in governmental grants or programs established to provide training for computer crime investigations. As these often are federally funded, the training is often based on Federal training models which may be initially viewed as impractical by state or local agencies (duration of training, locations offered, or programs offered in a series). While the Federal model may not match that of a local agency, perhaps the policies of the local agencies need to be reviewed in order to accomplish the long-range mission. In essence, the author's recommendation is that managers *make time* for training as any inconvenience in scheduling is offset by the benefits of having a trained staff.

An additional practice suggested would be to have an "in-house apprenticeship", in which a trainee observes practices and performs tasks under the scrutiny of seasoned investigators. This process should be documented in order to verify the level of training and skills possessed by the trainee. Implicit in this are formal evaluations and reviews, and if necessary, testing of basic skills and knowledge.

Conclusions

One suggestion I offer is that the *"acquire, archive, analyze,* and *attest to"* characteristics of a cyber investigator's responsibilities be expanded to include *"anticipate"*. The investigator should anticipate, preempt (if possible) and respond to attacks on the protocols and methodologies used in conducting his investigation.

While the CNF matrix provides a framework against which we can determine what education and training needs are required for a particular role, managers need to be aware that the matrix has greater significance if the roles can be structured as they appear in the matrix. Oftentimes an organization's needs may preclude adherence to such a matrix. At other times, reality will determine which role is required, despite the capability of personnel present at the scene. There are other issues for which one cannot train: analysts have a high degree of likelihood in testifying in a court (hence the need for the legal issue training), however some very technically competent people will not make the best expert witness. These intangible factors should be considered as part of the personnel selection process, as often the reliability of the work-product (analysis report) is not as important as the credibility of the analyst.

As I indicated, my opinion on the issue of certification has changed in recent years, largely due to the emergence of standards tools, as well as the nature of the maturing field of cyberforensics. While previously computer forensics was almost a black art, practiced by those versed in arcane practices, currently the need for forensics specialists is growing, and the scientific community reflects that, as it establishes accepted practices and standards as with other forensic sciences. Managers need to consider developing staff accordingly, and at the same time walk a fine line between building staff skills while increasing staff marketability to other organizations.

In closing, training is necessarily an ongoing process and needs to be managed proactively, and not left to the discretion or suggestion of the practitioners. The reason for the manager's body of knowledge as cited by Dr. Yasinsac is so that the manager can plan an appropriate training regimen. While the manager need not have the depth of technical knowledge, the position demands a breadth of knowledge, and not solely confined to the technology: training in personnel management, project management, risk management, budgeting as well as "people skills" are desired. Managerial challenges often arise, and often the manager will be frustrated as he strives to justify ongoing training, dictated by the rapid changes in technologies.

Managers should bear in mind that missions often change after plans have been formulated and implemented, and that training should be considered for potential and future requirements so as not to be behind the technology curve and in order to remain mission-capable.

References

Berghel, H. (2003). The discipline of internet forensics. *Communications of the ACM, 46*(8), 15-20.

International High Technology Crime Investigation Association (HTCIA). www.htcia.org

Malinowski, C. (2004). Information systems forensics: A practitioner's approach. *Proceedings of ISECON*, Newport, RI. [Electronic Version - http://isedj.org/isecon/2004/3232/ISECON.2004.Malinowski.pdf]

Robbins, J. (2004). *An explanation of computer forensics*. Incline Village, NV: National Forensics Center.

SANS (System Administration, Networking and Security) Institute. www.sans.org

Vacca, J. (2005). *Computer forensics* (2nd ed.). Charles River Media.

Yasinsac, A., Erbacher, R., Marks, D., Pollitt, M., & Sommer, P. (2003). Computer forensics education. *Security & Privacy Magazine, IEEE, 1*(4), 15-23.

Additional Sources

Azadegan, S., Lavine, M., O'Leary, M., Wijesinha, A., & Zimand, M. (2003, June 30-July 2). An undergraduate track in computer security. *Annual Joint Conference Integrating Technology into Computer Science Education, Proceedings of the 8th*

Annual Conference on Innovation and Technology in Computer Science Education, Greece (pp. 207-210). New York: ACM Press.

Bacon, T., & Tikekar, R. (2003). Experiences with developing a computer security information assurance curriculum. *Journal of Computing Sciences in Colleges, 18*(4), 254-267.

Campbell, P., Calvert, B., & Boswell, S. (2003). *Security+ guide to network security fundamentals.* Boston: Thomson-Course Technology.

Crowley, E. (2003). Information system security curricula development. *Proceedings of the 4th Conference on Information Technology Curriculum* (pp. 249-255). New York: ACM Press.

Holden, G. (2004). *Guide to firewalls and network security: Intrusion detection and VPNs.* Boston: Thomson-Course Technology.

Mackey, D., (2003). *Web security for network and system administrators.* Boston: Thomson-Course Technology.

Nelson, W., Phillips, A., Enfinger, F., & Stuart, C. (2004). *Guide to computer forensics and investigations* (2nd ed.). Boston: Thomson-Course Technology.

NSTISSI, (1994). *No. 4011— National training standard for information systems security (INFOSEC) professionals.* The Committee on National Security Systems. www.cnss.gov

Schwarzkopf, A., Saunders, C., Jasperson, J., & Croes, H. (2004). Strategies for managing IS personnel: IT skills staffing. *Strategies for Managing IS/IT Personnel* (pp. 37-63). Hershey, PA: Idea Publishing Group.

Tikekar, R., & Bacon, T. (2003). The challenges of designing lab exercises for a curriculum in computer security. *Journal of Computing Sciences in Colleges, 18*(5), 175-183.

Troell, L., Pan, Y., & Stackpole, B. (2003). Forensic source development. *Proceedings of the 4th Conference on Information Technology Curriculum* (pp. 265-269). New York: ACM Press.

Chapter XV

Digital "Evidence" is Often Evidence of Nothing

Michael A. Caloyannides, Mitretek Systems Inc., USA

Abstract

Digital data increasingly presented in courts as evidence is mistakenly viewed by judges and juries as inherently unalterable. In fact, digital data can be very easily altered and it can be impossible for this falsification to be detected. A number of common ways are described whereby data in one's computer can enter without the computer owner's knowledge, let alone complicity. The same applies to all digital storage media, such as those used in digital cameras, digital "tape" recorders, digital divers' computers, GPS "navigators", and all other digital devices in common use today. It is important for judges and juries to be highly skeptical of any claims by prosecution that digital "evidence" proves anything at all.

Introduction

Unlike conventional analog data, such as the shade of grey or the subjective recollection of a witness, whose believability and validity is scrutinized in depth, digital data which takes one of two very unambiguous values (zero or one) is misperceived by the average person as being endowed with intrinsic and unassailable truth.

In fact, quite the opposite is true. Unlike conventional, analog, data and evidence whose tampering can often be detected by experts with the right equipment, digital data can be manipulated at will and, depending on the sophistication of the manipulator, the alteration can be undetectable regardless of digital forensics experts' competence and equipment.

The reason is quite simple: The ones and zeros of digital data can be changed and, if some minimal precautions are taken by the changer, the alteration leaves no traces of either the change or the identity of the person who made the change.

Stated differently, computer forensics can determine what is on the suspect's digital storage media at the time of the forensics investigation, but is never able to determine who put it there, when, how, or whether or not the data has been changed. The only possible exception is if the suspect elects to confess, but even that is proof of nothing given the long historical record of coerced false confessions worldwide.

The potential for miscarriage of justice is vast, given that many defense lawyers, judges and juries are unaware of the esoteric details of computer science. Worse yet, malicious prosecutors may take advantage of this ignorance by courts and defense lawyers by falsely asserting that digital evidence is "proof" of the guilt of the accused.

This "dirty little secret" about digital "evidence" is conveniently soft-pedaled by the computer forensics industry and by the prosecution, both of which focus on those *other* aspects of the process of collecting, preserving and presenting digital data evidence which can indeed be unassailable *if* done properly, such as the "chain of custody" portion of handling digital evidence.

Let's take a common example of "computer evidence". A suspect's hard disk is confiscated, subjected to forensics analysis and a report is generated for the court which states that the hard disk contained this or that file, and that these files dates' were this and that, that these files were renamed or printed on this and that date, thereby appearing to negate the suspect's claim that he or she did not know of the existence of these files.

A typical judge or jury will accept these facts at face value. In fact, it should not; for the following factual reasons:

1. The data found in someone's hard disk could have entered that hard disk (or any other digital data storage media, such as USB keys, CD ROMs, floppy disks, etc.) through any one or more of the following ways without the suspect's knowledge, let alone complicity. All of these paths for surreptitious data entry are very commonplace and occur on a daily basis. Situations where this happens routinely include the following:

    a. The hard disk was not new when the suspect purchased it, and contained files from before the suspect ever took custody of it. This applies even in the case of purchases of "new" computers because they could have been resold after being returned by a previous buyer. Even if that hard disk had been "wiped" by the seller and the software reinstalled, there is no physical way to guarantee that some data were not left behind; this is why the militaries and security services of most countries will never allow a disk to leave a secure installation, but will physically destruct it instead.

b.   A large amount of software packages today (referred to as "ad-ware" and "spy-ware", take it upon themselves to secretly install unadvertised files and a capability for the software-maker to snoop on the individual's computer through the Internet or other network. If this "snooping" capability is exploited by a third party hacker who routinely scans computers for this "back door entry", then files can be inserted on the suspect's computer at will.

c.   Obtaining full control of anyone's computer through the Internet does not even require that such "ad-ware" or "spy-ware" be installed. Microsoft has been admitting on a near-weekly basis for the last decade to numerous existing security flaws in its operating systems and applications. This applies especially to Microsoft's Internet Explorer, that allow anyone to gain full control of anyone else's Internet-connected computer and insert files in it without the victimized computer's owner knowing anything about it. Discoveries of new online "back door entries" to anyone's computer have been appearing at an average rate of at least one every week for the last several years.

d.   When any of us "browses" the Internet, it is not uncommon to mistype and to end up inadvertently and unintentionally on a Web site which is often an adult site. Even without mistyping at all, however, one can still end up at an incriminating site for the following reason: hackers have often doctored up entries in the domain name servers (DNS)[1], which amounts to doctoring-up the directory which is accessed every time we type the name of a Web site we want to see.

e.   Even in the absence of any of the foregoing, the fact of life is that the Internet is largely free to the user; since nothing in life is really free, the revenue source for many "free" Web sites we visit on the Internet comes from advertising in the form of pop-up ads, scrolling text, images, etc. Often these advertising images are not ones of facial crèmes and vacation packages but of unclad underage persons; the presence of such images in one's computer is enough to cause someone to end up in prison in an increasing number of countries these days. While one can rapidly go to a different Web site, the fact is that, unless one has gone to the trouble to change the Web browser's default settings (of storing Web pages on the disk) to not storing anything, these images get stored (cached) in one's hard disk drives by default. Over a period of time, enough to them collect in any of our computers and an overzealous prosecutor can claim that there is an "obvious pattern or proclivity to child pornography that stretches over a few years". A hapless defendant will have a very difficult time convincing a technology-challenged judge or jury that he/she knows nothing about how those images got there, especially in today's culture.

f.   Unless one lives by oneself and never admits anyone to his/her house, chances are that one's sons, daughters, spouse, or some friend or relative, will use one's computer during a computer's typical lifetime of a few years. In that case, it is not inconceivable at all that such other persons could have visited Web sites that you or I would not have patronized; cached images from such Web sites will stay in our computers until we actively overwrite those files whose existence we don't even suspect.

g.   Unsolicited e-mail (spam) is as common as the air we breathe. Many of them peddle get-rich-quick schemes, weight loss schemes, eternal youth recipes, pyramid schemes, sex, and just about everything else. Most people ignore them; many delete them. But here is the problem: aside from the fact that deleting does not delete anything (it merely tells the computer that the space on the disk occupied by that file or e-mail, which is in fact not erased at all, can be used in the future if the computer feels like it), hardly any of us goes to the trouble to delete *attachments* that often come with such unsolicited e-mail; and even if we did, the attachment would still remain on our hard disks for the same reasons. Perhaps nobody, other than computer experts, will go to the trouble of *overwriting* the offensive attachment, because Windows does not include any provision to overwrite anything; one has to buy special software for this and most people don't. And even if one did go to the heroic step of overwriting a file with specially purchased software, the name of the file, which could be quite incriminating in and by itself, and which is stored in a different location than the file itself in our hard disks would not be overwritten, to the delight of the forensics investigator who has a vested interest in finding something incriminating. Again, the hapless defendant will have a very hard time convincing a non-technical judge or jury that such offensive files were not solicited (or even tolerated). Even if one went to the heroic steps of overwriting unsolicited e-mail attachments and their separately stored names (and nobody does *that*), fragments of these incriminating files may still be found by forensics investigators in the "swap" file (also known as "paging file").

h.   The Wi-Fi (802.11a,b,g,x) route. Wireless access- is increasing at an explosive rate worldwide. It can be found at McDonald's, Starbuck Coffee, many airports, many hotels, and most important to this discussion, in our homes where we may like to access our high speed Internet connection from anywhere in the house without running wires all over the place. The literature is full of the technical details of how insecure this "standard" is; "out of the box", Wi-Fi hardware is configured to require no password, no encryption, and no security at all; most users do not tinker with those default settings; the devices work "as is" out of the box. Now, radio travels over far larger distances than what these boxes claim, and it is not uncommon for a home Wi-Fi to be accessed up 5 miles away if one builds a directional antenna and drives around town looking for other people's home Wi-Fi's to connect to, a practice known as "war driving". In fact, there have been documented cases of unmodified Wi-Fi "access points" having been accessed a full 20 miles away! Once connected, which is trivial since there is no security, the unauthorized user of the victim's Wi-Fi access point has full access to that victim's computer *and* Internet connection. This means that files can be placed into or removed from the victim's computer, and it also means that the unauthorized user can leave a long trace of illegal Internet activity in the victim's Internet Service Provider's (ISP) records. Now imagine the very common situation where the victim is at home, is the only person at home, and the unauthorized user uses the victim's computer to engage in any one or more of the multitude of illegal activities that can be conducted over the Internet. The accusing finger will be pointed at the victim as being the "obvious" perpetrator;

good luck convincing a typical technology-challenged court that the victim was a victim and not the perpetrator.

    i.   Computers crash sooner rather than later. The typical course of action for one is to take the computer to some repair person in an effort to be able to access one's prized personal and business data. Computer repairmen have every opportunity to place potentially incriminating data into the repaired computer (such as hacking tools used by the repairman to diagnose and/or repair that computer). A few years later, the owner of the computer is likely to have forgotten about the repair altogether and never bring it up in his/her defense if accused of having hacking tools in that "personal" computer.

2.   Computer forensics examiners like to substantiate their findings by pointing out the time/date stamp[2] associated with different computer files, as if those time/date stamps were kept in a vault that is inaccessible by mere mortals. This is patently false. The date/time stamp, as well as every single bit of data in a computer's magnetic media can be altered undetectably so that the "evidence" found by the forensics investigator will substantiate what one wants it to appear to substantiate. All it takes is a readily and widely available software known as a "disk editor", which is openly available (e.g. in Norton Utilities), to change any metadata (data about data, such as who did what and when) in a computer, whether date/time, or anything else.

3.   Unlike conventional film-based photography where a competent investigator can usually determine if it has been doctored, digital images (such as those taken by any surveillance camera) can be altered in a manner that no expert can detect, if the alteration was done professionally enough. Noise and blur can be digitally added to the end result to further hide any digital tinkering that might have been detectable at the individual pixel level by even an expert. The old adage, "Pictures don't lie" is itself a lie; digital pictures can lie with impunity; we are all familiar with the ease that any of use can "doctor up" an otherwise dull digital photograph into a stunning one by using Adobe Photoshop or other powerful image manipulation software packages.

4.   As with digital photography, so with digitized sounds. Unlike analog sounds of yesteryear (e.g. the infamous gap in the tape recordings of Nixon's office), where a careful study of the background noise can detect alterations of analog recordings), digitized files of sounds can be altered at will; if the alteration is done professionally enough, it will be undetectable by even a competent forensics examination of the digital file.

In summary, we are witnessing a new phenomenon in today's courtrooms. All of us store in our computers more and more information about our lives and activities. This has resulted in an explosive increase in computer forensics on confiscated or subpoenaed computers on the incorrect assumption that "what is in the computer is what *we* put in it". An entire cottage industry of computer forensics investigators, some more qualified and competent than others, has sprung up to service the insatiable appetite for such services by all.

The legal and societal problem with this social phenomenon is that most individuals in the legal and law enforcement professions are unaware of (or choose to ignore) at least some of the many ways I summarized above whereby the data they present as evidence is really not evidence of anything because it is routinely placed in one's computer without the knowledg—let alone complicity—of the owner or the (often different) user of the computer.

Independently, "evidence" presented which is based on one's Internet Service Provider's records is, similarly, evidence of nothing because one's Internet account can be (and routinely has been) accessed by third parties without one's awareness or complicity, even if one was the only person at home when the alleged Internet access occurred.

In summary, defense lawyers and judges should get urgently needed remedial education in the shortcomings of digital forensics. Since one cannot require such technical competence on the part of randomly selected juries, knowledgeable judges have to inform juries explicitly that digital "evidence" may not be evidence at all, despite overachieving prosecutors' claim to the contrary. Digital evidence should be viewed with extreme suspicion, regardless of the competence or qualifications of the computer forensics expert witness who has a vested interest in appearing to be an impartial witness when, in fact, he/she is not due to the obvious conflict of interest involved. While the "chain of custody" portion of how the evidence was handled may (or may not) have been impeccable, the raw digital data itself on which a forensics analysis was done can be easily and undetectably tampered with by anyone with the right background. Digital evidence is often evidence of nothing.

Endnotes

[1]   The Internet does not "understand" names such as www.cnn.com and only understands addresses in number form, such as 123.456.789.012; the translation from a name to a number is done each and every time we type a URL name (such as www.cnn.com) by the Domain Name Server network (DNS) which is a network or computer servers around the world that does just that for a living.

[2]   The time/date stamp is part of the *metadata* of a file, i.e., the data about the file itself, and it may also include the declared registered owner (not necessarily the real owner nor the user) of the particular copy of the software that created the file, the version of that software, etc.

This chapter is based in part on related, but much shorter, articles in the *Keesing Journal of Documents* and on IEEE's *Security and Privacy* magazine.

About the Authors

Panagiotis Kanellis (kanellis@bcs.org) is currently a project director with Information Society S.A. in Athens, Greece. Previous to that, he held senior consulting positions with Arthur Andersen and Ernst and Young. He was educated at Western International University in business administration (BS), at the University of Ulster in computing and information systems (post-graduate diploma), and at Brunel University in data communication systems (MS) and information systems (PhD). He is a research associate in the department of informatics and telecommunications at the National and Kapodistrian University of Athens and an adjunct faculty member at the Athens University of Economics and Business. Dr Kanellis has published more than 50 papers in international journals and conferences. He serves on the board of the Hellenic Chapter of the Association of Information Systems (AIS) and is a member of the British Computer Society (BCS) and a chartered information technology professional (CITP). He is also a certified information systems auditor (CISA).

Evangelos Kiountouzis is professor *emeritus* of information systems with the Department of Informatics of the Athens University of Economics & Business, Greece. He studied mathematics at the University of Athens and received a PhD in informatics from the University of Ulster, UK. His professional and research interests focus on information systems analysis and design methodologies and information systems security management. He has published numerous papers in international conferences and journals including the *Computer Journal, Computers & Security, Information Management* and *Computers Security*. He is the author of several books on the topics of information systems and information systems security management.

Nicholas Kolokotronis is currently a visiting professor with the Department of Computer Science and Technology, University of Peloponnese, Greece. He received a BS in mathematics from the Aristotle University of Thessaloniki, an MSc in computer science, and a PhD in cryptography from the National and Kapodistrian University of Athens. He has been a consultant for private companies and public organizations (ministries, regulatory authorities), focusing in the design of security solutions for e-government and e-procurement applications, as well as, in the analysis of e-commerce technological and legal framework. He has published several articles on cryptography and systems security in international journals and conferences. Among others, his research interests include cryptography, combinatorial theory, error correcting codes, finite field theory, electronic commerce, network security protocols, Web services, public key infrastructures, and digital forensics.

Drakoulis Martakos is an associate professor with the Department of Informatics and Telecommunications at the National and Kapodistrian University of Athens, Greece. He received a BS in physics, an MS in electronics and radio communications, and a PhD in real-time computing from the same university. Professor Martakos is a consultant to public and private organizations and a project leader in numerous national and international projects. He is the chairman of the Hellenic Chapter of the Association of Information Systems (AIS) and he is the author or co-author of more than 70 scientific publications and a number of technical reports and studies.

* * * *

Sos S. Agaian is distinguished professor (The Peter T. Flawn Professor), College of Engineering, University of Texas at San Antonio (USA) and an adjunct professor with the Department of Electrical Engineering, Tufts University, Medford, Massachusetts. He has written more than 300 scientific papers (more than 100 refereed journal papers), four books, six book chapters, and has 12 patents. He is an associate editor of the *Journal of Real-Time Imaging, the Journal of Electronic Imaging,* and an editorial board member of the *Journal Pattern Recognition and Image Analysis.* His current research interests lie in the broad area of signal/image processing and transmission, information security, quantum signal processing, and communication.

Michael A. Caloyannides earned a PhD in electrical engineering, applied mathematics, and philosophy from the California Institute of Technology (Caltech) in 1972. After 14 years as senior scientist at Rockwell Int'l Corp., he worked for 13 years as chief scientist for an agency of the U.S. Government where he won the "Scientist of the Year" award. Since 1999, he has been senior fellow at Mitretek Systems Inc., a think tank near Washington, DC. He has published three books on computer forensics and countless technical papers. He also has a U.S. patent on high speed modems. He is also an adjunct professor in information security at Johns Hopkins and George Washington universities, a consultant to NASA, and a frequently invited lecturer on information security and computer forensics worldwide.

David R. Champion is an assistant professor of criminology at Slippery Rock University (USA). He is experienced in juvenile community corrections and is a former military police investigator. He holds a doctorate in criminology from Indiana University of Pennsylvania. Dr. Champion has wide-ranging interests in issues of crime and justice and has published and presented work in topics ranging from criminal psychology to policing to terrorism.

Thomas M. Chen is an associate professor with the Department of Electrical Engineering at Southern Methodist University (USA). He received a BS and an MS from MIT, and a PhD from the University of California, Berkeley. He is associate editor-in-chief of *IEEE Communications Magazine* and a senior technical editor of *IEEE Network*. He is the co-author of "ATM Switching Systems." He received the IEEE Communications Society's Fred Ellersick best paper award in 1996.

Caroline Chibelushi is a research associate at Staffordshire University, Stafford, UK. Her research interests is in developing text mining techniques which combine linguistics and artificial intelligence methods to analyze spoken and written language in the areas of decision making and crime detection. She is the lead researcher on the ASKARI project. She is a member of IEE and WES.

Philip Craiger is the assistant director for Digital Evidence at the National Center for Forensic Science, and an assistant professor with the Department of Engineering Technology, University of Central Florida (USA). Dr. Craiger is a certified information systems security professional and holds several certifications in digital forensics and information security.

Chris Davis, CISSP, CISA, is co-author of *Hacking Exposed: Computer Forensics and the Anti-Hacker Toolkit.* He has managed worldwide teams in security architecture, design, and product management. His contributions include projects for Gartner, Harvard, SANS, and CIS, among others. He has enjoyed positions at Cisco Systems, Austin Microsoft Technology Center, and currently Texas Instruments (USA). He holds a bachelor's degree in nuclear engineering from Thomas Edison, and a master's degree in business from the University of Texas at Austin.

Dario Valentino Forte, CFE, CISM, has been active in the information security field since 1992. He is 36 years old, with almost 15 years experience as a police investigator. He is a member of the TC11 Workgroup of Digital Forensic. His technical articles have been published in a host of international journals and he has spoken at numerous international conferences on information warfare and digital forensic. He worked with international governmental agencies such as NASA, and the U.S. Army and Navy, providing support in incident response and forensic procedures and has resolved many important hacking-related investigations. He has lectured at the Computer Security Institute, the United States D.H.S. and D.o.D., the Blackhat Conference, the DFRWS (US Air Force Rome Labs), and POLICYB (Canada). Dario has given interviews with *Voice of America, Newsweek, the Washington Times and CSO Magazine*. At the moment he is adjunct faculty at University of Milano at Crema and provides security/incident response and forensics consulting services to the government, law enforcement and corporate worlds. For more information, visit www.dflabs.com.

Steven Furnell is the head of the Network Research Group at the University of Plymouth (UK), and an adjunct associate professor with Edith Cowan University, Western Australia. He specializes in computer security and has been actively researching in the area for 13 years. Dr. Furnell is a fellow and branch chair of the British Computer Society (BCS), senior member of the Institute of Electrical and Electronics Engineers (IEEE), and a UK representative in International Federation for Information Processing (IFIP) working groups relating to information security management, network security and information security education. He is the author of over 160 papers in international journals and conference proceedings, as well as the books *Cybercrime: Vandalizing the Information Society* (2001) and *Computer Insecurity: Risking the System* (2005).

Zachary Grant has dedicated his career to developing and deploying security solutions for both healthcare and financial institutions. Grant is an IT manager/security engineer for a large healthcare company headquartered in the southwest. In addition to his endeavors in the private sector, Grant servers as a captain with a state law enforcement agency, where he oversees the communications for the agency. His work with the state agency has lead him to integrate with many different local, state, and federal agencies where he concentrates his day to day security efforts bridging private industry security techniques into training and investigation methods for law enforcement.

Connie Hendricks received her BS in criminal justice from the University of Central Florida (USA). She currently serves as a senior digital forensics research assistant at the National Center for Forensic Science, where she conducts research on cyberterrorism.

Pallavi Kahai (pkahai@cisco.com) received her BE in electrical engineering from Yeshwantrao Chavan College of Engineering, India (2000). She received an MS in electrical and computer engineering from Wichita State University, USA (2005). During her master's program she worked on various research projects, focusing on statistical analysis, information security and computer forensics. She presented her work at International Federation for Information Processing (IFIP) Conference on Digital Forensics, 2005, Orlando, FL. She is currently working as a software engineer at Cisco Systems (USA) and works on IOS development and feature testing for Broadband Edge and Mid-range Routers.

CP (Buks) Louwrens has a BMil (BA) from the University of Stellenbosch (1985) and a PhD in computer science from the University of Johannesburg (2000), formerly known as the Randse Afrikaanse Universiteit. Professor Louwrens has more than 25 years experience in the fields of military intelligence, security, information security management, disaster recovery, business continuity management, and lately, digital forensics. He was appointed as part-time professor in the Academy for IT, University of Johannesburg in 2004 and is currently lecturing computer forensics at honors level. Professor Louwrens is involved in further research into digital forensic frameworks, in conjunction with Professor Basie von Solms. Professor Louwrens is employed by Nedbank Limited in South Africa as an executive in Group Risk Services, responsible for information security management, digital forensics, and business continuity management.

Christopher Malinowski (BS, police science, John Jay College of Criminal Justice; MS management engineering, Long Island University) retired as a lieutenant from the NYPD after 20 years. Having started on patrol, he spent more than a dozen years as a systems programmer/supervisor on IBM mainframe computers in MIS. In 1996 he became the commanding officer of the new computer crimes squad in the Detective Bureau, responsible for responding to investigative technical needs for the NYPD and investigating computer-based crimes in New York City. He has served on committee for the Department of Justice sponsored National Cybercrime Training Partnership and has lectured on cybercrime related topics to various organizations. Currently he is an associate professor for the Computer Science Department at the CW Post Campus of Long Island University (USA).

Moira Carroll-Mayer (BA, MA, LLB, LLM) (moiracaroll2000@yahoo.co.uk) is a PhD research student with the Centre for Computing and Social Responsibility at the Faculty of Computer Sciences and Engineering, De Montfort University, Leicester, UK.

Chris Marberry is currently a senior digital forensics research assistant to Dr. Philip Craiger at the Nation Center for Forensic Science. He has graduated from the University of Central Florida (USA) with a bachelor's degree in information technology and is planning on pursuing a master's degree in digital forensics.

Andreas Mitrakas (andreas@mitrakas.com) is a legal adviser at the European Network and Information Security Agency (ENISA), Greece. He has previously been senior counsel at Ubizen (a cybertrust company) and general counsel at GlobalSign, (Vodafone Group). His research interests include the legal and organisational implications of technology in business and government. He is a qualified attorney (Athens Bar) and he has been visiting lecturer at the University of Westminster and the Athens University for Economics and Business. He has (co-)authored over 85 publications including *Open EDI and law in Europe: A regulatory framework* (Kluwer, 1997) and he is co-editor of *Secure Web Services in eGovernment* (IGP, 2006). He holds a PhD in electronic commerce and the law from Erasmus University of Rotterdam, a master's degree in computers and law from Queen's University of Belfast, a diploma in project management from ParisTech (Grandes Ecoles d'Ingenieurs de Paris) and a law degree from the University of Athens.

Kamesh Namuduri (kamesh.namuduri@wichita.edu) received a BE in electronics and communication engineering from Osmania University, India (1984), an MTech in computer science from the University of Hyderabad (1986) and a PhD in computer science and engineering from University of South Florida (1992). He has worked in C-DoT, a telecommunications firm in India (1984-1986). Currently, he is with the Electrical and Computer Engineering Department at Wichita State University (USA) as an assistant professor. His areas of research interest include information security, image/video processing and communications, and ad hoc sensor networks. He is a senior member of IEEE.

Peter Norris is a teacher fellow and principal lecturer in computer science at De Montfort University (UK). His background is in technical computing, initially with British Steel in the early 1980s, through the design of non-conventional machine tool (ECM, EDM and Laser) automated machine vision systems during the mid 1980's and into academia in the late 1980s. His entire academic career has been devoted to constructing curricula which give students access to software where they are free to experiment and make/recover from mistakes in safety. For the last six years, this has been in the provision of pre-configured, open source, Web application development software. Most recently, this has involved the specification of the faculty's Forensic Computing Laboratory.

Ravi Pendse (ravi.pendse@wichita.edu) is an associate vice president for Academic Affairs and Research, Wichita State Cisco fellow, and director of the Advanced Networking Research Center at Wichita State University (USA). He has received a BS in electronics and communication engineering from Osmania University, India (1982), an MS in electrical engineering from Wichita State University (1985), and a PhD in electrical engineering from Wichita State University (1994). He is a senior member of IEEE. His research interests include ad hoc networks, voice over IP, and aviation security.

Golden G. Richard III holds a BS in computer science from the University of New Orleans and MS and PhD degrees in computer science from The Ohio State University. He is currently an associate professor in the Department of Computer Science, co-founder of Digital Forensics Solutions, a private digital forensics corporation, and a technical advisor to the Gulf Coast Computer Forensics Laboratory (GCCFL), a consortium of local, state, and federal law enforcement agencies. Dr. Richard is a GIAC-certified digital forensics investigator and teaches digital forensics and computer security courses at the University of New Orleans (USA).

Benjamin M. Rodriguez holds a bachelor's degree in electrical engineering from the University of Texas at San Antonio and a master's degree in electrical engineering from the University of Texas at San Antonio. He is currently pursuing a PhD in electrical engineering from the Department of Electrical and Computer Engineering, Graduate School of Engineering and Management, Air Force Institute of Technology (USA). His research is in the areas of image processing, wavelets and fractal based compression, digital signal processing, applied statistics, steganography, and steganalysis.

Vassil Roussev holds a BS and MS in computer science from Sofia University in Sofia, Bulgaria and MS and PhD degrees in computer science from the University of North Carolina, Chapel Hill. He is currently an assistant professor in the Department of Computer Science at the University of New Orleans (USA). His research interests are digital forensics and collaborative applications.

Hanifa Shah is a professor of information systems at Staffordshire University (UK) and a fellow of the British Computer Society. She has led a number of research projects funded by academic and commercial organizations. Her interests are in the design and development of information systems, knowledge management, IT for strategic management and facilitating university-industry collaboration.

Bernadette Sharp is a professor of applied artificial intelligence at Staffordshire University, Stafford, UK, where she heads the Informatics and Technology Research Institute. She is also a fellow of the British Computer Society. Her research interests include intelligent agents, text mining, natural language processing, and knowledge management. She has managed a number of research projects with industrial collaboration and has received funding from EU, EPSRC, and industry.

Sriranjani Sitaraman is a PhD candidate in computer science at the University of Texas at Dallas (USA). Her research interests are in the field of digital forensics and computer security. Sriranjani received a Bachelor of Engineering in computer science from Bharatiar University, India (1998) and an MS in computer science from UT Dallas (2001).

Bernd Carsten Stahl is a senior lecturer in the faculty of computer sciences and engineering and a research associate at the Centre for Computing and Social Responsibility of De Montfort University, Leicester, UK. He is interested in philosophical issues arising from the intersections of business, technology, and information. He is editor-in-chief of the *International Journal of Technology and Human Interaction*.

Jeff Swauger holds a Bachelor of Science in physics, a graduate certificate in computer forensics, and is also a certified information systems security professional (CISSP). Mr. Swauger has over 25 years of experience in the areas of information security, information warfare, modeling and simulation, and advanced weapon system development.

Kyriakos Tsiflakos, PhD, is the technology and security risk services partner in Ernst and Young Southeast Europe. Tsiflakos coordinates the delivery of technology and security risk services in the context of external and internal audits, regulatory compliance, IT due diligence, IT project risk management, information security, business continuity planning, and other engagements. He holds a bachelor's degree in engineering from the National Technical University of Athens, a master's degree in management information systems from Cranfield University, UK, and a PhD in operations research & computing from Imperial College, University of London. He is also a certified information security manager (CISM). As a researcher in the areas of information systems and operations research, Mr. Tsiflakos has published extensively and delivered presentations at conference and company venues throughout Europe, North America and the Far East.

Subbarayan Venkatesan (Venky) received MS and PhD degrees in computer science from the University of Pittsburgh (1985 and 1988, respectively). He joined the computer science program at UTD in January 1989 where he is currently an associate professor. Venky has been a consultant for a number of companies in the Dallas area and has worked for Cisco Systems and Rockwell Collins. His research interests are in digital forensics, wireless networks, distributed systems, fault tolerance, and sensor networks. His work has been funded in part by numerous grants and contracts.

SH (Basie) von Solms holds a PhD in computer science, and is head of the Department of the Academy for Information Technology at the University of Johannesburg, South Africa. He has been lecturing in computer science and IT related fields since 1970. Professor von Solms specializes in research and consultancy in the area of information security. He has written more than 90 papers on this aspect most of which were published internationally. Profressor von Solms is the present vice-president of IFIP, the International Federation for Information Processing, and the immediate past chairman of Technical Committee 11 (Information Security), of the IFIP. He is also a member of the general assembly of IFIP. Professor von Solms has been a consultant to industry on the subject of information security for the last 10 years. He is a member of the British Computer Society, a fellow of the Computer Society of South Africa, and a SAATCA certified auditor for ISO 17799, the international Code of Practice for Information Security Management.

Jeremy Ward is services development director for Symantec in Europe. He has been with Symantec for five years. Previously with 18 years experience in the UK government, he has been a manager on large IT projects, has developed policy on personnel and telecoms security, and acted as an advisor on information security to the UK Prime Minister's Strategy Unit. Dr. Ward serves on a number of national and international bodies that produce policy and advice on information security.

Warren Wylupski has over 15 years of private sector leadership experience. He holds an MBA and is pursuing his PhD in sociology at the University of New Mexico (USA). His academic areas of specialization are sociology of organizations, criminology, and program evaluation. Mr. Wylupski's research and consulting interests are in the areas of police operations, organizational and white collar crime, organizational effectiveness, and process improvement.

Damián Zaitch (zaitch@frg.eur.nl) is a lecturer and researcher with the Department of Criminology, Erasmus University, Rotterdam. For the past 10 years he has researched and published on organized crime and drug policies in The Netherlands and Latin America. He earned his PhD (2001, *cum laude*) at the Amsterdam School for Social science Research, University of Amsterdam, with an ethnographic research on Colombians involved in the cocaine business in The Netherlands (Trafficking Cocaine [2002], Kluwer Law International) for which he obtained the Willem Nagel Prize in 2003. He is currently focusing his interests on other forms of cross-border transnational organized crime such as cyber crime in Europe and on corporate crime in Latin America. He is founding member of CIROC, the Centre for Information and Research on Organized Crime.

Index

wi-fi 235, 337
WildList Organization 36
WildPackets' iNetTools 8
WinDump 13, 69
WinInterrogate 56, 62
wired equivalent privacy (WEP) 323
WMATRIX 163
WORDNET 163
worm 17, 27
write-blockers 62
WU-FTPD attack 149

X

X-Ways Forensics 62

Y

Yahoo 20
Yahoo mail 232
Yasinsac 319